OUTSIDE ETHICS

OUTSIDE ETHICS

Raymond Geuss

PRINCETON UNIVERSITY PRESS   PRINCETON AND OXFORD

Copyright © 2005 by Princeton University Press
Published by Princeton University Press, 41 William Street, Princeton,
New Jersey 08540
In the United Kingdom: Princeton University Press, 3 Market Place,
Woodstock, Oxfordshire OX20 1SY
All Rights Reserved

ISBN: 0-691-12341-1
ISBN (pbk.): 0-691-12342-X

Library of Congress Cataloging-in-Publication Data

Geuss, Raymond.
Outside ethics / Raymond Geuss.
p.   cm.
Includes bibliographical references and index.
ISBN 0-691-12341-1 (hardcover : alk. paper) —
ISBN 0-691-12342-X (pbk. : alk. paper)
1. Ethics.   2. Liberalism.   3. Philosophy.   I. Title.
BJ1031.G48 2005
170—dc22   2005006802

British Library Cataloging-in-Publication Data is available

This book has been composed in New Caledonia

Printed on acid-free paper. ∞

pup.princeton.edu

Printed in the United States of America

10   9   8   7   6   5   4   3   2   1

Contents

Acknowledgments

ALL OF THE ESSAYS in this volume, except one, have been previously published, although some only in a shortened form and some only in German. I am extremely grateful to Nicholas Walker for his excellent translation of "Genealogy as Critique" (Essay 9); I am responsible for the English versions of the other essays originally written in German.

I have tried to list the most important particular intellectual debts I have incurred at the end of each essay, but this does not adequately express a much more general debt I owe to some individuals. Hilary Gaskin has given me the benefit of her own impeccable judgment and brought significant improvements to every one of the following texts. I am also grateful to John Dunn, Zeev Emmerich, Michael Frede, Istvan Hont, Susan James, and Quentin Skinner for continuing intellectual support in a very wide range of contexts.

Because the origin and publication history of some of the essays is complex, there follows a summary of their provenance.

Essay One: originally written in German as a set of lectures delivered at the University of Saarbrücken in December 2000; first published as "Das Unbehagen am Liberalismus" in *Deutsche Zeitschrift für Philosophie* December 2001; this version appeared in English as "Liberalism and Its Discontents" in *Political Theory*, June 2002.

Essay Two: first published as "Weder Geschichte noch Praxis" in *Mittelweg 36*, February/March 2003; this version appeared in English in *European Review*, vol. 11, no. 3, August 2003.

Essay Three: originally a lecture at the University of St Andrews (April 2002); published in *European Journal of Philosophy*, January 2002.

Essay Four: originally presented at Joint Sessions in Liverpool (July 1995); published in *Proceedings of the Aristolelian Society: Supplementary Volume*, 1995.

Essay Five: originally written in German as an article for *Frankfurter Rundschau* (29 September 1998); expanded and published in *Arion*, spring/summer 2000.

Essay Six: originally a lecture at a conference on "Democracy and Human Happiness" in Kyoto (April 2002); published in *Arion*, spring/summer 2002.

Essay Seven: originally written in German as a talk published as "Leiden und Erkennen bei Adorno" in *Dialektik der Freiheit: Frankfurter Adorno-Konferenz 2003*, ed. Axel Honneth (2005).

Essay Eight: published in a shortened version in *The Early Frankfurt School and Religion*, ed. Kohlenbach and Geuss (Palgrave, 2005); this version is a translation of the full German original.

Essay Nine: original published as "Kritik, Aufklärung, Genealogie" in *Deutsche Zeitschrift für Philosophie*, February 2002, and reprinted in *Michael Foucault: Zwischenbilanz einer Rezeption*, ed. Honneth and Saar (Suhrkamp, 2003); this version, slightly abbreviated from the original, was translated by Nicholas Walker and appeared in *European Journal of Philosophy*, August 2002.

Essay Ten: published in *European Journal of Philosophy*, 1999.

Essay Eleven: published in *Arion*, spring/summer 2003.

Essay Twelve: published in *Arion*, winter 2004.

Essay Thirteen: previously unpublished.

Essay Fourteen: published in *Arion*, fall 2004.

OUTSIDE ETHICS

Introduction

MOST OF THE FOLLOWING essays are *pièces d'occasion*, responses to concrete invitations to address a particular topic in a specific forum, and my primary hope is that as many of them as possible will be able to stand on their own as illuminating contributions to the understanding of whatever particular topic or topics each treats. However, it is, I hope, not mere whimsy to collect them into a single volume. There are various connections between the topics the different essays discuss: a number of them deal with the relation between ethics and politics, between individual values and the structuring of human social life, or with liberalism as a political philosophy; others are concerned with such central political and ethical values as freedom, happiness, or suffering, or with the idea of the success (or failure) of an individual human life or of a collectivity. Finally, several of the essays are concerned with the possibilities of radical social criticism, including the possibility that certain forms of historical inquiry or of art might have a critical potential. These are obviously closely related issues.

What strikes me most on rereading these essays, however, is a certain unity of attitude. One of the things that holds the essays in this collection together most closely is their shared skepticism about a particular way of thinking about what is important in human life which I take to be characteristic of contemporary European societies. By a "way of thinking" I do not, of course, mean a specific belief or even a characteristic set of specific beliefs, such as the belief that the earth is (roughly) round (or: flat), that witches must be burned at the stake (or: that there are no witches, and in any case no one ought to be punished by being burned at the stake), or that all species of plants and animals evolved gradually through natural selection (or: that they were all created, each in its unchanging form, at a particular point in time by an omnipotent deity). Rather what I have in mind is a very amorphous and ill-defined tacit assumption or set of assumptions about the nature of the human world, what is important in it, and how we can conceptualize it.

In the late eighteenth century Kant spoke of the distinction between a "cosmopolitan" and a "scholastic" conception of philosophy.[1] The scholastic con-

---

[1] The discussion of Kant that follows conflates his two treatments on this topic: *Kritik der reinen Vernunft*, ed. Raymond Schmidt (Hamburg: Felix Meiner-Verlag, 1956; hereinafter *KrV*), B866–68, 832–35, and *Immanuel Kants Logik*, ed. Gottlob Benjamin Jäsche, in *Kant, Werke*, ed. Wilhelm Weischedel (Wiesbaden: Insel, 1958), vol. III, A23–29. It is obviously influenced by Heidegger's *Kant und das Problem der Metaphysik* (2nd edition, Frankfurt/M: Klostermann, 1951), pp. 185–88. I have a brief further discussion of this issue in my "Morality and Identity" in C. Korsgaard et al., *Sources of Normativity* (Cambridge: Cambridge University Press, 1996), pp. 189–93.

ception was one which was limited to specifying the internal goal of philosophical activity: in Kant's view, the attempt to attain and justify a maximally extensive but unified system of knowledge of the world, without concerning itself with the intrinsic value of such activity, or its relation to any further human goals. Philosophy in the cosmopolitan sense, on the other hand, is concerned with the relation of knowledge to the final or essential ends of human reason, or, as Kant also puts it, with things that are necessarily of interest to every rational being. In the twenty-first century one might be inclined to wonder whether it makes any real sense of speak of the "essential ends of human reason," but Kant is firmly convinced that this is more than a metaphor expressive of what would have been for him an uncharacteristic state of exuberance. Human reason itself, he believes, has an essential interest, and this interest is summed up in the asking and answering of three questions:

1. What can I know?
2. What ought I to do?
3. What may I hope for?[2]

Philosophy as a cosmopolitan enterprise, then, is metaphysics (answer to question 1), ethics (answer to question 2), and religion (answer to question 3). Philosophy as a whole, or various detached parts of it, might have any number of, as it were, "collateral" benefits, such as contributing to the general training of the mind or helping to resolve particular problems that arise in the domain of one of the special sciences. However, to focus exclusively on these instrumental contributions philosophy can make to human life is to miss the point, which is that the asking and answering of these questions has value in itself for human beings. It is, Kant thinks, self-evident that there is a specifically moral "ought" which binds our actions, and it is self-evidently important for its own sake to know what limits human knowledge has, how we "ought" to act, and whether the hopes for an afterlife held out by religions are or are not justified, or, if not exactly positively warranted, rationally permissible.

Kant saw himself and was taken by various of his contemporaries and some of his successors as a revolutionary figure ushering in a new age, but from the vantage point of the early twenty-first century, eighteenth-century Prussia belongs to the very distant past, and the Kantian construct, rather than being especially forward-looking, is the last and most elaborate monument of a pe-

---

[2] As Heidegger points out (*Kant und das Problem der Metaphysik*, p. 187 f.), in the text edited by Jäsche from Kant's lectures (*Immanuel Kants Logik*, A26) Kant adds a fourth question, "What is man?," and states that in a certain sense the three other questions all "relate to" the fourth. Kant never actually makes much of this connection, however, and Heidegger seems to be right to claim that this is not an accident, but rather *"das Ungedachte in seinem Denken,"* and that too clear and sustained a focus on this issue would have dissolved the Kantian philosophy from the inside.

riod of our history that looks in retrospect both brutally archaic and exceptionally decadent. The three great Kantian *Critiques* are like an elaborate set of stained glass windows, highly original in their genre perhaps and intended to last for centuries, but completed just in time to be smashed by Puritan mobs, motivated by new ideals and energies that put an end forever to the world to which they belonged, and in which alone they made sense. They may be of great interest to the archaeologist or art historian, and retain a certain appeal because of their scope, the boldness of their conception, and the delicacy of their filigree, but they are of no direct relevance to us.

Although we might congratulate ourselves on having left behind Kant's world of metaphysics-morality-religion, *Privatdozenten*, wigs, copper engravings, Euclidean geometry, public hangings, and enlightened (or unenlightened) royal absolutism, this self-congratulation is premature and unwarranted because the dominant worldview in contemporary Western societies is not as distinct from the doctrines of Kant as one might expect or as we might wish. In fact, it shows some distinct similarities with basic Kantian structures.[3] It, too, is oriented around three kinds of question, and a set of answers to them:

1. What do I want? What do you want? What do they want?

2. What do we know?

3. What restrictions ought there to be on the actions people perform, particularly on those that affect other people?

To put it very crudely, people in contemporary Western societies recognize three broad categories of "things" as unproblematically important:

a) individual subjective human preferences; these are generally construed as prima facie hard, brassy, externally opaque, and atomistic, and as being expressed through word and deed

b) useful knowledge, especially warranted, empirically supported belief that tells us how the world is, how it can be predicted to change, and how we might use it (i.e., science); to a lesser extent, also certain highly formal disciplines like mathematics that are thought—perhaps, of course, incorrectly—to be about helping us deal with the surrounding world

c) a restrictive set of demands on action that could affect other people and that are usually construed as some set of universal laws or rules or principles; in particular, a set of universal laws on which "we" would all agree (under some further specified circumstances)

Knowledge and universal moral rules, as with Kant, are of intrinsic interest

---

[3] I am not asserting that the modern tripartite division is derived historically from Kant or the result of the direct influence of Kantianism, but am using the parallelism merely as an expository device.

and value, but in place of religion we have individual human preference. Everything else that can have any claim to our automatic and serious interest, it is assumed, must be in some way reducible to one or another of these three categories, or at any rate must be best approached through one or the other of them. Anything that does not is a delusion or at best something marginal and unimportant. Completely outside the three groups, however, there is thought to be only darkness.

When I say that a set of assumptions about the exclusive importance of these three categories in human life constitutes the final framework for most modern thinking, I do not mean that every modern person understands each of these categories clearly or even in the same way, or would necessarily affirm in an unprompted way the general statement that whatever does not fit into the tripartite schema must not be important. The assumptions in question form the tacit background of thinking and debate rather than a set of explicitly held views. We are familiar with political debates, in which different parties disagree so heatedly and, apparently, so radically on specific points that for those standing too close to the debate there seems to be little agreement or common ground between them. People do obviously differ very significantly in their specific conceptions of knowledge, morality, and human preference, and in their views or assumptions about the relation between them, and their relative importance in human life. However, if one is able to stand back, many, if not most, of the disagreements that loom so large for the participants themselves and their contemporaries can be seen to be differences within an overarching agreement of which the parties themselves might not be fully aware. Trotsky versus Stalin, Augustine versus Aquinas, Tiberius versus Piso, Rousseau versus virtually any contemporary of his one might wish to name; from a sufficient distance the similarities are more salient than the differences. There is no view-from-nowhere, and it is perhaps more difficult for us to step back from our own life and beliefs and the social, historical, and political matrix within which they are located than it is for us to take a detached view of people and movements in any case far removed from us in space or time, but that is no reason to think that a relatively abstract attitude is strictly impossible for us to adopt toward ourselves and our contemporaries, or that it would not be worth the effort to try to attain what cognitive distance from ourselves we can. Contrary to the *fables convenues*, this is, I think, one of the central theses of Nietzsche and of Foucault, and one I wish to endorse: one can reject the absolutist Platonic conception of the world and our knowledge of it without succumbing to Protagorean relativism.[4] Another common thread in these essays is the consideration of the implications of this thesis.

Within what I claim is this modern shared framework one can distinguish a wide variety of specifically differentiated positions: puritanical views that

[4] See "Nietzsche and Genealogy" in my *Morality, Culture, and History* (Cambridge: Cambridge University Press, 1999) and also "Genealogy as Critique" below.

give absolute priority to (c), positivist views that give priority to (b), and sybaritic views that give priority to (a); realist and instrumentalist views of knowledge; consequentialist and non-consequentialist accounts of morality; etc. One particular political configuration that will play an important role in several of the following papers is liberalism.[5] One of the central pillars of most contemporary liberalism is anti-paternalism, which in most of its forms presupposes that individual preferences in politics are to be taken as they come and not questioned.[6] Depending on the specific version of liberalism one considers, this view about preferences might be connected with a commitment to some universal moral principles.

Differences in the way one construes human preferences, how one thinks they relate to human knowledge and moral principles, or what weight one should give them in human life are extremely important, and much of modern philosophy is rightly devoted to trying to develop coherent, plausible positions on these topics, but looked at in broader terms, many of the controversies that preoccupy contemporary philosophy concern no more than different ways of distributing roughly the same pieces on the same board. I am suggesting that there might be some enlightenment to be gained from looking at the board and the pieces from the outside, even if one finally decides to return to one of the usual games.

All the essays in this collection are devoted in one way or another to trying to undermine what I claim to be the usual contemporary way of looking at and thinking about the world, showing its deficiencies both as a schema for understanding significant portions of human life and as a matrix for making evaluations. The essays share the view that there are many things that are of the greatest importance but do not fit comfortably into the tripartite scheme. The world is full of "things" that are not obviously subjective preferences, things that derive (or purport to derive) their value from being the objects of existing subjective preferences, moral rules, or bits of knowledge. In some societies at some times, and most notably and relevantly for us, in Western societies until about the middle of the nineteenth century, religion was a phenomenon that very notably escaped the tripartite division I have been describing. Religion was not a matter of personal preference—perhaps it has become a matter of mere preference in advanced Western countries now, but that is a sign of how far it has departed from its traditional vocation—nor a matter *merely* of a set of rules by which we live together. The same is true of music and poetry, and of society, history, power, politics, and existential choice.

[5] See also Raymond Geuss, *History and Illusion in Politics* (Cambridge: Cambridge University Press, 2001), pp. 69–109.

[6] As I try to show in my *History and Illusion in Politics* (Cambridge: Cambridge University Press, 2001), "liberalism" has become such a broad church that it is difficult to make any generalizations about it at all. There are versions of "liberalism," such as that developed by Joseph Raz, which do not hold to the strictest forms of anti-paternalism.

Although it would be natural to use the term "ethics" to refer to the third of the categories—rules that contain restrictions on the ways in which it is permissible to act toward other people—and I myself occasionally use the term in this way, I will also use the term in a more general way to refer to this whole way of seeing the world and thinking about it. The title "Outside Ethics" indicates in a narrow sense a rejection of the Kant-inspired view that the correct account of a good human life would give special prominence to universal rules, but in a wider sense it also indicates an attempt to step outside the whole triadic structure.

I am aware of the fact that the tripartite scheme I have described is extremely vague and ill-defined, but, as it were, that is not necessarily my fault. It would be a great mistake, and one it is only too easy to make when studying historical or ethnological material, to ascribe too much precision to that which is inherently imprecise. The need to avoid inappropriate, excessive, or fraudulent clarity in studying the human world is perhaps another general preoccupation that holds these essays together. In the mainstream of Western philosophy, and then also Western culture, since Parmenides one finds a very striking incremental glorification of a set of interrelated properties that are counted as virtues: clarity and consistency of thought, speech, and action, the ability to reflect, to detach oneself from prevailing opinion, to ask questions, to give reasons. By now this has developed into a series of highly structured disciplines—our arts and sciences—and sedimented into our everyday ways of thinking and acting, but it also seems rooted in human nature and is self-evidently of great value. Many of us strive for clarity and we do this for many of the excellent reasons the philosophic tradition has expounded in great detail. We tend to attribute to others an equal striving for and attainment of clarity with respect to their own beliefs, although the apparent generosity of this impulse sometimes can be suspected to mask a certain slyness, because it warrants us to put words in others' mouths, the better thereby to catch them out and trip them up. Socrates, of course, was an unsurpassed master of this technique, and his example remains in this regard paradigmatic for much of contemporary philosophy.

However, as Nietzsche very powerfully pointed out, humans do not always exhibit maximal interest in clarity and explicitness, and they are right not to. Clarity is often of no use to us at all, and can in some circumstances be a positive hindrance to attaining various important human goods. In addition to our desire for clarity and definiteness, humans exhibit a second set of properties that are perhaps equally important, are very inadequately understood, are very little under our control, and are seriously underappreciated. These are the powers of forgetting, ignoring, failing to ask questions.[7] Similarly,

[7] See Friedrich Nietzsche, *Vom Nutzen und Nachteil der Historie für das Leben*, in *Kritische Studienausgabe (KS)*, ed. G. Colli and M. Montinari (Berlin: de Gruyter, 1967), vol. 1, pp. 245–

when Heidegger speaks of the original conception of truth as "aletheia" the philology might be poor, but one of the points he is trying to make is, I think, correct.[8] What we can "know"—that about which we have "beliefs"—is something we must pull out of the darkness into a clearing that has been made. Determining the relative relation of the light and darkness which we attribute to other human agents requires a nice power of discrimination and judgment.

If this is the case, the result is an upgrading of the role of contingency, history, and "politics" (in the small "p" sense of the term). If we are capable of stepping back from our own beliefs and the usual standards we use to evaluate them, and looking at them in their wider historical and social context, we will notice that what we believe depends on who asks what question, how exactly formulated, and making what assumptions at what time, and in what order. This is *not* in itself an argument against the existence of "truth" or in favor of that philosophers' will-o'-the-wisp "relativism," but a simple generalization about how human life is constituted.

The first two essays in the collection, "Liberalism and Its Discontents" and "Neither History nor Praxis," treat the most well-entrenched, and one of the most pernicious, forms of contemporary political thought, the highly Kantianized liberalism originally popularized by Rawls. I am particularly keen to emphasize that it is a mistake to moralize politics or to construe it as "applied ethics" in the Rawlsian way. The essay entitled "Outside Ethics" discusses a line of historical development in European thought that bypasses the tripartite schema. The rest of the essays deal with various topics—freedom, happiness, human suffering, religion, forms of criticism—with an emphasis on the extent to which they do or do not fit into what I claim is the modern worldview. Religion, as I have mentioned, was one of the most important traditional phenomena that provided a general framework for large parts of the world during long historical periods, but which does not lend itself readily to assimilation to the modern tripartite schema. For a number of institutional and sociological reasons, and because of the inherent implausibility of its belief-structure, religion can, I believe, no longer play the role it once did, but it still needs urgently to be understood correctly both because of its historical significance and because of the nostalgic hopes for reviving fragments of the

---

334; *Jenseits von Gut und Böse* §§ 68, 217 (*KV*, vol. 5, pp. 86, 153); *Zur Genealogie der Moral*, Essay I, § 10, Essay II, § 1 (*KV*, vol. 5, pp. 273, 291–92); also Harald Weinrich, *Lethe: Kunst und Kritik des Vergessens* (3rd ed., Munich: Beck, 2000). What, one might wonder, would have happened if Oedipus had listened to his mother (*OT* 1056 ff) and stopped asking so many bloody questions. The plot of *Parsifal* turns in the reverse direction, depending as it does on the imbecility of the main character ("*der tumbe helt*," as he came to be known, or as Wagner has it, "*der reine Tor*") and his failure to ask questions.

[8] See Martin Heidegger, "Aletheia (Heraklit Fragment 16)," in his *Vorträge und Aufsätze: Teil III* (Neske, 1954), pp. 53–78.

original religious worldview that resurface again and again in the modern world.

The two essays on poetry might seem from their ostensible topic to be only tangentially related to the other essays in the collection. They are devoted to arguing that poetry has no essence; it is a changing historical configuration of different elements, projects, forms, and conditions, but in particular it is not (universally) a form of knowledge in any interesting, distinctive sense, nor does its value lie directly and exclusively in the fact that it satisfies the "preferences" of many humans. Its relation to rules for dealing with other people is indirect and so highly mediated that it requires special analysis, and can never be taken for granted.

These essays, then, aspire to be antiliberal, antipositivist, and antireligious in equal measure. Although their focus is on the supersession of the particular tripartite conception I have described as characteristic of modern thinking, this naturally raises the general issue about how one can criticize well-entrenched general conceptions, and about getting cognitive and moral distance from ourselves that would allow us to "improve" our situation, whatever "improve" might turn out to mean. To "go beyond," to "step outside of," to "overcome," to "transcend," to "sublate": although these terms have had an important traditional usage in certain areas in philosophy, they have had perhaps an even more important career as central concepts in many religions, and it would be reasonable to wonder to what extent they retain religious associations.

One of Nietzsche's most important legacies to us, I have suggested above, is his claim that it is desirable and possible to dismantle the Platonic apparatus of Forms, Absolute Truth, the Idea of the Good, etc. and its historical derivatives, such as Kant's transcendental philosophy, and that this can be done without fear of falling into "relativism." There is, however, a second and slightly different set of issues that also arises in part from the increasing implausibility of Platonist and Kantian approaches to philosophy, but more directly from the decline of traditional religions. The members of the Frankfurt School felt it important to deny that we had to choose between traditional transcendental religion and "positivism."[9] There is no God and no God's-eye view, but this does not imply that we are trapped in the present, condemned merely to mirror the "facts" of the world that surrounds us, or to engage at best in merely piecemeal criticism of our social institutions, as, according to the members of the Frankfurt School, "positivists" would have it. Nietzsche seems sometimes to replace the "transcendence" which stands at the center of traditional accounts—the existence of a transcendent God, or, failing that, a transcendental viewpoint—with that of a continually transcending activity

[9] See Raymond Geuss, *The Idea of a Critical Theory* (Cambridge: Cambridge University Press, 1981).

("*Überwindung*" in one of the senses in which that term is used).[10] There is no single, final perspective, but given any one perspective, we can always go beyond it. I merely note that to take this as implying a guarantee that we will *always* (necessarily?) be able to go beyond any given position we might occupy, would be to fall back into a theological view. For Nietzsche, whether or not we will be able to "overcome" the one-sidedness of a perspective in which we find ourselves is an open question, for him a question of one's strength. One need not endorse Nietzsche's late-Romantic glorification of "strength" to accept his view that there are no guarantees of the requisite kind in the nature of things.

The essays stand in what I take to be the tradition of the early (i.e., pre-1970) Critical Theory of the Frankfurt School, although the specific version of the Critical Theory which I favor contains a stronger Nietzschean component than most other versions. The early members of the Frankfurt School wanted to put together retention of some orientation toward a transcendental perspective with naturalism (although they call it "materialism"), a sort of religiosity without *any* of the dogmatic content of any particular religion. It is, of course, highly questionable whether they did succeed in giving a coherence to this, but then it is also an open question in my view whether or not such coherence is required of a position that by its nature is intended to be merely negative. I feel considerably less sure about my own position on this issue than I do about Nietzsche's rejection of Plato. The relation between Critical Theory and Nietzsche/Foucault is in any case a further recurrent theme in the essays in this volume (and one that I treat more thematically and extensively in my *Glück und Politik: Potsdamer Vorlesungen* [Berliner Wissenschaftsverlag, 2004]). The essays do not propose positive theories, but they attempt to analyze, point out reservations, and criticize; they make no apology for this. They do not even assume that there *must* be answers. The idea that all problems either have a solution or can be shown to be pseudo-problems is not one I share.

These essays invite consideration of what there might be outside the artificially illuminated circle of "Ethics." One must, of course, resist the temptation to assume that there must be *just one* "thing" outside ethics, but one of the things there might be is a humanly important notion of "enlightenment." The notion of being an "enlightened" person does not reduce simply to that of being a person who has highly developed cognitive abilities or disposes of a vast stock of knowledge; neither does it reduce to the idea of being a morally good or socially useful person. "Enlightenment" is not a "value-free" concept because it is connected with some idea of devoting persistent, focused attention to that which is genuinely important in human life, rather than to mar-

---

[10] Friedrich Nietzsche, *Also sprach Zarathustra: "Von der Selbst-Überwindung"* (in *KS*, vol. 4, pp. 146–49).

ginal or subsidiary phenomena, to drawing the "correct" conclusions from attending to these important features—whatever they are—and to embodying these conclusions concretely in one's general way of living. It involves a certain amount of sheer knowledge, an ability to concentrate and reflect, inventiveness in restructuring one's psychic, personal, and social habits; but to be enlightened is not to "have" any bit of doctrine, but to have been (re)structured in a certain way. This is a value-laden concept because it depends on some notion of what is important. To say that it is value-laden is not to say it is arbitrary or "merely subjective," because the values relative to which we pick out what is important are generally embedded in a network of factual and other beliefs and are themselves perfectly amenable to revision on the basis of new information and further reflection. The idea of some perfect or universal Enlightenment in which one has got everything that is important in the right perspective with the right consequences probably does not make sense, but what follows from that is that there are different degrees of enlightenment and perhaps different ways of being enlightened, not that the concept does not make any sense at all. "Enlightenment" in the sense in which I am using it now does not function the way many other *idées directrices* in the history of philosophy, such as "truth" or Kantian "duty," have done. A proposition is true or false (and that is the end of it); according to Kant, something is my duty or not (and that is the end of it). One difference between such concepts and "enlightenment" is that it makes little sense to say categorically that a certain way of behaving of or living is "enlightened;" the *context* that needs to be specified in order to make this a meaningful statement is all-important. The context that needs to be supplied in order to make sense of the claim "That is an enlightened way to treat children" is very different from that presupposed by "That is an enlightened way to organize the health services in a rural area of this kind" or "They are enlightened employers." One can, of course, admit that there is a coherent notion of enlightenment while yet leaving open the question exactly how important this notion is, although at this point the discussion immediately becomes reflective: How important is it to live a life that in some sense responds to those features of the world which you perceive to be important?

These essays will have served their purpose amply if readers come to agree with me that a historically informed and contextually sensitive approach to those areas of philosophy that are directly concerned with our human world is an exceptionally good way to contribute to further human enlightenment.

1

Liberalism and Its Discontents

I

Agents in contemporary Western societies find themselves in an odd situation. On the one hand, we seem to have no realistic alternative to liberalism; that is, we know of no other approach to human society and politics that is at the same time as theoretically rich and comprehensive as liberalism and also even remotely as morally acceptable to wide sections of the population in Western societies, as they are now in fact constituted.[1] Liberal ideas permeate our social world and our everyday expectations about how people and institutions will and ought to act; they constitute the final framework within which our political thinking moves. Prima facie nonliberal forms of habitual belief, such as those associated with certain religions, forms of nationalism, residual class enmities, and so on, still, of course, exist, but they seem to be, at best, isolated and localized foreign bodies in a universe, the overall structure of which is essentially liberal; in societies that are or are aspiring to be "Western," even these nonliberal ideological fragments sometimes adopt protective coloration in the form of the best veneer of compatibility with liberalism they can muster.

On the other hand, there are signs of a significant theoretical, moral, and political disaffection with some aspects of liberalism. Liberalism has for a long time seemed to lack much inspirational potential; it is good at dissolving traditional modes of life and their associated values, but less obviously good at replacing them with anything particularly distinctive or admirable.[2] It fits all

This text is a revised version of an article I wrote in German and published in December 2001 in the *Deutsche Zeitschrift für Philosophie* under the title "Das Unbehagen am Liberalismus." The original German article in turn was the content of a series of three talks I gave at the University of Saarbrücken in December 2000. My thanks to Professor Wilfried Hinsch of Saarbrücken for the kind invitation to speak there, and also to the colleagues in Cambridge with whom I have discussed this topic most frequently; John Dunn, Zeev Emmerich, and Quentin Skinner. I also owe a great debt of gratitude to Hilary Gaskin and to the two anonymous readers for this journal who helped me to correct several mistakes and significantly improve the original German version of the essay.

[1] John Dunn, *Western Political Thought in the Face of the Future*, 2nd ed. (Cambridge: Cambridge University Press, 1993).

[2] Alasdair MacIntyre, *After Virtue* (London: Duckworth, 1981); Friedrich Nietzsche, *Jenseits von Gut und Böse*, in *Kritische Studien-Ausgabe* (*KS*), ed. Giorgio Colli and Mazzino Montinari

too comfortably with some of the more ignoble aspects of commercial society. What contribution could liberalism conceivably make to thinking about the general degradation of the planetary environment? Liberal ideals like individualism, toleration, or limitation of state power seem either short-sightedly confused or mere covers for hegemonic designs. As the Harvard political scientist Samuel Huntingdon notoriously wrote, "What is universalism to the West is imperialism to the rest."[3] Older criticisms of liberalism have also lost none of their power and plausibility: that it has no clear remedy for poverty, for reprehensible forms of inequality of power, of conditions of life, and so on. To the extent to which liberalism is committed to the principles of individual initiative and the defense of private property, it is hard to avoid the suspicion that it is rather part of the problem than part of the solution. Political theories, however, which, like liberalism, are deeply anchored in the social institutions, the mentality, and the form of life of large and wealthy populations cannot easily be shifted by even the most vigorous forms of intentional human action. This inertia even in the face of massive and telling criticism is not merely the disreputable result of the brute power of the past; rather, in an uncertain, dangerous, and unpredictable world there are good general reasons not to embark on radical changes in one's social formation unless one is forced to it by demonstrable overwhelming necessity.

The title of this essay is modeled on that of a late essay by Freud.[4] For Freud we moderns are condemned to suffer from cultural imperatives and regulations that do not allow us to lead a biologically fulfilling life, but that we are also not able simply to throw off. "Discontent" with civilization is an unavoidable fate, given the incompatibility between our biology and the necessary demands of any form of specifically human society, and Freud thinks that it is strictly impossible to do away with it altogether; the best we can do is try to mitigate some of its worst effects. In contrast to this, the discontent we feel with liberalism is of a different type, if only because we can be sure that changes in the world around us, in our politics, our social arrangements, our economic circumstances, or perhaps simply an improvement in our powers of theoretical imagination, will sooner or later dissolve liberalism and render it as irrelevant to us as feudalism or theories of morality based on honor. In the meantime, though, we are stuck with a political and social regime and a set of associated doctrines whose deficiencies are palpable.

Historically, liberalism is an invention of the nineteenth century.[5] "Liberal"

(Berlin: de Gruyter, 1980), vol. 5, § 260, and *Zur Genealogie der Moral* (*KS*, vol. 5), Essay II, §§ 11–12.

[3] Samuel Huntingdon, *The Clash of Civilizations and the Remaking of the World Order* (London: Simon & Schuster, 1977), 184.

[4] Sigmund Freud, *Das Unbehagen in der Kultur*, in *Studienausgabe*, vol. IX (Frankfurt: Fischer, 1974).

[5] See also chapter 2 of my *History and Illusion in Politics* (Cambridge: Cambridge University Press, 2001).

was originally a word used to designate a political party; it seems to have been used for the first time in about 1810–11 to refer to a group in Spain whose members advocated a limitation of the privileges of the king and the introduction of a constitutional monarchy on the British model. *Ex post*, a legitimizing prehistory of liberalism has been constructed in which Spinoza, Locke, Montesquieu, Adam Smith, and others are made to feature prominently as theoretical precursors. Since at the latest the middle of the nineteenth century, then, "liberalism" refers both to a relatively abstract theoretical structure—a collection of characteristic arguments, ideals, values, concepts—and to a social reality, a political movement that is at least partially institutionalized in organized parties. Janus-faced historical phenomena of this kind that encompass both conceptual or theoretical elements and real social forces pose special difficulties for traditional forms of philosophy. Since its beginning, philosophy has oriented itself primarily on the analysis and evaluation of relatively well-defined arguments, but the struggle between competing political groups is not a seminar discussion. Questions of definition and of purely theoretical consistency are often not the most relevant ones to ask in politics.[6]

II

Classical liberalism is best understood as a negative phenomenon, a reaction against certain events, theories, and social and political tendencies in the late eighteenth and early nineteenth centuries that early liberals identified as especially dangerous.[7] In addition, this was a twofold reaction, a kind of war on two fronts. In one direction, as it were, vis-à-vis the past, liberalism opposes absolutism and also the cameralist idea that the state has the duty and the right to care for the positive well-being of its members in an extensive sense. In the other direction, facing the future, classical liberalism strongly rejects the exaggerated moralization of politics that it sees as propagated by the French Revolutionaries. The ideological precursors of liberalism in the eighteenth century were staunch opponents of the subordination of politics to theology, and to the extent to which an absolutist ethics simply stepped into the place that now-discredited theology once occupied in the political and social sphere without changing the existing structures, it too becomes an appropriate object of liberal criticism. Rousseau's theory of the republic as the

---

[6] See also my *History and Illusion in Politics*, 1–13 and 69–73.

[7] I'm particularly interested in four theorists as representatives of classical liberalism:Wilhelm von Humboldt (especially his *Ideen zu einem Versuch, die Grenzen des Staates zu bestimmen* [Stuttgart: Reclam, 1967]), Benjamin Constant *(De la liberté chez les modernes*, ed. M. Gauchet [Paris: Hachette, 1980]), Alexis de Tocqueville (*L'ancien régime et la revolution* [Paris: Gallimard 1967]), and J. S. Mill ("On Liberty," in *"On Liberty" and Other Writings*, ed. S. Collini [Cambridge: Cambridge University Press, 1989]).

embodiment of a unitary general will opens up a highly insalubrious, specifically modern possibility, that of clothing political decisions with the mantle of an unlimited, secular moral authority. Kant's attempt to ground politics on a non-naturalist categorical ethics is understood by liberals as a parallel phenomenon and correspondingly condemned. Thus, for the early liberal Benjamin Constant, Robespierre's *"republique de la vertu et de la terreur"* is a natural outcome of taking Rousseau's central conceptions at face value, and absolutist ethics of the Kantian type is just another, slightly etiolated version of the same basic position.[8]

There are four chief components of the classical liberalism of Constant, Mill, and Tocqueville. First, liberals assign a high positive value to toleration, as the cardinal virtue of human societies. This is the oldest layer in the liberal synthesis. Second, liberals attribute special normative importance to a particular kind of human freedom. Society should consist as much as possible of voluntary relations between people, and in particular, the free assent of the members is the only source of political authority. Third, liberals are committed to individualism: a society is good only to the extent to which the individuals in it are well off. Fourth, liberalism is characterized by a particular kind of anxiety, the fear of unlimited, concentrated, or arbitrary power. Limitation of such power is thus always a goal of liberal politics. These four elements constitute the political substance of the traditional liberalism of the nineteenth century.

Since my intention is to start from liberalism as a historical phenomenon, it is important to try as far as possible to avoid anachronism, that is, to avoid narrating the history of liberalism from an endpoint in the present that is positively valued and assumed teleologically as the natural goal of the historical process. Precisely this kind of anachronistic view seems to me to have become increasingly common in late twentieth-century liberalism, especially under the impact of the work of John Rawls. Starting in the later 1950s, Rawls's work gave impetus to a revival of political philosophy, a discipline that had been pronounced moribund by some of its most distinguished practitioners a few years before, and his early achievement, especially as documented by *Theory of Justice*,[9] led to a corresponding attempt to reinterpret the history of liberalism retrospectively in the light of his position. This had some peculiar results, given that *Theory of Justice* (and the associated early writings) represented a significant departure from what had been the main line of liberal thinking in a number of important respects.

First of all, as the title of Rawls's major early work indicates, he placed the concept of justice at the center of attention. Since "justice" for him is the chief virtue of a human society, it is understandable that he organizes his political

---

[8] See below, footnote 16.
[9] Cambridge, MA: Harvard University Press, 1971.

philosophy around a "theory of justice." This, however, is a rather surprising development. To be sure, justice was of great importance to a number of pagan thinkers in the ancient world—the qualification "pagan" is important here because the Pauline strand of primitive Christianity once again demoted justice (and the "law") in favor of "grace"[10]—but I think it is fair to say that no particular saliency had been attributed to "justice" in the political philosophy of the modern period. The two originators of modern political philosophy, Machiavelli and Hobbes, set the tone. For Hobbes, security and self-preservation are the basic political virtues and the highest goals of politics. "Justice" is a mere word, the content of which is given by the law laid down by the sovereign; it is thus a highly derivative and not very significant phenomenon. Machiavelli recognizes the variety of disparate goals that humans pursue and a corresponding variety of different conceptions of the good and of the good life—there is the life of piety, of wealth accumulation, of politics. Even within the realm of politics, a political community is the object of praise on account of its "greatness," not its justice (in the *Discorsi*), and an individual is "*virtuoso*" by virtue of being able to attain fame, honor, glory, praise, and so forth, rather than for being "just" in matters of the distribution of goods or the administration of given laws. The theoretical upshot of the work of these two theorists is that justice is a minor property of subordinate administrative systems rather than the chief virtue of a society as a whole, and that "being just" is the appropriate defining character trait of the administrator, functionary, or bureaucrat rather than of the politician or citizen. To jump forward by several centuries from Hobbes, Marx, too, treats justice as an epiphenomenon. Each socioeconomic formation generates the conception of justice it "needs" to allow production to proceed as smoothly as possible, and this conception remains dependent on and has no standing outside the mode of production in question. This relative theoretical insouciance about the concept of justice is not merely a general feature of much of the most interesting modern political philosophy, but it seems especially characteristic of classical liberalism. After all, for Humboldt, Constant, J. S. Mill, and Tocqueville, toleration, freedom, and individualism were focal issues, but justice was either completely invisible (Constant), or at best a minor side-issue (Mill), or finally an object of some suspicion because it could be thought to presuppose a unitary, centralizing view of society that was a danger to individualism (Humboldt). Prima facie, it seems highly unlikely that the analysis of a concept like "justice," which is so highly dependent on shifting forms of economic activity and on historically extremely variable conceptions of the good life,

---

[10] See, for instance, Alan Badiou, *Saint Paul: La fondation de l'universalisme* (Paris: PUF, 1997), esp. chapter 7. This element becomes even more prominent in the work of the "*Ultrapauliner*" (Günter Bornkamm, *Paulus* [Stuttgart: Kohlhammer, 1969], 24) Marcion, about whom the best work is still Adolf von Harnack, *Marcion: Das Evangelium vom fremden Gott* (Leipzig, 1924, reprinted Darmstadt: Wissenschaftliche Buchgesellschaft, 1985).

could give one any real grasp on the central phenomena of politics. If this is correct, the Rawlsian project was headed in the wrong direction from the start, but even if Rawls's reorientation of political philosophy around the concept of justice was on its own terms a philosophically fruitful move, it represents a singularly unfortunate position from which to try to rewrite the history of liberalism, a movement whose members overwhelmingly had very different concerns.

The second main element in Rawls's early program was a remoralization of political philosophy. For him, in contrast to most nineteenth-century liberals, political philosophy was "applied ethics," and the "ethics" in question is a complex and original construction. Rawls is not in any interesting sense a Kantian because he has no room in his theory for such central Kantian doctrines as that of the "a priori," but he is also at pains to emphasize a certain continuity between his position and Kantian ethics, particularly on two issues: the centrality of individual "autonomy" and the priority of the right to the good.[11] Earlier liberals, however, characteristically viewed with great suspicion the intrusion of specifically moral categories into politics, and in particular they rejected the Kantian ethics on principle. Rawls's work had the curious effect of advancing Kant to the position of a kind of patron saint of liberalism. This is mildly paradoxical, because Kant had been seen for most of the nineteenth and early twentieth centuries by the main philosophic proponents of liberalism (Constant, J. S. Mill, I. Berlin; also Bentham and Dewey) as an arch antiliberal.

Pre-Rawlsian liberals had two main objections to Kant. First of all, the concept of the a priori, which is structurally indispensable for all forms of Kantianism, is not acceptable to liberals. Kant's abstract conception of reason (which can in some sense be seen as the source of his doctrine of the a priori) constitutes an attempt to absolutize accidental forms of thinking that happen to be socially important at some particular time, and thus to freeze human development at some given level. Because people at a certain time and place all think that murderers should be executed, that all forms of telling an untruth are intolerable, or that the rights of property are incompatible with taxation, and cannot perhaps even coherently imagine any alternatives, these beliefs will be stylized as universal principles and circumflexed with the hyperbolic radiance of the a priori. An a priori philosophy is for liberals a fetter on human progress. A Kantian ethics of unvarying a priori principles is incompatible with the openness, flexibility, and willingness to revise one's view and adapt to the realities of the situation demanded of liberal politics. Second, although both Kant and classical liberalism are committed to the value of freedom, their respective conceptions of freedom are radically different.

[11] See *Theory of Justice*, § 40, for the first of these and *Theory of Justice*, p. 31 n. 16 and throughout for the second.

Most liberals are highly suspicious of Kantian freedom-based-on-reason and, in fact, strongly suspect that this "positive" conception of freedom can be used to justify forms of totalitarianism.[12]

To avoid any possible misunderstanding on this point, I am certainly not claiming that a Kantian-style philosophy is absolutely incompatible with any form of liberalism. To make an assertion like that would be to make precisely one of the mistakes I am suggesting that (some) modern liberals make, that is, to assume that there is an essence of liberalism and an essence of Kantianism and that the two can be compatible or incompatible. If "liberalism" and "Kantianism" are open concepts, it is not excluded that after a sufficiently long period of time, it might be possible that the two could be made to converge.

Similarly, nothing prevents us from using our present concepts anachronistically if we wish to do that, especially if we can give some plausible reason for wanting to do it. What I do wish to assert, though, is that as a matter of fact the majority of liberal theoreticians in the nineteenth century, and a not insignificant number in the early twentieth century, saw Kant as an opponent of their basic project and that this is a fact that liberals who wish to be Kantians should recognize and take some kind of position on rather than ignoring. If they were wrong, why exactly were Constant, J. S. Mill, Dewey, and Isaiah Berlin wrong about the compatibility of Kantianism and liberalism? Whatever the best way forward for liberals in the twenty-first century might be, neither Kant nor Rawls provides an illuminating mode of cognitive access to the *historical* phenomenon of liberalism.

III

To pass now from the history of liberalism to its present state and possible future, one sometimes hears the claim that liberalism differs from other political philosophies through its recognition of the plurality of potentially valuable modes of life. This is a highly misleading assertion. First of all, liberalism has no monopoly on the praise of pluralism. After all, Marx, too, was convinced that the capitalist economic formation made it possible for individuals to develop and participate in a wide variety of diverse forms of life. Second, the multiple forms of life which liberalism recognizes are always assumed to be embedded in an overriding consensus that has a latent moral significance. What is distinctive about liberalism isn't, therefore, so much its openness to pluralism as its view that all societies should be seen as capable of attaining consensus, despite a lack of homogeneity in the manners, beliefs, and habits of their members. Can one give any reasons for adopting this attitude toward consensus? It is not completely clear what "consensus" means.

[12] See Isaiah Berlin, *Four Essays on Liberty* (Oxford: Oxford University Press, 1969).

The term vacillates between descriptive and normative uses in a way that is confusing. One can distinguish four kinds of case. The first is the case of simple empirical agreement. We are both standing in the rain, and under normal circumstances I will assume that you too know it is raining. The second kind of case is that of adaptive behavior, conformism, acquiescence, or modus vivendi. People do as others do in some particular area of life without giving it much thought, or because they think they must bow to *force majeure*. Thus, certain Islamic groups in the United Kingdom no longer circumcise their young women because they don't want problems with the British police and courts, despite the fact that they by no means agree that they should give up this practice that they take, to use the now fashionable jargon, to be partly constitutive of their "identity." They just think they have no choice. A third group of cases concerns formal agreements, as in the paradigmatic case of contracting. In a contract all parties explicitly affirm that they will behave in a certain way, usually by transferring certain resources or performing certain services. However, all parties to a contract need not have equally good reasons to enter into it, and they certainly need not have the *same* reasons. Two people can agree on state-enforced vegetarianism, the one for religious, the other for medical or sociopolitical reasons. The fourth possible case of consensus is one in which the participants have the same reasons for agreement. Even if the agents have the same reasons for agreeing, it does not follow from that fact alone that the agreement has any particular normative value or standing. Two thieves can have the same reasons for wanting to cooperate in a burglary. If one agrees that increasing the number of persons involved does not change the standing of any agreement, it isn't clear that even the existence of universal consensus need be anything more than one fact among others.

One standard liberal line of argument tends to run the notions of "consensus" that are prominent in these different cases together. Effective coordination of action is highly desirable if humans are to survive and live a life any of them will find worth living, but coordination of action requires that some kind of at least minimal and tacit agreement in values and normative conceptions exists between the cooperating parties. If the parties did not share a large number of such values, cooperation would break down. Therefore, it is claimed, there exists in every society a basic consensus that can serve as the basis on which further agreements could be reached, thereby expanding even further the human social sphere in which freedom and normativity peacefully intertwine. From this the further conclusion is drawn that it is always possible and rational for humans to try to reach consensus with their fellows, or at any rate with those with whom they must regularly deal.[13]

[13] To be sure, one must perhaps distinguish merely apparent consensus, pseudo-consensus, from real voluntary agreement, but this is a minor correction that changes nothing in the basic structure of the argument.

To be more precise, there are three variants of the liberal thesis. First, an empirical version: in fact, in every functioning society there is, one way or another, a basic consensus. Second, the political thesis: it is always possible "in principle" to elaborate the basic consensus on which social life rests so that peaceful resolution of conflicts is possible. The third, moralizing variant has a stronger and a weaker version. The stronger asserts that we are all in some sense obliged to reach consensus or that it is always rational for us to try to reach consensus; the weaker that it is always a good idea to try to reach consensus.

Against these liberal positions, Marxists and Nietzscheans can make common cause. Nietzsche sees human society as a field of potential and actual conflict, although the "conflict" in question may not always be a matter of fisticuffs but may involve only the exchange of arguments and witticisms. In the real world, Nietzsche argues, any existing "consensus" can be no more than a momentary truce entered into for pragmatic reasons and with no moral implications, and to expect anything more is a utopian hope.

Marxists in any case have always been of the opinion that irreconcilable conflict, continuing disagreement, and social division are the normal states of all forms of society that have existed up to now. Apparent public consensus is merely the false (and thin) ideological cover that hides a chasm of division that is as deep and unbridgeable as anything in the human world can be. In its classic form, Marxism teaches that every class society is divided into groups that not only have no common good but have diametrically opposed basic interests. What is good for the capitalists is bad for the proletariat, and vice versa. Only a classless society could lack socially entrenched insoluble conflicts of interest. In capitalist societies, politics-as-usual is a pointless activity for members of the proletariat, and the only sensible way to act in the long run is to engage actively in the class struggle.

For a variety of reasons, the above analysis nowadays seems out of date. The thesis that the economically and politically relevant structure of a modern society can be exhaustively described by the contrast between capitalists and proletariat is no longer plausible. This should not, however, be taken to imply that liberal conceptions of social harmony and the unlimited possibility of peaceful consensus have become any more convincing, because the main problem of the Marxist analysis is that it oversimplifies the sources of conflict and division in the modern world. Instead of one main contradiction between workers and capitalists, there is an almost unsurveyable variety of groups that are potentially or actually in conflict with each other, groups that in some cases have very sharply defined, completely incompatible interests and control over considerable powers and resources.

In a given case, it may *sometimes* be possible to attain agreement about some points of dispute in real or hypothetical discussion. Sometimes there is neutral ground or a ground constituted by shared beliefs to which one can withdraw to find compromises—sometimes, not always. In every society there are both areas of consensus and areas of conflict. Both should be understood naturalistically, and individuals, social groups, and institutions must learn to deal with both. Naturally we often—but not always—have perfectly good reasons for taking part in discussion, especially when the alternative is physical violence with opponents who are stronger than we are, but whether the reasons we do (or do not) have in a particular case are good, less good, or ridiculously bad is an empirical matter.[14]

None of the three liberal theses about consensus seems to me at all plausible. First of all, it seems obvious that many societies are perfectly well able to maintain themselves although their members do not take part in a consensus that is in any way normatively binding; many people in many societies simply put up with existing arrangements that they must endure as best they can. Second, the claim that it is "in principle" always possible to attain consensus is completely uninformative until one knows, in more detail than has ever been provided by liberals, what exactly "in principle" means. Furthermore, even if the claim were true, why should a statement about a consensus that "could be attained" under some fictive or hypothetical circumstances have any direct relevance to a given real political situation? Finally, it is always an open question whether or not it is a good idea to enter into discussion or attempt to reach consensus. If I am dealing with a small group of armed fanatics, it is by no means clear that I ought to argue with them rather than immediately and unilaterally disarming them. To be sure, I will probably have various reasons for trying to do this with as little use of force myself as possible, but even if I use minimal force I won't be *discussing* anything with them, and a priori I can't know that any particular level of application of force will be sufficient.

IV

Which parts, then, of classical liberalism deserve to be further developed and cultivated? In the first place, the criticism of theocratic conceptions of society or, what is another form of the same thing, of absolutist (that is, explicitly or implicitly theocentric) forms of ethics. The Kantian philosophy is no more than at best a half-secularized version of such a theocratic ethics, with "Reason" in the place of God. This does not amount to much more than a change of names.[15] The pure normative standpoint that Kant's ethics tries to occupy,

[14] See also my *Public Goods, Private Goods* (Princeton, NJ: Princeton University Press, 2001), 96–104.

[15] It was a commonly held objection to Kant in the late eighteenth century that his criticism of traditional theology was substantively radical in name only. The whole content of traditional theology could be reintroduced simply by renaming it "Postulates of Pure Practical Reason." This

a standpoint in which we consider only the normatively relevant features of a possible world, abstracting strictly from the real world and the empirical accidents of concrete situations, is an expression of what Dewey called "the quest for certainty."[16] In an insecure world, weak humans struggle convulsively to reach some kind of stability; the a priori is an overcompensation in thought for experienced human weakness.[17] This is one of the origins of Kant's notorious rigidity, his authoritarian devotion to "principles," and his tendency to promote local habits of thought to constituents of the absolute framework within which alone (purportedly) any coherent experience was possible; thus, Euclidean geometry is declared the a priori condition of human experience, and sadistic remnants of puritanism become demands of pure practical reason.[18] Classical liberalism rejected Kant's practical philosophy, but perhaps this is not enough. Perhaps one should also reject the very idea of a pure normative standpoint.

This might be thought to be a rather extreme suggestion. Kantians have some human failings like everyone else; these need not be thought to reflect negatively on the pure normative standpoint. Is there any reason to think that the very idea of a pure normative standpoint implies the attempt to absolutize accidental existing habits of thought?

Rather than trying to give a direct answer to this question, I would like to approach it by discussing two examples. Both are drawn from the work of John Rawls. As I said, Rawls was never a strict Kantian, and as his thought developed, he moved further and further away from commitment to any form of pure normativity. This is a further reason to use him as an example: if some of the deficiencies inherent in adopting a pure normative standpoint are visible even in a philosopher who has moved as far beyond Kant as Rawls has, this seems to me to give further weight to suspicions about the normative standpoint as a whole.

To start with the first example, in *Theory of Justice*, Rawls claims to be de-

---

was not exactly fair, because not *all* of traditional theology would survive Kant's attack. A later version of basically the same line of thought occurs in Stirner's criticism of Feuerbach (Max Stirner, *Der Einzige und sein Eigentum* [Stuttgart: Reclam, 1967]). Feuerbach, Stirner claims, doesn't, as he pretends, radically detheologize religion, he simply uses the words "human essence" in place of the word "God." The structure of Feuerbach's theory and the content of the moral obligations it imposes on individuals, though, remain the same as that of traditional theology.

[16] John Dewey, *The Quest for Certainty in John Dewey: The Later Works 1925–1953*, ed. John Boydston (Carbondale: Southern Illinois Press, 1988), vol. 4; similar thoughts in Theodor Adorno and Max Horkheimer, *Die Dialektik der Aufklärung* (Frankfurt: Fischer, 1969).

[17] In a complex industrialized world, there is a further reason for adherence to fixed and rigid general principles: efficiency and simplicity of administration. See my *History and Illusion in Politics* (Cambridge: Cambridge University Press, 2001), 150–52.

[18] For Kant as "gallows-philosopher," see Jacques Lacan, *Séminaire VII: L'éthique de la psychanalyse* (Paris: Seuil, 1986), and also Adorno and Horkheimer, *Dialektik der Aufklärung*.

scribing the "reflective equilibrium" that would be attained by certain fully rational agents who engaged in discussion under certain idealized conditions. This state of reflective equilibrium is best understood as a kind of successor to the pure normative perspective. After all, the point of one of the main constructions—the introduction of the "veil of ignorance"—is precisely to exclude from consideration empirical information that might prejudice the overriding normative force of the outcome. It is, then, extremely striking, not to say astounding, to the lay reader that the complex theoretical apparatus of *Theory of Justice*, operating through over 500 pages of densely argued text, eventuates in a constitutional structure that is a virtual replica (with some extremely minor deviations) of the arrangements that exist in the United States.[19] It strains credulity to the breaking point to believe that "free and rational agents" (with no further qualifications), even if they were conducting a discussion behind an artificial veil of ignorance, and assuming that they were to agree on anything at all under those circumstances, would light on precisely *these* arrangements. Some critics might fasten on this as an indication of the essentially conservative bias of Rawls's discussion: the theoretical imagination is employed not to think about *alternatives* to the *status quo*, but in order to reproduce it schematically in thought, presenting it as the outcome of full, free, rational discussion.[20] This might seem grossly unfair, given Rawls's evident intention to produce a work that would have some powerful redistributive implications. If, however, one thinks it at all reasonable to judge what is after all presented as a political philosophy by its actual political effects, it is hard to see how Rawls's perfectly genuine redistributive hopes could have any chance of being realized—and not merely because Rawls has no theory of political *action* or agency, although that is also true. The actual effect of Rawls's theory is to undercut theoretically any straightforward appeal to egalitarianism. Egalitarianism has the advantage that gross failure to comply with its basic principles is not difficult to monitor. There are, to be sure, well-known and unsettled issues about comparability of resources and about whether resources are really the proper objects for egalitarians to be concerned with, but there can be little doubt that if person A in a fully monetarized society has ten thousand times the monetary resources of person B, then under normal circumstances the two are not for most politically relevant purposes "equal."

Rawls's theory effectively shifts discussion away from the utilitarian discussion of the consequences of a certain distribution of resources, and also away from an evaluation of distributions from the point of view of strict equal-

[19] Of course it is not at all difficult to see how Americans might find it plausible that any rational agents discussing politics under favorable conditions would agree on these arrangements.
[20] See Theodor Adorno, *Der Positivismusstreit in der deutschen Soziologie* (Berlin: Luchterhand, 1972), "Einleitung;" see also my *Morality, Culture, and History* (Cambridge: Cambridge University Press, 1999), 69–76.

ity; instead, he focuses attention on a complex counterfactual judgment. The question is not "Does A have grossly more than B?"—a judgment to which within limits it might not be impossible to get a straightforward answer—but rather the virtually unanswerable "Would B have even less if A had less?" One cannot even begin to think about assessing any such claim without making an enormous number of assumptions about scarcity of various resources, the form the particular economy in question had, the preferences, and in particular the incentive structure, of the people who lived in it, and unless one had a rather robust and detailed economic theory of a kind that few people will believe any economist today has. In a situation of uncertainty like this, the actual political *onus probandi* in fact tacitly shifts to the have-nots;[21] the "haves" lack an obvious systematic motivation to argue for redistribution of the excess wealth they own, or indeed to find arguments to that conclusion plausible. They don't in the same way need to prove anything; they, *ex hypothesi*, "have" the resources in question: *"Beati possedentes."*

How, however, are the have-nots—or intellectuals speaking in their name—supposed to make an argument that depends both on convincing others of the general plausibility of Rawls's approach *and* in addition on what cannot be more than a highly speculative evaluation of a complex counterfactual claim? That Rawls's early views have had no real redistributive effect is not merely a result of the usual difficulty of implementing political theories in the real world. The second example comes from Rawls's late work, *The Law of Peoples*. In this work in which Rawls discusses certain aspects of international relations, he introduces the category of an "outlaw state," a "regime that refuses to comply with a reasonable Law of Peoples" (p. 90), and writes that "France, Spain, the Hapsburgs—or more recently Germany" were instances of "outlaw states" (pp. 105–6). "Outlaw state" is a slightly more refined variant of the term "rogue state," which has come to fashionable use in the context of the attempt by the Bush administration to justify its missile defense program,[22] and Rawls's claims about "outlaw states" are the philosophical pendent of former U.S. President Reagan's characterization of the Soviet Union as an "evil empire." At this late point in his career, Rawls has moved very far indeed away from Kantianism, but this is still the sort of easygoing, but narrow-minded, moralization that some of the most interesting political theorists of the nineteenth and early twentieth centuries—Hegel, Marx, Nietzsche, Freud, Dewey—wished to put an end to and replace with more highly differentiated modes of dealing with history and politics. For Rawls, it seems a truth too self-evident to require mentioning that Spanish hegemony over Latin America in the eighteenth century was something utterly different from and much worse than North American hegemony over the same re-

[21] This is not a logical point.
[22] See Noam Chomsky, *Rogue States* (London: Pluto Press, 2000).

gion in the early twentieth century. The British Empire did not always use kid gloves in dealing with competitors and subjects, but for Rawls it was, in contrast to France, apparently never an "outlaw state." It also does not seem to occur to him even as an abstract possibility that the United States might be considered by some an "outlaw state," despite a history of annihilation of indigenous populations, slavery, and repeated military intervention in Central America (and elsewhere). It is hard even for those of us who belong to the privileged, inherently nonoutlaw, Anglo-American world to resist the conclusion that this part of Rawls's theory is significantly influenced by ethnocentrism. Naturally there are massive differences between the Spanish Empire of the seventeenth century and the British Empire of the nineteenth century—who would deny that? It is also true that politicians have a strong interest in distinguishing as sharply as possible between their own policies (and the actual effects of these) and those of their analogues in other states— what is firmness of purpose with us is repression in them.[23] Nowadays most modern governments will have huge staffs of experts, lawyers, and researchers who are paid to seek out grounds for making the appropriate distinctions as vividly and convincingly as possible. The fact that occasionally in some particular extreme cases one can't find any convincing differences is not really an argument for the political relevance of the strictly normative standpoint. In those extreme cases in which adopting this standpoint does deliver a practically useful answer, we usually have sufficient nonmoral reasons to make whatever decision we make, and in most run-of-the-mill cases normativity gives us a clear decision that seems plausible only because the analysis that must precede the normativity judgment renders a complex situation artificially simple and perspicuous. This analysis, which eventuates in the judgment "this is murder," "this is fraud," and so on, is what is actually doing the work.

The historical struggle against theocracy, absolutism, and dogmatism has left behind in liberalism a thick deposit of skepticism not only vis-à-vis all-encompassing worldviews, but also vis-à-vis universalist political theories of any kind. On this point Constant, Berlin, Popper, and Rorty (and also, of course, Burke) are of one accord. Classical liberalism did not wish to be an all-encompassing, universal worldview but merely a political program aimed at eliminating specific social and political evils.

In its origin, liberalism had no ambition to be universal either in the sense of claiming to be valid for everyone and every human society or in the sense of purporting to give an answer to all the important questions of human life. There is no clearly developed single epistemology for classical liberalism, but it would seem that a liberal would have to believe that liberal views are eas-

---

[23] Sometimes, of course, politicians have the reverse interest, one in presenting their programs as being as like as possible those of some favored model.

ily accessible to humans who have no special expertise or epistemically privileged position. The ideal of liberalism is a practically engaged political philosophy that is both epistemically and morally highly abstemious. That is, at best, a very difficult and possibly a completely hopeless project. It is therefore not surprising that liberals succumb again and again to the temptation to go beyond the limits they would ideally set themselves and try to make of liberalism a complete philosophy of life. For complicated historical reasons, in the middle of the twentieth century, Kantianism presented itself as a "philosophical foundation" for a version of liberalism, and liberals at that time were sufficiently weak and self-deceived (or strong and opportunistic) to accept the offer. Even with the infusion of a significant dose of the Kantian philosophy, however, liberalism has not succeeded in producing a position that is "universal" in any relevant sense. Neither has it demonstrated an ability to remain faithful to its original theoretical and moral abstemiousness without losing political effectiveness.

Rorty has made the extremely astute and important observation that the a priori, theocentrism (even in its attenuated form as a "philosophy of reason"), the purely normative standpoint, and a specific form of the "spirit of heaviness"[24] all naturally go together. A consistent liberalism would have to turn its back on all of them.

Unfortunately, Rorty strongly suggests an interpretation of this observation that does not do justice to it, and he seems to draw from this interpretation two false consequences. First of all, Rorty is obviously keen to promote irony as the most appropriate attitude for a contemporary liberal. While, however, it is true that the rejection of a theocentric view of the world will most likely bring with it a discrediting of a certain number of human attitudes that were closely associated with it—automatic deference to authority, attraction to certain kinds of solemnity, unctuousness, and obscurantism—irony is not the only alternative to piety. Another alternative is to adopt an extremely businesslike attitude, to identify oneself fully with various projects in the world, and so forth. Indeed, looking at the matter historically, there would not seem to be any particular natural affinity between liberalism and irony. If one considers the most significant ironists of the modern period—Pascal (in the *Lettres provinciales*), Swift, Voltaire, Kierkegaard—only Voltaire seems in any important way a precursor of liberalism, and I think one would search in vain in the writings of the major figures of liberalism (Humboldt, Constant, Mill) for traces of irony. In fact, the only obvious "ironist" among the political philosophers of the nineteenth century is Maistre, who was anything but a liberal. When Maistre in a famous passage[25] reports that the executioner after

---

[24] Nietzsche, *Also sprach Zarathustra*.

[25] Joseph de Maistre, *Les Soirées de Petersbourg* (Paris: Edition du Vieux Colombier, 1960), 40.

discharging his function returns home in a self-satisfied mood, saying to himself, "No one can break a man on the wheel as well as I can," this is an archetypical instance of what we usually call irony. Maistre is inviting us here to look at this situation simultaneously from three distinct perspectives that conflict. There is the point of view of the executioner himself ("the only man who wears gloves in church"); the point of view of (post-Beccarian) common sense, which finds the executioner (and his family) repellent and his self-satisfaction nauseating; and finally the point of view of God, who sees the executioner as the necessary central point of any society, holding it all together and making civilized life possible. "Ironically," the executioner is (from God's point of view and, therefore, also Maistre's to some extent) right, not perhaps right to be *self*-satisfied, but right to glory in the efficient discharge of a dignified and commodious office. The examples of Maistre and Kierkegaard also show that irony is not in itself inherently incompatible with a theocentric view of the world.

Rorty to be sure would be unmoved by all this, because he is not using "irony" in the normal sense in which we use that term—which is admittedly hard to grasp—but is engaged in the project of "using old words in new senses"[26] so as to break down existing vocabularies. Rather, for him an ironist is someone who has doubts about the existing "final" vocabulary in use in society and "does not believe that her vocabulary is closer to reality than others, that it is in touch with a power not herself."[27] On this use of the term, neither Plato, Maistre, nor Kierkegaard are ironists, a consequence that I think Rorty would welcome. Nor, although I think Rorty would disagree with me, is Hegel.[28] Most oddly of all, Heidegger turns out on this reading to be an ironist, a claim that will not, I think, immediately recommend itself to anyone who has followed the earth-heavy footfall of the Sage of Messkirch through any of his works and who retains a grasp on any of the senses "irony" has had in European life since antiquity.[29] None of this, again, would bother Rorty—of course, breaking down the old vocabulary will generate paradoxes like this, and my pointing them out is just part of *my* strategy of being, in Rorty's eyes, conventional and boring, or of rejigging the meaning of "irony" to suit my own purposes. If, however, "irony," in the traditional or the Rortyan

[26] Richard Rorty, *Contingency, Irony, and Solidarity* (Cambridge: Cambridge University Press 1989), 78.

[27] Ibid., 73.

[28] Hegel did change his mind on a number of things during his philosophically active life, but the one thing he never gave up was the commitment to a form of absolute knowledge (couched in a final vocabulary) and also a rejection of what he called "irony" (which he saw as instantiated in the work of Friedrich Schlegel).

[29] It is, of course, also the case that Heidegger is not a liberal, and is a paradigm of those attitudes of wilful obscurantism, authoritarianism, and sanctimoniousness that liberalism should terminate.

sense, is not the only possible attitude we can adopt if we want to avoid piety, and if "irony" in Rorty's sense is rather different from what tradition would have called "irony," it is hard to avoid asking why we should accede to Rorty's suggestion. And to answer this in turn, it might be useful to think about what motivates Rorty to make this suggestion and what the consequences of adopting it would be. This brings me to the second place in which he seems to me to point us in the wrong direction. I think his motivation is to detach us as much as possible from trying to approach politics theoretically and to denigrate political action in a very subtle and sophisticated way. Irony stands orthogonal to any form of active, practical engagement with the world. It is a luxury of people who do not pressingly have to act, the kind of people Rorty calls with admiration "bookish intellectuals," and whom he wishes to encourage to find self-realization in private life, not politics.[30] This is why it is particularly impressive that Socrates and Kierkegaard, who thought they did in some sense have to act, also allowed themselves to indulge in irony. An "ironic" execution is either no execution at all (but a literary or theatrical event), or a form of attempted additional mockery of the victim, or both at the same time: "This is Jesus, King of the Jews." The Christian thinks that this is doubly ironic, and that the joke is finally on Pilate.

The liberal who gives up the sanctimoniousness of the purely normative standpoint will perhaps, as Rorty correctly recognizes, stand at a certain kind of distance to some kinds of beliefs, but the attitude involved in this does not seem appropriately captured by calling it either "irony" or (another older contender) "skepticism." With this, one is returned to the issue from which I started, namely, what attitude we should adopt toward liberalism. This cannot be completely separated from questions about the intentions of liberalism and how to describe the kinds of attitudes that are, have been, or might easily be or have been associated with existing forms of liberalism. Irony will not allow the right kind of theoretically reflective, engaged political practice.

Some will (correctly) object that the demand that I made earlier that anachronism be avoided is an ideal impossible fully to attain. Of course, the account of "liberalism" I have given is a selective one—an ideal type—that arises from emphasizing certain features and downplaying others, and the choice of what to emphasize to some extent depends on what I judge to be philosophically fruitful and morally and politically valuable. We all have no alternative but to construct the past in the light of what we take to be a viable future, but it does not follow from this that all constructions are equally enlightening or that the usual empirical and documentary standards for judging historical accounts are irrelevant. The anti-Kantian and anti-Rawlsian perspective has, in my view, a twofold advantage. It is a better guide to liberalism as a historical phenomenon, that is, one that allows us to attain a fuller,

[30] Rorty, *Contingency, Irony, and Solidarity*, 65.

more detailed, and more correct understanding of its history, and it also at the same time provides a more promising orientation for thinking and acting politically in the future.

As long as the real social, economic, and political institutions and circumstances of our life do not change,[31] we cannot expect to rid ourselves completely of our discontent with liberalism. This might, however, even be thought to be a vindication of one strand in the liberal tradition, the strand that is action-oriented but reflexively anti-utopian and asserts that no system of either action or thought is perfect. This should hold as much for liberalism as for anything else. This kind of discontent, then, might be not necessarily an objection but a sign of the continuing vitality of this tradition.

---

[31] *"Le Libéralisme n'est évidemment pas une idéologie ni un idéal. C'est une forme de gouvernement et de "rationalité" gouvernementale fort complexe."* Michel Foucault, *Dits et écrits,* vol. IV (Paris: Gallimard, 1994), 36.

2

Neither History nor Praxis

THE RECENT DEATH of the philosopher John Rawls makes it especially appropriate, but also particularly difficult, to reflect on the peculiarity of his life, work, and influence, and try to assess what long-lasting contribution he might have made to our understanding of politics and society. Rawls by all accounts was a remarkably saintly man, a devoted teacher of many highly successful students, and a concerned citizen. Under these circumstances any discussion of him and his work, especially at this time, is likely to take place in an atmosphere of mild hagiography. The body of work he left behind is large and intricate, and has been the object of literally thousands of pages of exegesis, criticism, and further elaboration, some of it highly technical in character. Many academics have sunk large amounts of intellectual capital into mastery of the details of his position, and the "correct" reading of it. However, precisely because Rawls was a public philosopher of unrivaled influence, natural piety should not take priority over the demands of the piety due a philosopher: uninhibited discussion of his work and approach, and the attempt to give a global account of the status of his theory, its overall structure, and its historical location, without getting lost in details.

Between 1988 and 1992 Steve Pyke photographed several dozen philosophers and asked each to write a brief statement describing his or her "philosophy" to accompany the respective photo. Most of the entries are the sort of thing one would expect to find—philosophy is a form of self-knowledge, a way of asking certain basic questions, an attempt at systematic exercise of human reason, etc. Rawls's response takes the form of an autobiographical sketch:

> From the beginning of my study of philosophy in my late teens I have been concerned with moral questions and the religious and philosophical basis on which they might be answered. Three years spent in the US army in World War II led me to be also concerned with political questions. Around 1950 I started to write a book on justice, which I eventually completed.[1]

I am deeply grateful to a number of colleagues who have helped me over the years to think about the issues discussed in this essay: Martin Bauer, Rüdiger Bittner, John Dunn, Zeev Emmerich, Hilary Gaskin, Susan James, Christine Pries, Quentin Skinner. Needless to say, none of these persons necessarily agrees with any particular claim I make.

[1] S. Pyke (1993) *Philosophers* (Manchester: Cornerhouse Publications, 1993), no pagination

The book Rawls started in 1950 appeared in 1971 as *A Theory of Justice*. It is a densely argued treatise of over 500 pages dealing with institutional structure and the principles of distribution that ought to hold in what Rawls calls a "well-ordered society." Conceivably, the autobiographical statement to Steve Pyke is simply a way of elegantly evading the question "What is your conception of philosophy?," but it is just possible that Rawls thought that this description of the development of his interests threw some light on the nature of his philosophy. After all, there is a tradition going back to the ancient world which insists that philosophy and life are connected and are to be integrated in various distinctive ways. It is not just that Stoics and cynics hold and try to defend different theories or propositions, but the life of a Stoic has a different shape from that of a cynic.[2] This tradition is not as strong now as it once was, and in the contemporary world conceptions of philosophy modeled on mathematics, natural science, or some form of social problem-solving are more common, but the older view retains what force it has—understandably—in areas in which ethics, politics, and philosophy touch or overlap.[3]

Perhaps Rawls did have the modern, scientific model of philosophy in mind. For whatever reason, on this model one picks a topic to work on, and tries to do one's best with it. There will probably be specific biographical reasons for the choice of topic, but they will be of no relevance, provided the topic itself is of inherent interest.

---

in this volume, but the philosophers photographed are listed alphabetically and this autobiographical statement is on the page facing the photo of Rawls.

[2] The ancients tended to focus on one side of this integration: from the theoretical beliefs held to the kind of life lived. The Stoic and cynic lives differ *because* of the difference in the beliefs the respective philosophers held. The nineteenth century added to this an increasing appreciation of the other direction in which the equation could be read. Thus, in 1797, Fichte announced that the philosophy one chose depended on what kind of person one was, and by the middle of the century it was a commonplace idea among the Young Hegelians that a philosophy arose in part out of a reflection on the state of the world and the outstanding issues of the day (*sub specie universalitatis*). To identify what are the outstanding questions of the day is by no means a trivial task, but rather one that requires both a certain cognitive exertion and moral courage. Although this is to some extent the precondition of philosophy, the process of philosophizing itself does not merely give one answers to the questions with which one started, but can change one's understanding of what is questionable or problematic. A philosophical life is one in which this reflection and the results to which it leads inform the attitudes the philosopher takes toward this world, one in which an original, relatively naive and immediate diagnosis of the times is transformed into a considered position.

[3] No one much cares that the logician Frege was an early and ardent admirer of Hitler. After all, among other things, he died in 1925 and never took any public position on politics. Discussion of the philosopher Frege is discussion of his attempt to ground mathematics on logic, his definition of a number, his new notation for logic, or his philosophy of language. On the other hand, it seems wilfully blind to overlook Heidegger's National Socialism, given that his work is clearly, in some sense, intended not to provide a formal definition of some mathematical construction, but to tell us something about how to live. See Hans Sluga, *Heidegger's Crisis* (Cambridge, MA: Harvard University Press, 1993), esp. chapter 4.

No one can object to this free choice of topic for investigation or to the simple activation of theoretical curiosity that is not motivated by any compelling personal or social experience. It is, however, at least possible to read Rawls's statement as trying to connect a certain characteristic set of human experiences in the twentieth century and a set of topics and ways of going about philosophy, which he presents as attempts at finding appropriate responses to those experiences.

How one reacts to Rawls's presentation of this possible shape of a philosophical life is a good indication of one's own sensibilities. Some philosophers, apparently most philosophers in the English-speaking world, see it as a perfectly comprehensible moral and intellectual *cursus vitae*, and an instance of the philosopher being socially responsible in a particularly laudable way. There is, however, a small group of people, of whom I am one, who find this autobiographical statement odd in a way that is revealing about what we experience as the eccentricity of Rawls's work. To people like me, a philosophical life like the one Rawls outlines simply doesn't make sense, so we do not find it surprising that Rawls's philosophy doesn't make much sense as a contribution to understanding or dealing with the social and political world.

There is another old tradition which holds that philosophy is characterized more by the questions it asks than by the answers it gives to those questions. One can easily imagine a person confronted with the events of the Second World War being motivated to ask various questions, for instance about European history, about the dynamics of political systems under stress, about the economics of competitive international markets, about human social psychology and the structure of collective action. What, however, would one have to believe about the world to think that "What is the correct conception of justice?" is the appropriate question to ask in the face of concentration camps, secret police, and the firebombing of cities? Are reflections about the correct distribution of goods and service in a "well-ordered society" the right *kind* of intellectual response to slavery, torture, and mass murder? Was the problem in the Third Reich that people in extermination camps didn't get the slice of the economic pie that they ought to have had, if everyone had discussed the matter freely and under the right conditions? Should political philosophy really be essentially about questions of fairness of distribution of resources? Aren't security and the control of violence far more important? How about the coordination of action, the sharing of information, the cultivation of trust, the development and deployment of human individual and social capacities, the management of relations of power and authority, the balancing of the demands of stability and reform, the provision for a viable social future?

A *Theory of Justice* introduces Rawls's major intellectual innovation. This is the device of trying to understand "justice" as the content of possible agreement reached by all the members of a society in a discussion conducted under certain idealized circumstances. Rawls introduces two technical terms to refer to these idealized circumstances: the discussion is said to be conducted "in the original position" under a "veil of ignorance." Suppose, as a thought-experiment, that all the members of a society freely discuss the social arrangements which will regulate their mode of living together as if it were simply up to them to decide what institutions to create. That is discussion "in the original position." The people in this position are said to conduct their discussion "under a veil of ignorance" because we imagine them to be specifically deprived of empirical information about the society in question and their own place in it. In particular, they are not to know its economic or political situation or the level of civilization and culture it has been able to achieve.[4] They are also supposed not to know their own situation in the society, what generation they belong to, what assets, abilities, and general conception of the good they have; they have no knowledge of their concrete identity, save as purely rational deliberators. The participants in the discussion are like Platonic administrators who imagine they have a whole society at their disposal, and must decide how best to structure it. They themselves and the conditions under which they conduct the discussion have also been specifically idealized in such a way as to nullify any political relations that might be thought to exist between them, and thus to render these relations irrelevant and without influence on the final outcome. Justice is what such agents would freely agree to under such conditions. Rawls's book tries first to argue that the construction of such a discussion in the "original position" is the proper way to approach justice, and then to determine what agents in the original position would agree to. Although there is no politics in the original position, agents in that position in deciding how they will live together must, of course, agree on a political structure for the society they will inhabit. Rawls's conclusion is that in the original position the idealized free and rational agents he describes would agree on a set of constitutional arrangements very much like those now current in the United States as the basic political framework for their society, plus a set of fairly abstract principles to govern the distribution of liberties, opportunities, and goods and services in the society.

One main question is why we would have any reason to suppose that agents in such a situation would *agree* on anything at all. No matter how long they discussed matters, there might remain at the end different groups with different views.[5] A second question is why, even if they did agree, this decision should have any relevance whatever to us, who do have concrete "identities," parts of which sometimes can be of importance to us, and who live in a concrete situation in a complex real world, *not* in the idealized world of the orig-

[4] J. Rawls, *A Theory of Justice* (Cambridge, MA: Harvard University Press, 1971) p. 137.

[5] The variant of this that has been most widely discussed is the differences that might remain between people who were more risk-averse and those who were more willing to take risks. See R. Tuck, "The Dangers of Natural Rights," *Harvard Journal of Law and Public Policy*, 1997, 20(3), 690–93.

inal position. This type of theory appeals to traditional prejudice among philosophers in favor of purity, autonomy, formalism, and abstractness. The theory certainly purports to be pure of contamination by the facts of history, psychology, economics, sociology, and political science, but it is highly questionable whether *this* type of abstractness is conducive to real understanding of the world we live in, and at least equally questionable whether we can have a useful practical philosophy, or even a useful set of normative rules, without such grounded understanding.

Rawls's theory presents itself as egalitarian, although—at any rate in the original form—it comes equipped with a catch so large that it seems unsurprising that the real political effect of the theory has been close to zero. The catch, called the "difference principle," specifically allows departure from equality if the resulting inequality is one that improves the state of the least advantaged members of the society. It turns out to be extremely difficult to assess in practice whether or not a certain existing inequality is or is not allowed by the difference principle. Furthermore, one might wonder whether accepting the difference principle would not, in practice, lead to much more significant concessions to inequality than Rawls seems to expect.

Finally, it is perfectly possible to find the basic idea behind the difference principle—that increases in the absolute standard of living of the poor can, in principle, justify great inequalities—morally very repellent.[6]

Rawls's later work moves away from the Never-neverland of this early model with its glorification of the ignorance of agents in the original position, but it never gets very far, and pays for its minimally increased connection to the real world of American politics with a significant loss of scope and theoretical power. Thus his last systematic work, *The Law of Peoples*, is a treatment of international relations.[7] He distinguishes five kinds of society: (a) liberal, (b) decent,[8] (c) outlaw states, (d) societies burdened by unfavorable conditions, and (e) benevolent absolutisms.[9] Outlaw states are those that "refuse to comply with a reasonable Law of Peoples."[10] Examples of "outlaw states" include, in the early modern period, "France, Spain, and the Hapsburgs" and "more recently, Germany."[11] "Outlaw state" is clearly Rawls's theoretical equivalent of a concept that has become one of the cornerstones of U.S. foreign policy during the past 20 years, and has appeared in a variety of

[6] J. Dunn, *The Cunning of Unreason: Making Sense of Politics* (London: Harper-Collins, 2000), pp. 279–80.

[7] J. Rawls, *The Law of Peoples* (Cambridge, MA: Harvard University Press, 1999).

[8] A "decent society" for Rawls is one that is not liberal but still deserves to take its place as a member of a Society of Peoples under a reasonable Law of Peoples. See J. Rawls, *The Law of Peoples*, p. 4.

[9] Ibid., p. 4.

[10] Ibid., pp. 5, 90.

[11] Ibid., pp. 105–6.

guises, from Reagan's proclamation that the Soviet Union was an "evil empire" to the very emphatic use of the term "rogue state" by the current Bush administration. Rawls's claim that certain nonliberal societies (decent and "benevolent" ones) deserve some recognition and ought to be "tolerated" by liberal societies[12] is a significant and welcome advance over the strict dichotomization that seems to dominate much thinking in U.S. government circles today. It strongly suggests disagreement with the position of U.S. President George W. Bush, that those who are not "with" the United States belong to an "axis of evil." Still, Rawls does not think that liberal societies should extend their tolerance to outlaw states. Outlaw states may not be exterminated ad libitum, but "liberal" states have a right to keep and deploy nuclear weapons for deterrent purposes, and may attack outlaw states with military force under certain circumstances if that is necessary to prevent violation of human rights.[13] This does not even purport to be a view from an anonymous universal "original position," but is, even on the most superficial inspection, a specifically American political position—more enlightened, perhaps, than that of George W. Bush or Condoleeza Rice, but generically the same kind of thing. Of course, no one can object *in principle* to citizens helping to elaborate the national ideology (provided it is not actively vicious), but philosophy has in the past often aspired to something more than this.

Rawls's influence in the U.S. academy grew most rapidly in the late 1970s and 1980s, during a period that saw the start of a major and lasting downturn in the world economy,[14] a significant increase in inequality in the world, and a distinct turn to the political right in most advanced Western countries. This conjunction is an extremely striking phenomenon, but one that has failed to attract the attention it deserves: as Rawls's purportedly egalitarian theory became more entrenched and more highly elaborated, social inequalities in fact increased drastically in virtually all industrialized countries.

Four lines of hypothesis suggest themselves to explain why Rawls's stock rose as the world moved firmly and distinctly in the direction precisely opposite to the one apparently indicated by the theory. The first is that Rawls's theory gained in attractiveness as a compensatory fantasy.[15] The mechanism would be like that analyzed by Feuerbach for the origin and development of religion.[16] Weak humans cannot easily tolerate clear recognition of their de-

---

[12] Ibid., Part II.

[13] Ibid., pp. 9, 80–81.

[14] See R. Brenner, *The Boom and the Bubble: The U.S. in the World Economy* (London: Verso, 2002).

[15] For a general discussion of recent Rawls-style political philosophy along these lines, see A. Badiou, *Ethics: An Essay on the Understanding of Evil* (London: Verso, 2001), especially pp. liii–lvi, 90.

[16] L. Feuerbach, *The Essence of Christianity* (New York: Harper & Row, 1957), translated by M. Evans (George Eliot).

ficiencies and so invent an imaginary agent—God—whom they endow with the powers they lack. In just the same way, fantasies about the original position become more plausible to agents the more the world demonstrates to them their inability to understand or exercise any control over its movements. This would be comprehensible and unobjectionable enough if, unlike the fiction of a God, the theory of the original position actually directed us toward learning to deal with our weakness, but the continuing redistribution of resources from the poor to the rich indicates that it hasn't. Does one perhaps need to adopt a more long-term perspective, that of 400 or 500 years? Do we then have to adopt a similarly long time frame for evaluating claims about a possible "pure" Islamic Republic, Marxism, or the Situationist International?

The second line of hypothesis starts from a sharp distinction between the basic properties of scientific theories and those of a political philosophy. Scientific theories can be understood as abstract entities with relatively transparent internal structures; they use clear, well-defined concepts, and it is often relatively easy to specify what assumptions they make, and under what conditions they can be applied. Thus, a certain theory might be true of absolutely pure gases, and might apply in a real industrial situation to the extent to which some gas could reasonably be treated as if it were pure.

A political philosophy, in contrast, is not really an exclusively theoretical construction, but it must also be seen as an attempt to intervene in the world of politics: the consequences of acting on it ought thus never to be considered matters of complete indifference in evaluating it. Since, under modern conditions, proponents of a certain political theory must be in a position to argue for it in a plausible way, they will have a strong interest in presenting it to its best advantage. The image of the theory and its virtues that is projected in public debate will be unlikely to be complete in all details and may well be seriously misleading or even completely inaccurate. Since a political theory is also only in the rarest of cases the sort of thing that can be fully formalized, its advocates may in all innocence be very imperfectly aware of some of its basic structural features or their implications. In the long run, though, when a theory is widely believed and has come to inform the way large groups of people act, deeply hidden structural features of it can suddenly come to have a tremendous political impact.

Thus, in the middle years of the twentieth century, a series of liberal thinkers, including I. Berlin, J. L. Talmon, K. Popper, and F. Hayek, developed an influential account of Jacobinism and Marxism-Leninism. On the surface, these political doctrines presented themselves with a certain prima facie plausibility as theories committed to promoting human freedom, and many Jacobins and Marxists were subjectively keen and genuine partisans of human liberation in all its forms. Nevertheless, these liberals argued, a deeper account of their political views would reveal hidden authoritarian elements, such as commitment to a "positive" rather than a negative notion of freedom.

It was eventually this hidden structural kernel of the theory, not the private motives of its supporters, that had the last word in the real world of politics. Marxists did not get the world they consciously pursued and longed for as an ideal, but rather the one that was fated to arise under the given historical, economic, and political conditions when Marxism took hold of a whole society and succeeded in transforming it. The Soviet Union as it actually was, was the real content of Marx's "positive liberty."

The second kind of hypothesis applies this general schema of interpretation to Rawls's theory. It is not enough to look at the forms of self-advertisement of the theory, its superficial claims, or the intentions, motives, and personal character traits of its advocates. The best way to see what the theory is really about is to study the systematic, long-term effects of applying it. At some level, a widely accepted theory gets the world it really wants or, at any rate, the only world that is realistically possible if people hold the theory in question and act on it. The surface appearance of Rawls's theory—its apparent egalitarian content, standing, and implications—is deceptive, because the world that has arisen as the theory has established itself more and more firmly is one of increasing inequality.

The liberal thinkers like Berlin who gave their penetrating historical and conceptual analysis of Marxism in the middle of the last century realized that understanding a political philosophy involves taking account of a wide variety of factors that have no parallel in the case of strictly empirical theories. These include hidden structural features of the theory, various assumptions the people who are going to act on the theory make, and the actual institutional, economic, and political reality of the world into which the theory is trying to allow us to intervene (even if that intervention is at the level of a mere normative assessment).[17] Liberalism ought to have applied the theoretical sophistication which it had acquired in its critical struggle against Marxism to the task of understanding itself better in terms of these factors. The Rawlsian approach itself, of course, particularly in its "veil of ignorance" version, discourages the development of such theoretical self-consciousness, and that is perhaps its most basic deficiency. A third possible hypothesis starts by denying that there is any important connection between social and economic movements in the wider world and the increasing intellectual hegemony of Rawls-style political philosophy. Rawls's system, after all, is intricately elaborated and self-contained, and it also claims to embody a particularly well-grounded moral view of the world. Perhaps the pleasure in discussing such an aesthetically attractive and purportedly morally serious construction, and the associated sense of being part of an elite group of people who are both very clever and highly righteous, is a sufficient explanation of the omnipres-

---

[17] See J. Dunn, *The Cunning of Unreason: Making Sense of Politics* (London: HarperCollins, 2000).

ence of the theory. Explanations of the first *or* second type would be much too optimistic because they assume that Rawlsianism is potentially a genuinely activist theory, but actually it is a mere object of academic exercises. The advocates of the theory do not need compensation because they have no abiding interest in the state of the world outside universities and similar agencies anyway, and hardly notice it. They may in fact not even be aware that the world is moving ever further away from egalitarianism. Since whatever minimal political activity they may engage in is of no significance, the second kind of explanatory hypothesis—that in acting they are allowing a hidden "deep-structure" of the theory to realize itself—is otiose.

The final possibility is that Rawls's theory is supposed to be a strictly normative theory, and thus only a tool for honing individuals' moral sense and judgment. They may (or may not) then use it as a guide to their action, and may be more or less successful. Perhaps those who believe in the theory do not really feel the need to act in a way it seems to recommend, or perhaps they have simply been failures for completely contingent reasons. The fault is not with the theory, but with its supporters or the "others" in a world that is too powerful to be changed by well-meaning academics. None of this, one might argue, reflects badly on the theory, which is supposed to tell us only what "ought" to be the case. Nothing that (merely) happens to be the case is at all relevant to the validity of a strictly normative theory.

These four groups refer only to families or types of hypothesis, and the types are specified in such general terms that they allow a wide variety of actual theoretical accounts. A real analysis might well be a complex story embodying compatible elements of more than one of them for different parts of the account, but then the relation of a theory to its world is at least as complex as any of the other things history tries to enlighten us about.[18]

[18] Thus one important feature that would have to be kept in sight if one were trying to understand the prominence of Rawls's views at the end of the twentieth century is the spectrum of what were thought to be the possible alternatives. This is, I think, a general characteristic of much of the history of ideas, and one that was recognized very clearly by Nietzsche (and also Max Weber). When Nietzsche says that humans would rather will nothing than not will at all (*Genealogy of Morality*, Third Essay, § 28), this implies that in a number of areas people would prefer to hold onto even self-evidently shoddy theories rather than have no view at all. Another way of putting this is that skepticism or suspension of belief (in these particular areas) is almost always an achievement. Another possible line or explanation, then, runs as follows. For a variety of reasons that had little or nothing to do with Rawls and his views, existing alternatives—Marxism, utilitarianism, psychoanalysis, Critical Theory, anarcho-syndicalism, and in fact virtually the whole of modernist higher culture—were taken, correctly or not, to have been refuted or rendered irrelevant (by events); this is possible because they were at least sufficiently connected with *some* kind of reality that changes in the world could be taken to bear on them. Rawls's combination of sundry Kantian leftovers, New England Protestant ideals, and U.S. folkways was then virtually the only thing left on the board. It survived partly because it was sufficiently detached from actual politics not to seem (at least to many American readers) tarnished by anything that actually happened in the world, and yet it seemed vaguely and comfortingly familiar, which of

Despite the conscientious angst of Rawls the man, and his openness to well-focused criticism of individual sections of his work, the structure and ethos of this theory as a whole is deeply complacent, not to say smug. We who have the great good fortune to live in countries that are sufficiently like the United States in structure have got our politics basically right; all we really need to do is fine-tune our economies in various ways, particularly so as to maximize equality (while respecting the principle of difference) and struggle against any existing "outlaw states."

Rawls's students and followers incline to the fourth kind of hypothesis, and would presumably think that anyone who asks the questions I have been asking in this essay has lost the plot completely. Is it, though, or should it be, of any significance that the "normative" moral and political theory of the Rawlsian type has nothing, literally nothing, to say about the real increase in inequality, except perhaps "so much the worse for the facts?" This is not a criticism to the effect that theoreticians should *act* rather than merely thinking, but a criticism to the effect that they are not thinking about relevant issues in a serious way.

If casual reports by some of his former students are correct, toward the end of his life Rawls had a vague awareness of the gross discrepancy between the aspirations and self-conception of his theory and the way the world was going, and was disturbed by it. This does him credit. He did not, however, seem to have the conceptual tools to be able to make any real sense of it. He seems, that is, to have interpreted it in a characteristically displaced and distorted way as a problem about the lack of influence of his theory: his views were not taken with sufficient seriousness or were resisted, they were not acted on, his students were not adequately appreciated and promoted, etc. That such an exceptionally honest, personally modest, scrupulous, and self-critical man could have suffered from such a complete misapprehension of the situation makes it hard to avoid the conclusion that Rawls was up against the inherent limitations of his basic approach to the world and of the kind of theory he was trying to develop. After all, the problem cannot really have been lack of influence, because it is hard to imagine *any* philosophical theory that has had as much influence as Rawls's had in the second half of the twentieth century, at any rate in the Western capitalist world.

For a small number of English-speaking philosophers, then, the only way to make discernible progress in political philosophy is by studying history, social and economic institutions, and the real world of politics in a reflective way. This is not incompatible with "doing philosophy;" rather, in this area, it is the only sensible way to proceed. After all, a major danger in using highly abstractive methods in political philosophy is that one will succeed merely in

---

course it was, being simply a more coherent reformulation of some widely held North American views.

generalizing one's own local prejudices and repackaging them as demands of reason. The study of history can help to counteract this natural human bias. Politics depends, to a great extent, on judging what is actual relative to what is possible.[19] Is the actual regime of penal servitude, the family structure, or the system of compulsory school a good thing or a bad thing?

Answering these questions responsibly means thinking about them in a space organized around possible alternatives to the present existing state of affairs.[20] However, we have an inherently weak grasp on what is "possible" and most societies are not set up so as naturally to improve this, or actively to make us aware of possibilities we may have ignored or taken with insufficient seriousness. One of the great uses of history is to show us what, because it has in the past been real, is a fortiori possible. This can give rise to various illusions. Something can be thought to be politically possible now because it actually existed in the past, but it may have been possible in the past because of circumstances that have meanwhile changed.[21] This is a case in which further development of the very historical consciousness that gave rise to the problem will contribute to clearing it away.

For those of us with views like these, Rawls is not a major moral and political theorist, whose work self-evidently deserves and repays the most careful scrutiny. Rather he was a parochial figure who not only failed to advance the subject but also pointed political philosophy firmly in the wrong direction.

A perhaps apocryphal story has it that Rawls once gave to a visiting European historian the draft of a paper about modern politics "since the Treaty of Westphalia in 1548." When the historian mentioned that the accepted date was 1648, Rawls replied mildly "Oh, really?" and changed the offending digit with a single stroke of the pen. Despite myself, I cannot help finding this rather sublime. From the point of view of the original position, the difference between the sixteenth and the seventeenth century is completely insignificant, actually invisible. Of course, one tries to get things right, if one can, but nothing else in the work at all depends on this kind of correctness. No further part of the paper needed to be changed apart from that one digit. We should, however, resist the temptations of this kind of sublimity in politics and morality.

---

[19] To have kept this point sharply in focus is one of the singular virtues of the Critical Theory. See H. Marcuse, *One-Dimensional Man* (Boston: Beacon, 1963).

[20] See Max Weber's discussion of "the ethics of responsibility" in M. Weber, *Politik als Beruf* (Berlin: Duncker & Humblot, 1977).

[21] See B. Williams, *Ethics and the Limits of Philosophy* (London: Fontana, 1985), chapter 9.

3

Outside Ethics

THIS PAPER ARISES out of a sense I have had for many years that the German philosophers in whom I am most interested (Hegel, Marx, Nietzsche, Adorno, and Heidegger),[1] while obviously in some sense deeply concerned with human life in its practical aspects, are very difficult to situate in the established contexts of what we now usually think of as "philosophical ethics." Their theories don't seem easily to fit into the usual categories, and to the extent to which they can be read as instances of deontological, consequentialist, perfectionist, eudaimonistic, or any of the other standard types of theories, the results can easily seem shallow or extremely implausible. So in standard accounts we are told that Hegel put great emphasis on the fact that human action took place within a social, historical, and institutional context, as if this was something to write home about, or that Nietzsche believed we should all lead lives of maximal self-aggrandizement. In this paper, in any case, I would like to explore a possible explanation which has come increasingly to color my thinking about them. "Philosophical ethics," as it is now constituted, I have come to suspect, is a discipline structured around the asking and answering of a rather small set of questions. Part of the reason much of the German philosophy of the last 150 years can seem platitudinous, misguided, or eccentric, that is, part of the reason it can be difficult to assimilate this body of philosophical work, is that the philosophers in question were not centrally concerned with asking an easily recognizable member of that small set of questions that "philosophical ethics" in its most common contemporary form addresses. Even if this hypothesis were to be true, that would not, of course, in itself amount to a vindication of the particular views propounded by any of the German figures discussed here, but it might suggest that if we wished to see whether there was anything to be learned from them, it would behoove us to approach them in a way that is different from the ones that are customarily in use.

We are all familiar with the oft-told story of the history of modern ethics. We start at the end of the medieval period in Europe with a Christian world-

I'm extremely grateful to David Archard, Rüdiger Bittner, Elisabetta Galleotti, Hilary Gaskin, Istvan Hont, Terry Irwin, Robert Louden, Fred Neuhouser, Robert Pippin, Fred Rush, and John Skorupski for comments on this essay.

[1] Two other important post-Kantian philosophers, Kierkegaard and Lukács, although not Germans, belong to the same tradition.

view, which, if considered from a sufficient distance, was as coherent as such things ever are. Despite, that is, vigorous disagreement on details, in the period between the sixth and fourteenth centuries most of the people who had any reflective views about such matters at all agreed that the final, basic framework within which human life should be located was a theocentric one. The human being was a finite creature, totally dependent on, and fully subject to, an omnipotent God. One way in which God and humans were related was via his direct commands to us, that is, in the first instance via injunctions to each individual about how each of us ought to live. Each individual was in some sense free to choose how to act and could expect to be rewarded or punished (infinitely) according as he or she had obeyed or failed to obey these absolute commands. Although expectation of reward or punishment was not construed as the most laudable and appropriate motive, it was of the highest, indeed of strictly transcendental importance to each individual that he or she know what God commands. The basic ethical situation, on this view, that is, the situation which moral philosophy was to explore and elucidate, was thus one in which I ought always to be asking myself "What ought I to do?" where this is further glossed as meaning "What has God commanded me to do?" Part of the task of moral philosophy was to give a direct answer to this question, to help me decide on one of the possible courses of individual action which are open to me. For simplicity of reference I will call this question in its unglossed form ("What ought I to do?") the privileged or central ethical question; it is at any rate the question that has priority in the period that follows the end of antiquity in the West.[2]

During the Middle Ages the realm of human action was not considered to be a free-standing, self-sufficient domain which could be the object of self-contained, strictly philosophical ethical inquiry because the full correct answer to the question "What ought I to do?" was thought to require some reference to religious beliefs of a certain kind, a knowledge of the intentions and commands of an omnipotent entity who created us and who stands outside the domain of normal human experience.[3] This is connected with a theory of grace, faith, revelation, and conversion which purports to give an account of

[2] "What ought I to do?" is one of the three questions which, according to Kant, constitute the whole interest of reason (Kant [1956], B832/3). Other questions around which ethics could be centered include: "What kind of life should I lead?" (which is formulated in such a way as to leave open the possibility that there might be no distinct bearing of ethics on individual actions, only on types of life), "What is the good (or, happy) life (for me)?," and "What is the good?"

[3] This, of course, is only part of the full Christian story. It is one which leaves out the Pauline element in Christianity, a story about faith, forgiveness, and reconciliation, but although this is an abstraction, it is a truth-preserving one. In any case, to the extent to which one adds this Pauline element, the whole view becomes even more other-worldly than my sketch above suggests, and in all but the most heterodox, antinomian strands the Pauline element is taken to be compatible with a continuing prominence of the central ethical question. See Harnack (1985), Bornkamm (1969), and Badiou (1997).

how we access this extraordinary point of view on the world, which is of ulti-
mate importance to us in deciding how to live our lives. We do not, that is,
and cannot, come to know the full answer to the question "What ought I to
do?" simply by appeal to our untutored "intuitive" beliefs and existing social
customs, nor by appeal to any version of such beliefs and customs modified
by using our existing normal social practices of argumentation, criticism, and
justification, nor finally by reference to any revision of such beliefs and customs as modified by any simple reflective extension of those practices of criticism and justification. Ancient attempts to lead a fully good life based on
human reason alone are at best radically inadequate and at worst instances of
reprehensible human pride. At some level grace and revelation must represent a real break with human reason.[4]

There are two distinct issues here: first, what question should be central to
our thinking about human life in its practical aspect? Second, what is the relevant domain which is to be taken into account in asking and answering practical questions; from what possible standpoint can these questions be asked
and answered with any hope of success; what methods can be used in trying
to find an answer to these questions? Is this domain the secular, naturalist,
immanent realm of human action or something more transcendental, extra-
empirical, or otherwise significantly *outré*? Is the method to be that of (perhaps enlightened and extended) common sense, pure reason, empirical inquiry, or some other method?[5]

The contrasting terms in which I am trying to formulate the second issue—
immanent versus transcendent, naturalist versus extra-rational and extra-em-
pirical, etc.—are admittedly extremely vague and hard to grasp, and probably cover a variety of different distinctions and variants. Common to all of
them, though, is a basic contrast I think it is useful to try to mark. I can perhaps illustrate the kind of thing I have in mind by reference to the contrast
between the early aporetic dialogues of Plato (for instance, *Charmides*,
Laches, *Lysis*) and the *Republic*. In the aporetic dialogues, there is, characteristically, a series of exchanges between Socrates and one or more inter-

---

[4] There is, of course, much disagreement about whether revelation "merely" goes beyond
human reason or actually contradicts it in its common employment. That is, whether human reason by itself merely gives an incomplete answer to the question of what I ought to do, or a completely incorrect one. For the purposes of this paper, these disagreements are immaterial, although I should not perhaps fail to note that my view of historical Christianity is closer to
Augustine's than to Thomas Aquinas's. Historically speaking (see Assmann [1997]) it is a significant departure from the original motivation of monotheism to admit that humans without revelation can lead lives that are in any significant sense "good."

[5] One might wonder whether there is any connection between these two issues. It would not
be at all surprising if there was. Taking a certain question to be central might reasonably be
thought to preempt the question of what method ought to be used in trying to answer the question and what domain it would be relevant to consider. I cannot pursue this here.

locutors; Socrates typically deploys in an especially vivid and relentless manner the usual commonsense modes of evaluating propositions, testing them for internal consistency, inherent plausibility, coherence with everyday experience and received opinion, etc. There is no special, distinct method, no appeal to any unusual or exotic forms of experience, esoteric insight, or technical training[6]—just a more systematic, clearheaded, and energetic use of the sorts of commonsense methods people normally use in talking to one another. By the *Republic* the situation seems to have changed completely. In the myth of the cave (514a–521b) we are given to understand that in order to have a correct understanding of the world the potential philosopher must undergo a painful, enforced conversion from our everyday mode of life to a completely different one (515c–516a; 515c "ἀναγκάζοιτο" and "ἀλγοῖ;" 515e "ὀδυνᾶσθαι," 525d6 "ἀναγκάζει," etc.), must undertake a rigorous course of formal study of higher mathematics and dialectic which not everyone can expect to be able to complete successfully, and must eventually have a kind of experience of the idea of the good in a "place beyond the heavens" (ὑπερουράνιος τόπος, as Plato calls it in *Phaedrus* 247c) which is very different from anything Socrates will have encountered among the people selling fish in the agora, etc. The fully developed philosopher will have views that are *so* much outside the accepted mold that he or she on returning to the world of everyday life will meet nothing but hostility and aggression from those who have never left. The *Meno* represents a clear transition from the immanentist perspective to one that is "outside." In the first part, Socrates shows that even an untutored slave-boy can be brought by a series of commonsense steps to knowledge of an elementary proposition of geometry. From this the conclusion is drawn that the slave-boy must, like all other humans, have "seen" the objects of geometry in an existence before birth.

Christianity gives one a similarly extraterritorial viewpoint from which to study and evaluate the human world as a whole. This point of view did not comprise merely a more or less sophisticated, reflective, and generalized formulation of the standards in common use, nor even one that resulted from ruthless internal criticism of those standards, but a view that was radically *from outside*—dependent in part on some form of divine revelation—and which allows one to evaluate any given society, even the society to which one belongs oneself, completely independently of the society's own forms of self-assessment. In principle the Christian can reject any society, and even "the world" as a whole (*mundus* or *saeculum*), root and branch. From the Christian point of view, even if *per impossibile* pagan Rome had instantiated per-

---

[6] The account I suggest here is at variance with that presented by Foucault (2001). Foucault holds that ancient philosophy was dominated *from the start* by the idea that any access to truth required an antecedent form of cultivation or transformation of self.

fect, infinite justice, it would still have been a pestilential swamp of human sinfulness, its greatest men inherently and irremediably inferior to the most humble Christian.[7]

The familiar story now moves on to tell of how this medieval Christian ethical worldview was transformed in the early modern period. As one would expect, part of the medieval Christian synthesis was retained, part was dropped, and part was modified. At least in one important strand of development the part of this Christian way of thinking that was retained was the central formulation of the ethical question. Ethics continued to be construed as being about the asking and answering of the question "What ought I to do?"—that is, as focusing on a particular individual who is located in a particular situation and who must decide between possible alternative courses of action. It is assumed that the answer to this question is of great significance. In the beginning it was also assumed that the best answer to the question would be a clear imperative, which bindingly shows the individual which course of action is the one to be chosen.[8] What is, by and large, abandoned is the theocentric framework. Rather than seeing human life as a terrestrial spectacle, open on all sides to and fully encompassed by the divine presence, a play in which each actor must constantly consult a nonsecular authority in order to be sure he or she is moving within the outlines of the divinely intended script, human action forms a self-contained, secular realm within which the central ethical question can be asked and answered. Instead of a theologically based moral doctrine, philosophy takes over the task of elaborating responses to the basic ethical question that are independent of theological dogma. Philosophers disagree, to be sure, about the source and exact content of ethical injunctions, that is, about what will replace the God of the traditional Christian scheme, but not that the replacement will be something nontheological, immanent, and secular, the mode of access to which is not radically different from, or wildly beyond, our everyday experience.

One widely favored candidate is "reason," but there are others. Eventually there might be consensus among philosophers on the reasonableness of softening slightly the imperative character of such ethical directives—perhaps they are mere recommendations of what is "best" in a particular situation, rather than strictly and uniquely obligating commands—and perhaps there are complex or hard cases to which there is no univocal answer, and these shifts may seem as further progress down the path of a fully secular, free-

---

[7] Augustine (1928/9), Book XIX, chapter 26.

[8] Actually I think that this is merely one, albeit the more important one, of two strands in early modern ethics. The other is a strand that descends not from Christianity, but from international diplomacy, and is centered on finding general rules and procedures for governing the relations between political entities, especially states. Part of the appeal of Kant is to combine the two: the answer to the question what I ought to do is to give myself a potentially universal rule or law of action.

standing, self-contained ethics. With secularization the ethical realm is construed not merely as freestanding, but also in some sense all-encompassing: I can and must ask the basic ethical question in *any* context in which I find myself in which action might be called for; no domain stands outside the scope of ethics.

It is perhaps difficult to formulate this claim to all-encompassing universality in a clear and correct way. One thing implicit in it is that there is *no* separate religious (or other) realm that impinges directly on human life and action, and yet is not subject to ethical evaluation on the same terms as everything else. The Abraham of *Fear and Trembling*, that is, is excluded. Similarly there is no realm of habitual or traditional action that is exempt of ethical interrogation.[9] This does not, of course, necessarily mean that I need to go around compulsively and continuously asking about every *individual* action whether it is ethically permissible *before* I perform it. This is not merely an implausible view of how even humans who we think are morally good go about leading their lives; it is probably a strictly incoherent view. Most of our action is habitual, as even the Kantian need not try to deny. It is, of course, possible and necessary to develop habits which allow us to act "unreflectively." The claim to universality for "bourgeois" ethics is not the claim that I always ask and answer the ethical question, nor even that I ask a general question once and for all, and then adopt a policy which can become embodied in a habit of action which I need not question until I have reason to think circumstances have changed—after all, I have plenty of habits that have *not* arisen in this way, and that will be true even of a better person than I am. It is merely a version of the claim implicit in the enlightenment principle of universal criticism, that nothing is beyond the scope of ethical reflection, i.e., the claim that I cannot immunize some beliefs or forms of action from scrutiny. There are no taboos, hidden, inexpressible sacred doctrines, unquestionable *dicta ex cathedra*, etc. Asking and answering the question (as a philosophical question) is still considered to be of overwhelming importance.

The story of the transition from the medieval to the early modern worldview is told as the history either of a melancholy loss of sense, meaning, and orientation for human action, or of successive mutilations of the human spirit (Maistre, MacIntyre in most moods), or, more commonly, I think, with a pathos of liberation, emancipation, and human self-assertion (Kant). With whatever evaluation, whether positive or negative, there is widespread agreement that these are the terms in which we should see the modern predicament. In our societies serious-minded people continually ask the canonical modern ethical question ("What ought I to do?") in principle about all the situations in which they might be called upon to act, and they expect some kind of enlightenment about the possible answers to this question from an au-

---

[9] That this is a late historical development is emphasized by Horkheimer (1968), I.72–73.

tonomous philosophical ethics established as a discipline devoted to giving such answers in purely secular terms. Getting the right answer to this question is still thought to be one of the most important things in life.

I am not myself for the purposes of this paper terribly interested in whether the above sketch is plausible as an account of the history of ethics from, say, the twelfth to the end of the eighteenth century. What I am interested in claiming is that the most interesting and important strand in Central European philosophical thinking in the nineteenth and twentieth centuries is comprised of philosophers like Hegel, Marx, Kierkegaard, Nietzsche, Adorno, Heidegger,[10] who see the history of ethics in this way and who are determined to break with this "modern" variant of ethics. Central European philosophy cannot be seen as a positive continuation of this story. Rather, in a variety of different ways these central European figures were trying to demolish this modern consensus, although without, except perhaps in the case of Kierkegaard, returning to the older Christian view in its specifically theological or religious form. They were trying to take a different tack, or rather a variety of different tacks, on both of the two issues distinguished above (p. 42), that is, different from that pursued by the main line of modern ethics. On the second issue, these thinkers were trying to get outside the whole realm of ethics as conceived by the philosophers of the early modern period, either by finding a place to stand beyond it or by dissolving it, as it were, from within. On the first issue, they were trying to ask a different kind of question from that posed by the mainstream in modern ethics, and thus trying to avoid having to engage with philosophical ethics at all, except as an object of study, a fossil in a museum or a form of illness which was once deadly but is now a mere childhood ailment. In this way, I think, the Central European development really does diverge from the characteristic way in which ethics is now conceived in Britain, which still stands in what I have called the main line of the modern study of the subject.

With these preliminaries, then, I will turn to Hegel.[11] Philosophy for Hegel is both an inherently nonindividualistic and inherently speculative, that is, nonpractical, enterprise.[12] Philosophies are most interestingly understood as the products of specific forms of society; individual thinkers are the conduits through which spirit tries to attain reconciliation with its world.[13] Whatever

[10] Not, of course, the *only* strand. There have always been some philosophers, in Central Europe they tended to be Kantians, particularly in the period between 1880 and 1920, who did conform to the Enlightenment model of modern ethics, but they stand outside the main line I am describing. This does indicate the circularity between claims about what is the "main line" of history, what is "most interesting" in the past, and what we ourselves find most plausible; this is an unavoidable feature of the study of the history of ethics.

[11] Substantial recent works on the aspect of Hegel's philosophy which I will discuss here include Fulda (1968), Theunissen (1970), and Wood (1990). See also Pippin (2001).

[12] Hegel (1970), 8:20 and 7:12–13.

[13] "Reconciliation" is a term with definite religious connotations for Hegel deriving from its

spirit exactly is, it is certainly not identical with any individual human considered as a distinct biological entity, or an individuated subject, nor is it an abstract structure of ratiocination that can be neutrally instantiated by any one of a variety of individual thinkers. To say that spirit has attained reconciliation with its world means that the world has become, and can be seen to have become, the kind of place in which spirit can be at home with itself.[14] The "world" in question includes not merely the natural world, but also, and perhaps especially, the social world (and its history). Thus, to give an example of what it means for spirit to be at home in its world, since spirit is inherently free—freedom, Hegel writes in the *Lectures on the Philosophy of History*,[15] is its "substance" and its "essence"—it cannot feel itself at home in a world in which freedom is not recognized and realized in the basic social and economic institutions. No society in which slavery is admitted even as a marginal possibility is one in which spirit could conceivably be fully at home with itself.

Reconciliation is a historical achievement, and for spirit to attain it two distinguishable conditions must have been satisfied: first an "objective" condition, and then what for the moment I will simply call a "further" condition. First, the existence of a state of reconciliation requires that the world must be the kind of place in which spirit can be at home with itself. Since "the world" includes human society, this is not a condition which is in any sense trivially satisfied, even if one believes that nature was created by an omnipotent, benevolent god. For this first condition to be satisfied, it must be the case that spirit *has made* the (social) world amenable to its own purposes, that is, that the human social world has been transformed into a spirit-friendly place as a result of human action. This condition is called "objective" because it is concerned with the real results and actual consequences of human action, not with everyone's subjective intentions. It is in fact not necessarily, and will not usually be, the case that the "action" in question which has whatever objective results are in question is anything that could be performed by an individual person or even by any group of people at any given time—Spartacus would not himself have been able to end ancient slavery even if he had intended to do that (which, as far as we know, he did not), nor could indeed all the slaves in the ancient world, acting together, have put an end once and for all to slavery if the historical conditions were not ripe. The required objective transformations will therefore not necessarily be things that take place because any particular individual people or groups *intend* them (although in *some* cases they may); what is required is that slavery be absent, and that this

---

use in Christian, especially Protestant, theology. Hegel (1970), 3:569–71, 578–79; 12:385–87; 17:146–54, 329–44; 20:482–83, et passim.

[14] Hegel (1970), 13:50–52.

[15] Hegel (1970), 12:30.

in some sense be the effective result of human action, not that it have come about *because* any individual or individuals wanted or intended that outcome while it was being brought about. This then is one of the two components of "reconciliation."

In addition, however, a second condition must be satisfied: for spirit to be reconciled, it must not only be the case that its social world is one in which it can find itself at home, but spirit must have represented this to itself in an appropriate way.[16] That is, it is not enough that slavery in fact does not exist, but there must be a representation of this which makes it possible for us to see that it does not exist, and even perhaps to see (retrospectively) that it ended as a result of human action, even if the individuals whose action caused the end of slavery did not at the time intend that result (as seems to have been the case at the end of antiquity when feudal relations of dependence gradually and imperceptibly replaced forms of slavery). Hegel thinks that for spirit to be at home in the world, it must be able to represent to itself that *it* made the world have the right properties. This is turn means that "we" must have available to us a mode of representation which allows us to see history as a story of things "we" have done, although this requires a historically very encompassing notion of "we."[17] We represent to ourselves that "we" ended slavery, although we may know that those of our ancestors whose action brought about the end of slavery may never have intended that result. In fact we may still tell ourselves this story even if we know that the effective abolition of slavery was beyond the power of any well-defined group of human agents in the past—that it could have come about only as the result of a gradual, unintended process—so that at no point in the past would it have been possible to say in a non-utopian way that "we" intend to abolish slavery, using "we" to refer to any real, determinate, practically effective historical agent, who existed at the time in question. It is not an accident that Hegel characterizes (his) philosophy as inherently retrospective.

How then does spirit represent to itself that its world really is one in which it is at home?[18] Hegel's response to this question is that it takes place through the existence of artistic activity, religion, or philosophy; Hegel calls these forms of "absolute spirit."[19] Art, religion, and philosophy are (the) ways in

---

[16] Hegel (1970), 5:17; 20:454–55.

[17] Hegel (1970), 12:99.

[18] One must not confuse "representation" as a translation of "*Darstellung*" with another Hegelian concept which is unfortunately also sometimes translated as "representation," namely "*Vorstellung*." "*Vorstellung*" is a subjective, image-making human faculty, the activity of such a faculty, or the content which such an activity produces. It is only a slight exaggeration to say that "*Vorstellung*" is a derogatory term for Hegel; he most often uses it to mark the distinction between a mere thoughtless picture or opinion and something that is more substantive and the result of sustained thinking. See Hegel (1970), 10:256–83.

[19] See Hegel (1970), 10:366–78.

which spirit represents itself to itself. Of these, philosophy has a certain priority as the most complete and perfect way in which spirit can represent itself to itself. In all of the forms of absolute spirit, an organized institutional structure is an essential precondition and constituent of the collective human activity in question. The representation which spirit has of itself in art, religion, or philosophy is, thus, in one important sense not at all "subjective" because it is not best understood as the property or creation of any individual human subject; in particular it is not necessarily what we call a "belief" that is held by an individual.[20] To say that complete reconciliation has been attained, i.e., exists and is represented, is, for Hegel, to make a claim about a certain historical time and what has actually taken place at that historical time. It is to say that at that time society has attained a certain state of freedom, and that a form of organized philosophical activity existed in which that freedom was adequately represented. To be sure, philosophy, the thinking of the thoughts that constitute "reconciliation," will be an activity performed by one or more individuals, and in one sense it will not be adventitious that it thus operate through the activity of individuals, but it will be essential to this activity that it take place as part of a peculiarly self-referential social institution, and the relation of this process of reconciliation and representation to any *particular* individual will be almost entirely fortuitous, a matter of no philosophical or moral significance.

No individual can by his or her own actions act so as to make the world rational and amenable to spiritual comfort—just as no ancient politician could by his own powers have abolished ancient slavery—nor could any individual modern thinker by any amount of individual effort and ability have developed a mode of representing the modern world which allowed its inherently spirit-friendly structure to manifest itself adequately; philosophy, even in the modern age of moral and social individualism, is a collective, institutional enterprise.[21] An "ought" in these circumstances would not be very sensible. To be more exact, the speculative philosophy of right does reveal to us at the foundation of all things something which can in some sense be expressed in a lin-

---

[20] Hegel (1970), 14:142–44, and also 20:69. Of particular importance for this whole complex of issues, is, I think, Hegel (1970), 13:373–76, which discusses the phenomenon of the "objectivity" of a form of (artistic) representation. Art must in one sense be seen as a way in which the subjective and the objective are reconciled, but the form this takes cannot be one that has the traces of the individual subjectivity of the artist. To put it paradoxically, it is a kind of "objective subjectivity" that finds expression in the successful work of art. This idea that art is the locus of an "objective subjectivity" is a nineteenth-century commonplace (see similar discussion in Nietzsche [1980], 42–46). In general, I think the study of Hegel has suffered much from the neglect of his writings on aesthetics, which are a treasure trove of perspicuous insights into his central philosophical views.

[21] In fact, in one respect, modern philosophy is even more institutional than its ancient predecessor in that it is no longer a mere "private art" but a subject of required instruction for civil servants, see Hegel (1970), 7:20–22.

guistic form that makes it seem like an "imperative," and if one wishes one can call this imperative "categorical" (although I assume that Hegel himself would have preferred to call it "absolute"). This imperative, however, has a radically impersonal form—"Let Spirit be!" or "Let Spirit realize itself!"— and is not directed at any individual human person—at any of us in particular. It couldn't be an imperative given to us directing us to do something, because what it enjoins is beyond our capacities. Just as no individual can by his or her own efforts abolish slavery, so no individual can "realize Spirit" and, presumably, *ultra posse nemo obligatur*." More importantly, however, Hegel's doctrine of the "cunning of reason" implies that there is not anything any of us could conceivably do that would *fail* to contribute to the self-realization of spirit. "Let Spirit be!" is more like an inherently teleologically structured *conatus* of the world and history than like a genuine imperative; it is not an injunction directed at any individual human agent.

For Hegel the realm of "objective spirit" is the realm of human action, guided by will. This sphere is absolutely essential for human beings—we cannot live, nor can spirit realize itself, unless finite humans act on their projects and realize them in the external world—but it is also radically deficient, not at all the kind of place in which spirit can find the final satisfaction of its inherent needs. Objective spirit as a whole requires the existence of absolute spirit (art, religion, and philosophy) to give it final substance, stability, and warrant.[22] In particular this seems to mean that the Hobbesian project of a stable inherently secular state is doomed, and that a stable modern European state will require either the art-religion of Catholicism[23] or the cultivated Protestant conscience as a necessary support and source of legitimacy. Again this is a systematic claim about forms of society, not a claim about the psychological necessities or desiderata of individual life. Hegel, to be sure, held that just as religion in some sense supersedes art, philosophy supersedes religion. One might wonder, and indeed various Left Hegelians put this point forcefully, whether this view does not imply that philosophy could in the future take over the role of religion in providing a warrant for the state. Hegel explicitly and, as it were, exoterically, denies this, stating repeatedly that the state rests on the religious sensibility of its members, that religion is the substantiality of the state, etc.;[24] but perhaps he is being politically careful, canny, accommodating, or inconsistent here, or perhaps he is conforming to his own dictum that philosophy is always "its time grasped in concept,"[25] and is describing only the *present* necessities of the 1820s and '30s. Needless to say, they might not limit the possibilities of the late 1840s, not to mention the early twenty-first century.

---

[22] Ibid., 10:335–65, and 13:136–41.
[23] Ibid., 20:40.
[24] Ibid., 10:355.
[25] Ibid., 7:26.

However one unravels this knot about the relation between philosophy, religion, and the state, what is clear is that for Hegel there could be no direct movement from a speculative, philosophical warrant for the state to any interesting, philosophically distinctive answer to the question "What ought I to do?" Philosophy, as Hegel puts it, always comes too late. In the slightly brutal form in which Hegel states it in his most highly elaborated and public formulation, if you want to know what to do in some particular situation, consult your local authorities, judge, policeman, rabbi, imam, or priest. Asking the philosopher is pointless.[26] It is not the philosopher's job to tell anyone what to do, resolve conflicts or dilemmas, make us aware of new duties, or invent new ways of acting. This I take it is *not* merely a rejection of what used to be called "casuistry" as a proper task for philosophy. That is, it is not simply a denial that the theorist is always best equipped to analyze particular individual situations, but a denial of the claim that a philosopher by virtue of a special speculative competence is in any better position to give even general advice—"Do not kill; do not lie"—than anyone else.

In his *Philosophy of Right* Hegel presents the outline of a structure of objective spirit, of the rational institutions within which spirit can find as much reconciliation as is possible in the realm of human action (as opposed to the realms of art, religion, and philosophy), and Hegel points out that one *can*, if one wishes, associate with each feature of such a rational state a corresponding "duty."[27] However, the set of "duties" one can extract in this way has extremely limited significance. It is important to recall that Hegel's general philosophical approach is an assimilative one. Instead of trying to refute and reject all other philosophers' views outright, he claims to supersede them by incorporating all of them as partial, subordinate components in his own system. This means finding *some* place in his system for virtually every concept that has ever been seriously entertained by a previous philosopher, or that plays a part in everyday thinking. In reading Hegel, then, it is essential to try to keep one's attention on the load-bearing structural features of his view, such as the theory of spirit, and not to confuse them with the further material that is taken up into the system in the name of comprehensiveness. The fact that Hegel says that one can read part of his *Philosophy of Right* as a doctrine of "duties," then, doesn't in itself mean anything, except that he believes he can find a place for "duty" just as he can find one for physiognomy, the philosophy of Jacob Böhme, Zoroastrianism, oracles, fate, animal magnetism, and sundry other bits of historical detritus. What is important is not that his system contains things that can be construed as "duties," but that he thinks that construing these features in that way is a derivative, abstract, partial, and subjective way of looking at them, which does not give you the proper philo-

[26] Ibid., 7:13–14, 25–26, and also 8:47–49.
[27] Ibid., 7:297.

sophical understanding of them. In addition, these duties do not form a consistent system, but will constantly clash with each other, so knowing about one's duties won't always give one guidance for action. Finally, discharging these duties is not in any case the highest vocation of the human spirit, but is subordinate to the development of art, religion, and philosophy, although the form that this subordination takes is not one that imposes on any individual anything like an obligation to participate in artistic, religious, or philosophical activities. The "duty" aspect of these features—their potentially coercive relation to the subjective moral psychology of individuals—is not central to them.[28]

One might wonder whether Hegel could not be assimilated to the view I was ascribing to the main line of ethics (as represented by, say, Kant or Bentham), that is, whether the "outside" point of view from which Hegel's philosophy proceeds was not *really* "outside" of our everyday life. As I have tried to emphasize, "outside" can mean a number of different things: not secular, not naturalistic, not immanent, nonempirical, nonrational, outside common sense, etc. Isn't Hegel's own philosophical point of view, after all, something that arises from a clarification and a process of internal criticism of the standards we use in everyday life? Doesn't that make it in some sense merely a conservative extension of common sense? The correct answer to this, I think, is "no," because Hegel is deeply committed to the view that philosophy is not an extension of common sense, but common sense turned upside down, stood on its head. The first precondition to understanding his view is the ability to *leave behind* the use of the faculty which is all-pervasive and correctly deemed to be omnipotent in everyday life, the analytical power of the understanding ("*Verstand*": "*die verwundersamste und größte, oder vielmehr die absolute Macht*"),[29] and activate another faculty: "*Vernunft*." Entering the realm of *Vernunft* is abandoning the world of common sense, everyday rationality, the formal rationality of mathematics, and scientific rationality (in *our* sense of "science") completely.[30]

---

[28] I have been emphasizing aspects of the Hegelian philosophy that later figure prominently in the so-called "Right Hegelian" School, but I should note that even if one were to take a significantly more Left Hegelian reading—or, for that matter, a Marxist reading—that would not affect the particular point at issue here. In this I believe I differ from the view of Wood in his excellent (1990), esp. pp. 8–10.

[29] Hegel (1970), 3:36.

[30] Hegel (1970), 8:168–79. It is one of the basic sources of difficulty in Marx that he never seems to have been able to get clear about whether his own doctrine was a version of Hegelian *Wissenschaft*, i.e., activation of a cognitive power which, like Hegel's *Vernunft*, was radically different from our everyday understanding, or whether his view was simply a more clearheaded extension of everyday experience, like the empiricist account of (natural) science. I note that even those twentieth-century Marxists who are keenest to distinguish Marx from Hegel, those influenced by Althusser, need to introduce such a distinction, although, given their own essentially rationalist conception of "science," they can draw the line of what they call "*coupure episté-*

With that I am going to shift now from the first third of the nineteenth century to the final third, over the yawning gap that is constituted by the failure of 1848, of liberalism and idealism, and the unification of Germany under Prussia from above, from Hegel to the philosopher who is in some sense his antipode, Nietzsche. For a variety of reasons of varying quality, Nietzsche rejected the traditional conception of a philosopher as a person who developed a settled and systematically interconnected set of views on fixed problems and who derived from these a way of life which he instantiated. The Stoic sage— the man whose firm adherence to the principles of rationality and self-control makes him an unchanging, imperturbably virtuous citizen of the universe— is the epitome of what he rejected. Rather than being a Sage, Nietzsche tried to see himself as a *franc-tireur*, sometimes adopting one pose or mask, or another—e.g., the "free spirit"—but priding himself on not being fixed.[31] To be a philosopher is not to have an unchanging final opinion, or way of life, but to be able to move smoothly between a variety of different worldviews and ways of living.[32] He did not, of course, present this as an ideal for everyone, or indeed for every philosopher, but only as the one he wished to instantiate.[33] He famously remarked: "This is my way; what is yours?" This means that one can adopt two distinct approaches to studying his philosophy. First, one can consider the project of being thus flexible, never being tied to a single opinion, having only "short" habits (i.e., habits of short duration), etc.[34] Second, one can study one or more of the individual masks he adopts and then puts aside. I will be taking the second of these approaches and considering one such strand that can be found in his work, although there are others one could equally well examine. The question of which is the "real" Nietzsche is one he himself would have rejected—he may have been incoherent in this, but that is his considered attitude. Nietzsche's thought is radically different from Hegel's in any number of ways, most significantly perhaps in that it is consciously hyper-individualist. Nietzsche himself sees his historical significance to lie not so much in the fact that he gives any particular positive or critical analysis of morality, but rather in the fact that he asks what he claims is a series of questions of the form: "What is the value of ———?" In particular

---

mologique" between everyday experience and science, rather than between *Verstand* and *Vernunft*.

[31] Nietzsche (1980), 5:57–58, 59, 167–70, 229, 233–34.

[32] Nietzsche (1980), 3:415–16, 5:42–43, 233–34. One can wonder whether one can consistently hold this view, just as one can wonder if one can be a consistent skeptic. Adorno (1963, 152) remarks that all thinking is exaggeration—which remark is itself presumably an exaggeration intended to remind us that exaggerations can direct our attention to important features of the world that would otherwise be overlooked. Perhaps this is how this part of Nietzsche's work is best understood.

[33] Nietzsche (1980), 5:60, 163–65.

[34] Ibid., 3:535–36.

he believes that it is possible sensibly to ask "What is the value of morality?"[35] To ask this question, I am suggesting, is to position oneself outside the ethical realm, although in such a way, Nietzsche believes, as to remain, potentially at any rate, within a naturalistic framework.[36]

In common with most post-Kantian philosophy, including, notably, Hegel, Nietzsche rejects the very idea of a specifically moral "ought," giving a genealogical account of it as arising out of the natural reactions of people in positions of weakness; he hopes that giving this account will break its categorical hold over our imagination.[37] There is, then, no answer to the question of what I or anyone else "ought" to do—apart from an answer that refers to legal provisions or the hypothetical consequences of different forms of action. The "ought" in the sentence "I really ought to get this room painted" has a clear, nonillusory meaning, but a purportedly specifically moral use of "ought" does not. Nietzsche, then, thinks he has found a naturalistic replacement for the traditional ethical perspective and its questions, although, in my view, this naturalistic view is one centered not, as is usually thought, around the concept of "will-to-power" but around that of admiration. His view of humans, that is, takes them as standing at the intersection of certain forces and powers operating in the world—some of them operating on humans, and some through them—on the one hand, and, on the other, certain human reactions of admiration and contempt. Forms of morality are congealed and focused structures of human admiration and contempt.

It is important to see that Nietzsche does not first accept the central ethical question "What ought I to do?" and then go on to say, for instance, that each individual should perfect himself or herself, or maximally develop his or her will-to-power, or attain the highest possible self-aggrandizement. Rather he rejects the whole question on a number of grounds. First of all, asking the question presupposes that the agent, "Ego," is confronted with a decision in which there are a number of different possible alternatives between which Ego is free to choose. Nietzsche rejects the claim that this is in any sense the usual situation in which human agents find themselves. It is not useful to think of people as having a categorically free will (or a will that is in bondage). The whole dichotomy "free will/will-in-bondage" is a false one. People have wills that differ in their degrees of strength. Some have a strong will; others have

---

[35] Ibid., 5:249–53, 398–401.

[36] Ibid., 6:86. "*Man müßte eine Stellung außerhalb des Lebens haben, . . . um das Problem vom Wert des Lebens überhaupt anrühren zu dürfen.*" If this is the case, the position from which one can evaluate any given morality can only be one "within life" itself. There is nothing inherently wrong with thinking that one can adopt a position "outside ethics/morality" or "outside everyday reason" but which is yet "within life" or "within nature," but it must be admitted that the metaphorical nature of this whole way of speaking—as if "inside/outside" had a clear meaning in these contexts—may be an obstacle to clarity.

[37] Ibid., 3:377–78, 5:49–50, 66–67, 117–20, etc.

a relatively weak will.[38] If you *are* the right kind of person, one who has a strong will, you will not be terribly concerned with the question of what you *ought* to do. You will, to be sure, be looking for objects of appropriate commitment (*Hingebung, Bindung*), but that is just a fact about how a person like you is liable to feel the need to act, and the search on which you embark will be for something which you judge to be worth admiring. Such a search, however, has a completely different structure from that into what anyone "ought" to do. Also, if you are another kind of person—a kind of person Nietzsche does not admire and who has a weak will—asking the question what you *ought* to do will generally be pointless, because if you are weak there will be no significantly different alternatives open to you anyway, none, that is, that makes any real difference, just as for a certain kind of traditional Christian, a person in a state of sin does not have any freedom worth the name. A sinner can choose X or Y, but from the definitive religious perspective they will just be different versions of sin. Freedom to choose one sin rather than another is utterly unimportant, or rather it is a way in which an especially deep form of human bondage plays itself out. Nietzsche's own positive use of the term *"amor fati"* to describe a kind of character which he admires is an expression of this. To love one's fate is not something one ought to do, but something people sufficiently admirable will in fact do, and others will not be able to do, and in that ability and inability will lie the grounds for admiring them or despising them.

Nietzsche and Hegel, then, each in his own way, try to change the question which is at the center of modern practical philosophy, "What ought I to do?" Hegel and Nietzsche do *not*, of course, construe the shift they propose merely as an unmotivated change of topic or as the sort of thing that takes place when, say, fashions change, where fatigue and the desire for novelty are the driving forces; rather, the change is, they think, motivated by a view about the deficiencies of the old orientation, deficiencies which they describe and analyze at length in their work, and by the possibilities of a new kind of inquiry. In addition to this, Hegel departs from the second pillar of modern ethical thought by trying to describe a new extraterritorial perspective, one outside the realm of everyday reasoning, from which to see human life in its practical dimensions, the standpoint of *Vernunft*. Nietzsche's position on this second issue is to some extent unclear, given the unclarity about exactly how to construe such things as "the ethical realm" and "the realm of everyday reasoning about action." He seems, however, much less inclined to appeal to some distinct esoteric intuition or purported different type or kind of reason than Hegel is. At least in most of his work, he speaks as if it were some natural extension of the usual, empirical, scientific and historical forms of understanding that undermines the pretensions of ethics as usually pursued, primarily the pretension

[38] Ibid., 5:35–36; 6:95–96.

to have something of importance to say in answer to the question "What ought I to do?"

The general line of argument I have been trying to trace showed continued vitality in Central and Eastern Europe well into the second half of the twentieth century. Adorno held that advanced societies in the modern world were closed, total institutions that were radically implicated in evil. In such societies, no action could be, as it were, fully innocent,[39] and consequently demands that philosophy be connected with any kind of injunction to perform specific actions are themselves both forms of repression and an incitement to evil. Any attempt on the part of the individual to consider what he or she as an individual ought to do is a completely pointless exercise, and the only possibility remaining to us is to continue to reflect on the infinitely complex and subtle ways in which the falsity of the world as a whole poisons the possibilities of genuinely beneficial individual action and individual happiness. All that is left to us is a doomed attempt to maintain shreds of our subjectivity and spontaneity before they are finally crushed (like everything else), and to cultivate reflection so as to understand as fully as possible the complex structure of the evil in which we are necessarily implicated, no matter how we act. Beyond that we can have only a messianic hope in a total transformation of the society in which we live. This hope, however, would be for something that might come *from outside* the present and change our world utterly, that is, it is a hope for something that cannot even in principle be brought about by anything we could do.[40]

If anything we do, even the passive resistance we can muster to the forces of conformism, does in fact contribute to a messianic future, that contribution will be an indirect one in the long term about which we can now know nothing. What motivates us to try to see our social world as a whole "from the outside" is a combination of a holistic theory of society and the direct experience of certain kinds of exemplary evil—Auschwitz—or rather of the discrepancy between the technological capacity we have to turn the world into a paradise and the actual use we make of that capacity to produce Auschwitz or California.[41] If the world as a whole is an interconnected totality and Auschwitz is an integral part of that totality, we are strongly motivated not to remain within even the most widely based and reflectively developed version of the everyday moral consensus that is the basis of our social life. Adorno's epistemological position seems slightly different from Hegel's in that he claims a continuity between his own speculative construction of modern so-

---

[39] *"Das Ganze ist das Unwahre:"* Adorno (1951), 57; *"Es gibt kein richtiges Leben im falschen:"* Adorno (1951), 42. For the theological background, see Adorno's letter to Benjamin of 4 May 1938 in Adorno and Benjamin (1994, 323–29); see also Adorno (1970), 403–4.

[40] Adorno (1951), 167–69, 176–77.

[41] Adorno (1966), 352–56; see also Adorno (1970), 55–56, 65–67, 203–5; also Adorno (1951), 73–75.

ciety and "common sense."[42] The possibility of such a view of society as a whole from the outside is given through certain forms of experience of art which present the utopian image of a world that is radically different, although, given the nature of the world in which we live, that image can only be a "negative" one.[43] The "experience" in question, however, although not "absolutely different" from ordinary everyday experience, is not amenable to an empiricist analysis.

The strand of philosophizing I have described takes its most radical form in the philosophy of Heidegger. The young Heidegger was a Christian religious thinker who stood in the tradition of "negative theology," and thought that the vibrant, living "faith" of primitive Christianity, which was a way of life, not a set of doctrines, was calcified and distorted by being pressed into the preexisting intellectual schemata of Hellenistic philosophy. As Paul emphasized, the Christian message was "folly" to the Gentiles (1 Corinthians 1:23); it was thus, on Heidegger's reading, completely impossible to grasp the Christian faith and message in the categories of Greek philosophical thought (and a fortiori in those of its Roman and later European successors). The way back to something like that aboriginal faith is by "destroying the wisdom of the wise" (1 Corinthians 1:19), i.e., via a self-destruction of *all* forms of philosophical thought.[44]

The substance of Heidegger's thought changed in two ways over his long lifetime. First, he lost his religious faith. Strikingly enough, this seems to have had no influence on his basic philosophical project, although one might easily have thought it one thing to destroy human knowledge to make room for religious faith, but quite another to make tabula rasa of human reason in the interests of an empty place where faith once stood. Second, his study of the pre-Socratics convinced him that the much despised Hellenistic philosophy was itself a degenerate form of thinking which distorted an original vital Greek experience of Being just as much as it perverted and falsified original Christianity. To some extent, this pre-Socratic Greek experience of being would come to stand in the place which Christianity earlier occupied, as an object of rehabilitation to which access could be had only through destruction of the traditional forms of philosophical thought which perverted it (the whole of Western philosophy and all modern forms of conceptual thinking). There was, however, despite these continuities, one major shift in Heidegger's way of proceeding philosophically. His constant goal was the permanent disabling of philosophy, and thus also of any philosophical ethics. In the early

---

[42] Adorno (1969), 148.

[43] Adorno (1970), 55–56, 65–67, 348. Despite the appeal to "experience" here, it would, of course, be a complete mistake to assimilate this position to empiricism as it is usually understood.

[44] In 1971 Karl Löwith, who had been Heidegger's *Assistent* just before World War II, told me that at that time Heidegger repeatedly referred to himself, both in public and private, as a negative theologian interested in completely demolishing the pretensions of human reason.

period, this took the form of the victory of the Cross over the "wisdom of the wise"; later the victory of preconceptual experience over *any* form of conceptual thinking. The early Heidegger thought that this goal could be attained by thinking through transcendental philosophy to the point at which it would *itself* dissolve itself. This is the project of *Being and Time*. The second part of this work was supposed to show how the quasi-transcendental framework developed in the first part turned itself inside out and showed itself to be a perverted illusion.

Heidegger never finished the project to his own satisfaction, and his account of the reasons for this failure amounts to a recognition of the power and internal coherence of the project of conceptual thinking. Once one gives *any* houseroom to the concept, there is no way back. A complete destruction of the tradition and of all forms of philosophy would have to proceed in a different way from that envisaged in *Being and Time*. Thus the late Heidegger's work is more devoted to etymological speculations, interpretations of works of art, and various kinds of incantatory, non-discursive writing, all intended to break the hold the conceptual has on us.[45]

Heidegger, then, thinks that all forms of philosophizing, especially anything that can be seen as continuing to ask the transcendental question about a framework for human thought or action, are signs either of inauthentic existence (early view)—that is, of trying to run away from and hide from oneself the fact that human life is radically ungrounded, temporal, and finite—or of the forgetfulness of Being (later view). That is, to do philosophy at all, particularly transcendental philosophy, is to show that one is living in error about what it is to be human, where that "error" is both cognitive and quasi-moral; Heidegger sometimes calls this state *"die Irre."*[46] So simply to ask the questions "What are the conditions of the possibility of ———?" or "What ought I to do?" is to show that you are in such a state of cognitive and moral error or derangement (inauthenticity or forgetfulness of Being). For the early Heidegger it is the experience of extreme anxiety in the face of my own death that can bring me to see life and the world as a whole from an infinite distance, and to realize that everyday life is deranged and delusional because inherently constituted by a denial of this anxiety and what it reveals.[47] In the face of my confrontation with this anxiety the "ought" becomes irrelevant. The state Heidegger diagnoses as one of "for-

---

[45] There is one further aspect of Heidegger's search for an alternative to "philosophy." In addition to primitive Christian faith and pre-Socratic experience of Being, there is a strand of German poetry, particularly the poetry of Hölderlin, but also that of Trakl, Conrad Ferdinand Meyer, Rilke, Stefan George, Gottfried Benn, and others, that becomes the object of his interest as a possible source of a nonphilosophic, nonconceptual way of being and saying. See Heidegger (1951, 1960).

[46] Heidegger (1967), 91–94.

[47] Ibid., 1–19; also (1963): 184–91, 252–67.

getfulness of being" is one from which, as he put it at the end of his life, "only a god can save us."[48]

To ask "What ought I to do?" as a philosophical question is to assume that there could be some authoritative answer to that question. If, however, one understands the nature of human action and its place in the world, one will see that there is no such appropriate answer that combines authority with determinateness. We are tempted to ask "What ought I to do?," and to construe this question as one to which a philosophical answer would be relevant. This temptation is not in any interesting sense "natural" or unavoidable, but is a result of living in the epoch of the history of Being in which we do in fact live. The pre-Socratic Greeks lived in a world that did not yet know the distinctions between Being and Becoming, Being and Appearing (*Schein*), Being and Thinking, and finally, and in this context most importantly, Being and "the Ought" (*Sollen*). The final distinction is associated with a process in which Thinking extends its dominion (*Herrschaft*) over Being.[49] To the extent to which the aboriginal Greek experience is at all paradigmatic, then, it implies both a demotion of Thinking, and a redissolution of the various distinctions, especially (for present purposes) that between "*Sein*" and "*Sollen*." Whatever such a form would look like, it seems clear that it would be one that would have no place for philosophical ethics as we know it. Insisting on the centrality of a general reasoned answer to "What ought I to do?" strengthens the hold decadence, forgetfulness, and confusion have on us. Heidegger's own analysis does result in what he calls a "demand" ("*Forderung*"),[50] the demand for a new experience of Being, but this is not a moral or ethical demand for the various reasons that have already been reviewed—it does not result from common sense or traditional forms of philosophic thinking, it is not anything that could conceivably be in the power of any individual (or group of individuals) to do or not do, etc.

I have claimed that the main line of philosophic writing in nineteenth-century Central Europe rejects the received modern consensus, and tries to orient thinking about human life and action around a very different set of questions from the ones that preoccupy contemporary ethics. Continental philosophers reject either one or the other (or both) of the two pillars of contemporary ethics. As far as the first pillar is concerned, they take one or another of a variety of weaker or stronger views. Thus, they cast doubt on the centrality of the ethical question, holding the weaker view that knowing "What ought I to do?" is of distinctly subordinate importance in practical life, or that it is not a philosophically significant question. Alternatively, they hold the stronger view that it is actually a deep mistake or a failing to ask that ques-

---

[48] Heidegger (1976).
[49] Heidegger (1957), 149–50.
[50] Ibid., 153.

tion (at any rate, as a philosophical question). The second pillar of contemporary ethics is a kind of immanentism. Enlightenment "Reason" is an immanent category; Heidegger's *Angst* and Hegel's *Vernunft* are not. While some of these figures—like Nietzsche—actively embrace a form of naturalism that is immanentist, others look for a view outside nature (as usually understood) and the world of common social practices.

Even if one granted that the main stream of Central European philosophy rejected the modern paradigm of ethics, one might still wonder about its relation to ancient ethics. For every German philosopher since Schiller,[51] the "ancient option" has been a live one—"live" at least to the extent that it constituted an important part of the mental and imaginative space within which philosophic thinking took place, and which had a certain prima facie plausibility and attractiveness. Despite this massive cultural prestige of the ancient world (especially Greece), what is commonly taken to be the centerpiece of ancient ethics—the doctrine of "happiness"—is remarkable for its virtually complete absence as a serious structural feature of German philosophy in the nineteenth and twentieth centuries.[52] As far as I have been able to discover, no term that designates anything even vaguely like "happiness" occurs in any of Heidegger's writings. The early works (*Sein und Zeit*) are dominated by a glorification of "resoluteness" which is an active acceptance of the finiteness, guilt, and ungroundedness of human life, and, after the catastrophic disgrace of Heidegger's political involvement, the later works preach a radically passive attitude of listening to the voice of Being, letting-be, or "*Gelassenheit.*"[53] There is never any attempt, as far as I am aware, to connect any of this with possible human happiness. Nietzsche notoriously thought that humans didn't seek happiness (only Englishmen did). Hegel's most serious and sustained discussion of eudaimonism[54] essentially develops the Kantian thought that the idea of happiness is too contingent and too indeterminate to serve as any kind of serious framework for understanding human praxis or even guiding individual human endeavor, and as a human goal is always trumped by rational freedom. Some of his other random comments on "happiness"—such as that periods of happiness were the "empty pages" of world history or that the striving for happiness was "anodyne"[55]—leave little doubt of the contempt in which he held any attempt to make it central to thinking about human life.

[51] Schiller (1967).

[52] The era in the ancient world that made the deepest impression on the thought of Heidegger was precisely the pre-Socratic period, i.e., the period before systematic ethical thought oriented to "happiness" was firmly established. The same is true of Nietzsche.

[53] Heidegger (1959); see also Heidegger (1967), 145–94.

[54] Hegel (1970), 10:299–300; 7:71–73.

[55] "*Die Weltgeschichte ist nicht der Boden des Glücks. Die Perioden des Glücks sind leere Blätter in ihr*" (Hegel [1970], 12:42); "*Das Streben nach der Glückseligkeit . . . ist etwas Schales*" (19:289).

The one philosopher among the group that interests me who does make room, centrally and systematically, for a concept of "happiness" is Adorno.[56] Given Adorno's general views about the nature of contemporary society, full happiness, he thinks, is in fact unattainable. He does, however, have articulated views about what happiness would be, and very well developed analyses of the varieties of human unhappiness, and, most important perhaps, he does think that the fact that happiness is inaccessible to us is of great significance. A state of full-blown happiness would, he holds, be one of complete somatic satisfaction—sexual congress is its most exact image[57]—that had the property of complete spontaneity; it would not be "organized,"[58] but it would also not be merely accidental.[59] Finally, it would not be implicated in the evils of the world.[60] Adorno discusses two pale imitations of happiness, eudaimonoid but not eudaimonic states, which are not themselves the full-blooded phenomenon, but are nevertheless to some limited extent accessible to us. First, there are temporally transitory reanimations of certain infantile experiences of meaningfulness and satisfaction, experiences like that of the narrator of *À la recherche du temps perdu* with the madeleine. Adorno seems to think that the most intense of these are connected with our natural mimetic impulse, our inclination to depict or represent or to make for ourselves an imitation of the world. This impulse expresses itself most fully and directly in the work of art, which is thus a *promise* of utopian happiness.[61] This promise is bound to be unfulfilled, and the promise of happiness is no more happiness itself than a promise of relief from pain is relief from pain,

[56] This might seem paradoxical because Adorno is the member of the group of four who had the least interest in antiquity and for whom ancient philosophy, religion, and literature was of least systematic significance. As has often been noted, although Adorno's interest in and knowledge of literature, music, social theory, and philosophy was very broad and substantial, it was historically very limited. Essentially, for him relevant "history" starts with Haydn in music, Goethe in literature, and Kant in philosophy. Apart from the odd reference to J. S. Bach or the *Odyssey* ("*das Urbild . . . des bürgerlichen Individuums*" [1969, 50]) and isolated throw-away remarks about Plato and Aristotle, one finds no discussion of any work or figure before the middle of the eighteenth century. Nietzsche, on the contrary, was a trained academic expert in *Altertumswissenschaft*; much of Heidegger's later philosophy is transmitted through the medium of interpretation of various ancient texts; and the Greeks are a continual presence and a repeated object of treatment in Hegel's system. I wish to suggest, however, that this is not a paradox at all, but that it was precisely the *absence* of the Greeks from Adorno's mind and philosophy and his relative indifference to the cultural prestige of Philhellenism that allowed him the freedom to put "happiness" in such a prominent place in his thought without contortion.

[57] Adorno (1951), 291.

[58] Adorno (1951), 31–32, 73–75.

[59] Adorno (1966), 344.

[60] Adorno (1966), 343–45. "*In der falschen Welt ist alle ἡδονή falsch,*" Adorno (1970), 26.

[61] References to "*La beauté n'est que la* promesse *du bonheur*" (originally from Stendahl [1980], chapter XVII, but also discussed by Baudelaire [1971], 2.137) recur almost obsessively in Adorno's discussions of art, e.g., Adorno (1970), 26, 128, 205, 461, etc.

but even the mere promise can give us (some) pleasure and is of great value.[62]

The second kind of facsimile of happiness is associated with cognition. Thus Adorno takes as the motto of one of the three parts of his *Minima Moralia* a statement he attributes to F. H. Bradley: "When everything is bad, it must be good to know the worst."[63] In present circumstances this "happiness of cognition"[64] is self-undermining and bitter: if one knows anything in this world (in the emphatic sense of "know" which Adorno uses), one in some sense knows that true happiness is impossible. "Happiness" thus refers to some extra-ordinary, momentary form of experience, either the exceptional experience of art or the imagined content of a messianic transformation of the world, or to a form of intellectual life for which not everyone is suited, and which forces one to confront the final inadequacy of any form of life available to us. Happiness, then, is not a stable, possible object to be attained by individual action, or the final framework for living and evaluating one's mundane life as a whole.[65]

In describing these German philosophers as asking different questions from those asked by their British counterparts, I am *not* making a claim about incommensurability in the strict sense. Just because, say, Kant and Hegel ask different questions, that does not make it impossible, or useless, to look in Hegel's texts for answers to Kant's questions. In some contexts it is perfectly understandable that you might not be at all interested in the way the world looks to me—you may simply have perfectly legitimate, urgent concerns of your own that you think peremptorily require that one subordinate all else to their satisfaction. You may have no interest in the shape, structure, and perspective of my own map of the surrounding landscape[66]—if your needs are sufficiently pressing, you may wish to use whatever you can get in order to enable you to reach Oinville (like Roland and Corinne in Godard's *Weekend*) as efficiently as possible. On the other hand, we do not generally think it represents a very high level of intellectual curiosity or human sensitivity to act in this way when not under the pressure of events.

There is one sense in which Hegel had no ethics, and thought that approaching life in terms of ethics—by which he meant Kantian ethics, that is,

---

[62] Adorno (1970), 26, 204–5. On the proximity of "happiness" to infantilism, see Adorno (1970), 181–82, 503–4.

[63] Adorno (1951), 103.

[64] Adorno (1972), 68; Adorno (1951), 22–24, etc.

[65] It is, of course, not unusual in the modern period to use "happiness" to refer to a subjective state of satisfaction that is potentially of limited duration rather than a structural feature of a life as a whole. See further Geuss (2002). I am particularly endebted to Rüdiger Bittner for conversations and correspondence about Heidegger and Adorno; needless to say, he is not responsible for the use I have made of his help here.

[66] I merely note that this mode of speaking does not necessarily imply that philosopher's bugbear, "relativistic perspectivism."

living one's life taking Kantian ethics as the final framework within which to understand oneself and the world—was a mistake. There is, of course, another perfectly reasonable sense in which Hegel did have an ethics: he tried to express and justify a variety of claims we would call "value judgments," such as that slavery was wrong, that in cases of conflict the demands of the state take priority over those of the family, or that Protestantism was a more progressive form of religion than Catholicism. One can, that is to say, hold fast to the Kantian (the modern ethical) perspective if one wants to, and can torture Hegel's texts into giving you an answer to the questions that naturally arise when one presupposes that framework. To be sure, the Hegelian philosophy, as Kierkegaard pointed out very vividly, won't give you determinate answers in most of the cases in which you will be most keen to have purportedly authoritative advice: it won't tell you whether to join the resistance or stay at home to support your aged mother, won't tell you whether you should participate in the *coup d'etat* or revolution or not, won't give you a unitary way to evaluate Nero or Napoleon or Pol Pot. It will, however, tell you all sorts of things about the historical and valuational significance of the movements with which these people were associated. But what grounds do we have to assume that there will always be a single unitary way to give a definitive evaluation of a person, an event, or a course of action?

One might have the feeling that what I have described in this paper is a disorganized battery of various, very different, objections to different aspects of the way ethics has often been studied as an academic subject in the English-speaking world for the past hundred and fifty years or so, not a unified countertradition. I have described reservations about the possibility of a specifically philosophical ethics, objections to the assumptions made by the ethical question, doubts about the significance of choice and about the coherence or importance of individual action, and objections to a fully immanent approach to human life. That this is no coherent countertradition is, I think, no objection. Rather it is a conclusion I welcome.

If one is willing to entertain the line of thought I have suggested, one can go on to ask what the relevance of these nineteenth (and early twentieth-) century Central European projects is for us. Is the immanentist egocentric practical standpoint genuinely ineluctable—something to which we will be returned regardless of the misguided and sophistic attempts of philosophers to undercut it—or is it an artifact of the kind of individualistic, post-Christian society in which we live? Or finally, is it a kind of transcendental illusion, a complex mistake based on some form of natural egotism and as relatively independent of our specific history and form of society as it is immune to attempts to dissolve it? Is it at all coherent to look for a non-immanent standpoint from which to judge the present which is *not* finally theological, but is in some sense naturalistic? It may well be no accident that the line of thought I have been trying to trace has had such strong continuity in Germany. One may see it as a sign of economic, social, and political backwardness,[67] a pre-Enlightenment persistence of theological forms of thinking, and a feudal resistance to the view that commercial society and empirically based natural science are the final framework within which we must structure our lives. On the other hand, one might think that precisely the persistence of these relatively old-fashioned ways of thinking could have the advantage of allowing people a glimpse beyond a monolithic and massively entrenched status quo.

In conclusion, I would suggest a tripartite division of approaches to our practical life: skepticism, the project of modern ethics, and various forms of the view that there is something outside "philosophical ethics." The "outside ethics" views can either be old-fashioned theologically based ones, like those of Augustine or Kierkegaard, or they can have a more complex relation to traditional theology, like the views of Hegel, Adorno, and Heidegger. Skeptical elements play an important role in the philosophy of the figures with whom I am concerned—particularly in Nietzsche, in whom skepticism sometimes takes almost the robust ancient form[68]—but to the extent to which these German thinkers are not skeptics, they are devotees of one or another of the radical versions of thinking about practical life which I have called "outside ethics" views, not of any variant of the modern project.

The most widely influential form of ethical thinking at the moment—at any rate, the one that seems to play the most prominent role in international politics—is some version of a doctrine of natural human rights. It is, I think, fair to say that what are sometimes called the "normative foundations" of this theory are anything but clear (and convincing). The suspicion immediately suggests itself that the reason for this is that the project of finding a completely secular, immanent "grounding" for such a theory is incoherent: there simply is not any direct argumentative path from facts of nature and human psychology, as these are known to us through experience and the usual forms of scientific inquiry, the economic and commercial requirements of the kind of society in which we live, and some minimal principles of rationality, to the desired doctrine of natural human rights. Given the extremely weak cognitive grasp we have on the general area of practical philosophy, it would, I

---

[67] Setting aside, for a moment, the notion of social and political progress, the claim that Germany was economically backward during this period—which, after all, extends well into the second half of the twentieth century—seems highly implausible.

[68] Ancient Pyrrhonism, the view that on any topic there are equally strong arguments on either side, was also a central concern of the young Hegel, as is documented very convincingly by Forster in his (1989). See also Burnyeat and Frede (1997). Hegel held that, compared to this ancient form of skepticism, "modern" skepticism, for instance, views inspired by Hume, is a bloodless and ignoble form of dogmatism, accepting, as it characteristically does, any number of by no means indubitable assumptions, such as that we have impressions, that there is a distinction between thinking and being, etc.

think, be very rash at this point in time simply to dismiss all skeptical and non-immanentist views. In addition, there is a strong aspirational or self-constructive element to practical thinking. It is not merely the case that deciding to believe in or give one's allegiance to a particular view makes one a person of a certain kind, but retaining a wide spectrum of *views* under consideration also makes one a person of a certain kind, even if one thinks that one kind of view is strikingly more plausible than others. This is a basic Nietzschean claim that one can easily admit without moving at all far down the road to some of Nietzsche's other, more florid doctrines. Perhaps more importantly, retaining a wide spectrum of views in play makes a society a certain kind of place.

There are no guarantees in this area, and I have a certain amount of sympathy for the reader who might justifiably continue to object that even if human rights theory is in a parlous state, I have given no reason to think that any of the Central European theories I have expounded is any better off. The forms of radical practical thinking that descend from Paul and Augustine through Hegel to Adorno and Heidegger (and Badiou[69]) may turn out to be nothing more than self-imposed illusions, and settling back into our cosy world of cultivating the tiny garden of our own welfare and our "human rights" and those of other members of the global village, incoherent as the concept of a "human right" is, may well turn out to be in fact the final word for us. That would be extremely unfortunate—we would have become the creatures Nietzsche calls the "last humans."[70] I would like to think that my continuing to tell the story of nineteenth- and twentieth-century German practical philosophy in this way could have some potentially self-fulfilling effect in preventing that from being the case.

References

Adorno, T. (1951). *Minima Moralia*. Frankfurt: Suhrkamp.

———. (1963). *Eingriffe*. Frankfurt: Suhrkamp.

———. (1966). *Negative Dialektik*. Frankfurt: Suhrkamp.

———. (1969). *Stichworte: Kritische Modelle 2*. Frankfurt: Suhrkamp.

———. (1970). *Ästhetische Theorie*. Frankfurt: Suhrkamp.

Adorno, T., and W. Benjamin. (1994). *Adorno/Benjamin Briefwechsel 1928–1940*, ed. Lonitz. Frankfurt: Suhrkamp.

Adorno, T., et al. (1972). *Der Positivismusstreit in der deutschen Soziologie*. Neuwied & Berlin: Luchterhand.

Assmann, J. (1997). *Moses the Egyptian*. Cambridge, MA: Harvard University Press.

Augustinus, A. (1928/9). *De civitate dei*, ed. Dombart and Kalb. Leipzig: Teubner.

---

[69] Badiou (1998).

[70] Nietzsche (1980), 19–20.

Badiou, A. (1997). *Saint Paul: La fondation de l'universalisme*. Paris: Presses Universitaires de France.

———. (1998). *L'éthique: Essai sur la conscience du Mal*. Paris: Hattier.

Baudelaire, C. (1971). *Écrits sur l'art*. 2 vols. Paris: Gallimard.

Bornkamm, P. (1969). *Paulus*. Stuttgart: Kohlhammer.

Burnyeat, M. and Frede, M. (1997). *The Original Sceptics*. Indianapolis: Hackell.

Forster. M. (1989). *Hegel and Scepticism*. Cambridge, MA: Harvard University Press.

Foucault, M. (2001). *L'herméneutique du sujet*. Paris: Gallimard and Seuil.

Fulda, H. (1968). *Das Recht der Philosophie in Hegels Philosophie des Rechts*. Frankfurt: Klostermann.

Geuss, R. (2002). "Happiness and Politics," *Arion*, June, pp. 111–29.

Harnack, A. von (1985). *Marcion: Das Evangelium vom unbekanntnen Gott*. Darmstadt: Wissenschaftliche Buchgesellschaft.

Hegel, G. (1970). *Werke in zwanzig Bänden*, ed. Moldenhauer/Michel. Frankfurt: Suhrkamp. [Cited by volume and page.]

Heidegger, M. (1951). *Erläuterungen zu Hölderlins Dichtung*. Frankfurt: Klostermann.

———. (1957). *Einführung in die Metaphysik*. Tübingen: Max Niemeyer.

———. (1959). *Gelassenheit*. Pfullingen: Neske.

———. (1960). *Unterwegs zur Sprache*. Pfullingen: Neske.

———. (1963). *Sein und Zeit*. Tübingen: Niemeyer.

———. (1967). *Wegmarken*. Frankfurt: Klostermann.

———. (1976). "Nur noch ein Gott kann uns retten," *Der Spiegel*, vol. 30, no. 23 (31 May).

Horkheimer, M. (1968). *Kritische Theorie*. Frankfurt: Fischer (2 vols.).

Kant, I. (1956). *Kritik der reinen Vernunft*. Hamburg: Felix Meiner Verlag.

Marcuse, H. (1965). *Kultur und Gesellschaft*. Frankfurt: Suhrkamp (2 vols.).

Nietzsche, F. (1980). *Sämtliche Werke: Kritische Studienausgabe*, ed. Colli and Montinari. Berlin: De Gruyter. [Cited by volume and page.]

Pippin, R. (2001). "Hegel and Institutional Rationality," in T. Noon (ed.), *The Contemporary Relevance of Hegel's "Philosophy of Right"* (special issue of *Southern Journal of Philosophy*).

Schiller, F. (1967). *Über die ästhetische Erziehung des Menschen in einer Reihe von Briefen*, in his *Sämtliche Werke*, ed. Fricke and Göpfert, vol. V. Munich: Hanser.

Stendahl,.(1980). *De l'amour*. Paris: Gallimard.

Theunissen, M. (1970). *Hegels Lehre vom absoluten Geist als theologisch- politischer Traktat*. Berlin: De Gruyter.

Wood, A. (1990). *Hegel's Ethical Thought*. Cambridge: Cambridge University Press.

4

Freedom as an Ideal

ISAIAH BERLIN'S DISCUSSION of the two concepts of liberty[1] provides a convenient starting place for the topic I wish to discuss, namely the role conceptions of freedom play in structuring our human aspirations. Berlin assumes that "freedom" can be significantly ascribed either to human individuals or to groups, and he also distinguishes what he calls "negative conceptions" of freedom from "positive conceptions." An entity (whether human individual or group) is free "in a negative sense" to the extent to which there are no (external) impediments or obstacles to the action of that entity (in some particular domain); an entity (whether a human individual or a group) is free "in a positive sense" to the extent to which that entity is its own master, i.e., to the extent to which it rules or governs itself. One might think that these two distinctions (between individual and group freedom on the one hand and positive and negative freedom on the other) cut across each other so that actually Berlin's account recognizes four kinds of freedom:

a) negative freedom of an individual: if my hands are untied, I am to that extent freer than I was;

b) positive freedom of an individual: a Roman slave who was emancipated became free "in a positive sense;"

c) negative freedom of a group: a certain nomadic group might not be free to move in a certain direction because of frontier arrangements (Hadrian's Wall, for instance);

d) positive freedom of a group: if a colony successfully revolts against the metropolitan area and establishes itself as a separate political entity, it may sometimes be said to have attained a kind of (positive) freedom it lacked before the revolt.

As if this were not complicated enough, Berlin also claims that the positive conception of freedom (by which he seems to mean in this case the positive freedom of a human individual) is ambiguous. Sometimes "freedom" (of the individual in the positive sense) means "autonomy" or ability to give oneself the rule or principle of one's own behavior, but sometimes (positive) "freedom" means "self-realization," i.e., that the individual's "true" or "real" self comes to expression in action. Actually, neither of these two senses of "(pos-

My thanks to Prof. Martin Hollis for his extremely helpful comments on this paper.

[1] "Introduction" and "Two Concepts of Liberty" in *Four Essays on Liberty* (Oxford: Oxford University Press, 1969).

itive) freedom" seems the same as the sense in which the emancipated Roman slave has become free. An emancipated slave is a person who has been assigned a certain legal status: his or her actions are now recognized in a certain way, and certain kinds of action, such as appearing in court in one's own cause, are now possible that were not before. None of this implies that the former slave is now "autonomous," i.e., actually capable of regulating his or her own behavior or has attained "self-realization" (in any of the more emphatic senses in which that term was used in the nineteenth century).

The discussion can be clarified, I think, by introducing a further distinction which Berlin doesn't use. To return for a moment to the positive sense of freedom for a group, a colony that attains independence from a metropolitan area may be said to have gained a kind of positive freedom, but it does not follow from such independence that the former colony will be internally self-governing (by whatever standards one uses to determine this). I would like to say that the colony that becomes independent attains (positive) freedom "in an outward-looking sense"; "(positive) freedom in an inward-looking sense" then refers to political and social arrangements which nowadays will probably include the existence of a parliamentary system of government with regular elections, etc.[2] One can make an analogous distinction in the case of the positive freedom of an individual: the legal freedom of the emancipated former slave is positive freedom in an outward-looking sense, and it is an extremely important historical step when this notion of "being one's own master" is extended and internalized, giving rise to notions of (positive) freedom as self-control, autonomy, self-realization, etc., that is, to various conceptions of freedom in an inward-looking sense.

Berlin's own final position on freedom is not completely clear. He obviously thinks that the concept of freedom has suffered from a kind of "inflation" during the past several hundred years in the sense that people have tried to build more and more of the components of a fully good and satisfactory human life into the concept of freedom itself. In any case Berlin is clearly extremely concerned to counter this "inflation" of the concept of freedom as much as possible.[3] Thus he wishes to distinguish as sharply as possible between what belongs to the content of the concept of freedom itself and what properly belongs

---

[2] I would like to be able to give a clearer and more abstract account of the distinction between inward-looking and outward-looking senses of freedom, but can't. I hope the examples at least make my general intentions clear. "The positive freedom of a group in an inward-looking sense" doesn't yet designate a single well-defined concept, but rather a family of slightly different conceptions. Different more or less distinct concepts will arise by adding further specifications of what it means for a group to be "self-governing." I discuss some of these issues in more detail in my "Auffassungen der Freiheit" (in *Zeitschrift für philosophische Forschung*, 1995, pp. 1–14) and "Freiheit im Liberalismus und bei Marx" (in *Ethische und politische Freiheit*, ed. Julian Nida-Rümelin and Wilhelm Vossenkuhl [Berlin: de Gruyter, 1998], pp. 114–29).

[3] See *Four Essays on Liberty*, pp. xxxviii ff, liii ff.

only to the conditions under which freedom can effectively be utilized.[4] In fact Berlin at times comes close to suggesting that positive freedom itself in any of its various forms is not *really* a proper concept *of freedom* but a bloated amalgam, incorporating components of the concept of freedom with various other inflationary elements derived from conceptions of happiness, rationality, etc. Only, he suggests, the austere notion of individual negative freedom is the real unvarnished thing itself: certainly it is individual negative freedom which should be given strict priority in philosophical discussion.

The reason it is so important for Berlin to claim that the concept of individual negative freedom is in some sense the most basic concept of freedom[5] is that he believes there is a kind of elective affinity between positive conceptions of freedom and the legitimation of a certain kind of totalitarian oppression.[6] Only the positive conception of freedom, Berlin thinks, gives rise to what has been called "Rousseau's paradox," that is, the thesis that under certain circumstances one could force people to be free.[7] To believe that under certain circumstances people could be forced to be free is, however, to lack the conceptual resources to resist certain forms of totalitarianism.

To put what I take to be Berlin's argument in a series of steps:

1. To be negatively free means simply to be in a state in which one has unobstructed opportunities for action, but to be positively free means actually to live and act in a certain way.

2. If freedom is a way of life, someone else might know better than I do what constitutes that way of life.

3. Anyone who knew (better than I did myself) in what my positive freedom would consist could legitimately force me to adopt that way of life and in so doing would be forcing me to be free.

There are any number of difficulties with this argument.[8] Obviously nothing

---

[4] See *Four Essays on Liberty*, pp. xlix, liii ff. Accepting this distinction would exclude from discussion views that take power to be an essential component of freedom. "Freedom is an opportunity for action" (*Four Essays*, p. xlii), not a power to act or "action itself."

[5] See *Four Essays*, p. lvi.

[6] Berlin sometimes denies that he is asserting any special (in particular any logical) connection between positive conceptions of freedom and totalitarianism (cf. *Four Essays*, pp. xliii–xlix, 132), but this seems to me to be somewhat disingenuous. If the connection between positive conceptions of freedom and totalitarianism is really merely historical and contingent, it is hard to see what systematic point Berlin's discussion is supposed to have, beyond reminding us that "freedom" is used in a variety of different senses, not all of them compatible with each other.

[7] J.-J. Rousseau, *Du contrat social* (1762), Book I, chapter VII; cf. Quentin Skinner, "The Idea of Negative Liberty," in *Philosophy in History*; ed. R. Rorty, J. Schneewind, Q. Skinner (Cambridge: Cambridge University Press, 1984).

[8] Note for instance that it would be a mistake to assume that freedom in a positive sense must be an exercise concept, just because it is not a mere opportunity concept. "Freedom" (in a positive sense) might designate the possession of a faculty or capacity which may or may not be exercised.

at all like it could hold good for *all* positive conceptions of freedom, for instance a conception that saw freedom as residing in individual autonomy, because on such a conception it would be an integral part of the free way of life that the individual living it has chosen that life rather than being forced to adopt it.[9] At the moment, however, I would like to consider the third step in the argument. It is, of course, not true that if I know what would be good for you—even if I know what would be supremely good for you—this gives me a warrant to coerce you, especially not if the good in question is one which has value only if you chose it freely, so that in using coercion I destroy it.

The situation changes immediately, of course, if one adds to the three points listed above a fourth:

> **4.** There is a social agency (for instance, the State) who is really me (or: who is "the real me") and thus all of whose actions are really mine so that none of its actions against me can even in principle count as coercion.

Actually if one has 4 one doesn't need 3 to draw some strong and unpleasant conclusions. This suggests that Berlin has misdiagnosed the error which gives rise to an inability to resist the temptations of totalitarianism. The culprit is some thesis about the relation between individual and social agency—something like 4, or like what Berlin calls the "organicist" conception of society—and not the positive conception of freedom.[10]

It is striking that Berlin's whole discussion of freedom is structured by his interest in the limits of permissible social coercion.[11] Freedom for him is from the very start a police-concept. The possible justification of coercive social regulation of human action is not, however, the only context in which the concept of freedom plays a role. Another context is that in which individuals decide how they will lead their own lives. Whatever the importance of negative conceptions of freedom in the discussion of systems of public coercion, they are of little use in helping individuals structure their aspirations.[12] Since one is not necessarily going to be using conceptions of freedom to legitimize sys-

---

[9] Note that I could also force you to be negatively free by removing various obstacles to your action. Whereas before you had no choice but to stay seated (since you were tied to the chair), when I untie you you are forced to have the freedom of remaining seated or standing up. No one thinks there is anything conceptually odd about cases like this.

[10] Note that Thomas Hobbes has a relentlessly negative conception of freedom, but given his theory about the construction of social agency, the Leviathan, he arrives at strongly totalitarian conclusions. Note also that both Hegel and Marx specifically reject the "organicist" conception of society if by that is meant the view that human individuals are no more than accidents of the social substance or organs of a social whole. Cf. G.W.F. Hegel, *Grundlinien der Philosophie des Rechts* (Frankfurt/M: Suhrkamp, 1970), §§ 260, 261; also "Zusätze," § 273 ("Zusatz"). Cf. also Karl Marx, *Grundrisse* (Berlin: Dietz, 1974), pp. 375 ff, esp. p. 384.

[11] Berlin, *Four Essays*, p. 121.

[12] As Nietzsche writes, freedom as absence of constraints is perhaps a reasonable aspiration for slaves, but not for others. Cf. Friedrich Nietzsche, *Jenseits von Gut und Böse*, § 260.

tems of coercion, it isn't at all obvious that conceptual abstemiousness is the correct course. Nor does it follow from this that one can't take seriously Berlin's concern about excessive inflation of the concept of freedom; "freedom" needn't necessarily completely lose its profile and become indistinguishable from the vague general notion of "a completely satisfactory human life."

If "freedom" is not the same as "happiness," it is not the same as "morality" either.[13] So if one wants to make progress in the right direction in understanding freedom as an ethical ideal, one has to thread one's way through the minefield, some of the salient features of which I have just sketched. That is, one wants a conception of freedom which is a development of something rooted in everyday usage and practice which can serve to give clarity and focus to individual human aspirations but which is neither a police-concept nor so inflated as to be indistinguishable from the concept of the indeterminate sum of all human satisfactions, nor so thoroughly moralized that it is an analytic truth that anyone acting freely is acting morally.

There are, I think, a number of different paths through this minefield. I would like to mention four: (1) freedom as autonomy; (2) conceptions of freedom centered around power; (3) freedom as authenticity of desire; (4) freedom as self-realization. I will make some very cursory remarks about the first two, then some comments on authenticity and self-realization.

The full concept of autonomy can be thought of as being comprised of two components: I will be said to be "autonomous" if I

> **1)** have or exercise the capacity to set myself my own goals, give myself principles of action, etc.
>
> **2)** have or exercise a capacity for self-control, i.e., am able to refrain from acting on impulses I may experience if I know them to be incompatible with goals I have set myself or principles I have adopted.

This conception of freedom as autonomy has a long and distinguished history, although I would suggest that by itself it may seem slightly etiolated to those with a certain kind of modern sensibility. To use the standard example, the slave in chains may well be "autonomous" in the above sense, but we would perhaps hesitate to call such a slave fully free. One might think that one could deal with this consideration by claiming that the ideal of individual freedom comprises both full autonomy and maximal negative freedom.

If one reflects on the intuition that lies behind the negative conception of freedom, one might come to think that it was something like this: I am the freer the more possible courses of action stand open to me, thus any obstacle which closes off a course of action as a possibility for me is a restriction of my freedom. If this is the right way to think about freedom, then the central thing

---

[13] Despite the efforts of Kant and his followers to assimilate freedom and morality.

is the extent of the spectrum of possible courses of action that stand open to me at any given time. How many possible courses of action stand open to me, however, will depend on any number of factors; in many cases it will depend as much on how much power (of what kind) I have as on the existence or nonexistence of obstacles. "Obstacles" lose their salience in the discussion of freedom; there is in principle no reason why increase of my power might not lead to as great an increase in my freedom as the removal of obstacles would. This is the tack Marx takes when he cites the *Dictionnaire de l'académie* to the effect that *liberté* is most commonly used in the sense of *puissance*.[14]

Stalwart proponents of negative liberty can try to resist this line of argument by appeal to a certain moral intuition many of us have and which one finds expressed with great clarity in Rousseau's *Émile*, namely that we react differently to different ways in which our wishes can be frustrated. If our desires are frustrated because we lack the power to attain what we want or are prevented by some natural obstacle, our reaction will usually lack the quality of resentment and indignation it may well have if we are hindered by an obstacle created by another human agent (especially if this obstacle was created specifically to thwart us). Berlin, and those who take a similar position to his on the priority of negative liberty, argue from this Rousseauist intuition that only obstacles which are the results of human action (or even, of "deliberate interference")[15] count as restrictions of my liberty; natural obstacles or my own lack of power do not.[16]

It seems plausible that a conception of freedom which held it to consist in autonomy plus power could satisfy the conditions I outlined above. It could have a clear conceptual profile and be distinguishable from other ideals and it needn't be construed in an inherently moralizing way—I may well autonomously decide to use my powers in ways that do not satisfy reasonable standards of "morality."

One might still, however, think that a conception of freedom which took it to consist in autonomy plus power left something out. It has often been taken to be part of our intuitive conception of freedom that I can be called fully free only if I am doing what I really want. "What I really want to do" here refers not to some externally specifiable course of action, but to the kind of desire

[14] MEW 3.287, i.e., Karl Marx and Friedrich Engels, *Werke* (Berlin: Dietz, 1983), vol. 3, p. 287.

[15] Berlin, *Four Essays*, p. 122.

[16] Part of my intention is to try to break the hold on our imaginations exercised by an image Berlin (and some of his followers) tend to project, the image of a contrast between sober, responsible, more or less value-neutral negative conceptions of freedom and inflated, highly moralizing positive conceptions. (Cf., esp., Richard Flathman, *The Philosophy and Politics of Freedom* [Chicago: University of Chicago Press, 1987], pp. 50ff.) If the Rousseauist intuition did turn out to be part of the motivation of those who cling most tenaciously to a purely negative conception of freedom, this would be grist for my mill.

that gives rise to the action I perform. In this sense I am doing something I really want to do if my action is motivated by a desire that is genuinely or authentically mine. I'm free then, in this sense, if I am acting on a genuine or authentic desire.

Another way in which the same point is often put is to say that I am free only if acting on a desire with which I "identify." The most powerful contemporary analysis of what it means to "identify" with a desire is the one given by Harry Frankfurt in his classic paper "Freedom of the Will and the Concept of a Person."[17] This analysis starts from a distinction between first-order and second-order desires (and correspondingly first-order and second-order volitions). I identify with a given desire, roughly speaking, when I will that desire to be the one which moves me to action. Thus if I have a (first-order) desire to have a glass of wine, I will be acting freely in acting on that desire if I also have a second-order desire that that desire for a glass of wine be the one which motivates me to action; such a second-order desire is a second-order volition and means that I have identified with the given first-order desire. If, on the other hand, I have a first-order desire to drink a glass of wine and a second-order volition that that first-order desire *not* move me to action, then the desire to drink the wine is not one I have identified with, not one authentically mine, and acting on it will not be acting fully freely.

In a somewhat later essay[18] Frankfurt introduces a qualification to his account. If I have a second-order desire *not* to be moved to action by a particular first-order desire, I have not identified with the first-order desire in question, but it doesn't necessarily follow from the fact that I endorse a given first-order desire as motive for action that I have thereby identified with that first-order desire in any very significant sense. It may well be the case, for instance, that I have unresolved conflicts among my higher-order desires. After much backing and forthing I may reluctantly, with (proleptic) regret and many reservations, finally settle for the moment on a second-order volition that one particular first-order desire be the one that constitutes my will. In so deciding (and then acting) I don't fully identify with the first-order desire— all things considered, under these and these conditions, unfortunately, I endorse it for action this time around without any commitment or clear expectation that next time around I will not decide differently. This is the issue Frankfurt calls "wholeheartedness." It is obviously extremely difficult to give any kind of full and clear account of what it means to identify wholeheartedly with a desire, but Frankfurt is surely right to emphasize that one component of such an analysis is a commitment the agent makes vis-à-vis the

---

[17] Harry Frankfurt, *The Importance of What We Care About* (Cambridge: Cambridge University Press, 1988), pp. 11ff.

[18] "Identification and Wholeheartedness," in Harry Frankfurt, *The Importance of What We Care About*, pp. 159ff.

future; I grant the desire in question a continuing recognized place within the self.[19]

Reflection on wholeheartedness, identification, and authenticity gave rise in the nineteenth century to two contrasting ideals. The first of these is one which sees freedom to consist precisely in the absence of identification or wholeheartedness. The free spirit is bound by no fixed beliefs or commitments and stands related to desires in a way that is similar to that in which the ancient skeptic stands to beliefs. Desires, both first-order and higher-order desires, are there to be acted on in the given context, not to be the objects of identification. Genuinely free and deep people are those who love masks and are deft at changing them.[20]

As Hegel pointed out, though, in his criticism of Friedrich Schlegel,[21] the apparent rich multiplicity of possibilities open to the free spirit seems to be purchased at the price of an impoverishment of the self which is reduced to the single, empty, infinitely repeated movement of rejecting identification.

The other, diametrically opposed ideal is one which sees freedom to consist in identifying oneself wholeheartedly with a unitary, structured set of desires which constitute the core of a more or less enduring self.[22] Only then, so this line of argument runs, can there even be a self which might be said to be free or unfree in acting one way rather than another, namely acting freely if acting on a desire with which it identifies, otherwise not acting freely.[23]

It would, though, I think, be a mistake to think that one could understand freedom in the sense at issue here *merely* as action on a set of desires with which I can wholeheartedly identify. Even if the project of the "free spirit" in its more extreme versions isn't completely coherent, the proponents of this ideal did have something in mind that one can't simply dismiss: there can be a kind of naive, immediate, and unreflective wholeheartedness which we are not necessarily inclined to see specifically as a form of freedom. Hegel's idea that both reflection (which gives rise to the ideal of the free spirit) and identification (which gives rise to the ideal of wholeheartedness) are internal "mo-

---

[19] Cf. Frankfurt, "Identification and Wholeheartedness," esp. pp. 168ff. "Freedom of the Will and the Concept of a Person" deals with traditional problems of the mechanism of autonomy; "Identification and Wholeheartedness" deals with what came to be called "authenticity."

[20] This ideal is expressed with great brilliance at various places in Nietzsche's work (e.g., *Jenseits von Gut und Böse*, §§ 40, 284, 289).

[21] Hegel, *Grundlinien der Philosophie des Rechts*, § 140.

[22] Oddly enough, one finds extreme expressions of both of the two ideals in Nietzsche. (For an instance of something like this ideal of "wholeheartedness," cf. *Götzendämmerung*, "Sprüche und Pfeile," § 44). Part of the difficulty in understanding Nietzsche is a difficulty in knowing how to take this fact. Hegel has a complex theory of the way in which both of these ideals are (so he claims) rooted in aspects of the structure of the will and how they can be reconciled in a life lived in a fully rational state. Cf. Hegel, *Grundlinien zur Philosophie des Rechts*, §§ 5–7, 139–57.

[23] Kant doesn't use the language of "identification," but one might think of him as claiming that one should identify wholeheartedly only with the desire to act consistently.

ments" of freedom (correctly understood) seems plausible, but by itself leaves one without much clarity about how exactly the two will be related in full-blown cases of freedom.

Self-realization views of freedom shift the focus from the internal world of desire to the world of action. There are two slightly different versions of a self-realization approach to freedom. The first, which one can find perhaps most explicitly in Humboldt,[24] sees human beings not so much as creatures who have desires with which they identify or fail to identify, but as bearers of powers and capacities which they can exercise and develop. I'm free on this view to the extent to which I am engaged in a course of action in which I am exercising my powers and capacities in such a way that these powers and capacities are also at the same time being further developed. It is by exercising my capacity to play the piano that that capacity is further developed, and to the extent to which the exercise of this capacity is at the same time the development of that capacity, the course of action is free. In nineteenth-century capitalist industrial labor, workers performed simplified and highly repetitious motions for long periods of time; part of the reason why for Marx such labor was a form of unfree activity was that such simplified and routinized activity was the exercise of certain human capacities on the part of the individual worker which was not appropriately connected with the development of any powers or capacities.[25] Playing the piano an hour a day makes one progressively a better player but turning a screw in a certain position for an hour a day won't after the first day make one a better mechanic.

Often those who wish thus to understand freedom as the exercise and development of human powers and capacities hold that a fully free action will be one that is an integral part of an all-sided or universal development of human powers and capacities.[26] Since the development of some human powers and capacities is incompatible with the development of others, the coherence of the more extreme forms of this view has rightly been questioned.[27] There is also a slight difference, at least of emphasis perhaps, between this self-realization view and the view I mentioned earlier which identified freedom with power. The earlier view focuses on my ability to get what I want as the central part of freedom (where power is what lets me get what I want). In the self-realization views the emphasis seems rather to be on the transformation of my self which development of my powers and *capacities* brings

---

[24] W. von Humboldt, *Über die Grenzen der Wirksamkeit des Staates* (originally 1793; the most convenient modern edition is Reclam, 1967).

[25] MEW Ergänzungsband 1.454ff.

[26] MEW 3.74, 206, 237, 245, etc.

[27] Cf. G. A. Cohen, "Reconsidering Historical Materialism," *Nomos* 27 (1983), pp. 226ff. Obviously there are a number of different specific views possible here: that freedom consists in exercise and development of *all* of my powers and capacities, of any that are unique to me, of those that are in some sense characteristic of me, etc.

about; by developing and exercising my capacities and powers I become a literally more realized self and thus, the proponents of this argument claim, freer in my acting.[28]

The other variant of a self-realization view emphasizes that I am free only if I am acting in such a way as to be able to recognize (or perhaps recognize and affirm) myself in the action. Unfortunately it is tremendously difficult to give any kind of coherent reading of what "recognizing myself in my action" means which isn't either much too weak—"recognizing myself" means just having a certain feeling of familiarity or subjective belief, but one doesn't necessarily want to define freedom directly in terms of a mere subjective feeling—or really very strong indeed—if one, for instance, has a specific theory of the structure of the self and holds that free action is action in which I can see that particular structure of the self to be instantiated. I suspect that most of what is intuitively appealing about this version of the self-realization view can actually be accommodated by a judicious extension of notions of authenticity of desire or perhaps of the notions of authenticity plus development and exercise of my powers and capacities.

Autonomy, power, authenticity of desire, exercise and development of my powers and capacities all seem eminently reasonable objects of human aspiration; all of these seem reasonably clearly defined and none seems to have an inherent bias in favor of morality. I may autonomously set myself perfectly immoral goals, or authentically identify with desires that will move me to egregiously antisocial behavior, and the development and exercise of my capacities may be grossly incompatible with the continued existence of minimally humane conditions of life for large numbers of other people. Finally, none seems to be inherently a police-concept. Together with negative freedom, they seem to me to designate perfectly legitimate dimensions along which the discussion of freedom can proceed.

Earlier (footnote 16 above) I spoke of a certain image Isaiah Berlin's discussion insinuated: that "negative freedom" was a straightforward, sober, morally neutral concept, whereas positive conceptions of freedom arose out of an attempt to build highly controversial biases in the direction of one or another moral view into the very nature of freedom itself.

What "moral neutrality" might mean here isn't perhaps completely clear (nor why it should be a desideratum). I take it to be one of the great merits of Bernard Williams's work to have pointed out that "ethics" has traditionally meant two distinct things: (a) the attempt to say something about what the "good life" for me would be, and (b) the attempt to say something general about how people should regulate their behavior toward one another. "Ethics" widely construed refers equivocally to either task, narrowly construed to

---

[28] Note that the word "power" in the phrase "development and exercise of my powers and capacities" may not mean precisely the same thing as "power" meant in the earlier discussion.

the first; "morality" tends to be used to refer to the second. Western philosophy begins with the attempt to show the close connection between plausible answers to the two questions: the *only* way for me to live a truly happy life (it is claimed) is to do so in the context of acting toward others in morally well-regulated ways.[29]

"Negative freedom," I want to claim, gets its attractiveness if one is looking for a police-concept, that is, a concept to regulate the enforcement of morality. This doesn't mean one can't extract a concept of "negative freedom" from the context of moral inquiry in which it is embedded; of course one can, but outside this particular moral context the concept seems ad hoc and pointless.

It would be neatly symmetrical if I could now claim that the positive conception of freedom (or at any rate *some* of the various positive conceptions) has the property of "moral neutrality" falsely assigned to negative freedom, but I can't. This result should be undisturbing because one's whole interest in the concept of "freedom" arises from ethical concerns (very broadly construed), so it isn't obvious that all forms of moral neutrality are even desiderata. The positive conceptions of freedom I have mentioned describe individual aspirational ideals, but do so in such a way as to leave it an open question whether it is always good for each individual to attain his or her ideals (to become more free in one or another particular way) and also an open question whether or not (or to what extent) it would be a good thing for a society to be organized so as to allow its members maximal freedom in one or another of the positive senses.

[29] Cf. Bernard Williams, *Ethics and the Limits of Philosophy* (London: Fontana, 1985). For the persistence of this form of thinking in German Idealism, cf. Andreas Wildt, *Autonomie und Anerkennung* (Stuttgart: Klett-Cotta, 1982).

5

Virtue and the Good Life

THE COVER OF *How Should One Live? Essays on the Virtues*, edited by Roger Crisp (Oxford University Press, 1996), a collection of distinguished contributions to the contemporary debate about virtue-ethics, shows an engraving by Albrecht Dürer (figure 1). The engraving has come down to us without a title, and its iconography is difficult to make out. Some early commentators thought it depicted a cuckold (the man in the horned helmet) or the phenomenon of envy (*invidia*), or that it represented the struggle between chastity and unchastity. In a highly influential monograph from the early 1930s, the great German art historian Erwin Panofsky argued that the engraving was an illustration of the story of "Hercules at the Crossroads."[1] Accordingly, Oxford University Press gives the image the title *Combat of Virtue and Pleasure in the Presence of Hercules.*

Panofsky traces the original story back to Socrates' teacher Prodicus.[2] The youthful hero Hercules, so the tale runs, came one day to a fork in the road.[3] As he tried to decide which way to proceed he was approached by two women, "Virtue" and "Pleasure,"[4] who told him he must now decide in general what kind of life he wished to lead. They would lead him down one or the other of the two respective paths that lay open before him, the path of virtue or that of pleasure. He was completely free to choose whichever of the two paths and women he wished, but he would have only one choice.[5] He would have to re-

---

[1] Erwin Panofsky, *Hercules am Scheideweg und andere antike Bildstoffe in der neueren Kunst* (Leipzig: Tuebner, 1930).

[2] The oldest version is in Xenophon's *Memorabilia* II.1.21ff.

[3] So to speak of Hercules at the "crossroad" isn't, strictly speaking, correct. At a crossroad I will generally have three ways of going forward—straight ahead, to the right, or to the left. The story presupposes that Hercules is at a Greek τρίοδος, like the one at which Oedipus met and murdered his father, i.e., a place where the road forks. He has, then, only two choices: bear on down the right fork or bear on down the left.

[4] In Prodicus's original version, at least as reported by Xenophon, the two women were named "Virtue" (Ἀρετή) and Worthlessness (Κακία), although Ms. Worthlessness says her close friends call her "Happiness" (Εὐδαιμονία) and what she offers is pleasure (ἡδονή). It is significant that over the course of time "worthlessness" becomes increasingly identified with specifically sexual pleasure (*voluptas*), reflecting, no doubt, Christian obsessions with this phenomenon. In 5th-century Athens the main temptations against which people preached in this obsessive way seem to have been warm baths (cf. Aristophanes, *The Clouds*, lines 1043–54).

[5] In Xenophon he is called αὐτοκράτωρ, which in this context presumably means "his own master."

Figure 1. Dürer, Albrecht (1471–1528). Hercules at the Crossroads. Etching; courtesy Foto Marburg/Art Resource, NY.

main devoted to the woman he chose absolutely and unconditionally, and follow on the path she led to the end. What, then, do the two ladies have to offer?

At the bottom left of Dürer's engraving we see a couple that seems to have been interrupted while in the middle of an erotic encounter. He is a bearded, rustic figure with a fine pair of goat's legs. His right hand is resting loosely on the jawbone of a large animal (probably an ass); the gesture suggests that he has put aside for the moment this primitive weapon.[6] She has a very artfully arranged hairdo, and is naked save for a hairband which seems to be decorated with jewels. That is what Ms. Pleasure has to offer: if she is his choice, Hercules can have his way with her as the goat-man does. In almost the exact middle of the picture and dominating the scene, we see Virtue. She is fully clothed in an unadorned, pseudo-antique, flowing garment, and she has a knotted stick in her hands which she has raised above her head. She is about to strike Pleasure in the face with her full force. This is presumably an exactly calculated stroke and not a random blow. Even if Pleasure survives the attack, she will be mutilated; with a scarred face she will not be attractive, and will thus no longer represent serious competition to Virtue. Pleasure, half turned away from her goatish partner and toward Virtue, tries vainly to protect herself by covering her face with one of the folds of the garment she has laid aside.

We know how the story turns out, and Panofsky thinks that Dürer's image shows an episode of it which takes place *after* the decisive moment—Hercules' choice—has already passed. In the original version of the story, when confronted with the choice, Hercules is said to have hesitated, and sat down to think, not knowing which road to take (καθῆσθαι ἀπορουντα ποτέραν των ὁδων τράπηται, Xenophon *Memorabilia* II.1.21). On Panofsky's reading the choice has already been made: the Hercules in this engraving is *already* "something like a Paladin of Virtue," who thinks he can stand aside and wait because she is doing well enough on her own, but who is certainly ready to support her if she needs it. I wonder, though, whether it would not be possible to see the engraving differently. I find it difficult to see Hercules' gesture as one of *support*, even passive support, of Virtue, or one of patiently awaiting the outcome of Virtue's action. He seems to me rather to be trying to intervene to prevent manifestly unfair practice, i.e., to *stop* armed Virtue from attacking the defenseless semi-recumbent Pleasure. His gesture is a spontaneous reaction of simple humanity in the face of immediate, self-evident brutality. As the picture makes clear, this is clearly the young Hercules, not (yet) the mature, principled Knight of Virtue we know from such classical repre-

---

[6] In a woodcut which is thought to be from about the same time as this engraving (late 1490s) and which bears the explicit title *Ercules*, there is a figure just behind Hercules who wields an ass's jawbone as a weapon. Comparison of the way this figure holds the jawbone with the position of the wild-man's hand on the jawbone in the engraving gives further support to the view that Dürer is trying to represent the wild-man as disarmed.

sentations as the so-called "Farnese Hercules" (now in the Museo Archeologico Nazionale, Naples). The massively overdeveloped Farnese Hercules is stolid and completely immobile; he seems scarcely able to bear the weight of his own virtue and achievements, as he props himself up on his club (figure 2). Dürer's Hercules is by contrast a flyweight. His feet are wide apart and he is off balance, as if he has been surprised and is gauchely trying to hasten forward, fearing he may be too late to block Virtue's stroke; his mouth is open, as if to call on her to stop. It is very hard to see in this an *"abwartende Haltung,"* as Panofsky claims, but it makes sense if Hercules is taken aback by Virtue's savage intention and reacts impulsively. It also doesn't seem at all correct to describe this one-sided encounter as a "combat;" if anything, it is an attempted slaughter.

Who knows what Hercules would have decided if he had really had a genuinely free, unconstrained choice? Maybe he would have preferred to stay single and go his own way without any feminine company. In that case he might still have thought it wrong to treat Pleasure cruelly. It isn't, after all, her fault she is so attractive. Perhaps he would have liked to live with *both* women together, or alternatingly with one, then the other, if the redoubtable Lady Virtue had allowed this. To interpret the image as one in which Hercules has *already* chosen Virtue—because there is in some sense no question for him of any other choice—and is standing there as her totally superfluous "paladin"—unneeded because she seems, as Panofsky admits, to be doing fine on her own—is to deprive the picture of much of its dramatic tension and of much of its pathos. The dramatic interest and pathos consist not just in the fact that he hasn't yet chosen, but also that there is something to be said, if not exactly in favor of Pleasure—think of the *smell* of the goat-man—then at any rate against this kind of Virtue and her mode of proceeding. Perhaps the most humane outcome would be if Hercules were to be strong enough to keep Virtue in check and enforce peace between Virtue and Pleasure. That he must finally make an exclusive choice between the two is perhaps a sign of weakness, although Dürer might think this a weakness inherent in the human condition, and thus one not to be overcome even by Herculean strength.

For the contemporary viewer the most striking feature of Dürer's composition is its sadism. Virtue has her eyes closed; she doesn't see and doesn't want to see Pleasure or the wild-man. She is concentrating completely and collecting all her strength to smash Pleasure's face in. Nietzsche claimed that the Christian conscience and the Kantian concept of "duty" had their origin in sadism, but he also thought that the kind of sadism in question, one directed by the self on to itself, was the basic motor of all human progress.[7] Presumably he would have given a similar account of this kind of "virtue." After all,

---

[7] Nietzsche, *Jenseits von Gut und Böse* § 229, and the second and third essays in *Zur Genealogie der Moral.*

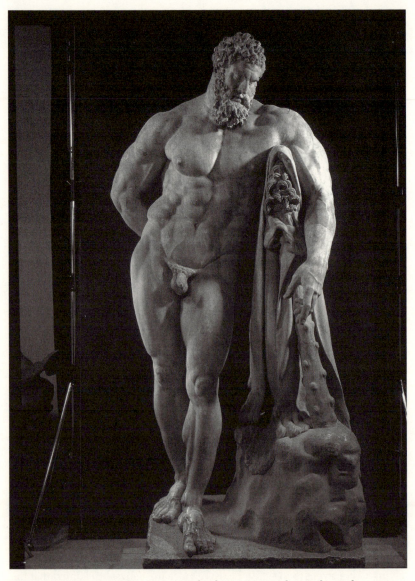

Figure 2. Farnese Hercules. Museo Archeologico Nazionale, Naples, Italy; courtesy Alinari/Art Resource, NY.

the specifically modern form of state terrorism began with Robespierre's proclamation of a *république de la vertu et de la terreur.*

Both the German philosophers Adorno and Horkheimer (in their joint book *Dialektik der Aufklärung*)[8] and the French psychoanalyst Jacques Lacan (in his essay "Kant avec Sade")[9] see de Sade as the figure who thinks through Enlightenment ethics, and particularly the Kantian duty-centered position, to its logical conclusion. Lacan memorably remarks that " *'La Philosophie dans le boudoir'* . . . *complète [et] donne la vérité de la 'Critique [de la raison pratique].'* " Adorno and Horkheimer emphasize that de Sade's universe is the systematically developed and organized model of the kind of abstract, fully self-consistent willing Kant saw as definitive of morality. One might be tempted to object to this that de Sade's view of the world is perhaps "rational" in that it is an instance of possible self-consistent universal willing, but it is completely inhuman. This line of objection is not, of course, open to Kant himself, because for him a feeling of "humanity" that was detached from, or anything more than, a conception of full rational consistency of willing is merely a "pathological" state of no standing whatever as a guide to moral action.

Perhaps the most disturbing further thought that results from this line of argument is that the real world of civilization which we inhabit *is really already* the world of de Sade—of universal sadism directed at self and others and of sadism's mirror image, masochism—if just a bit less fully and systematically organized, a bit less fully "rational" than *The 120 Days of Sodom.* To be sure, this sadism is usually very significantly sublimated, but "sublimation" itself, if Nietzsche is to be believed, is in origin itself a form of the same natural pleasure we take in watching pain being inflicted (although in the case in question it is pain we inflict on ourselves). It is not the least of the deficiencies of the Kantian moral theory that Kant has no doctrine of "sublimation" and no place for such a theory.[10]

The German poet Friedrich Schiller was an admirer of what he took to be the harmonious unity and coherence of life in the ancient world and particularly of the psychic integration the ancients enjoyed. Despite his general acceptance of Kantian ethics, Schiller fiercely opposed Kant's moral psychology, his image of the human soul as necessarily split between sensuous inclination and rational duty, and thus necessarily in a state of internal con-

---

[8] *Exkurs II: Juliette oder Aufklärung und Moral.*

[9] Reprinted in *Écrits I* (Paris: Seuil, 1966).

[10] If anything like this view, held by Nietzsche, Adorno, Horkheimer, and Lacan, is correct, it would cause rather serious difficulties for the form of liberalism associated with Judith Shklar (and tacitly endorsed by Richard Rorty), i.e., the view that cruelty is the worst thing in the world, that which is to be avoided at all costs. Cf. Judith Shklar, "The Liberalism of Fear," in *Liberalism and the Moral Life,* ed. Nancy Rosenblum (Cambridge, MA: Harvard University Press, 1989).

flict. He saw in this division a reflection of the fragmented, oppressed state of the modern social and political world. Schiller would have hated Dürer's engraving. German Idealism begins with the attempt to take seriously Schiller's visceral reaction against this Kantian image of an irremediably divided, alienated human psyche. The Idealists tried to find a way of showing that not only could there be a kind of "cease-fire" between the two ladies in Dürer's engraving, but that the two (or three, if one includes Hercules) "agents" in the picture could be brought to engage in a process of mutual accommodation in which they gradually modified each other, so that no further *casus belli* existed between them. Schiller proposes that "aesthetic education" could play an important, even perhaps an essential, role in implementing such a transformation.

"Sublimation" might be a name for one important component in such a process. It is only when the more utopian forms of hope about the possibility of such a relatively "peaceful" *total* transformation are dashed (after the political failure of 1848) that Nietzsche recurs to something like Dürer's image and tries to accept the sadism implicit in it. If there is to be sublimation it won't be entirely without coercion. This is not a simple return to Kantianism, because the Kantian view is a consciously static transcendentalist one—the split between the two components of the psyche, between sensory appetite and inclination on the one hand and pure reason on the other, like that between the transcendental and the empirical ego, is one to which temporal succession is of no relevance; it is unchanging and in some important sense "outside of time." For Nietzsche, rather, the image is one of historically successive processes of active aggression, which, if one is lucky, constitutes a way in which cruelty transforms itself into something "higher," especially into more sublimated forms of cultural activity. The split is there because it is continually reconstituted, although in an ever different form, and, again *if* one is lucky, in ever less *overtly* violent forms.

The past decade or so has seen the revival of an approach to moral philosophy which circulates under the general name of "virtue-ethics" and presents itself prima facie as a competitor to the two other approaches to moral theory that have been most influential in the twentieth century. These two approaches are consequentialism, the view that a human action is worthy of choice if it would have good consequences; and deontological views, which emphasize that the rightness or wrongness of a human action is to be judged by its compatibility or incompatibility with certain general principles. One of the most widely discussed forms of consequentialism is utilitarianism, which defines "good consequences" with the maximization of human utility. Kantianism, which specifies the general principles of right acting as those of consistent, rational willing, is one of the more philosophically influential recent versions of a deontological view. In contrast to this, virtue-ethics claims that the central items that are to be considered in making a moral evaluation should be not the actual consequences of a given action or general principles, but concrete human psychological dispositions, powers, and character traits. Ethics is not finally about what results a certain particular proposed course of action will be likely to bring about, or what general rules should serve as motivational guides for us when we are trying to decide what to do, but about what it is to be a courageous, temperate, truthful, just person, and how such a person would conduct his or her life. Much recent virtue-ethics takes as its source of inspiration the ancient discussions of the virtues and the good life, but the concept "virtue" has always been ambiguous, even in the ancient world. The Greek word usually translated "virtue" (ἀρετή) actually, as has often been pointed out, means something like "excellence, goodness, serviceability" and is used very widely, much more widely than we use "virtue." Thus the ancients seem routinely to have ascribed "virtue" to inanimate objects, and even to objects of everyday use. The "virtue" of a knife is its property of being an excellent, highly serviceable knife, i.e., of doing well what one expects a knife to do: cut. Just as there are various different ways of being excellent—to be a serviceable knife is quite different from being a serviceable hammer—so there are very different kinds of virtue. The same one might expect to be true of humans. Those persons have "virtue" or are "virtuous" who are excellent, good, serviceable. The question is: excellent in what respect, in what way serviceable, good for what?

Latin (and thus also English) deviate from this Greek etymological path by deriving "*virtus*/virtue" from *vir*, "man" as opposed to "woman," an Indo-European root which has left its trace in the English and German word: "*werwolf*" "man + wolf." "Virtue/excellence" for the Romans is in the first instance manliness. This is good news for Hercules, because manliness is one thing he possesses in abundance. But someone who, like Hercules, has to his credit large numbers of manly achievements—the destruction of various monsters, cleaning out in one day years of accumulated manure from the stables of Augeas, the impregnation of all fifty daughters of a minor local king in a single night—may also need to satisfy a man-sized hunger and thirst. Hercules may have sworn off pleasure, but his legendary capacity for eating and drinking is the stuff of which poets write.[11] In this respect, too, he outstrips everyone else. A great culture-hero need not be the most refined of houseguests. His riotous appetites are just one of the things one must simply put up with if one needs the benefits that can be conferred by a man of heroic virtue and achievement (figure 3).

Heroic virtue is not, however, the only kind; there are also bourgeois forms of virtue. The Homeric hero strives to excel in individual combat with his peers and is virtuous to the extent to which he has the properties, dispositions, and capacities which make him successful in this undertaking; the cit-

---

[11] *Cf.* Aristophanes, *The Birds*, 1583–1605; Euripides, *Alcestis*, 747–802.

Figure 3. Drunken Hercules. Hellenistic bronze. Galleria Nazionale, Parma, Italy; courtesy Alinari/Art Resource, NY.

izen of the ancient city-state didn't have to have heroic virtue—in fact, it would have been militarily extremely harmful if he had left the closed hoplite ranks to fight alone out front; what he had to do was follow the laws of the city and stay in his place in the line of battle. Heroic virtue is a matter of achievement and competition; bourgeois virtue, a matter of cooperation in a social context. One can deny that heroes, or "saints" (i.e., the heroes of Christianity), are "virtuous" only if one tacitly identifies "virtue" with the cooperative bourgeois virtues. If one does this, however, it becomes very hard to see any direct connection between "virtue" and the "good" life, unless, of course, one wishes to identify the good life with a life of smooth social cooperation.

Ancient ethics is structured around the question "What is the good life?," and the answer the main line of ancient ethical thought tried to get to this question was: the good life is that lived by the good person ("man"), and the good man is the virtuous man; increasingly ancient philosophers came to hold that the virtuous man is the man who has the cooperative bourgeois virtues of justice, truthfulness, self-restraint, and prudence. The identification of the good life with the life of the good man is so self-evidently false that it was recognized as a paradox by the ancients themselves, and an enormous amount of time and intellectual energy was devoted to proving that despite all appearances to the contrary, the virtuous man on the rack or the cross was really leading a good life.

"Virtue" is not really an active component of contemporary colloquial speech. To the extent to which the word "virtue" occurs at all nowadays outside philosophy texts, it would seem to designate a kind of highly self-conscious self-righteousness—not at all the sort of thing we admire nowadays. Some of the philosophers who have been most responsible for the revival of virtue-ethics have been concerned to emphasize the essential locatedness of virtues in existing social practices. Thus MacIntyre's dark view of the impossibility of leading a good life in contemporary society[12] would seem to derive from his assumption that a good life would have to be one of virtue; virtue would be a disposition for appropriate and effective functioning in a constituted set of social practices. Contemporary society, however, as Schiller thought, is so fragmented, it doesn't exhibit social practices of the right sort, and so lacks the framework within which full-blown virtues could develop or be exercised.

If virtue is effective excellent participation in given social practices, this suggests what may be a second worry many have had about virtue-ethics, i.e., a worry that may be distinct from the possible association of virtue with sadism.[13] "Virtue" seems to run the risk of being too closely associated with

---

[12] Alasdair MacIntyre, *After Virtue* (London: Duckworth, 1981).

[13] I can't discuss here whether conformism in some sense must be associated with sadism, or, if it need not be, whether there would be anything objectionable about it, and what the nature of the objections would be.

the set of dispositions that result from successful processes of socialization or normalization. We are all familiar with policies that are justified on the grounds that they are necessary for or conducive to making certain groups of people "useful members of society." The fact that such systematic attempts to make people "virtuous" have up to now always failed[14] is no cause for complacency or for self-congratulation. With increasing means of technological control over the natural and social world and corresponding political transformations, that situation might well change. One ought not either to despise the bourgeois virtues, just because they are boring. The former inhabitants of Foča, Zvornik, and Prijedor know that there are worse things than the bourgeois *Rechtsstaat* and the unexciting virtues of cooperation. The social practices that exist to make people predictable (within limits) and cooperative aren't *just* part of an apparatus of repression; to use what is now perhaps a slightly dated expression, they are "forces of production" of the first order. The approach to the study of this phenomenon which seems to me most enlightening, that initiated by Nietzsche in the late nineteenth century and represented more recently by the work of Foucault, is one that insists on seeing the enforcement of predictability, cooperation, and conformity in society as *at the same time* "productive"—giving us new powers and capacities we would otherwise not have—*and* repressive. To have a proper understanding of society means to see exactly how a multiplicity of diverse and normatively ambiguous elements interact to hold such a society together, and also to see what possibilities are implicit in this. This, in turn, need not imply that the bourgeois virtues have the last word in determining what the good life is or could be.

Hercules' choice remained paradigmatic for ancient moral philosophers, but given that his choice was, or soon came to be interpreted as being, one between Virtue and *Pleasure*, this left open the possibility of distinguishing

---

[14] Cf. Michel Foucault, "Le nuage et la poussière," in *L'impossible prison* (Paris: Seuil, 1980). This extremely important brief piece has been very seriously underappreciated in the literature on Foucault. In it he argues that the main point of his description of the "carceral society" in *Surveiller et punir* is *not* to claim that our society *is* a closed total institution of the kind Max Weber and the members of the Frankfurt School feared it was becoming. Rather, Foucault claims, imaginative models of such total closure were a central way in which we came to think about and plan for our society, *but* there is always a variety of incompatible models of this kind in a society at any time, and the implementation of any such model *always* fails radically. I would be inclined to say that for Foucault all such projects fail "for noncontingent reasons," although I could imagine that Foucault himself would have had reservations about any attribution of "non-contingency." It is for this reason that prison reform is virtually a constant; ever since there have been prisons there has been prison reform, because no prison reform ever works. This image of society as a plurality of incompatible, competing projects all of which *think* of themselves as absolute, definitive, and total, but no one of which is ever fully successful, is completely different from Weber's *stahlhartes Gehäuse* or Adorno's view of modern society as a closed, unitary *verwaltete Welt*.

between pleasure and the good life, or pleasure and happiness, and calling Hercules' life of strenuous and heroic virtue perhaps not exactly "pleasurable" or "pleasant" but in some sense "happy" (and thus also "good"). Some ancient thinkers then devote themselves to trying to develop techniques for making us pleased (i.e., "happy") to do what we have to do, what the social and cooperative virtues require of us, but those of us who inhabit the beginning of the twenty-first century may remain skeptical about claims that virtue and happiness can be made to converge effortlessly.

Different people clearly set themselves different goals in life and are committed to different values. Some people want to earn a lot of money; others are interested in others' good opinion. Many people seem to want to live a life which they would describe as "pleasing to God," and still others want as full and immediate a satisfaction of their physical needs as possible (as in Hercules' heroic gluttony). There are very different conceptions of what it is for a human life to be successful and good. If "virtue" is a question of those dispositions that make for effective excellence, it is hard, then, to resist the thought that there will be not only distinct, but incompatible virtues. No one will be likely to think that exactly the same set of human character traits will enable us maximally to earn wealth and lead a life that is pleasing to God.

It has often been pointed out that the very idea that there could be a multiplicity of different, equally good ways of living, and a corresponding multiplicity of virtues that don't form a single clear hierarchy, might have been thought to be mildly seditious in most of the ancient city-states. After all, the claim to political preeminence of the citizen-elite could be thought to depend on the view that there was a single unitary way of life that was ideally the correct object of human aspiration. Only *one* kind of human life, the life of an adult male citizen in a self-governing city, was really fully worth living. The virtues of such a citizen were *the* human virtues κατ' ἐξοχήν, and that the citizen exhibited these virtues was grounds for him to claim a position of leadership. Historical changes in the political, social, and economic world made many of the assumptions that underlay this way of thinking highly implausible, but the image of a single unitary human "good" was able to maintain itself for quite a long time, and didn't really begin to dissolve itself in a serious way until the nineteenth century. Although we may associate the idea of the irreducible plurality and incompatibility of human goods with Isaiah Berlin[15] and thus think of it as a typically liberal notion, one finds analogous conceptions in Marx, who, in the *Grundrisse*,[16] criticizes what he calls the "old conception" of the relation between the good life and productive activity which is characteristic of the ancient world. When compared with "modern" theories which put exclusive emphasis on industrial and economic development,

[15] Isaiah Berlin, *Four Essays on Liberty* (Oxford: Oxford University Press, 1969).
[16] Karl Marx, *Grundrisse*, 387–88.

this "old conception" can seem sublime and humane because it subordinates all activity to the human good. However, the good envisaged in the ancient world was deficient because it was construed as consisting in the production of some *one* pre-given human type in some particular narrow (*borniert*) "national, religious, political form"—the adult, male (Athenian) citizen. In contrast to this, the "modern conception" which subordinates the development of the full range and variety of different human activities to *no* pre-given standard (apart from development itself) is preferable. In a society in which there existed such a plurality of forms of activity not subordinated to a single overarching "good," a wide variety of virtues would flourish, not all of which would be obviously compatible with all others: the virtues of a good pugilist would not necessarily be compatible with the virtues of a good pianist.

In the ancient world, then, there are at least two distinct concrete answers that were given to the question "Who leads the good life?" There is (a) the good life in the sense of bourgeois virtue. I'm leading a good life if I follow the existing social rules, accommodate myself to the requirements of living with others, and keep the demands I make within the limits of what the other members of my society will tolerate. Then there is (b) the good life in the heroic sense, the life devoted to large-scale achievement. Not all heroes, however, as witness Hercules, will be likely to conform to all social expectations, and, what is more (in this context at any rate), not all of them need be especially "happy," if "happiness" is construed as having anything to do with subjective contentment. However, one of the most central traditions of ancient philosophy takes the good life to be essentially a *happy* life, so it would seem to be necessary to distinguish a third sense of the "good life": (c) the good life as the happy life.

If we shift our attention now from the ancient to the modern world, we will observe that although the ancients emphasized that various objective conditions would have to be satisfied in order to call a person truly happy (εὐδαίμων), philosophers in the modern period exhibit a very strong tendency to understand happiness as at least closely connected with specifically subjective forms of satisfaction, that is, a happy life is not necessarily one of maximal *pleasure*, but one in which my actual *desires*, whatever they might be, are as fully satisfied as possible. The use of the phrase "*as fully satisfied as possible*" leaves room for rather considerable disagreement about how to specify the space of "real possibilities" within which a happy life is located. Furthermore, one might also ask whether it is really appropriate to give special standing to my "actual desires," especially once one begins to become aware of the extent to which the desires people actually have may be inherently indeterminate or contradictory, the extent to which they may experience some of their desires as impositions to be resisted, and the extent to which the causal history of the acquisition of these desires may be disreputable. I may come on reflection to think that some desires which are in all behavioral senses "mine," in that I avow them, act on them, etc., are merely artifacts of my upbringing, and that satisfying them will not really make me happy. This, in turn, may make me begin to distinguish between desires I happen for whatever reason to have acquired and desires that are in some deeper sense "really mine," and to make this distinction in a way that is independent of the apparent motivational force of the desire in question. This can lead, then, to a fourth approach to the good life: (d) the good life is the life of "authenticity," i.e., one in which I discover who I really am and what I really desire, and try to structure my life around the pursuit of these desires (even if I don't succeed in fully satisfying them).

Unfortunately there seem to be at least two distinct standards for distinguishing which desires are "really mine"—(1) *underlying* motivational power, i.e., what really moves me to action, and (2) reflective endorsement, i.e., what I am really willing to identify myself with in an affirmative way—and the two standards do not coincide. In many psychoanalytic views, if I have understood them correctly, the desires I may finally uncover as "mine" will have the property that they are what is really fueling both significant and relatively trivial portions of my behavior (although they may be masked by various other factors, including kinds of rationalizations). Christianity and its Kantian extension can be seen as committed to (1) an especially sharp split between the two criteria, (2) an unwarrantedly (and self-defeatingly) negative attitude toward those desires in me that have real motivational power, but are not the objects of reflective approval, and (3) an especially narrow construal of what deserves to be endorsed reflectively. Simply to claim, however, that what reveal themselves to be my basic motives, what really move me to action, are "not me," at any rate not the "real" me, but the result of fallen human nature, original sin, mere empirical inclination, etc., turns out, as ample historical experience has shown, to be a very ineffective way of trying to live a good and satisfying life. It is not clear within what limits such basic motivational features might be at all effectively modifiable, and blanket denial and rejection of them deprives me of whatever chance I might have effectively to use what room for maneuver and modification might exist. For that matter, it isn't at all clear what sense it would make to claim that I could adopt a standpoint from which to begin reflection which stood completely outside and was completely independent of my fundamental motivational structure.[17]

One of the promises of psychoanalysis in its classical form, I am suggesting, was to realize in a clinically responsible way the great dream of German Idealism, that of making peace between Virtue and Pleasure. This requires abandoning the Kantian model of moral psychology illustrated by Dürer's engraving in which the forces of Reason/Virtue deny any affinity with pleasure—as "Virtue" in the engraving literally closes her eyes to it—and seek to

---

[17] Bernard Williams has made this point in a number of places.

mutilate or destroy her. The ideal is rather some process of reciprocal toleration and acceptance,[18] which will not be without tensions and conflict, not even without, perhaps, some coercion, but which will not be a war of extermination on either side, won't turn the psyche into a concentration camp, and will within limits be rationally manageable. From the fact that it is not easy to describe this process in a way we find theoretically completely satisfactory, it doesn't follow either that such a process does not or could not exist, or that it could not exemplify a kind of "rationality," although the "rationality" it instantiates will be of a very different kind from Kant's.

"Rationality" hasn't ever been a very clear or uncontested concept anyway. Thus, one of the basic differences between Habermas's "discourse-ethics" and the views of Michel Foucault, to take as an example the positions of just two influential recent figures, is a disagreement about rationality and its relation to "power." Habermas assumes that there is an absolute unbridgeable gap between the "exercise of power" (or: "coercion"), on the one hand, and the "discourse" or domination-free communication (*herrschaftsfreie Kommunikation*) which for Habermas is definitory of "rationality," on the other. For Habermas these two are like Pleasure and Virtue in the image. Foucault thinks this a naive view. Power, for Foucault, is omnipresent even in rational discourses aimed at reaching agreement about how to live, and its presence is not objectionable per se. If power is just the ability to get things done—I have the power to move my arm (by virtue of having a normal anatomy and physiology), to speak French (by virtue of having been taught), to take a book out of the library (by virtue of having acquired the right documents), to make a successful living as a beggar on the streets (by virtue of my engaging and unthreatening appearance and demeanor, my psychological shrewdness, my skill at banter in the local dialect, etc.)[19]—how can one have a *general* objection to it? Foucault holds that Habermas's *noli me tangere* attitude represents a fundamental misunderstanding of the phenomenon of power; the ex-

---

[18] Schiller differs from what came to be the main line of later Idealism in that he thinks virtue/duty/morality can be defined à la Kant by reference to principles of reason alone. Virtue's relation to the world of pleasure shouldn't be the belligerent one Dürer depicts, but there is also no *reciprocal* accommodation: all the give is on Pleasure's side. Virtue can get its own way peacefully, if it goes about things correctly. I discuss this at greater length in "Kultur, Bildung, Geist" in *Morality, Culture, and History* (Cambridge: Cambridge University Press, 1999).

[19] My attempts, in the spirit of scientific inquiry, to see whether I could make a living as a street beggar in New York in 1989 convinced me that successful begging is actually more difficult than it looks. Two colleagues, philosophers who have a keen interest in this issue, observed from the vantage point of a cafe table some of my overwhelmingly unsuccessful attempts to solicit money—the only people who gave me anything were some students of mine who happened to pass. They attributed my lack of success to the fact that those I approached could in some way discern that I didn't "really need" the money. I wore my usual attire and so could not, I think, have been reasonably deemed to be overdressed for begging. In any case, being "visibly needy" could at best be a necessary, not a sufficient condition for success in this profession.

ercise of power isn't usually at all like the stroke of Virtue's club. When I exercise some power I have, for instance my power of speaking to you in the English language, I am not generally doing something very much like assaulting you with a club (although certain politicians may be an exception to this general claim). Rather than seeing an abyss between, as it were, Virtue's club and Pleasure's complete reliance on her own inherent attractiveness,[20] Foucault thinks there is a continuum of ways of exercising different kinds of power, from forms of persuasion, through modes of indirectly inducing beliefs in a variety of ways, to directly compelling people to behave in certain ways. This spectrum includes forms of communication, ways of influencing people, threatening them, inducing emulation by providing attractive models, education, modifying people's environment or their beliefs, habits, and preferences, and so on. Virtue and Pleasure should be encouraged to give up the exclusive use of violence, on the one hand, and the display of the naked body, on the other, and to find more sophisticated ways of dealing with each other (and Hercules). A theory of "rationality" that would be appropriate for the moral and psychological domain would have to take account of some of these historically emerging ways of overcoming the alternative of slaughter or seduction.

A fifth approach to the good life (e) starts by questioning a certain assumption that might seem to be made by some of the more naive versions of the "authenticity" view ((d) above). This assumption is one made by those theoretists who speak as if for each human being a set of "authentic" desires (and an authentic self they constitute) is at any given time already in existence, and just waiting to be uncovered. In contrast to this, proponents of this fifth approach emphasize that my self is "constructed" all the way down and has no foundation in any preexisting, even if unconscious, desires. Thus Foucault (as usual following Nietzsche) is adamant in claiming that happiness cannot consist in discovering a preexisting hidden "real" self because no such thing exists.[21] He wishes rather to recommend that we try to discover and then deploy techniques of stylization which would allow us to give our lives a certain aesthetic form. Foucault's proposals for an aestheticization of existence through the development of new arts of living are not exhortations for a renewal of "virtue," at least in the bourgeois sense of "virtue." If the hero and saint are not "virtuous" (in the bourgeois sense), then the artist certainly isn't either, nor are those who attempt to give to their lives an aesthetic form. The above list of five approaches is by no means exhaustive of the various paths one can take to "the good life." Certain components of certain ways of un-

---

[20] In Habermas's version, to be sure, it is "rational argumentation" that is inherently attractive, not pleasure.

[21] Foucault, I think, tends to exaggerate the extent to which this assumption is a necessary part of psychoanalytic approaches.

derstanding the "good life" can appropriately be interpreted as "virtues," but to try to fit all aspects of all forms of the good life to the Procrustean bed of "virtue" makes as little sense as trying to define the good life as exclusively a matter of discharging one's duties or maximizing social utility.

We have a natural inclination to want to use the word "good" to give a definitive judgment on a person or a life. We seem to be able to do this in the case of objects like knives, why not also in the case of people? One reason may be that we make much more complex demands on human lives than we do on most objects (works of art may be partial exceptions). We can evaluate a person or a human life from a variety of different, even contradictory points of view. These diverse points of view aren't obviously commensurable. Would you choose to *be* this person or to live this life (if you had free choice—assuming it even made sense to speak of a "free choice" in a case like this)? Or, since virtually no one would, I think, actually want to be another person, perhaps the more relevant question is: Would you like or be willing to share a flat with this person, or live next to her? Would you like this person to exist in the world (although out of your sight) because he is obnoxious, but produces artistic works of transcendental beauty? Do you think we should try to persuade others in society to be like this person, or to avoid living this kind of life? How hard should we be willing to try to effect that? Even in my own case I can't always be sure what point of view is the appropriate one to take in evaluating some aspects of my life. If in the case of others it is sometimes easier to make a definitive judgment, that would seem to be simply because I am generally less interested in others and their lives than I am in my own.

The questions "Who is a good person? What is a good life?" are ones it is hard to avoid asking, but to think one can answer them definitively may well be a naive illusion. Philosophy might have to accept this situation in both its aspects. In addition to their inherent tendency to relatively unsublimated sadism, forms of Kantianism, including the so-called versions of "discourse-ethics" associated with Habermas, represent an understandable but defeatist position. They encourage us to give up the search for a philosophically enlightened substantial discussion of "the good life" and to limit our philosophical ambitions to describing—or perhaps also: claiming to "ground"—the minimal conditions of smooth human cooperation. It is indeed a great merit of virtue-ethics that it doesn't throw in the towel in this way. To be sure, given the connection between many forms of "virtue" and specific social practices, a modern version of virtue-ethics should ideally be embedded in a critical theory of society, although in the best case this would be a Critical Theory of the old type, and not of the etiolated Habermasian kind. It should also (ideally) be historically and psychologically more sophisticated than ancient versions could be. It can't be based just on a rereading of Aristotle, but must also take account of Marx's *Die deutsche Ideologie*, Nietzsche's *Zur Genealogie der Moral*, and Freud's *Das Unbehagen in der Kultur*.

Moral philosophy would benefit not just from locating its account of the virtues in a wider context of history, social theory, and psychology, but also from maintaining an openness to the concrete experiences people have over the centuries had in trying to attain a good life. Foucault's reflections on ethics at the end of his life point in two slightly different directions, both of which seem to me to be valuable. On the one hand, he reasserts the Nietzschean ideal of giving one's life an aesthetic form. The good life isn't a moral life, a useful life, a life of integrity or authenticity, or of "principle," but an admirable life. "Admiration," however, is an aesthetic category, and a life can be "admirable" in a variety of different ways.[22] On the other hand, he tries to redirect our attention to attempts made by thinkers in the past to deal with concrete aspects of life with the intention of improving our practice (in more or less the sense in which this was envisaged by pragmatism).

Without cooperation no sophisticated form of human life would be possible, and most human societies have practices and institutions designed to foster the acquisition of the cooperative virtues. One might almost say that there is a "natural" tendency in any society to overestimate cooperation. In addition, despite the iconography of Dürer's engraving, the virtues, especially the cooperative virtues, aren't *just* enforced upon us against our will by external social agencies, but are clearly in some way attractive to us. As Wozzeck says, virtue is a beautiful thing—who wouldn't be virtuous, if they could?[23] However, an excessive focus on the virtues of cooperation can have very unwelcome consequences. Cooperation is always cooperation *in* a particular society, and to some extent, then, *with* a particular concrete society. It is of some importance to know to what degree any given society deserves our cooperation, with which particular people we should cooperate and in what way.

Sometimes some people can't be or become virtuous because their circumstances makes the acquisition or exercise of virtue impossible, and sometimes it is not at all a good idea to exercise various of the specific virtues one might possess. No one will doubt the good intentions, the virtuous disposition, or the heroic efforts of many of the international aid agencies who operated in Bosnia during the recent war there, but to focus *simply* on the way in which the actions of the individuals and agencies in question were instances of the exercise of virtue might easily bring one to overlook the widely noted fact that in the broader context, the actual effect of this virtuous action was to further ethnic cleansing. Supporters of virtue-ethics might be tempted to claim that cases like this can't *really* be instances of exercising virtue because the exercise of virtue must always have only good consequences, but this

---

[22] I discuss this issue further in my "Nietzsche and Morality," originally published in *European Journal of Philosophy* (April 1997), now reprinted in my *Morality, Culture, and History* (Cambridge: Cambridge University Press, 1999).

[23] Alban Berg, *Wozzeck* 1.2.

seems extremely implausible. Of course, no one can be prevented from refusing to call something which has all the usual psychological (and other) characteristics and trappings of virtuous action "really" virtue, on the grounds that it has consequences that are not good and we wish to reserve the word "virtue" for dispositions and character traits that have exclusively good consequences; but to argue in this way is to adopt a kind of verbal immunization strategy rather than to tell us anything of substance about "virtue." If "virtue" is used in this sense, there may turn out to be no "virtues." The fact—if it is a fact—that caring for the aged, the helpless, and the infirm by taking them out of the line of fire actually contributes, *in these particular circumstances*, to the success of a reprehensible political policy—assuming for the sake of argument that "ethnic cleansing" even of a peaceful kind is a reprehensible political policy—in no way implies that those providing the care were not exercising virtue. After all, the members of the international agencies in question may not have had any real choice in Bosnia other than, on the one hand, acting (in many cases heroically) as they did, or, on the other, withdrawing or effectively doing nothing, an option that would also have been unlikely to stop ethnic cleansing and would certainly have resulted concretely in much more human suffering than actually took place. This indicates, I think, the need to see "virtue" in a wider historical and political context. From the fact that there is no obvious way simply to combine one's moral admiration for the action of many of these agencies with one's disapproval of the actual results to which they contributed (albeit perhaps unwillingly), so as to reach an unproblematic unitary general evaluation of what happened, is, I think, no argument against this position, but merely indicates the difficulty in evaluating real situations rather than the simplified "example" favored in some of the ethics literature.

One of the most important tasks of moral philosophy as the theory of the good life is keeping open a space for social criticism, so that necessary bourgeois cooperation does not transform itself into complicity with evil. This requires appeal to as much history, psychology, and social theory as we can muster. It isn't at all clear that a freestanding virtue-ethics can by itself discharge this task.

6

Happiness and Politics

AT THE HEIGHT OF THE TERROR during the French Revolution Saint-Just announced that "Happiness is a new idea in Europe."[1] Extracted from its context and interpreted very literally, this does not seem prima facie a terribly plausible opinion to hold. Surely many people before the eighteenth century had rather a clear idea of what they thought happiness was; many ancient philosophers, at any rate, such as Epicurus, Zeno of Kitium, and Aristotle, had views, sometimes elaborate and highly articulated views, about the nature of happiness, and about what human individuals might do to increase their chances of attaining it. What is more, Saint-Just will have known this.

Does Saint-Just, then, perhaps mean that the idea of "collective" or "public" happiness is a new thought? Does he think that ancient philosophers had views about the potential happiness of *individuals*, but none about what it would mean for a human community to be happy? "Happiness," after all, like that other great modern ideal, "liberty," is a term which in principle purports to refer either to individuals or to groups. I can speak of an individual human being, Alcibiades, Cavalcanti, or John Knox, as being happy (or free), but the Declaration of the Rights of Man and the Citizen (article one in the version of 1793) also speaks of the *"bonheur commun"* of a community as the goal of political association, and uses the level to which this "goal" has been attained as a criterion for evaluating a given polity.[2] If I follow this usage, presumably, I can say that the Roman Republic was "happy" whereas the *ancien régime* in the early eighteenth century was not, or that France in 1794 was happier than in 1744.

Margaret Thatcher once notoriously claimed that society does not exist, and this strong modern bias toward individualist conceptions might give further impetus to a historical argument to the effect that "happiness" (and also,

This paper is a slightly expanded version of a talk I gave at a conference on "Democracy and Human Happiness" in April 2002 in Kyoto. I wish to thank the sponsors of this conference, the Institute for the Integrated Study of Future Generations, and its president, Prof. Tae-Chang Kim, for the kind invitation to Kyoto. I am particularly indebted to John Dunn, Zeev Emmerich, Hilary Gaskin, Lawrence Hamilton, Istvan Hont, and Michael Sonenscher for discussions of the topic of this paper.

[1] *"Le bonheur est une idée neuve en Europe,"* in *Oeuvres Complètes de Saint-Just*, ed. Michel Duval (Paris: Gévard Lebovici, 1984), 715.

[2] Article One, *"Le but de toute société est le bonheur commun."* The documents show a parallel use of *"bonheur de tous"* and *"bonheur publique."*

by the way, "liberty") was originally used only of individuals, not of groups, and ought strictly still to be taken to refer in the literal sense only to individuals. Application to groups is a seemingly unwarranted metaphorical extension. To say that a city is happy is just shorthand for saying something that can be put more correctly as a simple aggregative statement about individuals, such as that most of the individuals in the city are "happy" (in whatever sense human individuals can be happy). This is a familiar phenomenon in political philosophy, and it is important to note that the process of "extension" can go in either direction. That is, terms that originally refer to individuals can be extended to groups, but terms originally used of groups can also come to refer to individuals. Thus "deliberation" seems originally to have referred to the processes by which groups of people discuss matters and come to a decision, and then it was extended to the presumed internal dialogue in which individuals may engage when they weigh up the merits and disadvantages of some proposed course of action.[3] Many people find this kind of extension inherently dubious and grounds for suspicion that some kind of category mistake is being made. I am suggesting that one try to see "metaphorical extension" not as a potentially dubious afterthought, but as the very lifeblood of all thought and language use.[4] As long as one is clear in each case about what one means, one can see this dual usage of "happiness" as potentially an enrichment of the vocabulary we have at our disposal to think about politics and the good life.

Unfortunately, if Saint-Just meant that the ancients had no conception of "public happiness," he was completely wrong. Ancient authors assume that one can speak equally of individuals or cities as being "happy."[5] Aristotle even goes further than this and specifically says (*Politics* 1324a5) that when one calls a group or an individual "happy" one is using the term *in the same sense*.[6] The argument he uses, however, which depends on the claim that "happy" in this respect is like "wealthy," does not convince completely, but rather should be seen as warning us of certain dangers.[7] Even if we assume that we know

[3] S. Hampshire, *Justice Is Conflict* (Princeton, NJ: Princeton University Press, 1999).

[4] Particularly if one takes a view of language like that which has been developed by Nietzsche and Wittgenstein and which deemphasizes the distinction between literal and metaphorical usage. This is clearest perhaps in Nietzsche's *"Über Wahrheit und Lüge in einem außermoralischen Sinne."*

[5] An example taken virtually at random: Pindar, *Isthmia* 7, line 1 (although the word there is μάκαρ, not εὐδαίμων).

[6] Aristotle does not, of course, have at his disposal the modern terminology of "meaning," so what he says is that the happiness of the city is the same as that of the individual.

[7] The conjunction of happiness and wealth is presumably not coincidental. The word which later gets established as the canonical one for "happy" (εὐδαίμων) does not occur in Homer, but when it does first appear it is paired with another word which seems to retain a strong connotation of "wealthy, prosperous" (ὄλβιος, in Hesiod, *Opera et dies*, 826).

what "wealthy" means in the case of an individual—originally, having many useful possessions, then having much money, and, perhaps nowadays, having large and secure entitlements and lines of credit—in applying the term to a group of people, a city, or a state, issues of distribution arise for which there are no analogues in the case of the individual. If the city is an organized po-litical association we can assume that the resources available will be divided among various individuals who make up the city, but that there will also be a sector of things held "in common" or "publicly." Various individuals in Cam-bridge (including me) may also own houses, but the City of Cambridge as a public corporation itself owns school buildings, police vehicles, tracts of land, etc. By virtue of what, now, would Cambridge count as a "wealthy" city? By virtue of what we could call the "private" wealth of the individuals who live there? Does this mean the total wealth or the average wealth? Or does Cam-bridge count as wealthy by virtue of the value of the resources owned by the corporation which is the City of Cambridge? Or perhaps by taking the sum of all the wealth in private or public hands in the city?

This is a serious issue not simply with reference to wealth, but also with reference to the concept of "happiness." Aristotle's breezy analysis seems to be trying to divert attention from this issue, but Plato faces up to it squarely at the beginning of book 4 of the *Republic* (419a–421c6), when one of Socrates' interlocutors, Adeimantus, objects to Socrates' whole mode of pro-ceeding in describing his ideal city. The ideal city is supposed to be an ide-ally *happy* (εὐδαίμων) city, that is, a city which instantiates and realizes what it is to be a city to the fullest, which is a fully flourishing specimen of what a city should be. Plato claims this is a city in which all the essential functions of communal human life are performed as well and efficiently as possible by distinct subgroups. Individuals are assigned to a given subgroup according to a highly developed principle of division of labor, so that each person does only that for which he or she has the greatest natural aptitude. Adeimantus, however, points out that in the city thus described, *none* of the people will be fully happy. This does not depend on surreptitiously shifting from Plato's technical sense of "happiness" (being a perfect specimen who is successfully, efficiently discharging one's task) to the common everyday sense of happi-ness (enjoyment or satisfaction), although we can well imagine that individ-uals in a Platonic city would not be terribly satisfied with their lot. Rather, although the Platonic city might instantiate fully what it is to be a city, none of the individuals would instantiate and realize humanity at its fullest, be fully flourishing instances of humanity; rather they would be locked into the exercise of particular social functions. Perfectly discharging one's task as a human being won't be the same thing as efficiently discharging one's specific role as a cobbler-in-the-ideal-city. The happiness of the city would then be quite distinct and would diverge in a significant way from the happiness of its members taken either individually or collectively.[8] For the purposes of the present discussion, the important point is that Plato seems to admit that happiness could, in principle, be a systemic property of the society as a whole that is not reducible to any straightforward summation of the states of happiness of the individual members. As Aristotle puts the point (*Politics* 1264b 19–20)—one he himself *rejects*—"happiness" is construed as being like "even" (as in "odd and even"). A given number, e.g., 14, can be "even" without it being the case that its constituents, e.g., 7 + 7, are themselves even. Perhaps it is not yet completely clear in what this "happiness" of the city as a whole as distinct from that of the individuals consists, but what is clear is that these ancient philosophers at any rate had a very robust sense of "public happiness" indeed.

No matter how one turns it, then, Saint-Just seems simply to be wrong. Perhaps we can make sense of what he says by considering the political context within which his claim was made. Saint-Just was speaking in favor of the enactments that have come to be known as the Ventôse Decrees. These decrees called for the expropriation of enemies of the revolution and the use of the resources thus made available to support "poor patriots." Measures like this, though, far from being a novelty of eighteenth-century France, have a very long history in the West. Demands for agrarian reforms that would have involved very extensive redistribution of lands to the poor were a recurrent feature of the political and social life of the Roman Republic at least from the time of the Gracchi (second century B.C.), and by the end of the Republic rival warlords were routinely using the expropriated land of opponents to reward supporters. Saint-Just's point, then, presumably would have been that the *reasons* he and the Committee of Public Safety gave for these measures depended essentially on some reference to human happiness, but that in the past arguments for measures like these depended not on appeals to happiness but on appeals to some other grounds. So to say that the idea of happiness was a new one would mean not that no one in Europe had ever had the idea of (individual or communal) happiness before, but that for the first time a systematic attempt was being made to adopt happiness as an explicit social goal in a politically effective way. Perhaps we can become clearer about what Saint-Just might have meant by "happiness" by contrasting it with other things which he might have thought people in the past would have used to support fundamental institutions or drastic forms of action. What sorts of other grounds, then, does he think his, and our, ancestors might have given for this kind of decree?

---

[8] Plato's response to this apparent objection is to emphasize the natural differences between individuals and to claim that although they are not happy *simpliciter*, they are as happy as they can reasonably be expected to be (given their natural endowments). This is then further developed in the myth of the metals (415)—one of the most repellent doctrines in the Platonic corpus.

One perfectly reasonable thing he might have meant was a contrast between the world of late eighteenth-century Europe and two other historical periods which preceded it and were widely considered to be completely distinct from it and each from the other: the Christian feudal era and the world of the ancient Mediterranean city-states and empires. The ancient world was one of perpetual war, and it is thus comprehensible that the most valued kinds of human properties were the active heroic ones of aggressive success, excellence, virtue, and glory. Such properties are characteristically displayed in zero-sum competitive contexts in which the success of one individual is the failure, or even death, of the other: Patroclus or Hector, Hector or Achilles, Pallas or Turnus, Turnus or Aeneas. The hero seeks always to be first and to attain glory. This heroic ethos is originally a moral code of individuals, but it can be extended to political communities, too: Athens or Sparta, Rome or Carthage. After all, such communities are as fully engaged in a network of competitive relations with other communities as individuals are with other individuals. When the city itself comes to be construed as a possible subject that can exhibit excellence, can succeed or fail, or gain glory, then these can become the goals of conscious political action. Thus agrarian reform in the ancient world could be thought to be connected with and justified by reference to the political power, strength, and security of the city.[9] For the city to be secure, powerful, and renowned, it needed soldiers. Under ancient conditions the best soldiers were expected to arise from the class of independent peasant farmers. Thus the city could have an interest in the redistribution of agricultural land which would turn the landless, and thus militarily useless, rural poor into prosperous farmers who were potential soldiers. This might have had nothing to do with the happiness of the individuals who were the beneficiaries of that redistribution.

Happiness, in any case, was not at all a necessary part of the heroic package. Achilles can choose a short, glorious life or a long, presumably comfortable life at home in fertile Phthia; Ajax is humiliated by the gods and commits suicide; Aeneas' life is a model of *pietas, virtus,* and *labor,* but hardly of happiness.[10] In ancient drama, "happiness" is the lot not of the heroic protagonist of tragedy, but of the anti-hero who is the central character in comedy—the Dicaeopolis in Aristophanes' *Acharnians* who wants peace, feasting, and sex, not war and glory. Thus it is not unreasonable to think that regardless of what a handful of politically marginal moral philosophers might have thought or said, real public action in the ancient world was characteristically conducted by reference to one or another of the complex of terms like basic security, virtue, success, glory. The claim that one would orient political action

---

[9] Public defense on these grounds is, of course, compatible with a determination to see to it that one's *own* partisans are the particular beneficiaries of the proposed policy.

[10] *Aeneid* 1.8–11, 12.435–36, etc.

toward "happiness" might then well be conceived to represent a historical departure.[11]

The Christian Middle Ages in Europe was no stranger to the politics of individual and dynastic competition, heroism, and the pursuit of glory. These seem de facto to have continued to inform the living and thinking at least of the politically dominant classes, but the advent of Christianity meant the recognition of another ideal: the quest for the salvation of the individual soul, or "beatitude." One might think of this as a recognition of two distinct concepts of happiness, a terrestrial kind ordered around the peaceful enjoyment of the goods of life, and a celestial kind, the possibility of which was disclosed to humanity by Divine Revelation, and the full realization of which could be attained only after death. There was wide disagreement on the relation between these two kinds of happiness, but even those most disposed to see beatitude and earthly happiness as compatible tended strictly to subordinate the latter to the former.

So one can, after all, make reasonable sense of Saint-Just's announcement. What is new in the eighteenth century is that "happiness" gets added to the possible list of freestanding grounds for public action.[12]

We can speak then of individual happiness or of the happiness of a group, and one can think of the happiness of a group in either of two ways. First, it can be thought of as some more or less simple aggregate of the happiness of the constituent individuals, just as one can speak of a city as "wealthy" if many individual citizens are wealthy or as "glorious" if many citizens are glorious. Second, one can think of the happiness of the group as something that is not thus reducible. That is, we can construe speaking of the "happiness" of a group in analogy to the cases in which we speak of a city as "wealthy," meaning by that to designate a high level of public wealth even if all the individuals are poor; or of a city as "glorious" if its armies or football teams defeat, by virtue of their extreme discipline and coordination, all comers even though no individual member is particularly glorious (or, if any glory an individual has derives from the glory of the army or team as a whole rather than the other way around).

This still, to be sure, leaves open the question of just what "happiness" means either in the individual or in the group case. I wish to distinguish three families of conceptions of happiness: first, externalist or objectivist views, second, desire-relative views, and finally, overall-assessment views.

To the modern temperament, the most convincing forms of externalist or

---

[11] Saint-Just does not claim that happiness is the *only* goal of the revolution. Other goals would include liberty, equality, and fraternity; also virtue, frugality, and glory (as mentioned, for instance, in the discourse on the reorganization of the army, *Oeuvres Complètes de Saint-Just*, ed. Michel Duval [Paris: Gérard Lebovici, 1984], 412).

[12] See A. Hirschman, *Rival Views of Market Society* (Cambridge, MA: Harvard University Press, 1992), 105–7.

objectivist conceptions of happiness are naturalist ones which start with some notion of basic forms of minimally healthy or especially vibrant or vigorous functioning of a human being, and then go on to define happiness as the exercise of these functions in a minimally viable or an especially vibrant and vigorous way. What counts as the healthy, robust functioning of an individual is in principle independent of the shifting beliefs, desires, feelings, and opinions of that individual. A human who was functioning in a vigorous way would be likely to know that and to feel pleased, but this might not invariably be the case, and even when it was, the feeling and knowledge would be secondary to the functioning.[13] Being happy would consist not in being pleased but in being well fed, fully mobile, able to work and reproduce, etc. The views of Plato and Aristotle are most naturally construed as having this structure. To move now from the individual to the collective case, we have seen how Plato's theory seems to posit a functioning of the whole which would in principle be distinct from functioning of the individuals. Despite our disinclination to take seriously the teleological metaphysics which underpins the Platonic and the Aristotelian view, there is something to be said for thinking of a society as a continuing enterprise that lasts potentially beyond the lifetime of any given individual and for countenancing it as a distinct level of functioning having its own integrity. Without *some* conception like this, albeit a nonmetaphysical one, it is very hard to see how we could even begin to think about, for instance, our relations to future generations.

Such an objective conception of happiness seems to play a role in some versions of the theory of the welfare state. Individual happiness may be connected with idiosyncratic forms of private enjoyment and may thus be both unpredictable and an inappropriate object of governmental action, but *public* happiness means providing some objectively specifiable set of accessible resources and services to all members of the society so as to ensure that each has at least a minimally defined standard of living: health care, food, shelter.[14] There is no need to be philistine about what this comprises; it can include an established church with extensive pastoral services, a national radio service that broadcasts performances of concerts, public picture galleries, and the satisfaction of various human psychic and emotional needs, as long as these can be shown to be objectively necessary for human flourishing. As noted above, on an objectivist view it need not invariably be the case that successful functioning was attended by enjoyment—some perverse people might not enjoy being healthy, but even so, health could retain its standing as a con-

---

[13] For further discussion of this with special reference to Aristotle, see Richard Kraut, "Two Conceptions of Happiness," *Philosophical Review* 88 (1979), 167–97.

[14] That the provision be presented as one that will be a universal distribution of equal benefits to all—or that North American *fata morgana* "equal opportunity for all"—is not a matter of any logical necessity, but merely a fact about what seems politically viable under modern circumstances where notions of equality have become ideologically deeply embedded.

stituent of public happiness—but this is compatible with there being an important range of aspects of human life in which knowing that the function was being successfully performed and enjoying that activation of the function was an integral part. It would then be an objective truth about our nature that *in some areas* we needed forms of activity that permitted this kind of self-awareness and self-affirmation. This can still be an "objective" conception if one thinks that it is true that one must have some kind of self-affirmation (in order to function in a healthy way) independent of whether one knows that this is the case or not.[15]

The second family of conceptions of happiness start from the idea that we humans are creatures of desire. These desires are real internal states of some kind that have a power to move us to do things in the world, although not necessarily an irresistible power—I might be very self-controlled or in the grip of another stronger desire. Desires are also highly variable and shifting, may stand in no relation to my basic forms of human functioning, and are not necessarily constrained by being directed at any natural object.[16] When I am hungry and eat, I can be said to be happy in a perhaps rather debased and rudimentary sense. I am happy, however, not because this is a natural function which I am performing but because at that moment eating was what I desired to do. Happiness should be understood as satisfaction of these desires, even if they happen, as they might, to have no relation to the basic needs or the functional imperatives of the human body and soul. I may desire things that in the short or long run are not good for me. To say that I am happy must essentially have something to do with my getting these desires that I have satisfied, whether or not that is even compatible with my physical well-being.

Desire itself is uncomfortable to experience—it might be various other things too, such as oddly, indirectly, or perversely satisfying, but this is in addition to being uncomfortable. As various philosophers, moralists, and religious figures have emphasized,[17] when a desire is satisfied, another one will arise and follow on the heels of the first immediately. It is the nature of human life that it is composed of desires that come and go, and the very idea of an absolute showstopping satisfaction of desire doesn't make sense. The idea of having all desires maximally satisfied is the idea of not having any unfulfilled desire, and that is very like the idea of being dead.[18]

As if this were not enough, many have argued that there is a distinction

---

[15] This was the view of the early Marx.

[16] Hobbes gives perhaps the most striking early modern theory of a form of desire that is in no way subordinated to an antecedent good, whether real or apparent; see *Leviathan*, chapters 6, 11.

[17] In particular Buddhists, and, among Western philosophers, Schopenhauer.

[18] Jonathan Lear, *Happiness, Death, and the Remainder of Life* (Cambridge, MA: Harvard University Press, 2000).

between a truly and fully happy life and a merely contented one. A happy life is not sufficiently characterized as one in which given desires are maximally satisfied, but must have a certain minimal richness, variety, complexity, novelty, and intensity. Thus some would say that a person with an exceptionally low level of desire and aspiration is less happy than a person with more complex and demanding desires, even if more of the first person's desires were in fact satisfied. Some have even claimed that a fully happy human life must be devoted in part to *developing* human powers. If this is the case, then the generation of new desires will be an integral part of the happy life,[19] and that means that a certain amount of nonsatisfaction will have to be part of a fully happy life, since "new" desires will by their very nature be ones I have not yet been able to satisfy. If this is the case, the pursuit of happiness might seem to require us to move in two incompatible directions at once: toward maximal satisfaction of the desires we have, and toward going beyond the set of desires we have evolved in the direction of as yet unsatisfiable new desires.

There is a degenerate form of the idea that happiness consists in satisfaction of desires which has played an important role in much recent social theory.[20] This approach identifies satisfaction of desires with satisfaction of one's *preferences*, where "preferences" are taken to mean *articulated* wants, i.e., what you *say* you want or what your behavior in highly controlled conditions (such as betting) indicates you want. There might be all sorts of good reasons to prefer preferences to desires as the basic entities with which to work in certain areas of life and politics—for a start, desires are frequently deeply buried, ill-formed, unfocused, and for various reasons not fully and clearly articulated or even articulable; preferences, on the other hand, are epistemically accessible and well defined in a way desires are not. One can thus work with them more easily, use them to evaluate the success or failure of various government programs, etc. However, it is also precisely this relative clarity and precision that makes them inappropriate as the final objects relative to which we think about such things as human *happiness*.

One major reason one might object to the whole ideal of public happiness is a difficulty in the very idea that there is anything at the collective level that *could* be sufficiently like a human individual as locus of desire for one to speak in a clear and coherent way about those collective desires being satisfied. The best one could get would seem to be some version of a collective analogue to

---

[19] See Wilhelm von Humboldt, *Ideen zu einem Versuch, die Grenzen der Wirksamkeit des Staates zu bestimmen* (originally 1792–95, now most conveniently in modern edition, Stuttgart: Reclam, 1967).

[20] Classic works in this tradition include: K. Arrow, *Social Choice and Individual Values* (New York: Wiley, 1951); and A. Sen, *Collective Choice and Social Welfare* (San Francisco: Holden-Day, 1970).

what I have called the "degenerate" form of happiness, a social welfare function.[21]

The third kind of conception of happiness takes it to consist not in the satisfaction of my desires, but in some form of self-approval. I am happy if I find my life worthy of approval as a life for me to live.[22] What is at issue here is an attitude or a judgment. This sense of "happiness" is clearly distinct from the previous two. It is obviously the case that I need not approve of healthy human functioning—lots of religious ascetics do not—nor must I approve of what I in fact desire, even ineluctably desire—many addicted smokers disapprove of smoking. One might expect that the judgment and attitude one has toward one's own life will not, as a matter of fact, be completely disjoint from the rhythm of origination and satisfaction of desire—I will be more likely to make a positive judgment about my life and say that I am happy if I have just satisfied a pressing desire than if I keenly feel an unfulfilled desire. This suggests that our attitude or judgment about our lives might be as shifting and unstable as our desires (and their satisfaction) are. The characteristic view of ancient philosophers seems to have been that one ought to try to find a stable attitude toward one's life *as a whole* which is based on a correct assessment of it.[23] This presupposes that I have at my disposal a standpoint from which I can see my life as a whole, even if only in recollection and imagination, and moreover that I have it in my power to see my life clearly and without illusion, to see it as it really is. Many ancient philosophers, especially Stoic philosophers, seem to have believed that, particularly with a bit of training and reflection, one can learn to retain such an attitude, even when in the presence of an otherwise disablingly insistent unsatisfied desire—like the ancient philosopher who claimed to be happy even while being tortured, because he knew he had given his life an overall shape of which he was right to approve. Modern people are perhaps less sanguine about this possibility. I may well never settle into a *fixed* judgment on my life as a whole, or I may not be able to attain fixity of judgment until it is too late for it to matter. By extension, not everyone may be in a position to adopt the Olympian, or perhaps I should say Mandarin, attitude of Zhou En-lai, who, when asked whether he thought the French Revolution had been a good or a bad thing, famously replied that it was too early to tell.

If the account I have given above is approximately correct, the prospects for individual happiness do not look encouraging: We no longer accept the

[21] To pursue this further would require discussion of Nietzsche's view of the Dionysian (especially in *Geburt der Tragödie*), and subsequent accounts by Durkheim, Freud, and Castoriadis.

[22] To judge that a life is worthy of approval as a life *for me to live* is not necessarily to judge that it is worthy *simpliciter*, so it is still possible to distinguish between "happy" and "good."

[23] Aristotle, *Ethica Nicomachea* 1098a16–17, 1099b9–1101a21, 1177b24–26. The modern philosopher who seems to have been most interested in this issue is the Heidegger of *Sein und Zeit* (see especially §§ 46–60).

natural teleology that underwrote the objectivist approach; the complete satisfaction of desire is radically unstable and even, to put it paradoxically, inherently unsatisfactory as a general human goal because any satisfaction of a given desire will give rise to a new desire. Finally, we are no longer so sure we will be able to come to a single, stable evaluative assessment of our lives as a whole, much less to one that has some property of "truth."

What kind of happiness then is at issue in the politics guided by Saint-Just's "new" European idea? Could a politics directed at happiness ever hope to be successful?

In his speech in favor of the Ventôse Decrees, Saint-Just says that by passing the decrees France will show Europe that it is no longer willing to tolerate "even one unfortunate (*malheureux*) or oppressor" on French territory.[24] It is perhaps not completely fanciful to see these two terms as designating slightly different dimensions of the "happiness" Saint-Just goes on to laud. On the one hand, the succoring of individual need is most naturally located within a program of public happiness which takes this to presuppose the maintenance of the minimal welfare of all individuals in the society. From the fact that the government cannot effectively undertake the incoherent task of rendering people positively happy by maximizing the satisfaction of their desires, it by no means follows that it cannot sensibly prevent distinct *"malheur"* by maintaining minimal standards of living. The second dimension of "happiness" refers to the absence of "oppression." "Oppression" is conceptually distinct from poverty. It seems but a step from the project of the elimination of oppression to democracy, as a political system in which equal citizens rule themselves. In its worst incarnations, "poverty" might be conceived as having an almost purely naturalist component even by people who are inclined to give great weight to the variability of human beliefs and the autonomy of human desire. Whatever public happiness is, and no matter what people's opinions are, we might think that public happiness is not compatible with gross malnutrition among large segments of the population. Public happiness as absence of oppression seems to fit most easily into the third of my three families of conceptions of happiness. That means that there must be a clear social locus or position or standpoint from which some general judgment about the society as a whole can be made, which will be like the judgment the individual was supposed to be able to make about his or her life as a whole. There must be a voice that gives this judgment or assessment embodiment or a clear social agent who can adopt the relevant attitude. If happiness is absence of poverty and of oppression, then there must be no poverty and some-

---

[24] "*Que l'Europe apprenne que vous ne voulez plus un malheureux ni un oppresseur sur le territoire français . . . ,*" *Oeuvres Complètes*, p. 715. The word I have translated as "unfortunate" above, "*malheureux*," of course, means "unhappy."

one has to have formed a moderately stable judgment to the effect that no oppression exists. If, when what is at issue is *my* happiness, then I am the final judge of that, so similarly when what is at issue is "our" collective happiness, "we" should make the final assessment of that. Who, though, is "we?" To say that "we" should be "everyone" is no answer to the question because that question is precisely the question of who speaks for everyone—that is, what real agency or instance is "our" real voice?

There are three candidates for this honor. The first is the governmental structure which is the designated official speaker for "us all." In a democracy like that of contemporary Britain, that is presumably the Parliament, or the Queen-in-Parliament, or perhaps the Cabinet, that is, nowadays effectively the Prime Minister. They will speak for us when they speak in their official capacity following all the established rules correctly. It might seem that if such a system is functioning properly it will instantiate a very quick and straight-forward way of moving from democracy to human happiness via a direct con-ceptual link. Democracies will by their very nature be happy polities in the most significant of the senses of "happy" that can be of concern to politics. After all, one might argue, a democracy is by definition a system in which whatever the society does is the result of a decision by its members. If what collective political life people have depends—as much as it can depend on any human agency—on what they themselves decide, surely in a democracy they have the best chance to live a collective life of which they will approve. In such a system, if it works, there are no individual "oppressors" like Louis Capet, or the members of the French aristocracy.

I think one should resist this shortcut because there is an important dif-ference between democracy as an ideal and as the designation of any real po-litical mechanism.[25] To speak of democracy as an ideal is to speak of a polit-ical system in which "the people have the power." In the ancient world of small direct democracies, it was perhaps relatively unproblematic to see what was being meant by saying that the people ruled: whatever decisions were made, were made by an assembly which in principle anyone could attend, and which many people did regularly attend. In contrast, to speak of any real mod-ern representative system of parliamentary rule as a democracy is to engage in an extremely contestable form of theoretical interpretation of what is going on when the system functions in its everyday way.[26] Do multiparty elections by themselves (or, for that matter, in conjunction with any specifiable further set of real political institutions) *ensure* that societies in which they exist are ones in which the people rule? Does Tony Blair necessarily speak for me

---

[25] See my *History and Illusion in Politics* (Cambridge: Cambridge University Press, 2001), pp. 110–28.

[26] See J. Schumpeter, *Capitalism, Socialism and Democracy* (New York: Harper & Row, 1950), esp. part 4.

when he repeatedly gives us and the rest of the world to understand that Britain under New Labor is a happy, morally admirable society? I submit that a moment's serious reflection on these questions will incline the thoughtful toward a negative answer to them.

The second candidate for the position of *vox societatis* is "public opinion." This seems to me a totally hopeless choice. Public opinion is exceedingly fragile, and its utterances can be very indistinct: more importantly, if the official political structures do not reflect my views about whether the life we are leading is worthy of approbation, why should I have any more reason to expect public opinion always to do so?

The third possibility is the voice of the people speaking directly, if raucously, in civil disturbance, riot, lynching, pogrom, eventually civil war or revolution, or alternatively in vivid expressions of approval—torchlight parades to see the troops off to the front, spontaneous celebrations of sporting victories, etc. Here again, if not literally everyone is out on the streets, that will mean that there are two sides to this story, and thus there will not be an obviously privileged position from which to make a definitive judgment. Even when the voice is strong, direct, and virtually unanimous, the message may be indistinct, and the transmission will usually be extremely intermittent.

Democracy raises the ideological stakes and human expectations, without necessarily commensurately increasing our ability to satisfy our desires, or to adopt a positive attitude toward our life as a whole. It is a standard liberal sentiment[27] that I might find it more galling to tolerate a situation in which someone *else*, some collective political institution, is effectively defining what *attitude* I am to have toward my own life and my assessment of my own happiness, than a situation in which money, resources, or services are straightforwardly extorted from me by an individual oppressor who makes no claims to be contributing to my happiness. This may be a relict of Christian religious views about the inviolability of the soul, but it is one that continues to have a firm hold on the minds of many in the West. Under what circumstances do I experience a "democratic" decision in which I belong to a defeated minority as a decision of "someone else?" This is obviously a question of capital importance for any democracy and one the answer to which will depend on a wide variety of factors, many of which are probably extra-political and few of which are at all well understood. It underlines the need to take the widest possible view of the context within which politics takes place.

The story has been told many times how, as he was led out to be guillotined, Saint-Just pointed to the Declaration of the Rights of Man and of the Citizen inscribed on the wall of the Conciergerie, and said: "After all, I was the one

---

[27] Given its classic formulation, although with specific reference to the concept of "liberty," not "happiness," by Isaiah Berlin, "Two Concepts of Liberty," *Four Essays on Liberty* (Oxford: Oxford University Press, 1963).

who did that."[28] In the debates that preceded the promulgation of the Constitution of 1793, Saint-Just took the view that the task confronting the Convention was simple: "If you want a republic, attach yourself to the people and act only for it. The form of its happiness is simple. Happiness is no further away from peoples than from the private person."[29] Saint-Just obviously took this to be an optimistic thought. I have tried to suggest here that it can equally be taken as a rather pessimistic one.

[28] "*C'est pourtant moi qui ai fait cela.*" K. Marx, *Die Heilige Familie*, in *Marx-Engels Werke* (Berlin: Dietz, 1980) vol. 2, p. 129. See also B. Williams, "Saint-Just's Illusion," in *Making Sense of Humanity* (Cambridge: Cambridge University Press, 1995).

[29] "*Si vous voulez la république, attachez-vous au peuple, et ne faites rien que pour lui. La forme de son bonheur est simple, et le bonheur n'est pas plus loin des peuples qu'il n'est loin de l'homme privé,*" in *Oeuvres Complètes*, p. 423.

7

Suffering and Knowledge in Adorno

SUFFERING, MANY REFLECTIVE PEOPLE HAVE THOUGHT, is simply an integral part of any human life; since there is no certain remedy for it short of death—which many believe carries its own disadvantages—one might as well learn to tolerate it as best one can. Some philosophers, to be sure, have thought that this reaction is too undifferentiated: if one wishes to think seriously about suffering one must begin by distinguishing different kinds of suffering toward which perhaps very different attitudes would be appropriate. Thus Nietzsche[1] distinguishes very sharply between suffering that has a meaning—the pain experienced during training by an athlete preparing for an important event—and "senseless" suffering. Humans, Nietzsche thinks, do not in general find the former kind of suffering problematic, but the latter is intolerable; so intolerable, in fact, that they will invent or accept the most ludicrous fantasies—stories about the will of imaginary gods, theories of antenatal existence and the transmigration of souls, the doctrine of original sin, etc.—to endow suffering with the appearance of "meaning."

Nietzsche further distinguishes very sharply between self- and life-affirming interpretations and life-negating or -denying ones. The suffering the athlete in training undergoes is not simply an incomprehensible series of random events that form no pattern and of which he can make no sense at all, but is part of a structured set of events that he or she can see is integral to a project of affirmation of self. Even if the athlete does not in fact win the race, the project is an affirmative one. In contrast to this, most traditional religious interpretations of the world have been life- and self-denying. Thus for the traditional Calvinist believer, too, the world and human life makes perfect sense. At the end of a long life of exhausting labors most people can look forward to sharing with the overwhelming majority of humanity (the *"massa damnationis"*) in an infinity of exquisite torments invented and inflicted on them by God. God, to be sure, has predestined us for this, but that is no excuse for us. Since, for whatever reason, we are in fact all sinners, this infinite punishment is also our just desert, and the meaning of our infinite suffering is that it contributes to God's glory. Not only, that is, will people make up the most implausible tales and theories to give some apparent meaning to their lives, they would also prefer even radically masochistic, self-abnegating interpretations

[1] Friedrich Nietzsche, *Zur Genealogie der Moral*, in *Kritische Studienausgabe*, ed. Colli and Montinari (Berlin: de Gruyter, 1980), vol. 5.

of the world to acceptance of its sheer irreducible fatuous pointlessness; they would rather make their own lives vales of tears than find them empty.

A third distinction that might seem to recommend itself is that between "avoidable" and "unavoidable" suffering. It is not difficult to imagine developing this distinction into the temptingly commonsensical thought that we ought to try to tolerate "stoically" only such suffering as is unavoidable, while trying to deal actively with suffering that is unnecessary or avoidable.

The view of human society proposed by various progressive political movements in the nineteenth and early twentieth centuries, including Marxism, gave a further twist to this discussion by distinguishing between historically superfluous and historically necessary forms of human suffering. In societies with low productive powers and rudimentary means of transport, hunger may be an unavoidable and virtually universal concomitant of human life; in modern societies we have the technological capacities to feed everyone, and so hunger is "objectively superfluous" in a way it was not in the Bronze Age.[2] Hunger in the modern world results from social and legal arrangements— the distribution of entitlements—that could in principle be changed.[3] The members of the Frankfurt School were not in any sense orthodox Marxists, but their Critical Theory stands in this tradition in that the main object of their theoretical interest was the continued existence of superfluous suffering in a world in which it could actually be abolished.[4]

Although "suffering" refers in the first instance to a set of somatic processes—the stimulation of certain nerve endings associated with what we call "pain"—in complex societies physical suffering can come to be "reflected inwardly" so that in addition to toothache we sometimes experience "heartache."[5] Prolonged grief, psychic disturbance, systematic humiliation, etc. are also forms of suffering even if they do not involved the direct infliction of physical pain, and, as such, they deserve to be taken seriously, too. Modern societies, so the proponents of Critical Theory believe, are integrated totalities in which all parts are inextricably interconnected and the more important structural features are hidden from direct view.[6]

A human society is not like a dead natural object, which has no end or goal in itself. A rock, a lake, a pile of sand have no inherent purpose, but a human society is a set of practices, structures, and institutions that are directed at making it more likely that certain states of the world are realized and that others are not. Agricultural societies have various methods for storing grain

---

[2] See Gareth Stedman Jones, *An End to Poverty* (London: Profile Books, 2004).

[3] See A. Sen, *Poverty and Famines* (Oxford: Oxford University Press, 1981).

[4] Adorno, *Negative Dialektik* (Frankfurt: Suhrkamp, 1966; hereinafter *ND*), p. 201; Adorno, *Ästhetische Theone* as vol. 7 of *Gesammelte Schriften* (Frankfurt: Suhrkamp, 1971; hereinafter *AT*), p. 55 f.

[5] *ND* 200–202.

[6] Adorno, *Minima Moralia* (Frankfurt: Suhrkamp, 1951; hereinafter *MM*), p. 29; *ND* 204.

which they implement in order to have enough food for the winter and prevent hunger. A society can be seen as a system directed at attaining, and in fact having the shape it does in order to attain, a certain kind of life which is thought by the members of the society to be "good." The use of teleological language is therefore licit in discussing social institutions, whereas it would not be so in discussing natural phenomena. If this is accepted, then, it might be argued, there is no reason in principle not also to accept the possibility that one of the things the society as a whole might be teleologically oriented toward doing is producing, not merely such things as an agricultural surplus or various industrial goods, but also certain beliefs in its members. Some of these beliefs might be true—it would be of clear utility to humans if their society had institutions devote to training medical personnel and inculcating in them correct beliefs about human anatomy; other beliefs, however, might not be true. In fact, the members of the Frankfurt School hold that modern societies can and must be seen as systems that are structured so as to produce misapprehension of their own essential mode of operation. It is not as if the central and essential features of the society, the basic mechanism that makes it work, as it were, accidentally fails to come to our notice, but the operation of the society is such that it systematically blocks off correct cognitive access to its own deeper structure, and generates illusions and distortions, presenting a façade that is actively misleading.[7]

All of this means that simple, old-fashioned approaches to the elimination of suffering will not work. Direct, individual intervention to relieve patent pain may be morally praiseworthy but cannot be more than a palliative measure, and will certainly not be sufficient to deal with the deep-rooted and systemic social and economic sources of suffering. One cannot directly observe the "real causes" of most suffering in such a complex society, and even the best empirical theories built up according to the canons of positivism will be superficial and misleading, taking the illusory surface a society produces for its essential structure. Correct cognitive access to society as a "totality" requires a philosophically informed mode of understanding which is not a competitor to observation and empirical theorizing, but which places empirical social research in its proper context. That context is provided by the nonempirical concept of "spirit," a concept analyzed most astutely in Hegelian philosophy. To be sure, Marx was right to emphasize the importance of the socioeconomic system—the capitalist form of production—in the generation of systematic forms of human suffering, but even "the economy" in the narrow sense could not be fully understood by a theory that was construed along strictly empirical, "positivist" lines. The most important structural features of

---

[7] One can, of course, perfectly reasonably ask *why* modern society should be structured in such a way as to generate such illusions, and one can try to give various answers to this, none of which I will go into.

our society, including its central economic institutions, are integrated into the social whole and reveal themselves for what they really are only when we view that whole as a form of "spirit," and that means analyzing it relative to what spirit requires of it. Only a theorist who is himself a philosophically reflective bearer of spirit has the necessary conceptual resources to make cognitive sense of the suffering our society produces. Only a theorist who has a correct spirit-based understanding of society can engage in radical social criticism effectively, and only such a person is capable of sustained intellectual resistance to the pressures to conformism and acquiescence in the status quo which is such a pervasive danger in modern societies. To be sure, active participation in "spirit" makes a person in some ways more susceptible to suffering, because more sensitive to the ways in which society fails, but this is the price one pays for the critical potential spirit gives. In spirit cognition, the possibility of criticism and resistance, and sensitivity to suffering are closely connected.

Thus it is not at all surprising, and is no objection, that the immediate point of departure for Adorno's Critical Theory is a series of experiences that could seem to be no more than minor irritations of the sensibility of a highly sophisticated but also extremely effete bearer of "Spirit." He presents his critical opposition to the society that surrounds him as having been set off by the observation that the semicolon is falling into desuetude,[8] that Alban Berg's *Violin Concerto* contains some tonal elements rather than being uncompromisingly atonal,[9] that modern doors generally have simple knobs rather than handles,[10] that large numbers of people rush to the cinema to see infantile films,[11] etc. This is not necessarily an evasion of more serious forms of suffering. The first task is a correct analysis of the causes of social suffering, and if society really is a totality that actively produces mystification about its own basic structure—a "false whole"—then *any* part, even the most seemingly insignificant, can, if properly analyzed, reveal the falsehood at the heart of the social world; an indirect approach through seemingly peripheral or insignificant phenomena may have more chance of success than an attempt to gain enlightenment by studying the traditional "grand topics" of social philosophy directly. The "grand topics" refer generally to precisely the parts of society that will be most deeply camouflaged and surrounded by thick smokescreens and false road signs.

Hegel devotes an important chapter in his *Phenomenology* to a form of spiritual life which he calls "the unhappy consciousness." This form of con-

---

[8] Adorno, *Noten zur Literatur I* (Frankfurt: Suhrkamp, 1958), p. 168.

[9] Adorno, *Gesammelte Schriften* (Frankfurt: Suhrkamp, 1984), vol. 18, pp. 499–501; see also *Der getreue Korrepetitor* (Frankfurt: Suhrkamp, 1963), p. 187, and *Gesammelte Schriften* (Frankfurt: Suhrkamp, 1984), vol. 13, pp. 349–50.

[10] *MM* § 19.

[11] *MM* §§ 5, 130, 231.

sciousness is one that it forced by its own internal constitution to generate
and measure itself against a set of standards which it can never fully satisfy.
What results is an intrinsically "split" consciousness which is in perpetual, uncomfortable motion, in a constant process of being painfully forced to recognize its own failure to live up to the standards it sets itself, and thus its own
worthlessness and insubstantiality. The pain caused by the keen awareness of
the unbridgeable gap between its real state and the ideals it sets itself poisons
and embitters this whole form of life. Examples of this "unhappy consciousness" are forms of self-lacerating religious consciousness, particularly various
forms of medieval Christianity.

Despite the evident massive differences between Hegel's idealism and
Critical Theory, Adorno has a number of surprisingly positive references in
his *Negative Dialektik* to Hegel's doctrine of "unhappy consciousness." In the
modern period the possibility of radical critique depends on the existence of
highly differentiated human individuals, but any individual consciousness,
Adorno claims, is "almost always and with good reason" an instance of "the
unhappy consciousness."[12]

Hegel's unhappy consciousness measures itself against standards it sets itself and finds itself wanting. For him "unhappy consciousness" is a transitory
phenomenon, a mere preliminary to the full maturity spirit attains when it
has completed its *Bildungsprozeß* and attained a full, affirmative awareness
of itself as what it truly is, and is thus in a position to comprehend and affirm
the world around it, including its social world. Adorno claims that Hegel has
a "strategic aversion" to the unhappy consciousness and that the reason for
this is his desire to "render impotent the critical moment"[13] which is inherent in unhappy individual consciousness; criticism must for Hegel be a mere
passing stage on the way to final affirmation.

Adorno, by contrast, does not suffer the painful self-laceration of a consciousness divided against itself, but judges the society he encounters against
the highest exigencies of spirit, and condemns it for failing to live up to these.
The standards of criticism are, Adorno claims,[14] rooted in demands that the
society can be seen tacitly to make of itself—why go to the effort of building
complicated barns and silos, if one is going to look on with equanimity when
the silos fall down, ruining the harvest? Nevertheless, in point of fact the standards of criticism have their concrete location in Adorno's sensibility. The society is said to fail because it fails him, that is, it fails to live up to the very
highly pitched requirements and expectations he, as archetypal bearer of
spirit, imposes on it. Adorno's philosophy can be seen as a philosophy of suf-

[12] *ND* 53, see also 200–201.

[13] *ND* 53.

[14] This is what is meant by the claim that the theorist must transform the concepts he uses
into those "the object itself" provides. See Adorno et al., *Der Positivismusstreit in der deutschen
Soziologie* (Neuwied and Berlin: Luchterhand, 1969), pp. 7–79.

fering spirit, a way of articulating the pain spirit experiences when confronted with a world that thwarts its aspirations,[15] and as such, a criticism of that world.

The main question I wish to consider in this essay is what role cognition, and the philosophic theory of cognition (epistemology), might play in a philosophy of suffering spirit. The established procedure which philosophers have followed since antiquity would prescribe beginning with a formal definition of the central relevant concepts—"suffering," "spirit," "cognition," etc.—moving on to the substantive discussion only when the task of defining terms was satisfactorily completed. Just as Hegel did before him, Adorno completely and utterly rejects this way of proceeding in no uncertain terms. "Definition" in the traditional sense depends on a number of logical and epistemological presuppositions and has a number of implications which make it inappropriate as a method for discussions of any important phenomenon in the realm of spirit. Thus, for instance, a definition was traditionally supposed to contain a specification of a finite set of invariant features that would allow one reliably to distinguish the definiendum from other kinds of things. Definitions were supposed to satisfy strict conditions of noncircularity: the definiens was not to contain any item the definition of which itself required reference to the definiendum. "A cat is a feline animal" is not a satisfactory definition if one's only definition of "feline" is "a cat." Furthermore, it was supposed to be possible to distinguish clearly between a "definition," which gave the mere meaning of a concept, and empirically or theoretically contentful statements in which the definiendum occurred. Definitions were not, traditionally, supposed to have empirical content: "A triangle is a closed, three-sided, geometric figure" tells you nothing about the world, whereas "The topiarist has produced a row of almost perfect triangles" does tell you something about a particular garden. If these conditions—and a number of further ones I have not mentioned—are not satisfied, no definition in the traditional sense is possible.

In the case of spirit, Adorno claims, none of these conditions is fulfilled. The only way to get to know what spirit is, is not by mastering a list of distinguishing invariant features it exhibits, but by participating in the process by which it constitutes itself. How then do we enter into this process? Adorno takes over from Hegel the further claim that this is the wrong way to pose the question because we already *are* spirit,[16] an integral part of an uninterrupted, socially located, reflective activity. Thus all we need are some indirect, inexact, and, logically speaking, circular pointers to draw our attention to what it is we already are, and what it is we are already doing. The process will seem

---

[15] *ND* 27.

[16] G.W.F. Hegel, *Phänomenologie des Geistes*, in *Werke in zwanzig Bänden*, ed. Moldenhauer and Michel (Frankfurt: Suhrkamp, 1970), vol. 3, pp. 68–69.

to have two stages: pointing out what it is that we, as spiritual beings, are doing already and then making sure we do not misunderstand what it is we are and are doing. The first part of this will seem in some sense trivial, and perhaps even in some sense simpleminded and unenlightening. The second will consist of a long sequence of increasingly complex and convoluted negations, refutations of various incorrect (and usually reductive) theories that have been propounded about spirit: spirit is *not* this, *not* that, *not* some third thing. Overall the procedure will look very much as if it violates another tacit assumption of traditional procedures of definition, in that one will seem not so much to be saying what the *definiendum* is, but merely (at excessive length) what it is *not*. In the realm of spirit, though, the approach through a negative dialectic is the only one appropriate.

Although we cannot *define* spirit, we can continue to engage in a process of gradual, reflective, internal clarification or explication—literally "unfolding"—of it. Another way to put this is that we cannot define it, because it is itself nothing other than a continuous process of self-definition in which we participate. For Hegel and Adorno, then, in philosophy we do not begin by defining, rather we plunge in *in medias res*—well, "plunge in" is the wrong metaphor because if we were not already "in" up to our necks, the whole issue would not arise. There is no shore to stand on from which to initiate our jump, only the ever-rolling ocean of spiritual reflection.[17] Hegel was an optimist about this: *Plus léger qu'un bouchon nous dansons sur les flots*. There is no need for nostalgia about *"l'Europe aux anciens parapets"*—although the sea stretches limitlessly in every direction, we will soon realize that we are not bobbing helpless, but ensconced on the barque of the modern State. The barque is sound, and seaworthy, and even if not opulently appointed, contains ample facilities to allow us to pursue those activities that give human life meaning and value—religion, art, and philosophy; it is thus all the home we need. Adorno's view is bleaker. We are adrift in a leaky, foundering *"ponton."* The best we can hope for is that we are able to scribble a few philosophical texts before we go under. These texts are messages-in-bottles[18] that may or may not eventually find readers. That Adorno was capable, under the circumstances, of complaining about the room service, the tuning of the piano, and the quality of the pictures on the wall of his cell in the prison-ship is a sign of his characteristic combination of high philosophic purpose, extreme self-absorption, and gross bad faith.[19]

"Spirit," although it in some sense has instantiation in individuals, refers to ways in which humans live together with special reference to the formation

---

[17] The imagery in the following obviously comes from Rimbaud, *"Le bateau ivre"* (*Oeuvres completes* [Paris: Gallimard, 1972] pp. 66–69).

[18] *MM* § 133.

[19] See G. Lukács, *Theorie des Romans* (Neuwied and Berlin: Luchterhand, 1962), forward to the second edition.

and satisfaction of absolute needs. Our primary, absolute need as spiritual beings is for what Hegel calls "reconciliation"[20] or what Adorno calls "truth in an 'emphatic sense.'" This need cannot be satisfied for human beings once and for all by any individual action they might take, as individuals or as a group, or by coming to hold true any individual proposition or doctrinal system, but only through the development of a set of historically changing social practices: art, religion, and philosophy.

This characterization is not a traditional definition because spirit and the forms of generation and satisfaction of needs that constitute it cannot be specified independently of each other: the only way to explain spirit is by entering into substantive discussion of religion, art, and philosophy, but art, philosophy, and religion can only be fully and correctly understood as "spiritual" phenomena, that is, as formations essentially directed to concretely shaping and satisfying our absolute needs. The continual reference in this discussion to "needs" indicates very clearly that spirit is *not* a strictly epistemological category. Adorno admits that it does contain important "intellective elements,"[21] but they are only components of a larger structure. Spirit is very definitely not intended as merely another word for the transcendental subject of the epistemological tradition—the agency of a purely representational activity of thinking directed at mirroring reality as exactly as possible. Rather it is supposed to designate a historical process with a strong social dimension in which voluntative, impulse-based, intellective, and other elements come together, each influencing the other. In fact, blind drives seem to have a certain priority in the final constellation: in *Negative Dialektik*[22] Adorno writes that everything in the realm of spirit is nothing but "modified somatic impulse" and that the precursor (*Vorform*) of spirit is the impulse (*Drang*), not the image, the percept, the word, or the judgment. Cognition itself is an exceedingly important, perhaps teleologically the most important, "moment" of spirit, but only a moment nevertheless.

Even to speak of needs is to presuppose a teleological framework, one of which the speaker is very often fully conscious. If I tell you I need money, I will in general also be ready to tell you what I need the money *for*. For instance, I need money in order to buy food. Very often the object that I claim immediately to need (e.g., money) is clearly distinct from the state of affairs which forms the final object of my teleological intention (e.g., the state in which I have something to eat). The object can be defined, recognized, striven for, and attained independently of the state of affairs, and vice versa. Notoriously one cannot eat money. If the basic form of a need-statement is

---

[20] See M. Hardimon, *Hegel's Social Theory: The Project of Reconciliation* (Cambridge: Cambridge University Press, 1994); see also "Art and Theodicy," in R. Geuss, *Morality, Culture, and History* (Cambridge: Cambridge University Press, 1999), pp. 78–115.

[21] *ÄT* 138.

[22] *ND* 200.

"I need x in order to y," it would seem that a certain kind of relativity was built right into the concept of needing. The concept of an absolute need would then seem to be a contradiction in terms. An absolute need would have to be either one for which the question "You need x *for what?*" never even arose, or conceivably one in which to raise the question was itself to answer it. Once again, I think that what is important here is to see that Hegel and Adorno would be perfectly happy to grant that discussion of "absolute needs" is and must be circular. Such circularity is a basic characteristic of spirit and thus of any serious philosophical treatment of spirit. So when one asks "Why do humans need art?" the answer is "The need for art must be satisfied so that spirit can continue to exist." Spirit, however, cannot be understood and the demand that spirit must continue to exist cannot be in any way explained or justified without reference to the need for art (and the ways in which that need might be satisfied). Rather than seeing this circularity as an epistemic or moral deficiency, Hegel and Adorno regard it as a sign of distinction: spirit is an irreducible end in itself and gives itself its own laws autonomously in its own realm. Human needs and the ways in which they are satisfied have their foundation in the human body, but to the extent to which such human needs reach up into the realm of spirit, they can come to count as "absolute" despite their historical variability.

This might still seem to be an evasive and unsatisfactory account of "absolute" needs, and so it is perhaps useful to locate it in a slightly larger context. Kant initiated a certain tradition in philosophy that was based on the claim that there was a strict distinction between actions that were performed for their own sake and actions that were performed for the sake of something else, between categorical imperatives and hypothetical imperatives, between action that was empirically motivated and action motivated by respect for the moral law, or, to use Max Weber's terminology, between value-rational (*wertrational*) and end-rational (*zweckrational*) modes of acting. These distinctions are obviously not all the same, but the slightly hysterical insistence on the importance of one or another of the versions of them probably has its roots in a widespread character deformation that also inclines those who suffer from it to be susceptible to religious or quasi-religious views about the absolute distinction between the numinous and the profane and to the observation of various kinds of taboos and rituals. For the Kantian, in any case, the clear separation between what he calls "pathological" or "empirical" motivation and motivation derived from pure respect for the moral law is the *conditio sine qua non* of any form of morally responsible human action.[23] For Marx, Dewey, Adorno, and other progressivist opponents of Kant, the very distinction between that which is an end in itself and that which is instru-

---

[23] Kant, *Kritik der praktischen Vernunft*, Erster Teil, I. Buch, 3. Hauptstück, "Von den Triebfedern der reinen praktischen Vernunft" (Hamburg: Felix Meiner, pp. 84–104).

mentally useful is *itself* merely relative and not absolute. As Adorno puts it, the intellectual does not recognize the "alternative: work/recreation."[24] Societies in which these dichotomies are especially deeply rooted or strongly institutionalized show by this very fact that they are repressive or underdeveloped. When someone who belongs to this anti-Kantian strand of philosophizing calls a certain need "absolute," this should be understood to mean that in our society this need is strongly autotelic—people want to satisfy it "for its own sake"—but this is taken to be fully compatible, on the one hand, with a recognition that this need has had an empirical genesis, and, on the other, with the possibility that the whole distinction between the autotelic and the heterotelic—that done "for its own sake" and that done "for the sake of something else"—might come to seem utterly pointless in a fully developed and emancipated human society.

The "needs" that contribute to constituting spirit can be seen, then, from a different point of view, as demands made on the world. Humans are not "pure spirits," as angels were thought to be in certain religious traditions, but also biological systems, and thus in addition to the need for art, "reconciliation," and truth, humans also need bread and water. Spirit, to be sure, for both Hegel and Adorno, inherently strives to "raise" itself above nature, including its own nature, above its own material and somatic needs, in order to become free and autonomous. Adorno disagrees with Hegel only in that he thinks this striving is both unavoidable and fated from the very start to complete failure. Fortunately, dialectical thinking is able to accommodate this without missing a beat: spirit, Adorno claims, is "something mediated in itself, at the same time both spirit and non-spirit."[25] For Hegel, by contrast, spirit is not merely "real" or "actual" (*wirklich*) but it is also "Reality" ("*die Wirklichkeit*") in Hegel's technical sense of that term, that is, it is an ontological structure that lies at the base of the world and is capable of reproducing itself according to its own laws. When spirit claims absolute validity for itself, Hegel believes that this claim is true and that this means that absolute knowledge of the world as spirit is in principle possible. We can thus come to see that the world is *au fond* not mere dead matter circling contingently in a primal void, but an essentially spiritual reality and thus of kindred nature to us. This is what Hegel means by "reconciliation." Ontology gives us a guarantee that "reconciliation" is accessible to us. For Adorno there is no absolute knowing and no guarantee of any kind; his whole theory is structured around the impossibility of a lasting, nonillusory satisfaction of our spiritual needs under any non-utopian circumstances.

It is not an accident that Adorno repeatedly cites Stendhal's claim that art is a "*promesse de bonheur.*"[26] In this sense art is typical of the forms of spirit.

---

[24] *MM* § 84.
[25] *ND* 197.
[26] *ÄT* 128.

All spirit is a promise of happiness.[27] One must not, of course, confuse the promise with the fulfilment of the promise; that, in a way, was Hegel's error. The happiness promised in art is not a highly satisfactory experience of a further work of art, but a fundamental change in all aspects of human life. Similarly, the promise spirit holds out is not a mere improvement in religion, philosophy, painting, and music, but satisfaction of *all* needs, somatic as well as "absolute." This promise was destined in the past to remain unfulfilled, because it is in fact completely unfulfillable in any society known to us.[28] Nevertheless it would be a mistake simply to ignore the promise of spirit entirely, to trivialize it, or to construe it as no more than uncontrolled fantasy proceeding from the subjective imagination—this is the mistake positivism makes. Rather one cannot understand human life at all without taking account of the fact that it is irrevocably oriented toward the pursuit of this promise.

Spirit, then, is neither a natural phenomenon nor a purely self-referential structure of thought, which is abstracted from real acts of thinking and put forward as if it were ontologically independent. It is perhaps in some sense an imaginary domain, but, if so, it is most definitely not a mere thing of fancy; the "imagination" in question is as much a social or institutional as an individual phenomenon. Spirit is not anything "subjective"—not a play performed in the *theatrum internum* of any individual human soul—but a realm in which somatic and other needs and modes of need-satisfaction are integrated and transformed, and as such it has a certain social objectivity. Spirit, in fact, necessarily embodies itself in real social structures such as publishing houses, churches, chamber orchestras. It arises out of the interaction of these structures and institutions with each other and yet can contribute to systematically transforming them: musical life in the eighteenth century starts out with church organists, choirs, and bands of court and municipal musicians, playing fugues and performing dances and ceremonial music, and ends up with entrepreneurial impresarios, traveling virtuosi, string quartets, symphonies with first movements in sonata form, and large-scale piano concertos. *How* in detail this process proceeds, is, no doubt, a matter of extreme complexity, but the defenders of "spirit" would point out that the story cannot comprehensibly be told without reference to the interplay of institutional and more individual subjective factors. Just as spirit needs embodiment in social structures, it also needs individual bearers. There would also be no art without artistically talented people and without a potential audience of human beings interested in art. There would equally be no "truth" in Adorno's emphatic sense without human subjects who attempt to orient themselves on this truth.

[27] *ND* 205.
[28] *ÄT* 204–5.

The most significant subjective bearer of spirit in the modern era—the bourgeois individual—is a product of, and structurally reflects, the dominant form of property in our society.[29] To be more exact, Adorno thinks, the modern individual is a product of the market: each individual is essentially defined and constituted by his or her own "self-interest," which is the form the impulse toward self-preservation takes in a market society. By the middle of the twentieth century the modern individual in this sense was already an anachronism, well on its way to being "liquidated" by the same economic powers that had originally produced it.[30] In any case, as we have seen, for Adorno spirit was *never* full, actually given, immediate reality,[31] not even in any idealized past: neither in ancient Athens nor in the Vienna of Haydn, Mozart, Beethoven, and Schubert. In the middle of the twentieth century, however, spirit was confronted with its own *total* dissolution. In earlier periods, spirit was a promise that was never fully realized; now the promise itself begins to fall into oblivion. Even for the spiritual elite of the generation to which Adorno (born 1903) belonged, spirit had at best a certain residual validity.

What is the point of cognition in a world of suffering spirit? Again, the best way to understand what Adorno is trying to do seems to be to follow him along the *via negativa*. The model for "cognition" is not the scientific theory which has possible technological application; Adorno very definitely rejects the view, which he takes to be characteristic of positivism, that "knowledge" is the state of having or acquiring propositional knowledge of the world. He also rejects the view which he attributes to various "irrationalists" that to know something is simply to have any kind of special, direct intuitive acquaintance with something that cannot be expressed in words or concepts. Finally he rejects all forms of pragmatism that claim that cognition is simply "know-how," the ability to act in an intelligent and successful way in a wide variety of circumstances. Cognition for Adorno is essentially a process of interpreting something; it is like the aesthetic interpretation of a work of art, or the psychological interpretation of the actions and intentions of a human agent, or the religious interpretation of the cosmos as a whole, when the believer recognizes God's omnipotence in the motion of the heavenly bodies.[32] Such an interpretation is intended to present the emphatic, not merely the factual, truth about the state of affairs at issue. It will in general be connected in various complex ways with strict forms of propositional knowledge, and may also be associated with direct acquaintance and with various ways of acting intelligently in the world, but it will not be reducible to any one of them, certainly not as they are theorized by positivism, any of the forms of irrationalism, or pragmatism.

---

[29] *MM* § 99.

[30] *MM* §§ 83, 88.

[31] *ÄT* 136.

[32] For reasons I cannot go into here, I think it is important not to confuse Adorno's notion of "interpretation" with that of his slightly older right-wing contemporary Hans-Georg Gadamer.

The concrete interpretation of some individual phenomenon always starts from a "concept" of the phenomenon which contains within itself certain demands. Thus, for instance, the use of the concept "democracy" in its contemporary sense contains implicitly the requirement that the society so characterized will be one in which "the people have the power." Making this demand or imposing this requirement will make sense only in the context of a further set of valuations that can be seen as presupposed. These additional valuations must be capable of being seen as in some sense "(naturally) going together with or belonging to the concept." The demands made in or by the concept will generally be rather abstract and indeterminate, or at any rate subject to further interpretation. One will not necessarily know in advance which concrete political institutions will have to be present in a society in order that the demand for "people's power" be realized, and one will certainly be unlikely to know in advance what further implications the full realization of "democracy" will have for the educational system, the art world, the economy, the religious institutions, etc. of a given society. Thus social democrats have argued plausibly since the nineteenth century that the effective political power of the people is incompatible with any large-scale economic inequality. Economic equality is neither a clear component of the very concept of democracy—certainly not one that could be extracted from it by simple semantic analysis—nor a mere empirical addendum. Rather it seems to be a further demand that was in some sense implicit in the rationale for the original concept, but which could emerge clearly only when it was possible to investigate concrete cases in which people tried to realize "democracy" in particular social formations. One might be inclined to think that we are faced with a strict alternative: *either* a demand that was already very clearly present, although, perhaps, hidden, is laid bare, *or* a new demand is being added. Adorno's point—and Hegel's point before him—is that accepting this as a strict alternative makes it impossible to understand what is actually going on when large groups of people attempt to apply basic political concepts to the structuring or restructuring of their society.

Trying to give an "interpretation" that tells one the emphatic truth is a dialectical process in several senses. First of all, a good interpretation will uncover the nonidentity between a set of relevant general concepts and the individual case that is being subsumed under these concepts. No "really existing" society in fact satisfies the demands of democracy in full measure, and an adequate interpretation points this out concretely. Second, the procedure is dialectical in that the concept or concepts from which one starts, together with the demands that are contained within them, undergo a systematic transformation during the course of the interpretation. It is only *post factum*—after one has confronted the concept with the purported individual instance—that one comes to see clearly the demands which ought to have been made of the individual case from the very beginning. We find out what "democracy" "really" means—as we say—only after we have investigated concrete cases in which people have attempted to instantiate the concept. If we investigate correctly and pay attention to what is happening, we will notice that the concept we are using has itself changed in a structured way during the process of investigation. The investigation is dialectical if two processes are conjoined in it: on the one hand, the individual case (or cases) shows itself to be deficient relative to the demands contained within a concept we are using, but on the other hand, the concept itself develops by unfolding successively various of its (normative) implications. Adorno's philosophy is a sustained, unitary process of interpretation through which we are supposed to come to recognize *both* in what respects our world is radically deficient *and* what demands spirit makes on the world. Cognition does not reconcile us to our world and the suffering it contains. In fact, it makes us more aware of that suffering, and thereby increases it. Attaining correct cognition is, however, an inherent *conatus* of spirit.

An interpretation can and must ignore many of the mandatory principles of epistemological asceticism dear to Kant and the positivists. For positivists, feelings, impulses, and emotions have no proper role to play in cognition, and wishful thinking is absolutely taboo. For Adorno, on the contrary, wishful thinking, fantasy, feelings, and instincts are constituent parts of spirit, and hence also of any unconstricted, freely flowing process of interpretation. In any case Adorno holds that *all* thinking is exaggeration, and he takes it to follow from this that every interpretation is in some sense a metaphor.[33] In the realm of spirit "nothing is . . . meant literally."[34]

To be sure, an interpretation presupposes a certain, at least minimally correct, perception of that which is to be interpreted. The emphatic truth is exaggerated and metaphorical, but it is not completely invented, and is not intended to annihilate, repress, utterly ignore, or cancel the facts. Even if one holds, as Adorno does, that there is no such thing as "the facts, unvarnished," but only the facts as interpreted one way or another, it does not follow that any interesting interpretation can be pure and unvarnished, unsullied by the attempt to get the sheer givens of our world right, and deficient when it fails to do this. It might be tempting here to think of this in terms of the Kantian distinction between "intuition" (blind without concepts) and "concept" (empty without intuition),[35] each of which needs the other to result in "cognition." This would not be completely incorrect, provided one kept in mind Adorno's Hegel-derived belief that Kant got it right when he pointed out the interconnection of concept and intuition in any real cognitive process, and

---

[33] *MM* §§ 79, 82, 127, 128; see also T. W. Adorno, *Eingriffe* (Frankfurt: Suhrkamp, 1963), p. 152.

[34] Adorno et al., *Der Positivismusstreit in der deutschen Soziologie*, pp. 44–45.

[35] Kant, *Kritik der reinen Vernunft*, ed. Raymund Schmidt (Hamburg: Felix Meiner, 1956), B75/A51.

wrong when he tried nevertheless to insist on a strict dichotomy between the two. One of Adorno's intentions is to dissolve as much as possible the distinction between concept and intuition, thinking and perceiving. Impulses, acts of imagination, and exaggerations are all integral parts of thinking, and perception/intuition is no mere act of passive reception of that which is immediately given. Even the most rudimentary perception is shot through with imaginatively laden anticipations, wishes, anxieties, and desires, and preformed by expectations that depend on the concepts and theories we have.[36]

Adorno replaces Kant's simple dichotomy between thinking and "intuiting" with a more highly differentiated, context-specific set of instruments: the identical and the nonidentical, the general and the particular, the concept and the nonconceptual, finitude and infinity, the immediate and mediation, etc. Traditional philosophy labors under a fundamental illusion; it "takes the concept just as fetishistically as the concept takes itself, when it explicates itself naively within its own realm: as a totality that is sufficient unto itself."[37] In doing this philosophy gets caught up in an empty process of reflection, "confusing an image [of itself, i.e., of philosophy] with concreteness."[38] When this happens, philosophy loses its content—"*die Sache selbst*"[39] or the "nonconceptual" which is the true referent of all concepts[40]—completely. One cannot break out of the *circulus diabolicus* of purely conceptual reflection by activating a purportedly "pure" intuition of the "nonconceptual," but only by a "full, unreduced experience"[41] of concrete, individual things. Such an experience will contain both intuitive (or perceptual) and conceptual "moments," but there is no reason to expect it to be particularly "intuitive" in the sense in which, for instance, the contemplation of a picture is "intuitive."[42] Adorno states that the goal of his philosophy is to grasp the nonidentical cognitively, but he always adds that this cannot be done in a process that is completely nonconceptual. One can only "get beyond" given, inert conceptual structures *by using concepts*. The "utopia of cognition" consists in "opening up the non-conceptual with concepts, but without assimilating it to them,"[43] and this seems clearly to assign a certain priority in cognitive processes to concepts over intuitions.

Adorno opposed one of the basic pillars of positivism, the philosophical primacy of epistemology, and he consistently denied the possibility of a completely freestanding theory of knowledge.[44] Lenin was right, he thought, to

---

[36] *MM* § 79.
[37] *ND* 21.
[38] *ND* 23.
[39] *ND* 203.
[40] *ND* 21.
[41] *ND* 23.
[42] *ÄT* 141–54.
[43] *ND* 19.
[44] Adorno, *Zur Metakritik der Erkenntnistheorie* (Stuttgart: Kohlhammer, 1956).

accuse "subjective positivists" of "complicity with the powers that be,"[45] but he ought not to have used this as an excuse to refuse to enter into detailed discussions of epistemology. Theory of knowledge is a perfectly proper subject for philosophical reflection. This reflection will treat epistemology as part of an overarching theory of society, and will thus of necessity have a political dimension. The negativity of Adorno's reflective analysis—the dialectical movement back and forth between concept and instance which never terminates in identity—is the counterpart of real social antagonism, of the fact that our social reality does not satisfy the demands of spirit and we suffer from this.

Since Critical Theory attributes to truth itself a temporally-specific historical kernel, taking seriously Hegel's claim that philosophy is "its time grasped in concepts,"[46] it is hard to avoid asking what contemporary relevance Adorno's thought can have today, thirty-five years after his death. Is "spirit" at all a useful or even a comprehensible category? Can it still serve any of the functions Adorno ascribed to it: furthering our understanding of society and enabling us to resist certain reprehensible social pressures? Instead of trying to answer this question directly, I would like to discuss briefly the contemporary relevance of two related aspects of a dialectical epistemology of suffering spirit.

First of all, it is of the utmost importance to recall that Adorno's "negative dialectic" had as its goal resistance against what were thought to be almost intolerable pressures to intellectual, moral, social, and political conformism that had developed during the central portion of the twentieth century. Opposition to social pressure toward uniformity of belief and mode of life has, of course, a long pedigree in liberal political theory, but Adorno holds no brief for liberalism. He generally follows the main line of post-Hegelian theorizing in Germany which takes traditional liberalism to be naively and unreflectively fixated on the individual as something like a naturally given monad. This, he believes, is never going to allow one to understand contemporary society in a way that would give one powers of resistance against the economic forces that are dissolving the bourgeois individual and all his works.[47] In particular, he presents a very sharply pointed and extensive criticism of one particular thesis which he takes to be characteristic of liberalism. This is the "liberal fiction that any thought can be promiscuously communicated,"[48] i.e., the view that

---

[45] *ND* 203.

[46] G.W.F Hegel, *Grundlinien zur Philosophie des Rechts* in *Werke in zwanzig Bänden*, ed. Moldenhauer and Michel (Frankfurt: Suhrkamp, 1970), vol. 7, p. 26.

[47] The situation is actually slightly more complicated and less clear than I have presented it in the main text. Partly this is because "liberalism" is not actually a concept Adorno uses in a systematic way. He thinks the important categories are: "bourgeois (thought)," "enlightenment," "progressive (thought)," etc. See, however, *MM* §§. 97, 88.

[48] *"die liberale Fiktion der beliebigen, allgemeinen Kommunizierbarkeit eines jeden Gedankens"* (*MM* § 50; see also *MM* §§ 5, 93).

in principle *anyone* can understand *any* thought. This "fiction" is a form of oppression and a prop of social and political conformism. The real function it serves in contemporary societies is to impose censorship, preventing the expression of thoughts that go beyond, or against, what "everyone" thinks they know anyway, and what "everyone knows" will be overwhelmingly innocuous banalities and unthreatening bits of whatever is the dominant ideology. Eventually external censorship of the expression of idiosyncratic, nonstandard, or deviant thoughts will tend to be internalized into a form of self-censorship with the result that one cannot even think for oneself what is in any way original, or potentially subversive. Part of the political significance of the hermetic strand of avant-garde art since Mallarmé is that it puts into question the principle of easy, universal communicability.[49] Truth itself, at any rate emphatic truth, seems to have an exoteric dimension: "Only those thoughts are true that do not understand themselves."[50] To criticize society radically is to break out of the existing social consensus and its complicity with the status quo. Adorno thinks that only dialectical thinking will make this possible. To orient oneself or one's philosophy on "consensus," whether an actually existing consensus, a possible one, or even an "ideal" one, means to internalize conformism.

Is it really true, as Adorno claims, that only an epistemology that is centered on the concept of spirit and takes the form of a negative dialectic is capable of allowing us to resist and criticize our society so that we come to be in a position to abolish historically superfluous suffering? This history of the Frankfurt School after Adorno's death seems to support his view: a "dialectical" approach was gradually replaced by an eclectic mixture of empiricist and neo-Kantian elements, and this went hand in hand with a distinct loss in critical power, and even a clear abandonment of the original critical intention of the School. The original program formulated by Horkheimer claimed that the Critical Theory was directed precisely *not* at making anything in this society function better, but at showing that radical social change was imperative.[51] By the 1980s Habermas had more or less reversed this, and was propounding theories that seemed directed at showing how to improve existing social life through improved communication. Nevertheless, this example is not a conclusive confirmation of Adorno's views about the connection between nondialectical theories and conformism. After all, there have been approaches that were very deliberately non-dialectical and would have no truck with any notion of "spirit," but which were certainly every bit

[49] This strand of politically motivated hermeticism can in fact be traced back, Adorno suggests, to Hölderlin. See *ÄT* 115, also *ÄT* 218, 475–7, *MM* § 93.

[50] *MM* § 122. Some of Adorno's biographers report the pride with which he used to report to friends and colleagues after a successful day of writing that he had written paragraphs which he did not (yet) understand himself.

[51] Horkheimer, "Traditionelle und kritische Theorie," in Horkheimer, *Kritische Theorie* (Frankfurt: Fischer, 1968), vol. 2, pp. 137–92.

as radical in their social criticism as Adorno was. Foucault is a good example of this.

This brings me to my second point. One strong current in contemporary liberalism shows a striking apparent similarity with two of Adorno's central—and negative—theses. Adorno is notoriously obsessed with what he calls the "prohibition of graven images" in art, religion, politics, and philosophy.[52] This prohibition forbids one to elaborate a positive image of utopia, and seems to have been derived in the first instance from Marx's strictures against "utopian" thinking. There was an anti-utopian component in some Cold War liberalism, where "utopia" served as a code word for revolution.[53] Another line to which some recent liberals seem committed has been the claim that liberalism is "neutral" in the struggle of ideologies, and that it has no specific positive values of its own or substantive conceptions of a "good life" it seeks to realize. That this claim is itself false and ideological seems to me too self-evident to require detailed discussion. The requirement, which is integral to this form of liberalism, that only "neutral procedures" be used in public decision-making, excludes from the very start any structuring of society based on transcendent religious values. This can be called "neutral" only in a Pickwickian sense. From another point of view it is also obvious that liberalism as a whole is oriented to a conception of a society of free and autonomous individuals, who pursue their own destiny without substantive reference to traditional patterns of behavior. This "liberal individual," whose preferences, whatever they may be, are not to be interfered with, is a very different potential social type from Adorno's ideal of the individual bearer of spirit as a creature of deep taboos that are the "sediments" of significant historical and cultural experiences.[54] Adorno does not, of course, claim that any part of his theory satisfies some abstract demand of "neutrality," and would not think much of a view that expected us to find a method of judgment or decision-making that would be equally acceptable to the ignorant and the informed, the perverse and the healthy, the selfish and the altruistic.

The second apparent similarity between Adorno and liberalism is one that is slightly harder to deal with. Contemporary liberalism rests on, and also fosters, an extremely highly developed sensitivity vis-à-vis the phenomenon of suffering, and seems recently to have contributed to a veritable cult of the suffering victim. One unedifying consequence of this is the highly visible contemporary spectacle of groups and individuals vying for the status of "most oppressed." It has also not escaped the notice of astute observers of contemporary politics that liberal theories that are focused on the alleviation of suffering nowadays function in fact as part of the justification for an apparatus

---

[52] See for instance *ND* 202–5.
[53] Perhaps the best known was Karl Popper's version in *The Poverty of Historicism*.
[54] *MM* § 8.

that uses extreme coercion to stabilize a worldwide system of oppression.[55] Recently many liberals have begun to support the so-called doctrine of "humanitarian intervention,"[56] which has been used to justify coercive economic and political measures, including military attack on sovereign states, on the grounds of the need to help suffering humanity.[57] The predictable response to this is that even the occasional misuse of a principle is not in itself an argument against the principle. A schema is not responsible for its own misuse. The simple imperative "Just abolish suffering" is not in itself discredited by being crudely, or even self-servingly, applied. Simple general imperatives, after all, do not usually apply themselves, but require focusing through an extensive panoply of empirical theories, and what empirical data we have available at any time depends in part on what we have thought it worthwhile to collect.[58] Thus one might well think that in many cases what seems to be an objection to the general principle of abolishing suffering is really an objection to one or another of the subsidiary assumptions that are being made. Human individuals and groups, one might think, are naturally self-centered, and tend to overestimate their own suffering, while underestimating that of others, especially of competitors, rivals, or members of what they take to be inherently inferior cultural formations. This, one might argue, is the main reason the principle of preventing and abolishing suffering seems to misfire. It is, of course, true that, to take a contemporary example, in Iraq casualties among the occupying forces are carefully recorded, even if they are not, for understandable, if not laudable, political reasons, publicized in a way that will allow them to have any significant public effect, while casualties among the natives are not, but it isn't clear that this is an exculpation of the principle rather than an additional objection.

One does not know what Adorno himself would have thought about any of this, had he lived to see the contemporary world, and perhaps the very idea of an Adorno of the twenty-first century does not make much sense, but philosophic positions that attempted to remain close to the central intuitions of Adorno's philosophy within the changed historical circumstances of the early

[55] See Alain Badiou, *L'éthique: Essai sur la conscience du Mal* (Paris: Hatier, 1998).

[56] For an austere and restrained analysis of some of the political difficulties associated with this doctrine, see John Dunn, "The Dilemma of Humanitarian Intervention," in his *History of Political Theory and Other Essays* (Cambridge: Cambridge University Press, 1996) pp. 136–47.

[57] This text was written in Britain during the summer of 2003 at the point at which the Blair government was beginning to shift its justification for the war against Iraq from the nonexistent weapons of mass destruction and the transparently hypocritical claims to be defending the will of the United Nations to a version of humanitarian intervention, conveniently overlooking the fact that much of the suffering of the population of Iraq resulted from the Anglo-American embargo on that country. For a philosophically informed treatment of this see Slavoj Žižek, *Iraq: The Borrowed Kettle* (London: Verso, 2004).

[58] See John Dunn, "The Dilemma of Humanitarian Intervention," pp. 136–47, on political *means*, including organization of sustained attention and will.

twenty-first century might be expected to call for a certain amount of skepticism about the politics of "alleviating suffering," as it is now envisaged and practiced. It is historically perfectly understandable that in the '50s and early '60s of the last century Adorno made the abolition of suffering in a rather unqualified sense one of the central motifs of his philosophy. However, even then that was an undialectical thought, and, one way or another, a mistake. One would hope that if Adorno were still alive, he would have tried to develop a more sophisticated and differentiated analysis of suffering than he did. Wouldn't it be most appropriate for contemporary dialectical thinking to try to overcome the one-sidedness of a philosophy of suffering, either of the liberal or the 1950 Frankfurt variety? Would Adorno's epistemology itself remain unchanged by this revision in its substance?

8

On the Usefulness and Uselessness of Religious Illusions

GENERAL, DISCURSIVELY STRUCTURED CRITICISM of the way in which humans conceive and imagine the gods reaches back to the very beginnings of systematic Western philosophy. Poems written by Xenophanes in the second half of the sixth century BC contain a remarkably modern-sounding analysis and rejection of religious anthropomorphism.[1] What is historically perhaps most notable about this is that Xenophanes in presenting his case against conceiving the gods as having human form does not appeal to any form of esoteric lore,[2] to intuition, revelation, or the inspiration of the muses,[3] but merely to comparative, empirical observation and to everyday forms of human reasoning. It is by virtue of this method of inquiry, more than the particular results to which he comes, that Xenophanes can count as an early representative of the general, pan-European movement members of the early Frankfurt School called the "Enlightenment."

Since the tradition preserves Xenophanes' verses only as disordered fragments, it is impossible to be absolutely sure about how his argument is to be reconstructed, but it seems that he proceeds by accepting first of all that all humans believe that the gods have a human form.[4]

[1] See W.G.F. Hegel, *Vorlesungen über die Geschichte der Philosophie*, in *Werke* (Frankfurt: Suhrkamp, 1971) vol. 18, pp. 81–113, 283–84; T. Adorno und M. Horkheimer, *Dialektik der Aufklärung* (Frankfurt: Fischer, 1969), p. 12; W. Burkert, *Griechische Religion in der archaischen und klassischen Epoche* (Stuttgart: Kohlhammer, 1977), p. 371–72.

[2] Homer claims to know (*Iliad* 20.74) that the river humans call "Skamandros" has a different name ("Xanthus") among the gods. If this had been widely known among his contemporaries, and not a bit of esoteric lore, he would not have felt the need specifically to mention the difference.

[3] Hesiod, *Theogonia* 22–35.

[4] It is peculiar that Xenophanes does not cite the hemitheriomorphic gods of Egypt in order directly to refute the claim that there is universal consensus on anthropomorphism. There are at least three possibilities here. First, Xenophanes simply had no knowledge of these non-anthropomorphic gods. Second, he did know about them, but perhaps simply for the sake of argument did not discuss them. Third, he subjected the gods of Egypt to an *interpretatio philosophica* about which we know nothing. As far as the third possibility is concerned, recall that two generations after Xenophanes, the polytheistic universalist Herodotus simply identified Egyptian with known Greek gods, or rather he felt compelled to tell the most outlandish and implausible stories in order to assimilate the two (e.g., II. 42.3–4; W. W. How and J. Wells, *A Commentary to Herodotus* [Oxford: Oxford University Press, 1912], ad loc. remarks laconically, "No native authority confirms Herodotus' story").

ἀλλ' οἱ βροτοὶ δοκέουσι γεννᾶσθαι θεούς,
τὴν σφετέρην δ' ἐσθῆτα ἔχειν φωνήν τε δέμας τε [DK14][5]

Such universal consensus, however, is by no means something one would naturally expect, since humans notoriously have widely divergent views on speculative topics. Isn't this unwonted unanimity, then, good reason for thinking that anthropomorphism is true? How else can one explain the universal consensus? Xenophanes' argument can be reconstructed in a series of steps:

1. The most important distinction between gods and men is that the former are "immortal" (ἀθάνατοι), whereas the later are mortal (θνητοί).

2. Thus the argument should be concerned not merely with the views of humans (ἄνθρωποι) only, even of "all" humans, but with the views of all "mortals" (θνητοί). The use of the word "βροτόι" in the formulation of the universal consensus on anthropomorphism in DK14 above is highly misleading, because it refers to "mortal men" (or perhaps better "men as mortal"). However, men are not the only mortal beings; animals, too, are mortal: they are θνητοί but not βροτοί.

3. We observe that the various distinct human tribes attribute to the gods in each case their *own* physiognomic peculiarities. African gods have dark skin and snub noses, Thracian gods, blue eyes and red hair.

Ἀιθίοπές τε <θεοὺς σφετέρους> σιμοὺς μέλανάς τε
Θρῆικές τε γλαυκοὺς καὶ πυρρούς <φασι πέλεσθαι> [DK16]

4. We can hypothesize that a lawlike regularity about the relation between mortals and their respective conceptions of the gods lies behind this observation: mortals imagine the gods according to their own image.

5. If the regularity postulated in 4 above holds, then we should be able to project it contrafactually to other mortals, for instance, animals:

ἀλλ' εἰ χεῖρας ἔχον βόες <ἵπποι τ'> ἠὲ λέοντες
ἢ γράψαι χείρεσσι καὶ ἔργα τελεῖν ἄπερ ἄνδρες,
ἵπποι μέν θ' ἵπποισι βόες δέ τε βουσὶν ὁμοίας

---

[5] I cite Xenophanes according to the sixth edition of Diels-Kranz, *Fragmente der Vorsokratiker* (1951; reprinted Dublin and Zurich: Weidman, 1996; vol. I, pp. 113–39). "DK 14" means fragment 14 in this edition. Diels assumes that Xenophanes composed (at least) two different poems Σίλλοι and Περὶ φύσεως. He ascribes fragments 14–16 to the first of these two poems, fragment 23 to the second. Diels gives no reason for this, and I will cite all of these fragments on equal terms. Fragment 14 in the form given in Diels is metrically extremely peculiar. The first line is an iambic trimeter, the second a dactylic hexameter. West (*Delectus ex iambis et elegis graecis* [Oxford: Oxford University Press, 1980, p. 276]) cites an anonymous emendation ("*nescioquis ut sit hexameter*"):

ἀλλὰ βροτοὶ δοκέουσι θεοὺς γεννᾶσθαι < ∪ — — >

which can be read as a fragment of a dactylic hexameter.

καί <κε> θεῶν ἰδέας ἔγραφον καὶ σώματ᾽ ἐποίουν
τοιαῦθ᾽ ὁἱόν περ καὐτοὶ δέμας εἶχον <ἕκαστοι> [DK15]

6. Animals, that is, would *not* conceive of the gods in human form; we, however, presumably do not notice this because they cannot communicate it to us. We, therefore, do not notice that there would be no consensus among all mortals on the form of the gods.

7. Thus we have no reason to believe that there is consensus among all mortals to the effect that the gods have human form.

8. The regularity noted under 4 in fact gives us a good reason to think anthropomorphism is false, while at the same time explaining why all humans unanimously believe that the gods have human form.

9. The common human opinion recounted in DK14 is an error: at any rate, the highest god has the form of no mortal being, and thus a fortiori does not have human form.

εἷς θεός, ἔν τε θεοῖσι καὶ ἀνθρώποισι μέγιστος,
οὔτι δέμας θνητοῖσιν ὁμοίιος οὐδὲ νόημα [DK23]

I consciously used the technical term of contemporary analytic philosophy "reconstruct" to describe setting out Xenophanes' argument in this way. One can reasonably wonder whether he would himself even have recognized as his own the thought structure which is ascribed to him here. Even if he did not, it is by no means obvious that this is relevant. One of the acknowledged goals of philosophy is to understand other philosophers better than they understand themselves. After all, Xenophanes proceeds in a not dissimilar way when he discusses anthropomorphism: because his contemporaries erected statues that looked like statues of humans and performed various ritual actions in the presence of these statues, and also told stories about the doings of the gods that seemed to presuppose that the gods are humans-writ-large, Xenophanes attributes to them a very sharply defined general belief—the belief that the gods have human form—and also an argument—*ex omnium consensu*—that is taken to serve as the foundation for this belief. Only when he has thus "reconstructed" their position does he set out to refute it.

One of the basic claims of the Critical Theory, in the form in which it was elaborated by Adorno and Horkheimer in the 1940s is that enlightenment is "totalitarian."[6] One of the central elements of this totalitarianism is the monolithically imposed requirement that human behavior be construed as articulating verbally expressible beliefs, and that means in fact that it be transformed as much as possible into a tacit form of expression of clear and unambiguously formulated "opinions." These "opinions" must be in principle capable of extraction from their original context and presented for general

[6] Adorno und Horkheimer, *Dialektik der Aufklärung*, p. 12; cf. F. Hegel, *Phänomenologie des Geistes*, in *Werke in zwanzig Bänden* (Frankfurt: Suhrkamp, 1970) vol. 3, p. 398–441.

discussion to determine whether they are argumentatively "justified" or not; a speaker is committed to the logical consequences of the opinions he expresses. These demands are by no means self-evident, but represent a distinctive historical development. Western philosophy, with its focus on the "argument" and an associated set of concepts ("definition," "cogency," "justification," "validity," "abstraction," etc.), has been a major force in promoting this enlightenment project. Just as for the grammarian all reality is grammatical, for philosophers everything in the vicinity becomes a possible or actual opinion for which an argument must be given, even things that might originally not have been intended as contributions to a disputation at all. Argumentation as we see it develop in the early Platonic dialogues is an agonistic procedure which is always directed at a potential "opponent" whom it is trying to refute or convince. Since genuine argumentation of this kind plays an infinitesimally small part in normal human life, using the procedure often involves inventing an argument which one attributes to an imaginary opponent, for the purposes of having something definite to take as an object of criticism.[7]

We are so familiar with this way of proceeding even in nonphilosophical contexts, that we scarce notice it. Thus above I cited fragment 16 of Xenophanes as given by Diels/Kranz, but the attentive reader will have noticed that Diels has added two words to the first line ("θεοὺς σφετέρους") and also two words to the end of the second line (φασὶ πέλεσθαι") and translates: "The Ethiopians *assert that their gods* are snubnosed and black. . . ."[8] Diels uses italics to indicate that these are his addenda. The original prose text (by Clement of Alexandria) from which this fragment was derived reads:

> τὰς μορφὰς αὐτῶν [*scilicet* τῶν θεῶν (DK)] ὁμοίας ἑαυτοῖς ἕκαστοι
> διαζωγραφοῦσιν, ὥς φησιν ὁ Ξενοφάνης, Ἀιθίοπές τε μέλανας σιμούς
> τε Θρῆικές τε πυρροὺς καὶ γλαύκους.

Diels fiddles with this text, inverting (μέλανας σιμούς → σιμοὺς μέλανας) and adding words (φασὶ πέλεσθαι) where necessary to produce two metrically correct lines of verse, but διαζωγραφοῦσι (in Clement's text) clearly means "to paint," *not*, as Diels's version reads, "to assert" (φασὶ πέλεσθαι = "*behaupten*"), unless, that is, one presupposes exactly what is at issue here, namely that a painting you make is adequate grounds for me to attribute to you a specific belief. From the fact that the Ethiopians paint pictures of black, snub-nosed humans, carry these images around with them through the streets of their villages, singing, dancing, and sacrificing to them, the conclusion is drawn that they *assert* that the gods have snub noses, black skin, and human form.

---

[7] For some similar comments on the relation between philosophy and poetry, see the excellent *Origins of Criticism* by Andrew Ford (Princeton, NJ: Princeton University Press, 2002).
[8] "Die Äthiopen *behaupten, ihre Götter* seien stumpfnasig und schwarz. . . ."

Given this general commitment of philosophy to doxaplasis[9] (the generation of opinions) and argumentation, it is in no way surprising that, when they come to think about religion, philosophers have considered it as a set of beliefs and opinions people hold. "Religious" beliefs, some philosophers have claimed, differ from other sorts of beliefs because of their purported content. "Cosmological" beliefs are beliefs about the structure of the universe; "biological" beliefs are about living things; "religious" beliefs are about the existence and properties of superhuman entities (gods). For traditional Western philosophy religion is essentially theology,[10] that is, it is a coherent, systematically organized, general discourse which purports to give some kind of knowledge of the gods and their relation to humans. To be sure, there are popular forms of religiosity that are not at all clear and coherent, but they can be seen as debased versions of "proper" religions.

There are some immediate objections to this conception of religion as fundamentally theology. First of all, this approach is not in general terribly illuminating when one tries to understand many non-Western religions. There are religions that have no gods and also religions in which gods are relatively unimportant. Thus Buddhists think that in the strict sense there are no gods—they are an illusion just as everything else in the world is. On the other hand, most Buddhists are prepared to tolerate various popular forms of the worship of gods, even of Buddha as a god. The reason for this is that the existence or nonexistence of gods is of no final significance, one way or the other. Buddhists are in a paradoxical sense pragmatists. They think that the only serious problem for human beings is how to find release from the unceasing cycle of desire and subsequent suffering. Speculating about the existence or nonexistence of gods is perhaps a slight distraction from what is genuinely important, but also in itself irrelevant and harm-

---

[9] See Xenophanes, "πλάσματα τῶν προτέρων" (DK1, l. 22).

[10] The Greek language, like, as far as we can tell, primitive Indo-European (see E. Benveniste, *Le vocabulaire des institutions indo-européenes* [Paris: Minuit, 1969], vol. 2, p. 265ff.), had no common single word for what we call "religion" (J. Harrison, *Prolegomena to the Study of Greek Religion* [Cambridge: Cambridge University Press, 1903], p. 2). Rather the Greeks made do with various circumlocutions such as "θεραπεία τῶν θεῶν" (J. Rudhardt, *Notions fondamentales de la pensée religieuse et actes constitutifs du culte dans la Grèce classique* [Paris: Picard, 1992], p. 141 with reference to Plato's *Resp* 327b), or "θεῶν τιμάι" (W. Burkert, *Griechische Religion in der archaischen und klassischen Epoche* [Stuttgart: Kohlhammer, 1977], p. 406; see also Plato's *Euthyphro*). The word "theology"—and by the way, also "philosophy"—seems to have been coined by Plato. θεολογία: *Resp.* 379a. Because the dating of the individual Platonic dialogues is controversial, it is impossible to say with certainty when the word φιλοσοφία was first used. On this whole issue see W. Burkert, *Griechische Religion in der archaischen und klassischen Epoche*, pp. 452–54, and W. Burkert, "*Platon oder Pythagoras,*" in *Hermes* 88, 1960, 159–77. The other side of the relation between philosophy and theology is of particular concern to Heidegger, who holds that traditional Western philosophy has by its very nature always been aspiring to be theology. See "*Die onto-theo-logische Verfassung der Metaphysik*" in *Identität und Differenz* [Pfullingen: Neske, 1957, pp. 31–69]).

less.[11] Buddhism then is a religion of "salvation" without a savior, in which the issue of salvation (from appearance/desire/suffering) is considered to be completely distinct from the question of the existence (or the properties) of god(s). In a similar way, many scholars describe Confucianism as a strictly this-worldly ethic which prescribes the cultivation of traditional rites and the development of a certain character for the sake of social harmony, and which lacks any requirement of "belief" in gods. Although both Confucianism and Buddhism have an internally complex theoretical structure, they are not essentially *theo*-logies in our traditional sense, that is, they have no constitutive doctrine of the nature of god(s); if they do express views about the gods, these are minor appendices, footnotes, condescending accommodations to popular beliefs, and so on.

Atheological religions like Buddhism and Confucianism deviate from the Western model because of their lack of interest in the existence of god(s), but they are highly sophisticated intellectual structures that present characteristic doctrines which they attempt to justify and develop through forms of argumentation. In the case of Confucianism this structure is a complex doctrine of the virtues, and in the case of Buddhism a metaphysics and epistemology and a set of ethical precepts about the best way in which the human will can extinguish itself, thus ending the cycle of desire and suffering.

There are, however, further objections against the traditional Western model of religion that go deeper than this. They share with this first objection the denial that theology is necessarily central to religion. However, the reason they give for this is different. They do not hold that it is fixation on the existence and nature of the *gods* that is wrong, rather it is the exaggerated fixation of traditional Western philosophies of religion on opinions, beliefs, doctrines, arguments *tout court* that is incorrect. The intellectualist attitude of traditional philosophy blocks the path to an appropriate understanding of the essence of religion. Religion is not essentially a matter of opinion, belief, dogma, and argument, at all, not even of naive, spontaneous, unreflective belief and opinion, but rather something essentially non-doxastic. Simplifying slightly, one could say that if "theology" means "conceptually articulated discourse" ("-logy" from λογος) "about god" ("theo-" from θεός), then the first objection rejects the claim that the essence of religion is *theo*-logy, whereas the three further objections I will canvas now reject the claim that theo-*logy* is the essence of religion. The three anti-theological lines of argument I will investigate now are distinct in that each understands the non-doxastic element which constitutes the essence of religion in a different way.

I will call the first of these three antitheological approaches the "socio-ethnological." Even rather narrow-minded philosophers must admit that most re-

---

[11] This is well captured by Brecht in his poem "Gleichnis des Buddha vom brennenden Haus" (in *Die Gedichte*, Frankfurt: Suhrkamp, 1981, p. 664).

ligions are not exclusively sets of beliefs and arguments, but also social institutions: systems of practices, rites, ritual, ceremonies, and habitual forms of behavior. An old tradition in philosophy in fact defines the "essence" of any phenomenon as that which is invariant in it in a variety of circumstances over time. If one were to take this philosophical view seriously one would have to locate the essence of religion in these practices and rituals, not in dogmas, because, as Nietzsche pointed out with great astuteness, the rituals and customs are historically much less variable than the "beliefs" of those who take part in religious ceremonies or rituals. In court we still swear on the Christian Bible, even if few people nowadays are "believers," and one could easily imagine our continuing to perform this important symbolic act in this way, even if virtually no one had any idea what the content of that book was.[12] Even the linguistic components of religious ceremonies are in large measure speech-acts, not doxastic claims put forward for argumentative evaluation or belief. Shouting "*hallelujia*," "ἰὴ Παιάν," "εὐφήμει,"or "ἄλαδε μύσται," speaking in tongues, intoning "oum," breaking out into the eastern and southern Mediterranean ὀλολυγμός, or saying "*ego te baptizo*" are not ways of propounding propositions.[13]

The second approach I wish to mention starts not from social institutions and organized forms of acting, but from purported features of human psychology. Those who take this second approach claim that there are religious feelings or experiences that are qualitatively different from other kinds of experiences or feelings.[14] These religious experiences are "*reale Objekt-Gefühle*,"

[12] On the "essence" of religion, see. F. Nietzsche, *Jenseits von Gut und Böse*, §§ 45–62 (in *Sämtliche Werke: Kritische Studienausgabe*, ed. Colli and Montinari, Berlin: de Gruyter, 1980, vol. 5; abbreviated *JGB*); on the concept of "natural history" see *JGB* §§ 186–94, 45; on questions of historical method and the concept of the "relatively persistent" see F. Nietzsche, *Zur Genealogie der Moral, Zweite Abhandlung* §§ 12–13 (in *Sämtliche Werke; Kritische Studienausgabe*, vol. 5; abbreviated *ZGM*).

[13] J. Rudhardt, *Notions fondamentales de la pensée religieuse et actes constitutifs du culte dans la Grèce classique*, pp.177–213. The Christian Credo, a speech-act with a consciously dogmatic content, is historically rather exceptional. Anyone who takes the philosophy of language of the late Wittgenstein at all seriously will in any case naturally be inclined to take the institutional framework within which speaking is performed to be of overwhelming importance in understanding it. The very intense historical and ethnological discussion of religion in the first half of the twentieth century overlaps in its interests with older philosophical discussions only in part. Early twentieth-century anthropology was interested primarily in the relation between ritual and myth (that is, τὰ δρώμενα and τὰ λεγόμενα) rather than in the older philosophical issue of the relation between myth and *logos* (or δόξα and ἐπιστήμη/θεολογία). On the question of "belief" in the ancient world, see B. Snell, *Die Entdeckung des Geistes* (Göttingen: Vandenhoeck & Ruprecht, 1980) chapter 2, and P. Veyne, *Les Grecs ont-il cru à leurs mythes?* (Paris: Seuil, 1983).

[14] "[W]enn überhaupt auf einem Gebiete menschlichen Erlebens etwas diesem Gebiete Eigenes und so nur in ihm Vorkommendes zu bemerken ist, so auf dem religiösen" (Rudolf Otto, *Das Heilige* [Gotha: Klotz, 1929], p. 4; see also p. 19); see also William James, *Varieties of Religious Experience* (London: Penguin, 1982) and Freud's discussion of the "oceanic feeling" (*Das Unbehagen in der Kultur*, in *Freud-Studienausgabe* (Frankfurt: Fischer, 1974), vol. IX, pp. 197–205).

states of feeling in which a nonhuman reality is directly present to or for us, and as such they are the origin and the "first element" of religion.[15] If one wishes to understand religion correctly one must focus one's attention on them. They are by their very nature "extra-ordinary," they represent extreme departures from the kinds of experiences we have in our everyday life, and they are radically a-rational, if not irrational. As such, they inherently resist simple, direct linguistic expression, or at any rate direct linguistic expression that would be in any way adequate to their content. They have an element of the confrontation with the unknowable and uncontrollable, with that which is radically other. Finally, they have a certain highly characteristic emotional timbre: a mixture of high anxiety and overwhelming admiration.[16] Religious statements, then, are by their very nature doomed attempts to react in an appropriate way to inherently nonrationalizable experiences. Thus that central religious statements do not make discursive sense is not, as the philosophical tradition assumed, a defect, but exactly what one would expect, if that-which-is-radically-Other did exist and did manifest itself to us in certain extra-ordinary experiences.

Rites, rituals, and ceremonies are attempts to deal practically with phenomena that are the locus of extreme states of anxiety. One strategy which seems to have been rather successful, given that it is found in a wide variety of times and places, is the separation of the conceptual, spatiotemporal, and social world into two distinct spheres: the profane, everyday, secular on the one hand, and the sacred, numinous, taboo, on the other. By maintaining a rigid distinction between the two spheres and inflexible rules about the access to the sacred and the way in which it is treated, one can hope to calm an anxiety which might otherwise spread in a paralyzing way.[17] The archaic formulae and rigid, stereotyped rituals that are characteristic of many religions are an expression of the primordial anxiety from which religions originally arose in prehistoric times. When anxiety is so extreme, *any* change is a potential threat, and tried and true methods can retain their hold on populations for very long periods of time.

To be sure, Freud points out that feelings all by themselves cannot constitute a religion.[18] Even assuming that feelings are of central importance, religions strictly so called arise only from interpretative reactions to particular experiences.[19] Nietzsche seems to agree with this when he speaks of religion as an interpretation (or misinterpretation) of a set of physio-psychological phe-

[15] R. Otto, *Das Heilige* (Gotha: Klotz,1929), p. 20n.

[16] Ibid., p. 43.

[17] E. Durkheim, *Les formes élémentaires de la vie réligieuse: Le système totémique en Australie* (Paris: Alcan, 1912), book 1, chapters 1, 3–4.

[18] S. Freud, *Die Zukunft einer Illusion*, in *Freud-Studienausgabe*, vol. IX, p. 166 f.

[19] See also R. Otto, *Das Heilige*, p. 5.

nomena.[20] This is no doubt true, but might be thought slightly to miss the point. To what extent, after all, can one hold sharply to a distinction between a feeling and an interpretation of a feeling? Do humans ever really have clinically pure, fully pre-doxastic feelings? Even if there are some basic emotional states, like anxiety, that occur without awareness of a specific object, isn't it also part of human nature, to the extent to which one can speak sensibly of "human nature" in this context, that we are constantly motivated to give experiences an interpretation? Isn't this impulse, and its partial frustration in the case of such feelings as anxiety, part of what makes the state so disorienting? Isn't it then more plausible to think that feeling/reaction/interpretation form a spectrum with unclear and shifting boundaries?

This need not imply a direct rehabilitation of the claims of theology as a set of interconnected, relatively abstract beliefs. First of all, an "interpretation" need not be fully linguistic or doxastic, but can be a form of behavior (such as hand-washing or certain other compulsions). Then, too, even if feelings naturally have a tendency to move over into linguistic form, the "beliefs" it generates might not be detachable from the original context of religious feelings and experiences in a way that would allow a traditional kind of theology to establish itself as a distinct, discursive discipline.

The third anti-theological approach focuses not so much on the origin of religion as on its goal, or end, or teleological orientation. What is most important in understanding religions is neither institutions, nor theological doctrines, nor phenomena of individual (or collective) psychology, but rather a particular human task and various attempts to discharge that task. Religion is concerned with human attitudes toward the whole of life, with the control of anxiety, the production of a sense of security, the satisfaction of the "metaphysical need," the attempt to find, discover, or construct a sense or meaning of life, etc. The attempt to give a theodicy or satisfy the metaphysical need in whatever way is what defines religion. This way of thinking about religion is completely different from that which focuses on the origin of religion in certain feelings or experiences, although reference to certain feelings of insecurity or anxiety may play a role in both approaches. It is one thing to say that an anxiety-tinged experience will give me some kind of quasi-cognitive way of encountering a nonhuman form of being, and quite another to say that anxiety might be part of the motivation I have (or "humanity" has) to set myself (or "itself") a task.

This approach centering on theodicy and the metaphysical need also is sharply to be distinguished from the traditional one which emphasizes theol-

---

[20] F. Nietzsche, *Menschliches, Allzumenschliches* §§ 108,132–41; *ZGM* III.16. In other passages (*Die fröhliche Wissenschaft*, § 353) religion is analyzed as an interpretation of a form of life.

ogy as a descriptive or explanatory ontological discipline. If the point of theodicy is that it make my world seem meaningful or allow me to accept the world (as good) despite the fact that the world contains much evil, many imperfections, etc. it is not at all clear that giving me a correct description of the world which explains most of its central features will at all serve. Nietzsche points to two very significant differences between what the metaphysical need demands and what discursive reason can provide. First, his analysis of pre-Socratic Greek culture in the *Birth of Tragedy* in intended to show, among other things, that a theodicy need not be discursive or linguistic at all. A statue of a Greek god which looks like a Greek man or woman is in itself a rudimentary theodicy; it satisfies a need we have to find order, beauty, and sense in human life.[21] Second, even in the case of discursive attempts to discover or create an existential horizon of sense for human life, the focus and structure of such attempts is different from that of traditional theology. For the theologian, the propositional content (and the truth) of assertions of religious dogma are what is essential, whereas for those who take the approach under discussion now, what is important is the aptness or suitability of certain statements to satisfy the metaphysical need or help us solve the riddle of life. Why assume, Nietzsche asks, that, for instance, appearance (*Schein*) or fiction are not more suitable than truth is to discharge the requisite function? Even if "truth," and not mere belief, is a necessary condition for satisfying religious needs, the "truth" seems here to have a functional, not, as for philosophic theology, a constitutive significance. Furthermore, even if some truth is functionally necessary, it does not follow that it must be a truth about gods. Buddhism, again, is an incontrovertible counterexample here.

All four of the approaches I have just canvased (religion as theology, as a form of social organization, as a distinctive kind of experience, as the attempted solution to the riddle of life) share in their more primitive forms a common assumption, namely that there is such a thing as a timeless essence of religion which can be formulated in a definition. Nietzsche, Wittgenstein, and Foucault have, each in his own way, subjected this assumption to massive criticism, so it is, to say the least, no longer unproblematic. As Nietzsche famously asserts: "Only that which has no history can be defined";[22] and religions, no matter what else might or might not be true of them, are eminently historical. Even at their most unitary they are configurations, contingent syntheses of historically changing elements. It is hard to avoid the conclusion that

---

[21] For the sake of simplicity of exposition I attribute this line of thought to Nietzsche because that is where most modern readers encounter it, but it is older, and can be found in a very striking form in Hegel. For further discussion of this, see "Theodicy and Art," in my *Morality, Culture, and History* (Cambridge: Cambridge University Press, 1999). Much interesting relevant material on this topic can also be found in Susan Neiman, *Evil in Modern Thought* (Princeton, NJ: Princeton University Press, 2002).

[22] F. Nietzsche, *ZGM* II. § 13.

no "definition" can give an adequate account of the sorts of things they are, or tell us how to understand them.

The definition of a concept was supposed *minimally* to give us a strict criterion for distinguishing those things to which the concept applied from those to which it did not.[23] It was to contain a specification of a property or a small and surveyable set of properties which all the positive instances of the concept have and which nothing else has which is not an instance of the concept. It is perhaps possible to give a definition in this sense of nonhistorical concepts. A triangle is always and everywhere a closed geometric figure that has three sides. Historical concepts like "religion" have a completely different structure. What we call a "religion" might not at all be any kind of unitary entity, but we might use the term to refer to a variety of different kinds of thing, each one an internally heterogeneous congeries of diverse components brought into conjunction only by the accidents of history. When we speak of "religion" we might have in mind a few instances which we hold to be paradigmatic, for instance Christianity, Buddhism, a certain idealized conception of "ancient polytheism."[24] These instances might have no common essence, no set of properties and features which they all share and which are shared by nothing that is not a religion. They might rather have at best a "family resemblance." To understand a certain religion does not mean therefore to discern in what ways the (general) essence of religion has been concretely instantiated but rather to tell the story of the events that have led to the contingent conjunction of ceremonies, forms of ecclesiastical organization, theological views, and customs which we call "Islam," "Christianity," "Baha'i," etc. If we encounter an otherwise unknown collection of practices, stylized rituals, and opinions for the first time, it will be a question of judgment whether or not we call it a "religion," and that judgment will depend on the extent to which we can perceive sufficiently important and salient "similarities" between the complex in question and the paradigmatic cases of what we call "religion." The judgment we make will not generally be "ungrounded," at least not in the sense that it will be completely random or arbitrary, or that we can give no account whatever of why it was made in this way rather than in some other way. After the fact we will be able to point to existing, not invented, similarities between the things we used to call "religions" and the new instances of this category we countenance, but *only retrospectively* will we be able to say that these similarities were relevant and sufficiently compelling to "ground" extending the term "religion" to these new cases. The philosophi-

[23] For reservations about this traditional view, see Kripke ("Naming and Necessity," in *The Semantics of Natural Language*, ed. D. Davidson and G. Harman [Dordrecht: Reidel, 1972] and the subsequent discussion.

[24] For a highly illuminating discussion of polytheism and ancient "monotheism," see Michael Frede, "Monotheism and Pagan Philosophy in Later Antiquity," in *Pagan Monotheism in Late Antiquity*, ed. P. Athanassiadi and M. Frede (Oxford: Oxford University Press, 1999).

cal discussion of religion should in any event start from a natural history of religion, just as Nietzsche's "science of morality" starts from a natural history of morality.[25]

Adopting the perspective of a natural history of the many varieties of religion makes the problem of criticism more complex than it was during the period of the High Enlightenment in the eighteenth century. If there were a unique essence of religion, there would be a clear target for philosophical criticism. If, however, a "religion" is a historically changing constellation of diverse elements, it is not so obvious where a fatal blow can be struck. There has always been criticism of individual points of religious practice, and much of this criticism can itself plausibly be claimed to arise from religious motives, and is therefore in no sense part of a radical criticism of religion itself—the Puritan iconoclasts who destroyed the stained glass in East Anglian churches certainly did not think of themselves as attacking "religion," but as attacking idolatry and defending true religion, and indeed it would be bizarre for us nowadays to try to make sense of what they were doing by viewing it as "antireligious." In the eighteenth century general criticism of religion was twofold. On the one hand, there was social criticism of the church as an institution; on the other, there was criticism of theology, as a purported discipline giving knowledge of things divine.

Criticism of established churches, theology, and the clergy is not necessarily also criticism of religion itself. "*L'infame*" which progressive thinkers in the eighteenth century vowed to root out was not the popular religious belief of ordinary Frenchmen and Frenchwomen; Voltaire, after all, thought it morally highly problematic and politically undesirable to enlighten the common people completely. Nor was abstract deism the target of the philosophers. What roused the fury of enlightened Europe was the attempt on the part of a devious and self-interested clerical hierarchy to exercise secular domination over the population through obscurantist mystification.[26] Intensive criticism of the church as a social (and thus political) institution was also an established inner constituent of various very highly developed religious movements in the West, and in no way an expression of antireligious sentiments.

The criticism of theology can see itself as the direct heir of a philosophical tradition that goes back to Xenophanes. If religion is essentially theology, and the kernel of theology is a set of dogmatic beliefs or assertions about god(s), then criticism is simple. All one needs to do is show that these assertions are

---

[25] F. Nietzsche, *JGB* §§ 186–203. Since I have discussed these methodological issues repeatedly elsewhere, for instance in "Nietzsche and Genealogy" (in *Morality, Culture, and History* [Cambridge: Cambridge University Press, 1999]) and in my "Replik" (in *Glück und Politik Potsdamer Vorlesungen* [Berlin: Berliner Wissenschaftsverlag, 2004]), this account is minimalist.

[26] See B. Constants, critism of "*réligion sacérdotale*" in *De la religion considerée dans sa source, ses formes et ses développements* (modern edition of volume 1: *Bibliothèque romande* [Lausanne], 1971), *passim*.

false or that they are groundless, or that they are "illusions" (that is, they have extra-epistemological motivation). In the first of these cases the appropriate conclusion to be drawn would be atheism;[27] in the second and third cases, skepticism, agnosticism, or some other form of suspension of belief.

There are two further complications in the case of Christianity that slightly muddy the waters. First of all, the Christian believer has a special epistemology of "faith" which is proof against certain naive forms of enlightenment criticism, such as that proposed by Hume.[28] For the Christian, or at any rate for one particularly highly sophisticated kind of Christian, the very use of the normal methods of rational argumentation in questions of religion—"rationalism"—is not the use of a "neutral" or impartial procedure but rather a stacking of the deck in favor of atheism. Only through "faith," so the Christian claims, can one obtain a proper understanding of or be in a position to evaluate the content of Christian theology. The ostensible "impartial" weighing up of arguments *pro* and *contra* is inappropriate in this area for reasons that have to do with the nature of the subject matter under discussion; even a momentary suspension of judgment is in fact a proleptic denial of the claims of theology, and thus a prejudging of the issue.[29]

Second, the restriction or even complete denial of theology, which is construed as arid speculation or scholastic dogma in the name of "living faith" is itself a recurrent, deeply rooted Christian motif. This can be seen to be operate even in the nineteenth century, when attempts by thinkers such as Ludwig Feuerbach to free Christianity from the distortions imposed on it by theology are really attempts to save religion, not to abolish it.[30]

The Christian epistemology of "faith" is a form of blackmail to which thoughtful non-Christians will feel no need to accede, but might try to assimilate for their own purposes. Thus Freud's own basic attitude in matters of religion seems to have been one of relative straightforward rationalist unbelief, but theoretically he embarked on a path of reorienting the study of religion away from the content of its dogmas toward a consideration of issues of motivation that was in some respects parallel to the trajectory of Christianity. Freud held that religious dogmas are illusions. That does not necessarily mean they are false; in many cases they are simply so indeterminate and have so little cognitive content, it makes no sense to call them either true or false. Did Lady Macbeth have a son or a daughter? If you are absolutely convinced she had a son, is that a true belief or a false belief? In any case, Freud

---

[27] Thus in the old Soviet Union there was a "Museum of the History of Religions and of Atheism" in the Church of Our Lady of Kazan (Leningrad, now Petersburg).

[28] For instance in his essay "On Miracles."

[29] See S. Kierkegaard, *Concluding Unscientific Postscript*, translated by David Swenson and Walter Lowrie (Princeton: Princeton University Press, 1941).

[30] Ludwig Feuerbach, *Das Wesen des Christentums*, in *Werke in sechs Bänden*, ed. E. Thies (Frankfurt: Suhrkamp, 1975), vol. 5.

thought, the central beliefs religious people hold are rationally completely unmotivated convictions. The reasons why people hold them have little or nothing to do with the normal reasons that operate in the rational forms of empirical belief-formation we find, for instance, in the sciences. If we were to allow the mechanisms of responsibly controlled formation of beliefs to operate as freely in matters of religion as they do in serious scientific inquiries, and were able to face accepting the results, we would have no truck at all with any form of religious belief. What disturbs the normal functioning of this mechanism is the urgency of some powerful components of our wish-structure. Religious belief, in short, is a kind of wishful thinking. We want to believe that there is an omnipotent, benevolent agency in charge of the universe, and the wish is the father of the belief.

This seems to take us back to the questions addressed in the third antitheological approach to religion. What is the task of religion? Can the need to discharge this task have any special urgency or any justificatory power? What human needs does religion satisfy? Is it even correct to approach religion from the direction of human needs? To put the point slightly differently: if we put aside the church as a social institution and also put aside theology as a purportedly cognitive discipline, what remains? Is there then anything left over as the object of a radical form of criticism of religion? What remains would seem to be what has been called variously "the metaphysical need," "the need for finding out the meaning of life," "the need for a higher orientation," or "the need for a theodicy." The full-blown metaphysical need, as it was described in the Christian philosophical theology of the early modern period, can only be understood by correctly grasping the three elements that were to be purportedly brought together when it is satisfied: (a) a metaphysical element—some account of the essential nature of reality, (b) an element of reconciliation—an account of how human life fits into the larger scheme of essential reality and why we must accept this reality, and (c) consolation— the assuaging of pain and the generation not merely of minimal acceptance, but of a positive attitude toward the world.

Although the present linguistic use of the term "metaphysics" rests on a gross historical misconception,[31] it is so deeply entrenched that it would be pedantic to object to it. The metaphysical is that which is purportedly beyond normal experience, or which refers to a reality behind, beyond, or outside of our empirical world.[32] Those who hold that all humans have a metaphysical need, believe that we have an uncontrollable urge to know what is beyond the

---

[31] "Τὰ μετὰ τὰ φύσικα" actually designates only a certain set of works by Aristotle by reference to their position in the standard ordering of his works; they are the books that come *after* (μετά) the books on physics.

[32] R. Otto speaks of the "Epékeina" of the mystic (*Das Heilige* [Gotha: Klotz,1929], p. 37). Etymologically what we now call "the metaphysical" should be more correctly called designated "the epekeinaphysical."

bounds of our everyday experience, and to find there a standpoint which is not of this world and which will allow us to see the reality in which we live and conduct our lives. Only when we see the "reality" of our lives and are able to locate them within a scheme that is not immediately accessible to everyday experience or knowable by science, can we see what meaning they could possibly have. The metaphysical need is the need for a kind of transcendentally grounded orientation in life which can be satisfied only by knowing what lies behind or beyond appearances.

The second aspect of the metaphysical need was of special interest to Freud. The orientation in life which religiously mediated access to the "world beyond" gives must also satisfy a further requirement. For Freud, human civilization imposes a very extensive set of prohibitions on all of us as a precondition of its survival. The real function of religious belief is to reconcile us, in one way or another, with the deprivations, the repression, and the forms of renunciation of the satisfaction of powerful human drives that are necessary if civilization is to maintain itself.[33] The need for a metaphysical worldview is the need for a way of coming to accept our necessarily painful social and cultural reality.

Third, it is not sufficient for religion, as it were, to tell us a metaphysical fairytale which makes everything in the world make sense to us, tells us what to do, and shows us that it all is necessary and must be accepted. In addition, a religion must offer some *positive* compensatory satisfaction, some imaginary happiness or image of possible happiness that will make up for all the real pain and deprivation we must suffer.[34] Religion must itself be or provide a positive "source of pleasure in suffering."[35]

If we then abstract from all the other aspects of religion, the various other functions it fulfils and has historically fulfilled, and consider it merely as an attempt to satisfy the metaphysical need, is it beyond criticism? There would seem to be two possible tacks a critic could take. One could try to criticize the metaphysical need itself, or the particular way in which this need is, or has been, characteristically satisfied by religions.

One might object that the first of these makes no sense. What would it mean to criticize a need? One either has a need or one does not, period.[36] That is not, however, the end of the story, because one can perfectly reasonably speak of criticism of needs in at least three senses. First of all, I can crit-

---

[33] S. Freud, *Die Zukunft einer Illusion*, in *Freud-Studienausgabe* (Frankfurt: Fischer, 1974), vol. IX, pp. 171–72.

[34] Ibid., pp. 171–72, 182, 204.

[35] Ibid., p. 216. There seems little reason to assume that all three aspects must necessarily occur together. Certainly a metaphysical account of the world as a whole need not be consoling in any interesting sense.

[36] On the concept "need," see D. Wiggins, *Needs, Values, and Truth* (Oxford: Blackwell, 1987), "Essay I: Claims of Need," pp.1–57.

icize the claim "X is a human need" (if X is not a human need). It might simply not be the case that *all* humans, as the devotees of religion claim, need transcendentally based solace. Second, one can criticize something which purports to be a unitary human need by showing that it can be dissolved into constituent parts that have little to do with each other. It isn't that there is a single need-for-consolation-through-metaphysics, but rather we have a natural human tendency to wish to see as much of the world in as interconnected a way as possible, a need for a general scheme to orient us in our life, and a need for consolation for various deficiencies, imperfections, and forms of suffering that are the concomitants of many human lives; but there is no need that these three separate things be connected in the particular way the doctrine of the "metaphysical need" requires. We don't need religion, but science, progressivist social action, and psychotherapy in varying combinations. Third, it is possible for humans to develop needs that they might have avoided acquiring, and which it would clearly have been better for them to have avoided acquiring. I can criticize a certain need, for instance the need for drugs, alcohol, or the particular kind of stimulation provided by gambling, by reference to their deleterious effect on other important aspects of human life, or I can criticize a particular person who by virtue of his or her own action develops needs that it would have been better not to have acquired, or I can criticize a society because it is structured in such a way that many people in it are not prevented from developing, or are even actively encouraged to develop, certain highly undesirable needs.

In the criticism of the metaphysical need, Nietzsche and Freud are allies. In one of his relatively early works Nietzsche analyzes the metaphysical need as a historically transitory phenomenon that arose under perfectly comprehensible conditions, but has now reached the end of its career and is in the process of dissolving itself.[37] The implication is that there is no reason now to be concerned about this development one way or the other. Rather than lamenting or trying to turn the clock back, it makes more sense to try to understand why the metaphysical has become irrelevant in the modern world. Freud's criticism is couched in the language of the scientific naturalism which he generally favored. It is, he thinks, in no way necessary to posit anything "outside" the empirical reality which science studies. Science itself is fully sufficient to give us secure orientation in life and a sense of meaning. Religious justifications for cultural prescriptions and demands can be completely replaced with no loss of effectiveness by rational ones.[38] The compulsive rigidity of religious beliefs and practices is a serious hindrance to rational conduct of life. Religious illusions are in any case a highly unsatisfactory source of

---

[37] F. Nietzsche, *Menschliches, Allzumenschliches* § 141; FW § 151.
[38] S. Freud, *Die Zukunft einer Illusion*, pp.174–79.

pleasure for intelligent human agents.[39] Freud, too, then seems to be un-characteristically optimistic: religion will dissolve itself and disappear if left to its own devices, because "in the long run nothing can resist reason and experience."[40]

Freud's argument seems to be an expression of a very strong confidence in science, human reason, and our capacity to distinguish very sharply, very clearly, and incontrovertibly between "scientific" forms of opinion-formation and wishful thinking/illusion. It also seems to rest on a very robust confidence in the psychological power of science to convince people and allow them effectively to resist the lures of the obscure and at best only partially articulated desires that lurk within us. Freud's own life shows very strikingly that it is possible for science or a "scientific worldview" to be powerful enough in exceptional cases to provide humans with all the "orientation" in life they require. The scientific worldview, however, is a worldview, that is, it is closer to a philosophical stance than to a specific scientific theory. Is the distinction between science and illusion really as clear, sharp, and well grounded as Freud seems to suppose?

"No, our science is no illusion," he writes at the end of the *Future of an Illusion*,[41] but he gives no reason for this claim. Freud himself, however, was one of those who taught us most persistently to be extremely skeptical of claims put forward like this with great conviction but *without any cited justification*. This is one point on which Freud and Nietzsche part company. Nietzsche had the highest esteem for empirical science, although he also pointed out that the systematic pursuit of scientific knowledge arose from a historically contingent "will to truth" that was in various ways problematic. It seems likely that Nietzsche would have taken the views Freud expresses when he is being philosophical as an instance of the naive faith in science Nietzsche was trying to put into question.

The term "need" is used in a number of different ways[42] of which two are immediately relevant here. First of all, it is used in a purely formal way to designate an instrumental relation that holds between some object in the world and a desire or want that I have. Thus, I "need" a Latin dictionary because I wish to discover what some word means. This is true if I do in fact wish to discover what the word in question means, if having a Latin dictionary will allow me to satisfy that wish, and if there is no *other* way in which I could equally efficiently satisfy that need in the given context—I don't know the word myself, no other Latinists are standing by to be consulted, etc. Assigning a "need"

---

[39] Ibid., p. 216.

[40] Ibid., p. 187.

[41] Ibid., p. 189.

[42] "I need" is also *sometimes* used simply to mean "I want very intensely (and do not propose to explain to you why)."

here is highly relative to a particular context. The second way in which "need" is used is one that adds to the above account that the wish or desire in question is not merely active, or even reasonable and subjectively pressing, but in some sense "vital," or that the purpose to which I wish to put the object I claim to need is urgent and objectively compelling. I will call this need in the "strict" sense. One can imagine someone denying that I really "need" a Latin dictionary—at any rate I clearly do not "need" it in the sense in which I "need" a certain amount of water each week to drink if I am not to die. In both of these cases, however, it is the instrumental structure connecting the object needed with some human wish, desire, purpose, or end that is the focus of attention in a need claim. Ascribing a need automatically marks out a sphere of utility, because there is nothing so "useful" as that which one needs. The category of the "useful," however, extends beyond the realm of that which anyone "needs" in the strict sense. I can find things "useful" that are not essential to my well-being, provided that they subtend to promoting recognizable purposes or satisfying comprehensible human desires.

Religion and Critical Theory have in common that they both deny that "utility," that fundamental category of the Enlightenment, ought to have universal dominion over human life.[43] The sacred is in no way useful, or, at any rate, not "useful" as humans can understand the term, and the religious separation between the realm of the "taboo" and the profane sphere of everyday objects that can be used ad libitum sets a limit to utilitarian forms of thinking. Magic is (empirically poorly supported) action directed toward clearly utilitarian goals, but this is precisely what is thought to distinguish it from religion. Religious actions are supposed not to be either useful or useless, but rather to belong to a sphere in which this distinction makes little sense.[44] The metaphysical need, its supporters claims, cannot at all be understood through categories like those of the "useful" or the "instrumental." It is not useful to experience the need and the need is not for anything that is "useful," certainly not for anything that is instrumentally useful. The appropriate categories for the metaphysical need are those of meaning, sense, and value; it is a need for that which has inherent meaning and value *in itself*. The metaphysical need is a need to participate in that which is inherently meaningful, not to use anything in any way. Presumably this would be one of the grounds on which a religious person would reject Freud's analysis and Nietzsche's. Freud, the religious person would claim, reduces the notion of finding inherent meaning in

[43] G.W.F. Hegel, *Phänomenologie des Geistes* (in *Werke in zwanzig Bänden* [Frankfurt: Suhrkamp, 1970, vol. 3]), pp. 414–19. See also G. Bataille, *Théorie de la religion*, ed. T. Klossowski (Paris: Gallimard, 1973).

[44] B. Malinowski, "Magic, Science, and Religion," in *Science, Magic, and Reality*, ed. J. Needham (New York, 1925). It is in fact also true that in many societies it is difficult to distinguish sharply between what we would call "religious" and what we would call "magical" practices, but that is not directly relevant to this discussion, which concerns *our* system of categorization.

life to that of finding mere empirical orientation in the world; a purely scientific worldview can perhaps give the latter, but not the former. Nietzsche, the religious person will claim, misunderstands completely by assuming that meaning can be *created* by us, rather than found or discovered, but, there is a contradiction in thinking humans can create the kind of meaning they need, since it is an inherent property of that kind of meaning that it can only be found, not created. Nietzsche, of course, would continue to hold that this begs the issue: Why assume humans can't create whatever meaning there could be?

In his programmatic statement of the aims of the Critical Theory, Horkheimer claimed that it had no interest in improving the way in which anything in contemporary society functions.[45] That, of course, is in principle compatible with thinking that what needs to be done is to replace contemporary society with another society that "functions" in an altogether superior way, and that a Critical Theory is instrumentally directed at bringing the "superior" kind of society into existence. So the opposition of the Critical Theory to narrow forms of utilitarian thinking—what is better for the functioning of *this* society, or what is useful for humans, given that they live in *this* society—does not necessarily imply a general rejection of principles of utility. This early position, as above specified, does not seem incompatible with various orthodox Marxist views, such as those Brecht affected for much of his life. The dynamic of the Critical Theory, however, was in the direction of more and more radical criticism of the whole notion of utility. To be sure, at *some* point this criticism of society will begin to ring hollow. I can ask whether one type of thermos is more useful on a trip than another, but once I begin to ask whether it is more useful for me to live or die, or for human society to exist at all or not, the question loses whatever sharp contours it might originally have had.

Although Adorno in some of his later and more hyperbolic rhetorical moments might seem to be calling for an utter rejection of any form of utility or connection with the world of instrumental reason, this cannot be what is intended. To oppose any form of utility or instrumental rationality root and branch would be just as one-sided, "undialectical," and false as to affirm Enlightenment claims about universal functionality and the absolute priority of utility. The Enlightenment makes in fact two related mistakes.[46] First, it distinguishes very sharply between two categories: (a) the "instrumentally useful" (or, "that which is done for the sake of something") and (b) the inherently valuable (or, "that which is done for its own sake"). Second, the Enlightenment develops very clear criteria for the rationality of instrumental action;

---

[45] M. Horkheimer, "Traditionelle und Kritische Theorie," in *Kritische Theorie* (Frankfurt: Fischer, 1968), vol. II, p. 156.

[46] The classical treatment of "Enlightenment" in the Frankfurt School is *Dialektik der Aufklärung*, written jointly by Adorno and Horkheimer (Frankfurt: Fischer, 1969).

such action is rational if guided by scientific knowledge which gives agents good reason to believe it will result in the satisfaction of desires or preferences they actually have. By failing, however, to give any equally clear criteria for judging what is inherently valuable, or for the rationality of that which is done for its own sake, the Enlightenment tacitly promotes or even glorifies instrumental action, and denigrates action directed at the inherently valuable. The "inherently valuable" becomes a residual category, and human desire in fact regresses to more and more undifferentiated and infantile forms. The appropriate way to resist this, Adorno thinks, is to reject the sharp distinction between action that is (merely) instrumentally useful and action that is performed for its own sake. A truly free society would be one in which this distinction had no purchase in reality and thus little cognitive plausibility. Actions would be performed both because they had useful consequences and because they were valued in themselves.[47]

To put it in the paradoxical way that seemed natural to some of the earlier members of the Frankfurt School, the utility of Critical Theory as a form of contemporary philosophizing consisted precisely in the fact that it was utterly "useless" in all the usual senses of the term, while it at the same time retained a certain inherent consistency, meaning, and intrinsic value. The same was also supposed to be true of the other two successors of Hegel's absolute spirit—art and religion. What for the rationalists of the Enlightenment, and particularly for utilitarians, was one of the main objections to religions—their apparent complete uselessness for all the usual purposes of human life—is, or at any rate could potentially be, an advantage in the eyes of the Critical Theory. Religion does not fit into the modern world of universal functionality, and thus could, under some circumstances, become a bulwark against the closed world of bureaucratic domination which resulted from the full realization of the Enlightenment project, that is, against what Adorno called "the administered world."[48]

Nowadays it is not so easy to be deeply, consistently, and relentlessly "useless" in the right way. To be really useless is not simply to drop out of the society completely into the underclass of delinquents, deviants, terrorists, or the long-term unemployed. In the larger scheme of things, as has often been pointed out, such groups clearly do have their uses. That which would be *properly* useless would have to instantiate an autonomous configuration of meaningfulness and value, and also effectively resist and maintain itself against the infinite ability of our society to assimilate and co-opt deviancy. De-

---

[47] See my "Freiheit im Liberalismus und bei Marx," in *Ethische und politische Freiheit*, ed. J. Nida-Rümelin and W. Vossenkuhl (Berlin: de Gruyter, 1998), and "Suffering and Knowledge in Adorno," essay 7, this volume.

[48] See Adorno's preface to *Der Positivismusstreit in der deutschen Soziologie*, ed. Adorno et al. (Neuwied-Berlin: Luchterhand, 1969), pp. 7–79.

spite Adorno's superficially modernist aesthetic[49] and his political suspicion of all forms of atavism, a certain susceptibility to the childlike, the historically bypassed, the archaic residue keeps breaking through.[50] Are the dusty, abandoned corners of modern life and the contemporary soul in which "religion" ekes out its thin, shadowy existence perhaps potential seedbeds for a form of human emancipation?

That religion is a stumbling block to the full development of fundamental features of modernity is not in itself a clearly sufficient reason to celebrate or even tolerate it. Not every relict of archaic times is a potential source of resistance to the present. To rehabilitate religion, Critical Theory would have to point out some distinctive features of it that have particular value. As far as I can see, the members of the Frankfurt School see two such features. First of all, religions are imaginative repositories of certain human values and aspirations which they express in a utopian form, and which humans would otherwise risk losing track of.[51] Second, religion cultivates the metaphysical need and keeps open the possibility of transcendence,[52] without which radical criticism of society would not be possible. Oddly enough, some crypto-Protestant motifs appear in this context, especially in some of the later writings of Horkheimer. The possibility of a society that would be utterly different from any we know is, Horkheimer says, not an object of any possible knowledge, only of a "longing." How is such a "longing" to be distinguished from "faith"? Is it in fact true that only transcendental metaphysics renders radical social criticism possible? If religion is no longer to have as its main task to provide comfort and consolation, but is rather to call constantly for resistance, it has become inherently political in a very definite sense. What could the political relevance of a religion oriented around "longing" be in the contemporary world?

The "classic" form of the Critical Theory developed by Adorno and Horkheimer has three characteristic features: (1) it maintains a firm grip on liberal taboos about the human subject, (2) it is committed to the continued cultivation of the metaphysical need, and (3) it exhibits a paralyzing and paranoid

---

[49] See his *Philosophie der neuen Musik* (Frankfurt: Europäische Verlagsanstalt, 1958).

[50] In *Ästhetische Theorie* (Suhrkamp, 1970) Adorno speaks of the *"Sympathie der Moderne für längst Vergangenes"* (p. 28). See also Adorno's *Beethoven: Philosophie der Musik* (Frankfurt: Suhrkamp, 1993), pp. 21–22, and my "Trauer, Hoffnung, Überdruß," *Deutsche Zeitschrift für Philosophie*, 1/2004, pp. 116–17. For a further strand of the same thing, see Adorno's *Amorbach* in *Ohne Leitbild: Parva Aesthetica* (Frankfurt: Suhrkamp, 1970), and *Negative Dialektik* (Frankfurt: Suhrkamp, 1966), pp. 364–66.

[51] See M. Horkheimer, *"Gedanke zur Religion"* (originally published in 1935, now in Horkheimer, *Kritische Theorie* (Fischer, 1968), vol. I, pp. 374–76.

[52] M. Horkheimer *"*Über den Zweifel,*" "Pessimismus heute," "Bemerkungen zur Liberalisierung der Religion,"* and *"Schopenhauers Denken im Verhältnis zu Wissenschaft und Religion,"* in *Sozialphilosophische Studien*, ed. W. Brede (Frankfurt: Fischer, 1972), pp. 122–55.

fear of instrumental reason. In all three of these respects it shows itself to be very similar to well-known properties of archaic religions. In contrast, philosophers who see themselves as the successors of Nietzsche and Foucault have no generalized fear of instrumental reason. They are willing to treat the liberal subject as one good among others, not as a fetish surrounded by a number of taboos. Finally, they have little interest in the metaphysical need except as an object of historical curiosity. This is the reason so many of our contemporaries believe that Nietzsche and Foucault are the true "progressive" heirs of the Enlightenment, whereas the representatives of the Critical Theory often run the risk, to modify a phrase of Nietzsche's, of choking while remasticating theological absurdities, or, like Habermas, of becoming the conformist defenders of the liberal social order in which we are at the moment forced to live. It must be recognized that the final demise of religion in Western societies, so confidently predicted for the past two hundred fifty years, has not yet taken place, but there seems little reason to congratulate ourselves on this. If anything, religious belief in 2005 would have to be even more wilfully obscurantist than it was in 1805 because it requires active suppression of so much of humanity's accumulated stock of knowledge and lacks the institutional support that was still intact in much of Europe in the nineteenth century. It is hard to see what the compensating benefits could be, even if one presupposes the widest and least utilitarian sense of "benefit."

9

Genealogy as Critique

I SHOULD LIKE TO ADDRESS the issue of "genealogy as critique" in terms of the question about the relationship between theory and praxis, between knowledge and its supposedly binding power. In the context of modern philosophy we can distinguish at least three basic types of critique which effectively correspond to three senses of the word "critique" itself.[1]

In an everyday sense the term "critique" describes a specific form of conduct, with two characteristic features, which I may adopt with regard to someone or something. In the first place, the term in this sense possesses unambiguously negative connotations. I am not criticizing a specific position if I merely ask for further clarification, for example, or if I offer additional arguments for the relevant position, but only if I assume a negative stand towards the latter. In the second place, I cannot be said to "criticize" a certain position if all I do is simply repudiate or oppose it. In order to exercise criticism I should also have to be able to say what I am objecting to and why, i.e., to provide reasons for my repudiation. But demanding, proffering, and accepting reasons, or repudiating them as the case may be, is a specific social language game, which may assume this or that particular form, and may be institutionalized with various degrees of strength. What counts as a valid "reason" or "ground" for something in a legal-juridical context may be quite irrelevant in the context of a literary or philosophical discussion. In the language game of proffering grounds and reasons, the processes of justification and critique usually function as reciprocally and internally related acts; they are, as it were, mirror images of each other. Justification implies the presentation of positive and convincing grounds and reasons; critique implies the effective presentation of negative ones.[2]

Translated by Nicholas Walker. I am particularly grateful to my Cambridge colleague Zeev Emmerich for some illuminating discussions of the questions explored in this essay.

[1] The word "critique" derives etymologically from the Greek verb *krinein*, meaning to distinguish, separate, or divide. In the ancient world the substantive *kritikē* was used in a very broad sense to designate a considerable range of cognitive abilities and accomplishments. "Critique" in this original sense therefore signifies "analysis" or "the (theoretical) breaking down of a given phenomenon into its elements." Cf. Liddell, Scott, and Jones (1968), Ritter (1971), Wissowa (1980), for the relevant entries under *krinein* and *kritikos*.

[2] Apart from the developed language game of justification familiar in the legal-juridical context, there is also the different but related usage encountered in aesthetic discussion. As a "critic" I may review a play without coming to a negative verdict. I may find it excellent and lavish ex-

For centuries philosophers have attempted to generalize "critique" in this everyday sense. This development reached an initial culmination in the Enlightenment, and most particularly in the philosophy of Kant. And this brings us to the second sense of the concept of "critique." Kant speaks repeatedly of the "Tribunal of Reason" before which all the "conflicts" of theoretical and practical reason alike are to be properly addressed. The juridical metaphor, the idea that the quest for authentic knowledge resembles a legal process of some kind, originally goes back to Plato[3] and characteristically permeates the entire Kantian argument. As in the case of juridical procedure, the conclusion of this trial aimed at discovering truth is a verdict that claims binding force.[4] This kind of legal process conducted before the Tribunal of Reason is essentially understood as something that possesses universal and absolute validity and binding force. At the same time, "critique" for Kant signifies the investigation of the limits involved in the proper use of reason, and thus the self-legitimation of reason in its juridical function within the limits as so determined.[5] One should not underestimate the significance of Kant's concept of systematicity for the entire structure of his theory: all experience is accommodated within a *single* system that is subject to the legitimate competence of the Tribunal of Reason itself.[6]

Critique in the first everyday sense is therefore a way of denying or saying no to something. For this reason it is implausible to suggest that Foucault understood his own works as "critical sciences" (in this everyday sense). We should rather assume that he intended to adopt the Nietzschean posture that finds expression in a remark from the *Gay Science*: "Let *looking away* be my only negation! . . . for I wish only, one day, simply to be a Yes-sayer."[7]

But how can we really entertain general reservations about saying no? Is not this capacity so fundamental and indispensable that no "objections" to it

---

travagant praise upon it, etc. My evaluation need not therefore be remotely negative, but it must, if it would be taken seriously, be supported with reasons. The language game involved in demanding, proffering, and accepting reasons is rather differently structured in this area compared with the legal-juridical context. For I may analyze the positive aesthetic characteristics and the weaknesses of the piece without actually coming to a straightforward definitive conclusion like "the piece is good/is bad."

[3] Plato (1961), 170d, 201 b/c.

[4] Cf. Kant (1933), B24112, where the objectivity of knowledge is defined explicitly in relation to the idea of "compulsion."

[5] The "judging function" consists, remarkably enough, precisely in acting *legislatively* here.

[6] This summary account ignores the fact that for Kant there are actually *two* different realms of validity involved and therefore *two* Tribunals of Reason as well: that of theoretical reason responsible for adjudicating empirical experience in general, and of the natural sciences; and that concerned with pronouncing the moral verdict of pure practical reason. It is not possible to pursue this complex of issues in the present context. But in both cases we are presented with internally unified and comprehensive realms of validity.

[7] Nietzsche (2001), 157 (§ 276).

could ever be ultimately convincing? However that might be, the most powerful objection is surely this:[8] to deny or reject something (at least in certain contexts) is to participate in a language game of proffering and accepting reasons and grounds, for negation or denial is a specific move in such a game. But what if one already harbors certain fundamental doubts concerning the language games of grounding, critique, and justification? What if one attempted to avoid, or undermine them, to call them into question, or perhaps suspend them? Kant believed that there was nothing of relevance outside the competence of pure reason, that it was impossible to undermine reason itself by calling it into question; or more precisely: that the very attempt to do so would logically lead to the sort of transcendental reflection that reveals the absolute and universal validity of the rationality implied in science, morality, and the associated language game of grounding and justifying. But what if this Kantian claim itself were nothing but another example of dogmatism? Is there perhaps simply a historical variety of different games of justification that do not constitute a single unified system?

How can I escape the jurisdiction of such processes of justification, or assume a position outside or beyond this realm? One possibility is the utopian activation of fantasy and imagination. If I compose some utopian novel or utopian piece of theatre, then I do not necessarily have to get involved in a discussion of knowledge claims and their justification, etc. Aristophanes's play *The Birds* (*Aves*) is not a systematic or scientific work but a Nietzschean "turning away" from the contemporary reality of Athenian life. This is a way of "thinking differently" (*penser autrement*), though it is one whose practical implications are very hard to determine.[9]

There is a passage where Foucault speaks of the "ethos of enlightenment"[10] and interprets it precisely as the questioning of all givens. To question something is naturally *not* necessarily to reject it. Foucault distinguishes this "ethos" very sharply from the Kantian attempt to define and determine

---

[8] There are also two other possible grounds for skepticism here. In the first place, one may raise objections to the negativity of this approach per se. One can thus claim that it is unattractive, fruitless, and exhausting to be *purely* negative because an exclusively negative response merely fetters human energies rather than releasing them (see Badiou [1998]). In the second place, there are certain objections with characteristically Hegelian rather than Nietzschean overtones. Someone whose *sole* purpose is the negation of an existing given can easily become entirely fixated on the latter. Negation can render us dependent upon what is negated and is therefore not always compatible with the pathos of total liberation from the experience of oppressive positivity. Since Foucault has little sympathy for projects of "radical liberation," it is rather improbable that objections of this sort carry any weight with him.

[9] This is not equally the case with all of Aristophanes' comedies. Thus I presume that one would have to evaluate the relationship to praxis implicit in works like *The Acharnians*, *The Birds*, and *The Frogs* in a different manner in each case.

[10] "Qu'est-ce que les Lumières?," in Foucault (1994), 571–78.

an all-encompassing, self-grounding realm of legitimate competence for pure reason. While we can and should preserve the ethos of enlightenment, the program of transcendental grounding is obsolete and should therefore be abandoned.

A comparison with Husserlian phenomenology may help to clarify the theoretical situation as I see it here.[11] Simplifying matters considerably, we may distinguish two fundamental elements in phenomenology. In the first place, Husserl presupposes, like Kant, that human experience forms an infinite but unified field for potential investigation, one which has the transcendental ego as its intrinsic correlate. In the second place, Husserl develops a method designed to encompass this field effectively in epistemic terms. The heart of the method is the so-called *epoché*, the systematic and universally applied procedure of bracketing, neutralizing, or suspending all reality claims in a specific domain precisely in order to facilitate the pure description of the phenomena that thereby remain for inspection.

Foucault wants to reject the first element of Husserl's program entirely. There is no transcendental ego, nor is there any valid realm of pure reason capable in principle of encompassing the whole range of empirical experience in a unified fashion. But he does wish to preserve the second element, namely the *epoché*, in a modified form. He has no intention of introducing his *epoché* in strictly universal fashion within the framework of an abstract philosophical investigation of the foundations of knowledge, but only intermittently and always in the limited context of a specifically defined project of historical investigation, although the word "historical" must be interpreted broadly enough to include the present in its purview as well.[12] The impossibility of providing a self-grounded legitimation of reason in no way implies a nihilistic view of our own cognitive resources. Language games of justification are themselves various and contingently produced forms whose emergence and disappearance must be identified and traced historically. In no way does it follow from this that they are somehow "invalid." What is more, the critical ethos of enlightenment, as it is understood by Foucault, is better seen as a tireless encouragement to go beyond the alleged limits of reason than as an attempt somehow to limit the exercise of the latter. And this also suggests another reason why any closure or systematicity in the Kantian or the Husserlian sense

---

[11] "L'intellectuel et les pouvoirs," in Foucault (1994), 750.

[12] The term "historical" signifies both (a) "singular" (in contrast to "universal") and (b) "related to the past (and not the present)." At the beginning of the Western tradition of historiography, in Herodotus for example, the first sense is actually the principal one. The Greek word *"historia"* generally simply signifies "research" or "inquiry" into something. Thus alongside investigations that are purely historical (in the modern sense), the historiographical writings of Herodotus also contain geographical studies, ethnological materials, myths, fragments of a theological character, political observations, etc. In the following discussion "historical" is understood in this broadly classical sense.

is already ruled out as impossible. Art, and especially literature, can contribute to the enhancement and consolidation of this ethos, but the transgression of limits attempted in Foucault's work is also intended to raise a potentially cognitive claim.

These reflections thus yield our third sense of "critique": critique as a way of putting into question or problematizing something. What does such a critical process look like concretely, and how does it effectively proceed? The principal targets of this problematizing approach are the apparently self-evident assumptions of a given form of life and the (supposedly) natural or inevitable and unchangeable character of given identities.

The existing language games of justification and legitimation are never entirely isolated and autonomously self-contained practices. On the contrary, they intersect with other language games, they perhaps harbor a certain potential for further reflection, and they are embedded in broader sets of practices. The latter sometimes facilitate the process of critique, but not every *potential* for reflection that is given in principle is *actually* realized in every particular case.[13]

Any given language game of justification and legitimation rests upon a complex structure of practical habits and routines. The regulated exchange of argument and counterargument, of reasons for and against, proceeds all the more smoothly the more the "self-evident" rules are tacitly observed by the participants, and the more the participants are acting in the context of well-established, pre-given, and apparently secure variables. Here I should like to offer a deliberately extreme example, and one that Foucault did not explicitly discuss in his own writings: that of an ecclesiastical court of the Middle Ages. The successful functioning of such a court presupposes a range of beliefs then regarded as self-evident, like the absolute truth of the Christian gospel and its saving message, and the necessary division of all human beings as orthodox Christians (or proper Catholics), heretics, and pagans.

The traditional philosophical discussion of Christianity, whether critical or apologetic, primarily investigates the truth of the Christian doctrine, or the potential justification of the Christian faith. These traditional investigations tacitly presuppose that something like Christianity already exists as a unified, internally coherent, given phenomenon that presents itself as an object for possible discussion. Genealogy is designed to render precisely this presupposition problematic.

To offer a genealogy is to provide a historical dissolution of self-evident identities. If we remain with our example, it is to place in question both the

---

[13] One should not interpret "reflection" here in a narrow idealist sense of the term. Over and beyond the pure and exclusively self-related movement of spirit itself, "reflection" can also signify the revision of our accustomed modes of thought in the light of new attitudes to life and fresh empirical knowledge.

identity of the ecclesiastical court and that of the parties presented before the court (as "sinners" for instance). The genealogy of Christianity is a historical analysis of the processes through which Christianity resulted from the inter-play of forces in time. Genealogical attention to the role played by contingent relations of power in the genesis of Christianity, including Christian dogma, for example, intrinsically serves to destroy the semblance of self-evidence and immediate givenness that attaches to it.

A genealogy is obviously not a critique in the everyday sense mentioned above, that is to say, it does not automatically imply the rejection of what is subjected to genealogical analysis.[14] Genealogical critique is not directly con-cerned with the binding truth or falsity of a first-order claim or proposition. It is therefore not interested in knowing, for instance, whether sinner George feels due contrition for his transgressions or not. To ask that question is to conceal the relevant genealogical question. What we want to know is: how do concepts like "contrition," "sin," "punishment," and "church" come to be binding and universally applied to all?

This is a question for which *neither* an empirically or hermeneutically ori-ented theory of knowledge *nor* any mere historical analysis of concepts can provide a relevant answer. The concept of "sin" relates perhaps to a clearly identifiable complex of modes of behavior and human reactions. It may be that George actually does feel "sinful." "Sin" therefore possesses a certain *fun-damentum in re* which survives normal empirical critique. George may well be deceived in falsely believing that the ecclesiastical court will pardon him, but he is not deceived in the same sense when he feels himself to be a "con-trite sinner." This latter identity is constructed, but it is not purely imaginary. "Sin" and "contrition" can thus possess an eminently *somatic* reality, which cannot simply be dissolved into a variety of concepts, convictions, attitudes, and perspectives. The genealogical question asks: how has a specific histori-cal process led human beings to develop and embody this sort of identity? Such a process is more than a series of episodes in which external forces shape the passive human being *ab extra*, for the emergence of a historically effec-tive identity also requires certain processes through which human beings "freely"[15] shape themselves. The genealogical task is directed towards nar-

---

[14] Some other remarks of Nietzsche seem particularly appropriate in this context. In book 5 of *The Gay Science* (§ 345) he writes: "These historians of morality (particularly, the Englishmen) do not amount to much. . . . Their usual mistaken premise is that they affirm some consensus among peoples, at least among tame peoples, concerning certain moral principles, and then con-clude that these principles must be unconditionally binding also for you and me—or, conversely, they see that among different peoples moral valuations are *necessarily* different, and infer from this that *no* morality is binding—both of which are equally childish" (Nietzsche [2001], 202–3). Nietzsche was therefore perfectly aware of the false step involved in what is generally called the genetic fallacy, and we can safely assume the same level of insight in Foucault too.

[15] Like Nietzsche, Foucault is firmly convinced that the concept of freedom, and any actual ascription of freedom, is always dependent upon some specific context.

rating this history as completely as possible, that is to say, with due attention to as many of the relevant aspects as possible.

Genealogy involves an indispensable historical element,[16] but one may well ask why such genealogical inquiry demands fresh historically detailed and specific analysis in each case. Why is it not sufficient simply to offer a single decisive abstract argument for theses like "everything is contingent," "there is no intrinsically necessary identity," "everything self-evident requires a prior framework"? To see why that is not enough, we must understand the internal relationship between genealogy and praxis correctly. As we have seen, genealogy is not conceived as critique in the everyday sense. It is not meant to encourage human beings to repudiate what is subjected to critique or even to regard it simply in a negative light. In a late interview Foucault says he was concerned with claiming not that "x is false" or "x is bad," but rather that "x is dangerous." The dangerous is what we must *preeminently* concentrate attention upon, what we must *before all else* take care to consider. The dangerous can indeed be attractive or even valuable, but in cases of acute danger, the aforementioned Nietzschean attitude of "looking away" is not always the best strategy. Genealogy as pursued by Foucault, on the other hand, is a way of concentrating attention on a given situation in the context of an imminent danger. The discrimination of what is more dangerous from what is less demands detailed historical presentation of the specific case.

Nietzsche speaks of the philosopher as lawgiver. Genealogy does not lay down the law, nor is it a policing discipline. Rather it is a summons to develop an empirically informed kind of theoretical imagination under the conditions of perceived danger.

In contemporary philosophical discussion the concept of normativity (along with the now almost automatically raised question concerning the "normative implications" of every theoretical proposal) is surely the most important "self-evident" notion that must be put in question. Foucault's work can be interpreted as an initial contribution to a genealogy of normativity,[17] and his writings will remain highly relevant until such time as the task is fulfilled.

References

Badiou, A. (1998). *L'éthique: Essai sur la conscience du Mal*. Paris: Éditions Hatier.
Foucault, M. (1994). *Dits et Écrits*, vol. 4. Paris: Gallimard.
Kant, I. (1933). *Critique of Pure Reason*. Translated by Norman Kemp Smith. 2nd ed. London: Macmillan.

[16] See footnote 12 above.

[17] Such a genealogy would naturally represent the exact opposite of Korsgaard's undertaking in Korsgaard (1996).

Korsgaard, C. (1996). *The Sources of Normativity*. Cambridge: Cambridge University Press.

Liddell, H. G., R. Scott, and H. S. Jones. (1968). *Greek-English Lexicon*, Oxford: Clarendon Press.

Nietzsche, F. (2001). *The Gay Science*. Translated by J. Nauckhoff and A. Del Caro. Cambridge: Cambridge University Press.

Plato (1961). *Theaetetus*. Translated by F. M. Cornford. In: *Plato*. *The Collected Dialogues*. Princeton: Princeton University Press.

Ritter, J. (1971–2000). *Historisches Wörterbuch der Philosophie*. Darmstadt: Wissenschaftliche Buchgesellschaft.

Wissowa, G. (1980). *Paulys Realencyclopädie der classischen Altertumswissenschaft*, neue Bearbeitung begonnen von Georg Wissowa, fortgeführt von Wilhelm Kroll und Karl Mittelhaus, unter Mitwirkung zahlreicher Fachgenossen, herausgegeben von Konrat Ziegler. Munich: A. Druckenmüller.

10

Art and Criticism in Adorno's Aesthetics

WHEN ADORNO LOOKED BACK at theorizing about art in the nineteenth and early twentieth centuries he saw it as dominated by a struggle between two tendencies.[1] There was a strand associated with Kant which put great emphasis on the autonomy of art and the irreducibility of aesthetic judgments to any other kind of judgment. Art followed its own laws which it gave itself: in particular, one couldn't evaluate a work of art *as art* by such criteria as whether it gives a good imitation of reality, whether it has contributed to social progress, or by moral criteria. Usually this claim that art is autonomous was taken to mean that art produces distinctive "forms" that are inherently significant and worthwhile, and that the experience of these "forms" is in all relevant respects self-contained. Obviously art arises only in a certain social context, but any attempt to relate art to anything outside the aesthetic experience itself—the experience of a certain response to formal properties exhibited by the work—and thus in particular any attempt to relate art to society or history is at best a case of missing the point or changing the subject (for instance, from experiencing a painting to doing art history), and at worst a serious confusion. The claim that art is autonomous in that it is governed by rules and laws which it gives itself is taken to imply a formalist normative aesthetics, that "good" art is good by virtue of its satisfying form.[2]

The second tendency can be associated with Hegel. One can see this line of argument as distinguishing between art in the common everyday sense and what Hegel calls "art 'in its highest human vocation.'"[3] Everyday art is the

I'm very grateful to Zeev Emmerich, Hilary Gaskin, Susan James, and especially Mark Sacks for comments on the contents of this paper.

[1] Actually there is also a third which emphasizes "expression" as the central aesthetic category. This becomes indirectly important for Adorno through its influence on the way Schönberg thought about what he was doing, but it plays little direct role in Adorno's more reflective theorizing.

[2] The "autonomy of art" can mean at least two analytically distinct things. First, it can be a sociological thesis about whether "art" is established in a certain society as a separate realm of human endeavor not subject to outside interference; second, it can be a thesis about the existence of standards of judgment and evaluative principles of a certain kind. It is natural to think that these two things will usually go together, but the fact that they don't in reality is one of the more interesting features of human history. It is also not self-evidently incoherent to claim that art is "autonomous" in that it has its own distinct criteria and standards while denying that the appropriate autonomous criteria refer merely to the *form* of works of art.

[3] Hegel (1970), vol. 13, pp. 20 f and 240 f.

skillful production of sensible appearances that engage humans' attention in various ways, give them pleasure, perhaps serve various utilitarian goals, etc. Art in its highest vocation, however, must be seen as a competitor to philosophy and religion (in their respective highest vocations), that is, art is to be seen as a potential way of reconciling humans to their society as a whole by telling them the truth about that society and causing them to see their world and the lives they are able to lead within it as worthwhile and good. To be more precise, art "in its highest vocation" must, according to Hegel, do two things at the same time:

> **1.** it must tell us the truth or bring us to a correct awareness of our (natural, historical, social, and political) world;
>
> **2.** by telling us this truth it must bring us to affirm our world as a fundamentally worthwhile place in which to live.

Only when these two elements come together successfully does one have "art" in the full sense. This isn't a return to the form of moralizing art criticism Kant rejected because the task of exhibiting the world to people as worthwhile is one that is in some sense "beyond" the realm of ethics altogether. To use Hegel's technical terminology, art belongs to the realm of "absolute spirit," while law, ethics, and politics are matters of objective spirit.[4] Art doesn't directly tell us what to do in the way a legal code or a set of moral precepts or guides to successful living do; it doesn't issue specific or general positive injunctions or imperatives, nor does it dissuade us from possible courses of action, nor even, finally, does it, like Socrates' inner voice, issue determinate warnings in particular cases without citing grounds. Since none of these things is part of art's essential vocation, moral criticism of art is adventitious. Art's essential task is to make clear to us how to understand the general (natural and social) framework within which we must act and live, and to help us to adopt the correct general attitude toward that framework. This general attitude, Hegel thinks, should be one of affirmation. That art is by its very nature socially affirmative is, for Hegel, no reason to be suspicious of it, because, after all, he thought that the world and the life humans could lead in it were (at any rate in the Europe of the early nineteenth century) essentially (and demonstrably) good. This part of Hegel's philosophy, however, created difficulties when his general scheme was taken over by Young Hegelians who did not share Hegel's thoroughgoing optimism. If one does not agree with Hegel that there is a metaphysical guarantee that the world is in order, but thinks rather that essential social and political reforms need pressingly to be carried out, then one can ask the question whether it is always such a good idea for people to come to affirm their social world, and be reconciled with it.[5]

---

[4] Hegel (1970), vol. 13, pp. 134–39.

[5] Hegel uses the term "reconciliation" to mean not just a grudging acceptance of the world as

For reasons like these, many of the Young Hegelians believed that full affirmation of nineteenth-century Central European society as it was would be inappropriate, but Adorno's objections to modern society go far beyond the criticisms formulated by even the most radical of the Young Hegelians. Marx, for instance, attributes the deficiencies of the modern world to an inadequate realization of the accepted principles of rationality, a failing which is to be explained by the needs of the present capitalist system to defend existing forms of economic privilege. What is wrong, that is, with capitalism is that by the middle of the nineteenth century it is no longer a maximally efficient and productive mode of economic organization. The basic idea of rationality as, roughly speaking, economic efficiency is not called into question in this analysis. What society needs is to be made more rational by having its underlying economic structure changed fundamentally, and this can be brought about by abolishing capitalism so as to allow society to extend and develop its powers and attain greater efficiency and productivity.

In contrast to the rather sober, scientific analysis Marx gives of the economic limitations of capitalism, Adorno holds that our society is not just less rational and economically productive than it could be, but is *radically* evil and doesn't deserve in any sense to be an object of affirmation. His grounds for this view seem ultimately to be not economic, but metaphysical or religious in nature.[6] Adorno puts particular emphasis on one aspect of Marx's theory, namely his criticism of the universal commodification which is characteristic of modern capitalist society; everything in such a society is a potential object to be bought or sold at a price which is only contingently related to its underlying use-value. This "contingency" can be seen as a kind of proto-irrationality. Adorno thinks, however, that the universal commodification analyzed by Marx is itself merely the superficial expression of a deeper-lying principle which he calls "the Enlightenment," and it is the Enlightenment, and a specific conception of rationality which is constitutive of the Enlightenment (and which Marx shares), to which Adorno objects.[7]

---

it is, but a process which terminates in a strongly and affectively affirmative attitude. For further discussion of "reconciliation" as a central Hegelian concept, see Michael Hardimon (1994).

[6] In correspondence with Walter Benjamin (Adorno [1994], p. 324) Adorno speaks of his own theological impulses. It isn't completely clear how to read this. Benjamin had an esoteric view of the relation between materialism and theology, and Adorno had an odd fixation on Benjamin. Perhaps Adorno actually did hold views like Benjamin's and was just letting the esoteric cat out of the bag in these letters to a fellow-adept, or perhaps this is just another part of his attempted intellectual seduction of Benjamin, which in this case was operating by pretending to a position closer to the one he thought Benjamin had than was actually the case, in order the better to prize Benjamin away from the dangerous views of Brecht (which Adorno took to be instances of "vulgar materialism") and attach him more firmly to Adorno's person and theoretical position.

[7] Subject to certain qualifications, such as that his criticism of the Enlightenment is to be correctly understood as a form of internal self-criticism of the Enlightenment project and not a return to some purported pre-Enlightenment state. In what follows, I am not going to be as care-

The Enlightenment project can be seen as having two components: first of all, a substantive commitment to certain ideals of human life—certain principles of humanity, noncoercion, rationality, the right of individuals to pursue their happiness; second, a particular view about how these goals can best be attained, namely by the systematic pursuit and implementation of a certain kind of knowledge. The Enlightenment construes the knowledge in question as having a number of interconnected properties. For present purposes we can distinguish three: (a) the Enlightenment takes genuine knowledge to be "identifying" knowledge, i.e., it assumes that knowledge is increased by finding general concepts under which individual things can be subsumed: something is considered to have been "identified" (and thus to be "known") if and when it has been brought under an appropriate general concept, and different instances of the same general concept can within limits be treated as if they were "identical" (i.e., one instance of a general concept can be substituted for any other under appropriate circumstances); (b) the Enlightenment takes genuine knowledge to be inherently instrumental, that is, to be the kind of thing which gives its possessor the ability to control the environment; and (c) the Enlightenment takes "meaning" to be essentially a category that is to be defined relative to the identifying, instrumental knowledge described in (a) and (b).[8] For a variety of complex reasons, Horkheimer and Adorno believe that "instrumental reason"—the pursuit of greater and greater control over the world through the accumulation and implementation of "knowledge"—has an inherent tendency to absolutize itself and to undermine the attainment of the substantive goals of Enlightenment. The ideals of the Enlightenment can't show themselves to be "rational" if "rationality" is *defined* as instrumental rationality, and the growth of scientific knowledge and associated instrumentally rational forms of industrial, commercial, and bureaucratic organization in fact undermine the actual ability of people in the modern world to attain individual happiness, self-determination, etc. In the final analysis, then, instrumental reason is the cause of the discrepancy between the paradise the human social world could be (given our technological possibilities) and the proto-Auschwitz it actually is.[9]

Associated with this general Enlightenment approach, Adorno claims, is a view of human society which takes it to be a set of homogeneously interchangeable parts. A society in which the characteristic views of the Enlightenment were fully and consistently implemented would be a society of uni-

---

ful as I should about distinguishing between "the Enlightenment," "the Enlightenment project," "instrumental reason," and even "positivism."

[8] In the first instance, Adorno seems to have in mind the verification theory of meaning in one or another of its early positivist forms, but he thinks this particular formulation was just an especially consistent development of a fundamental tendency of Western thought and society.

[9] This topic is treated at greater length in *Dialektik der Aufklärung* by Adorno and Horkheimer (1944). On the contrast between paradise and Auschwitz, cf. Adorno (1970a), p. 55.

versal fungibility. Nothing would be uniquely just what it was; nothing would be "for itself" but only for something else. Work of any kind would not be experienced as a specific activity of a qualitatively distinctive kind—gardening, sewing, washing dishes, distilling liquor, etc.—but just as a sequence of activated or exercised or invested units of abstract work-time, and a unit of work would be "for" the basket of subsistence goods that could be purchased with the wage one received for the work (and would in that sense be "identical" with any other unit of work of equal magnitude, qualitative differences being considered irrelevant). In such a society even a piece of coal would exist and be seen to exist (only) "for" the amount of energy that could be extracted from it, the amount of currency it would command if sold, etc. Any piece of natural scientific reasoning or of straightforward means-ends calculation, Adorno claims, can finally be seen as an attempt to enforce this universal commensuration.[10] The ills of modern society result from the unreflective institutionalization of Enlightenment conceptions of rationality; Marx, because he still accepted the Enlightenment concept of reason and its associated baggage (including a productivist ethos) without question, in one sense made the problem worse rather than solving it.[11]

If we accept for the sake of argument that our social world is evil, and that this evil has something to do with the dominance of instrumental reason, a number of immediate consequences follow for art. First of all, any form of art (or of religion or philosophy for that matter) that contributed to trying to make people affirm this world or think that life in it was worthwhile would not just be doing something unhelpful, but would be misguided in the most fundamental way possible. Such a form of art would be, as it were, "sinful." Just as in Christian doctrine "original sin" did not designate the individual trespass some particular person had committed, but referred to a basic corruption of the will that infected *any* natural form of human willing, so to live in a modern society is to live in a state of social corruption that is tantamount to sin. Any art which made us comfortable in the fallen and sinful state of our world as a whole, would be at least a quasi-moral failing. In a radically evil society one task of art must be to make people more consciously unhappy and dissatisfied with their lives, and especially to make them as keenly aware as possible of the dangers of instrumental rationality and of the discrepancy between their world as potential paradise and their world as actual catastrophe. Hegel, according to Adorno, was right to think that art had a higher vocation than just to provide entertainment, moral improvement, or even low-level criticism of specific social evils à la Dickens, but in Adorno's view that voca-

---

[10] The idea that to categorize two things as "identical" is to be committed (at least tacitly) to trying to *make* them become identical is one Adorno held very deeply, cf. Adorno (1966), pp. 147–61.

[11] For Adorno's view of Marx as trying to turn the whole world into a huge Victorian workhouse, cf. Adorno (1951), § 100.

tion is to be radically critical—negative, not affirmative. Hegel, however, was also right to think that art has an inherent tendency to be affirmative, that being affirmative was part of the "concept" of art.[12] Even the most critical art gives us *some* pleasure, and to take pleasure in art is to be close to being open to the possibility of affirming the society in which this pleasurable experience is possible. The implication Adorno draws from this is that for art to be *socially* critical in an appropriate way, it must be aesthetically radical, i.e., it must radically and to some extent successfully struggle against its own tendency to affirmation. It can do this, Adorno thinks, only if it is *formally* negative or critical. Eventually this notion of being "formally negative" will be explicated to mean that the work of art in question must internally subvert traditional aesthetic forms.

In addition to sharing a sense of the "high vocation" of art, Adorno is also deeply committed to another Hegelian doctrine, namely the view that philosophically serious criticism must be "internal" criticism. If I am a utilitarian and Joan a fundamentalist Christian, and we disagree on some policy issue, I may well criticize Joan on the grounds that her position on this particular issue is not one which will lead to the greatest happiness of the greatest number. This sort of thing is the bread and butter of everyday life and politics, but in a certain sense it is philosophically superficial (which doesn't, of course, mean that it might not be terribly important in some practical contexts). It is a form of what Hegel calls "external criticism": I bring the principle of utility to bear on Joan's position from "outside" that position. We have no reason to expect Joan to be impressed by what I say, because as a Christian (I assume) she doesn't share the (utilitarian) principle on which my critical evaluation is based. If I take a strongly and explicitly utilitarian tack with her, I won't just be making a mistake in rhetoric and thus failing to convince her, but I will have made a serious lapse of rationality by failing to be philosophically critical in the full sense. Joan will be *right* not to be impressed if all I can give her is an argument from premises she doesn't accept. The "internal" criticism at which philosophy should aim must take the form of arguing against Joan's policy by appeal to principles which are extracted from her own position, i.e., by appeal to principles to which she herself can in some sense be shown to be committed. Usually this will mean engaging in some complex reconstructive work to extract from the fundamentalist position some principles implied by it but which the fundamentalist may not antecedently be aware of holding. All social criticism for Adorno (and thus also the social criticism implicit in art) should have the form of such "internal" critique.

I have spoken rather blithely up to now of a work of art as "being critical," or "telling a truth," of "correct" forms of consciousness in art, of art as producing correct awareness of society, and of the "meaning" of a work of art.

---

[12] Adorno (1970a), p. 10.

This suggests some very strong claims about the cognitivity of art. However, Adorno also believes that this "meaning" and the "truth" that are at issue in art are not the kind of thing that can be grasped by the categories of "instrumental reason." Given that "instrumental reason" is construed in a very all-encompassing way, so as to include most of what we would usually think are paradigmatic cases of knowledge, it isn't at all obvious what this noninstrumental kind of cognition that art is supposed to give us might exactly be.

First of all, the claim that art should be critical or negative does *not* mean for Adorno either of the following: (a) art should be a form of propaganda directed at motivating people to engage in any specific form of political action, (b) a work of art is in some way "equivalent" to a proposition or has a propositional structure. The "internal" reason for (a), i.e., the reason from within Adorno's own general theoretical conception, is that if art really were a form of direct propaganda, it would stop being autonomous and become a thing for which instrumental forms of calculation might become appropriate, that is, one could then judge what was a good work of art by reference to its effectiveness as an instrument for social change. If art just was propaganda, one might even try to investigate in the usual empirical ways just how effective various different artistic forms were in producing whatever political action was deemed desirable, and the one that worked best would be the best form. This would reduce or eliminate art's autonomy and subject it to the categories of instrumental thinking. If instrumental thinking, though, is the root of the evil in the modern world, extending it in this way to one of the few spheres that still escapes its grasp is not a plausible strategy for helping art attain its highest vocation. This is the source of Adorno's criticism of some of Brecht's views.[13] Just as Brecht would have thought that someone like Dickens was insufficiently radical—by criticizing individual social evils while leaving the general capitalist framework of society unquestioned, Dickens could be thought tacitly to have contributed to the solidification of capitalist society—so Adorno thinks Brecht insufficiently radical, because by putting art in the service of revolutionary propaganda, he construes it as essentially instrumental. Art that conformed to the Brechtian canons would not give us sufficient distance from the main structural source of evil in our world and thus would not be genuinely progressive. As far as (b) is concerned, to think that a literary work of art is equivalent to a propositional statement is one of the more widely canvased forms of philistinism—as when the Duchess in *Alice in Wonderland* says that everything has a moral—and it seems difficult even to imagine what could be meant by claiming that a work of purely instrumental music could be equivalent to a proposition.

Works of art for Adorno are inherently useless objects which present an

---

[13] Brecht's *views* but not necessarily his actual theatrical practice, which, Adorno admits, was more sophisticated.

"image" (*Bild*) of a kind of meaningfulness and freedom which society promises its members but does not provide. The fact that art is both something many people find meaningful—even if it isn't clear what "meaningful" means—and yet something which by most of the standards of everyday life is useless, is already for Adorno a good sign, because it violates the Enlightenment principle of universal functionalism, that is, the principle that everything must be useful for something, and that the meaningful and the functional are inherently connected.

Adorno's most detailed account of the way in which a work of art can be said to present an image of freedom is to be found in his discussion of the freedom of the compositional subject in music.[14] He takes over from Hegel as his basic model that of a subject, a composer, who in trying to compose something confronts what Adorno calls alternatively an "object" or "the musical material." The composer will have certain skills, aesthetic predilections, and spontaneous reactions to musical configurations. The "material" the composer faces, is, as Adorno repeatedly states, not to be understood as a physical magnitude or a pure, acoustic phenomenon, but rather as comprising everything composers in the historical period in question have before them, including pre-given forms (inherited from previous compositional activity): "*die Tonalität, die temperierte Skala, die Möglichkeit der Modulation in vollkommenem Quintenzirkel [und] ... ungezählte idiomatische Bestandteile [der] musikalische[n] Sprache*" (*Gesammelte Schriften* 16.503). The basic claim now is that this material *itself* can be seen to have an inherent structure, exhibit tensions or tendencies, or even make demands. In the late nineteenth century there is a certain tendency toward expressive use of chromaticism. One can use this vocabulary of tensions, demands, etc. precisely because the "material" is not just neutral acoustic data, but the sedimented result of previous compositional activity including, as it were, the unfulfilled aspirations of previous composers (in the face of what they were able to accomplish with the historical material which they had at their disposal). Now *if* the composers in question have fully developed compositional powers, this will be partly because they have fully internalized the traditional material and associated practices, expectations, aesthetic preferences, etc., and this means that their own *spontaneous* reactions to the material will themselves "naturally" run in the direction of the "tendency" of the material itself.[15] In this happy state there will be a conformity between the inherent tendencies of the "material," what the "material" requires or demands (roughly, "objective" necessity), and what composers spontaneously want and like (roughly, subjective freedom). Doing what the material demands will not be experienced as conforming to exter-

[14] For instance, in his "Vers une musique informelle," now in Adorno (1978).

[15] Although, of course, in another sense there will be nothing "natural" about this at all. It will be an instance of what Hegel sometimes calls "second nature." Hegel (1970), vol. 7, pp. 301 f.

nal coercion or pressure, but as acting on one's own inmost spontaneous impulses; in this state, then, the composing subject will attain Hegelian freedom, finding itself "at-home" in its "other," the material.

This sounds very conformist, and so it is important to add that Adorno assumes that part of the demands the material makes, and correspondingly part of the spontaneous need a composer who was well brought up in the tradition will have acquired, is precisely a need for originality, for producing something new. This means, however, that the composer will be trying precisely *not* merely to write note-perfect specimens of works that satisfy all the acknowledged rules of one or another of the existing genres, but rather to write something both novel and unique. Ideally a composer with any ambition does not try to write a fugue just like the ones Bach wrote or, for that matter, just like what any later composer will write. The only way for a composer to be "like" Beethoven (in the sense of "like" which is finally decisive for aesthetic evaluation) is by writing works that don't sound anything like anything Beethoven *wrote*, because part of what it is to be "like" Beethoven is to write music unlike any previous music. Another way of putting this is that the composer can be seen as trying to violate a version of the principle of identity which is embedded in the traditional practice. This aspiration to uniqueness will at some level have to fail because absolute uniqueness, noncomparability with *any* other work of music, is not, I think, conceivable,[16] but Adorno is unmoved by the necessity of failure—in a way, everything that is most important in life is a necessary failure, after all—and he seems quite clearly to think that the aspiration itself is more important than the successful execution of it, and even perhaps in some sense sufficient. As he remarks in an oft-cited passage: "The new is the desire for the new."[17] Obviously it will be a contingent but tremendously important fact about a certain artistic tradition that it does inculcate a taste for the unexpected, the novel, and the original.

Now, Adorno adds, this coinstantiation of what the material "demands" and what individuals would spontaneously want is, or at any rate can be interpreted to be, an image of a utopian state of human society—where the demands of material life in the form of what we all need to do to live coincide with what we would spontaneously want to do. Furthermore, in some sense every human society, or at any rate any "modern" society (where "modern" means, roughly, "any European society between 1750 and 1950") tacitly appeals to the coincidence of these two in order to justify itself. That is, all modern societies feel the need to give a systematic justification of themselves to their members (and others), and in some sense all such systematic justifications can in the final analysis be seen as versions of the claim that the given social institutions and practices are justified *because* they are the nec-

[16] Marx (1983), vol. 3, pp. 425f.
[17] Adorno (1970a), p. 55.

essary framework for allowing maximal realization of freedom in this sense, i.e., maximal coincidence of what necessity requires with what people spontaneously want. If a given modern society can't quite summon up the self-confidence to claim that it has fully realized the coincidence of human wishes and material necessity, it will at least claim that it is striving as best it can (under unpropitious circumstances) to attain a state in which such freedom is maximally realized. All such claims, in non-utopian circumstances, and certainly in early twentieth-century capitalist societies, are unfounded. Obviously it is a very strong quasi-empirical claim that an important part of the self-legitimation of societies, or at least of nineteenth- and early twentieth-century Western capitalist societies, has taken this form, and it is an equally strong quasi-empirical claim that such self-legitimation fails. The suggestion made above that this particular form of self-legitimation might be limited to Western societies "between 1750 and 1950" is a proleptic reference to some important changes which Adorno believes have taken place in Western societies (and therefore also in the situation of art) starting in the middle of the twentieth century; I will discuss these changes and their significance later in this essay.

The work of art has "meaning" by virtue of its structure or form—this progression of sounds is a symphony or a fugue or a passacaglia or whatever. It criticizes our society by juxtaposing its own image of successfully realized unification of subjective spontaneity and objective necessity with the false claim our society makes that a similar unification of spontaneity and necessity takes place in our basic social institutions, too. The work of art thus causes us to confront in an unmistakable way the contrast between the two cases and thereby makes us very vividly aware of the shortcomings of our society and its utter inability to justify itself even on its own terms. It brings us to a correct awareness or tells us a truth by virtue of being a sufficiently fascinating and at the same time sufficiently irritating artifact that we are motivated to keep trying to interpret it, and a proper interpretation will take the form of the kind of account I have just given. The interpreted work of art, it is claimed, is a form of cognition because it tells us about what the (social) world is *really* like, what its real deep-seated nature is—it is radically evil in the ways specified—but a work of art is also not a form of cognition that accords with Enlightenment canons of rationality because it isn't empirically based in any recognizable way, won't let you manipulate anything in the world better, is not connected with any direct imperatives to action, and is striving to be utterly unique and escape from any kind of identificatory thinking.

There is one final twist of the dialectic which takes art to the very brink of utter self-dissolution. The modern world is so sinful that it has lost even the possibility of criticizing itself radically by confronting itself (through the work of its artists) with a utopian image of perfect freedom, to which it might appeal even if it could never fully attain it. Although Adorno never explicitly puts it in exactly these terms, one can understand his position best, I think, by attributing to him the view that art progresses through four stages, which can be roughly related to historic periods. First there are forms of art which are the simple, unmitigated glorification of what is—exemplified perhaps by the hyper-Homeric art of ancient panegyric: the deified Emperor is the ideal image and the reality of happiness, virtue, and goodness, and the panegyricist need only point this out. Then there is the Hegelian (and, according to Adorno, Beethovenian)[18] form of art as an affirmation of our world's sense conditional upon its realizing a set of ideal demands, which are potential sources of legitimacy and are expressible in utopian form (i.e., in an image of the ideal good life). These demands are at least in principle distinct from empirical reality so that it is an achievement to have realized them. Art affirms our social world on the grounds that our society is *fundamentally* oriented toward and striving to attain ideal freedom and happiness, and has to a very large extent—although not (yet) in *all* details—realized the most fully developed state of freedom and happiness which could reasonably be expected. This form of art is historically appropriate to the optimistic period of the rising bourgeoisie just after the French Revolution.

The third stage is the Schönbergian crisis in the early part of the twentieth century in which the split between the increasingly horrible world-as-it-is of incipient monopoly capitalism, on the one hand, and the residual images of the good (of human happiness and freedom) which society continues to project as part of its attempt at self-legitimation, on the other, has become infinite and seems utterly unbridgeable. The sense of desolation in works like *Erwartung* is an expression of the infinite unattainability of any real freedom and happiness in our world. To experience our state as one of desolation, however, implies that we still have some grasp of what a qualitatively better world would be like, even if the image we have of it is only negative: that it is *not* like this world in some essential respects. The freely atonal music of the final movement of Schönberg's Second String Quartet was originally experienced as especially disorienting precisely because people in 1908 still had a very clear sense of what it would be like to live in the unproblematic world of permanent C major.

Finally (in the fourth stage) the very idea that society *needs* or could conceivably have any justification of itself in terms that went beyond a mere redescription of itself (perhaps redescription of itself as slightly larger-than-life, with slightly larger GNP, level of consumption, more Olympic gold medals, etc.) becomes increasingly incomprehensible, and society loses its grasp altogether on *any* normative image of a qualitatively "better world" relative to which it could be evaluated. This development begins, roughly, after the First

---

[18] Adorno always emphasizes the similarity between Beethoven and Hegel, *cf.* Adorno (1993), pp. 31–46, 73–80.

World War and gains momentum after World War II, culminating in a form of society which is nothing but brute self-justifying fact. In such a situation art turns against its own ability to produce soothing images, aesthetically pleasing appearances, unified works, and produces formally fragmented and jarring "negative utopias,"[19] as in the work of Beckett. His negatively utopian works are the most radical forms of social criticism, because they confront a real society—ours—with its own inability to produce even an authentically convincing image of a possible utopian state to which that society could in any way be related, even if that "relation" was one of trying to live up to the utopian standard and failing.

It is slightly confusing that Adorno uses the term "negative utopia" in two slightly different ways, and also uses the term ("negative utopia") in one of its two senses to describe both a characteristic feature of the art of the third period and a rather different feature of art in the fourth period.

"Negative utopia" is ambiguous as between: (a) a dystopia, a (real) society which as a whole is irremediably bad, i.e., evil through and through, as bad as it can be, and (b) the idea of a society which is ideally good, which idea is however wholly without a clear specification of a positive content. Specifically modern art (i.e., art in the third and fourth stages) should be negatively utopian in both senses, i.e., it should show that the world in which we live is as bad as could be—because it is—and also show that the only (utopian) hope is for a society which we can characterize only negatively—all we can say about such a society is that it would be radically different from the one we now have. Adorno thinks that the works of Schönberg in his most radical period (the third stage) and those of Beckett (the fourth stage) are of this type. Still, there is a subtle difference between the two. Schoenberg presents a sinful world infinitely incapable of realizing a utopian state (which can itself be conceived only negatively, as radically different from our real state); Beckett, a world which is incapable even of conceiving that there could be any (even negatively specified) utopian state outside itself relative to which it could be judged.

A further reason that specifically modern art can present only a negative rather than a positive utopian vision (in the second sense) is that there has been a historical shift in the function of utopias: to the extent to which they do still exist at all, they have become dangerous in a way they were not before. Traditional art contained positive and contentful utopian elements, such as the vision of freedom, justice, and solidarity at the end of *Fidelio* or of community at the end of Beethoven's Ninth Symphony. Now, in the early twenty-first century, such positive utopian elements must be treated with the most extreme caution, because we have the technological powers to try to realize them fully all at one go. In fact they should be avoided altogether because of

---

[19] Adorno (1970a), pp. 55 f, 348.

our experience that attempts at the full implementation of them in the twentieth century have been a series of nightmares: the Nazi ideal of a perfectly homogenous ethnic community or the Soviet ideal of a classless society. In our historical period, then, it is appropriate for us to return to and strictly enforce the biblical prohibition of "graven images," that is, not to elaborate in detail any positive image of a utopian society.[20]

As I have already mentioned, Adorno thinks that radical social criticism depends on aesthetic radicalism, on working one's way out of an artistic tradition which must be sufficiently intact to give the new work a clear "meaning," but which the work itself must formally undercut. Art can be fully successful in the right way only if it remains true to its vocation and history. The history of art is one of increasing emancipation from all extra-artistic purposes, and in the modern world cultivating this autonomy turns out *also* to be the most effective way to be radically critical of society. Art is critical through its form.[21] The most radically negative kind of art would be one which did two things at the same time. First, it would, through exclusively artistic means, turn the most fundamental received laws of a certain kind of artistic activity upside down or inside out, and do so precisely by treating these received laws, principles, and rules of procedure with the highest seriousness and developing them consistently in a nonarbitrary way into their opposite. Second, a fully radical form of art would be one which by its internal negation of the artistic tradition also succeeded in inculcating into people an appropriately cognitively grounded negative attitude toward their own society.

This is the significance, for Adorno, of Schönberg's progress from Romanticism to atonalism. Romanticism was committed to some principles of musical expressivity and originality; it was also committed to the tonal system. Schönberg's development "shows" that this is an inconsistent set of demands and by showing this, tacitly criticizes Romanticism (and also, indirectly, the bourgeois society of which Romanticism is an expression): the tonal system had by the end of the nineteenth century become so "exhausted" that the expressivity and, in particular, the originality Romanticism demanded of music couldn't be attained by using tonal means. Taking the extreme chromaticism of late Romanticism "further," as earlier Romantics had taken existing earlier forms of chromaticism "further," eventually meant loss of the sense of tonal center altogether, and then abandoning the tonal system itself. In a way, Schönberg can be seen as merely drawing out the consequences of a historical situation, as showing that nineteenth-century music was tending to undercut, subvert, or destroy itself. That this is the case is part of the power and significance of his music.

---

[20] Adorno (1966), pp. 202 ff.

[21] "*Wodurch sie [i.e., die Kunst, R. G.] aber, als erkennende, richtet, ist die ästhetische Form.*" Adorno (1958), p. 119.

The sense in which Schönberg's music "shows" the inconsistency of Romanticism (and certainly the sense in which Schönberg's music can be said to criticize bourgeois society) is not one that will reveal itself if one simply considers any particular work of his fully on its own, in complete isolation from its historical context, and studies *just* its immediately perceptible properties, or analyzes its formal structure, although adequate understanding will, of course, require exact analysis of the formal structure as *part* of the overall interpretation. To appreciate the critical force of Schönberg one has to know the musical tradition and its place in wider social history and hear his music as part of that history. One has to hear that history itself as making demands or asking questions to which Schönberg gives what Adorno thinks can only be described as "the correct" or "the necessary" or "*verbindliche*" answers in his works. For anyone who is liable to listen to Schönberg's music seriously, though, this does not require going outside "the music itself" and bringing to bear some extraneous bits of learned lore, because in some sense the history of Western music is already in our ears, in their accumulated habits and expectations of hearing. If this wasn't the case, not only would we fail to see Schönberg's music as critical, we would fail to be able to make sense of it at all. To the extent to which we are knowledgeable about music, it will be because we are a part of this tradition and have built up the appropriate habits and expectations, and so, to some extent, we will be able to react to Schönberg's criticism without needing to have it explained to us. As competent auditors, we will recapitulate with our ears the freedom of which the music is an "image." In one sense early audiences may not have "understood" Schönberg's music. *Ex hypothesi* a certain kind of freedom and spontaneity of perception is required to follow genuinely *new* works of art, and this is just what contemporary people are prevented systematically from developing, because the general structure of society discourages any form of spontaneity. Early audiences' reactions of perplexity then were comprehensible—Schönberg's music is that complex and runs counter to some deep-seated habits of listening—but in another sense the Viennese public in 1913 understood Schönberg all too well. They didn't just dislike his music; it outraged them and inspired in them an active violent hatred. The shock, horror, and rage with which the music was received makes good sense if one assumes that earlier audiences did realize in some sense that their whole society and form of life were being assaulted.

Still, assault is not quite the same thing as internal criticism. Adorno also thinks that art needs philosophic interpretation as its necessary complement to develop its critical impetus into full-blown truth-telling,[22] and *this* need is not construed as a denigration of art's autonomy. If one wants a full and adequate understanding of Schönberg's music, it isn't enough to have an internal

---

[22] cf. Adorno (1970a), pp. 391, 193 ff.

analysis of the structure of whatever piece is under consideration and an account of how it developed out of the music (and society) of the nineteenth century, but one must go on to the kind of speculative discussion Adorno gives of the way in which the work of art fits into the philosophical history of failed attempts at emancipation in the West.

So the answer to the question how art can tell a truth, create awareness, etc. is that a work of art is by its very nature inherently irritating/stimulating and requires for its correct understanding and appreciation a process of interpretation. This interpretation will start from an account of the way in which the work internally exhibits "freedom" while at the same time radically negating various traditional practices (by turning them inside out), and then move on (eventually) to a historically based critical theory of our society. Furthermore, it isn't just the work of art in some undifferentiated sense, but specifically the *form* of the work which has this effect. What we call the "form" of a work of art is the locus of a kind of rationality—the highly precise and sophisticated kinds of musical analysis that are possible make this clear, Adorno thinks, beyond reasonable doubt, at any rate for music as an art—but this rationality is also sufficiently distanced from *instrumental* reason to allow, and indeed induce, radical criticism of the social world. The "interpretation" of a work of art is not a gratuitous addition, because the work itself demands interpretation in order fully to discharge its vocation; but the work of art can also have some kind of proto-critical effect—the *actual* effect of distancing people from their society—even when they can't give the full correct interpretation.

This seems to generalize tremendously from a highly peculiar individual case—Schönberg's music. For Adorno there is nothing wrong with this. He thinks there is a very determinate sense in which certain contemporary artistic practices can be said to be the technically most advanced ones, and the most advanced present artistic practice *should* throw light on all forms of art, including all art of the past. In a way, Adorno isn't looking for correct general theories, but for something like ideal types to guide aspiration. That is why Adorno says that "exaggerations" are the truest parts of a theory of society and culture.[23]

Adorno wants to deviate systematically from what he takes to be one of the main goals of traditional philosophy, which is to get a set of definitive theories that are atemporally true of the world, that is, that are as much as possible like a certain conception of theories in natural science—water has the properties it has at all times and places, and a good theory of it would formulate those properties. Whatever the merits of this kind of approach to the natural world, Adorno is interested exclusively in the human social and cultural world. He claims that this world is significantly constituted by history,

[23] Adorno (1951), §§ 82, 128.

and that a philosophy that wishes to engage with cultural and social phenomena in an illuminating way must reflect that fact and be radically histori-
cized. Furthermore, at least at higher stages of human cultural development,
the "objects" under investigation won't just be "historical" in some indefinite
sense, but will be constituted in part by particular human ways of theorizing
about them. So in some sense one won't be able to look at art (or religion or
the state) without at the same time looking at people's theories of art. Art, the
state, the prevailing forms of human motivation, religious belief, aren't the
same everywhere. Art, in particular, is constituted by certain human practices
that change over time, so it makes sense to try to incorporate some awareness
of this into one's theory of art.

This doesn't quite mean what one might think it means, namely that no
generalizations about the nature of art are at all possible—Adorno makes
general assertions himself all the time, and indeed it is hard to see how one
could systematically eschew making them—but it does mean that purportedly general statements about art should be made with an appropriate reflective awareness of their limitations. They should be seen as arising in a particular historical context and as referring primarily to an intended specific
historical situation, usually the present. When Adorno speaks of "art" he really means—and he knows he means—Central European music and literature in the period between 1770 and 1955, and he knows he is interpreting
that body of art in the light of his experiences in a Europe under the shadow
of fascism. That is the art that is most directly relevant to Adorno, and it is
both appropriate and unavoidable for him to have it primarily in mind. When
we make generalizations about "art," including art from as long ago as the neolithic period, we are seeing these generalizations to some extent through the
lens of what art has become for us; if art had had a different history—and,
presumably it could have had—we would see that neolithic art differently.
Neolithic cave painters couldn't have been expected to be trying either to affirm their society or to criticize it, although *we*, looking back at them and their
activity through our own concerns, may have no alternative but to look for
those aspects of their practice which eventually lead to the development of
the possibility (and necessity) of criticism.

Part of Adorno's reason for rejecting the Enlightenment and its notion of
rationality was fear of the repressive homogenization of the world which he
felt to be implicit in the Enlightenment project, a fear that motivated him to
try to defend what he called "the nonidentical": the unique, the qualitatively
specific, the unrepeatable, the "other," that which cannot simply be seen as
just one more indistinguishable specimen of a general category, interchangeable *ad libitum* with any other specimen. This "other" is that which slips
through the network of our concepts and theories. Art was to be a place where
the unique and unrepeatable could be experienced, and the task of philosophy was to mobilize the "otherness" and "nonidentity" of art for purposes of

radical social criticism. This strand of Adorno's theory, however, stands in a certain tension with his commitment to Hegel's dialectic and the Hegelian principle of "internal criticism." It isn't at all clear that Adorno was ever able to show effectively how experience of the "other" could coexist productively in a critical project that was basically structured by the Hegelian dialectic. The term "dialectic" is used by different philosophers in a variety of different ways, but the main characteristic of dialectic in Hegel's sense is that it is a speculative, retrospective ordering of the elements of a historically *closed* system, and tells a story which has an absolutely fixed and determinate end/goal: *us*.[24] Although any number of philosophers since Hegel have tried to reconfigure dialectics as open-ended, directed toward the future, perhaps even practical (rather than "speculative"), it is at least an open question whether any of these attempts has been successful.[25]

Concretely, the price Adorno pays for construing art as essentially a way in which a historically given society reflects on itself, either admiringly or critically, and for his commitment to the Hegelian principle of "internal criticism," is a difficulty in giving any plausible account of the possibility of appreciating the art of other societies. It isn't perhaps an accident that Adorno not only exhibited no interest whatever in any art except the recent art of Central Europe, but seemed to be as actively hostile to any attempt to engage with non-European forms of art as the Viennese public was to the original performances of works by the Second Viennese School. If the Viennese couldn't tolerate the "new," Adorno seems to have at least equal difficulty in accepting the "other": anything outside the musical and literary tradition to which he had been introduced as a child.[26] He was particularly scathing in his rejection of jazz as a possibly significant form of music[27] and expressed nothing but contempt for what he called "*Negerplastik*" even when it was a case of a Western artist like Picasso turning toward African masks for inspiration.[28] One philosophical reason for this, I think, is that one needs a coherent, highly self-conscious tradition, like that of nineteenth-century Viennese music, and

---

[24] Hegel (1970), pp. 12–13, 26–28. I discuss this issue at greater length in "Form and 'the New' in Adorno's 'Vers une musique informelle,'" in Geuss (1999).

[25] I can't even begin to deal adequately with this issue here, but I would like to point out that Adorno's complete disengagement from the world of praxis makes it especially difficult to see how he could get beyond Hegel's essentially speculative form of dialectics.

[26] Note that he was aware of this and had theoretical reasons, which he thought were derived from Benjamin's theory of childhood as a source of privileged access to experiences of meaningfulness and happiness, for failing to try to outgrow this. Growing up, as Hegel knew, means distancing oneself from such experiences and learning to deal with things that don't fit into the categories derived from them. The emphasis on retrospectively justifying such immediate childhood impressions leads to some of the more implausible parts of Adorno's *Beethoven* (1993, see pp. 21–22, and also Adorno [1994], pp. 344–45).

[27] cf. "Über Jazz," in Adorno (1964), pp. 84 ff.

[28] cf. Adorno (1958), pp. 136 ff; cf. (1951), § 32.

moreover one which takes itself and is taken by others in society with the utmost seriousness, if one wishes to give determinate sense to the idea that a
work of art could have a meaning that went beyond what was revealed by an
internal analytic specification of its formal properties. Another reason Adorno
might have given, though, is that the historical story one must tell about
progress and regress in order to have a proper understanding and appreciation of art, for instance in order to understand that Schönberg's music represents the self-dissolution of a certain European bourgeois tradition, must be
a *Whiggish* story, like the Hegelian one, at least to the extent that it must be
one that leads up to *us* by a series of steps that have a kind of retrospective
inevitability. One must see the work as having been produced by "one of us,"
another artist who stands in the *same* tradition in which one has oneself been
trained, for notions of *self*-affirmation, i.e., affirmation of our own society by
itself, or of internal *self*-criticism, to have application. If art is not to degenerate into entertainment, it must have an existential dimension, and it can
have that for us only if the drama it enacts is our own; and it must have a rational dimension, which means that the resources used in the criticism must
come from *within* the society and its traditions.

Here, however, as so often elsewhere, the question arises of who "we" are.
How far does the "we" extend? Who is included, who excluded, and on what
grounds? No given society, and no social "we," was ever as closed as the dialectical story must make out, and although this may not terribly matter if the
story is a retrospective one, it is of crucial importance if what is at issue is a
contemporary world considered under the perspective of a possible future,
whether that future is the future envisaged in various forms of political action
or the creation of a work of art of a kind that doesn't exist yet.

For Adorno the limits of sympathetic identification with the extra-Euro-
pean were narrow. Conceivably that was just a personal failing, but it is one
whose effects are exacerbated by the Hegelian framework Adorno uses. Still,
a satisfactory account of the critical use of art, and of the nonidentical in art,
can't just ignore the role of such things as African masks and *gamelan* or treat
them dismissively as Adorno does.

I began by contrasting Kant and Hegel. One way of putting Adorno's final
position is that autonomy and formalism are not a priori properties of all art
and of all artistic experience, as Kant thought, but historical features that have
developed in contingent ways. They also can't in themselves be strictly considered to be either wholly good and progressive developments or wholly bad
and retrograde developments. An appropriate analysis will find elements of
both good and bad in them (and won't be able to separate the two cleanly). I
have emphasized the positive features of autonomy, but Adorno, especially in
his later writings, is equally forthcoming about ways in which he takes autonomous art to have been complicit in the horror of history. Adorno unre-
servedly endorses Benjamin's claim that "every document of civilization is at

the same time one of barbarism."[29] The fact, though, that autonomy has historically had a tarnished origin in the unjust separation of manual and mental labor and has been used for good and bad ends is no argument against it, because of the overwhelming importance that is to be attributed to the possibility that art might satisfy its "highest vocation" (i.e., to radical criticism). Adorno believes that for art to serve its highest vocation (i.e., roughly, to do what Hegel thought it properly could and should do, at least at certain historical periods) it must retain its inherent autonomy and commitment to formalism (i.e., roughly, must hew close to the line centrally sketched out by Kant). We may, of course, wish to separate more clearly than Adorno does: (a) the vocation of art (either Hegel's positive one or Adorno's negative one), (b) formalism, and (c) autonomy (in various senses).

Hegel did to some extent acknowledge this distinction between autonomy, formalism, and the vocation of art. He held the view that art "as far as its highest vocation is concerned" was for us (that is, for Central Europeans at the beginning of the nineteenth century) a thing of the past,[30] but he also believed that this was a historical advance in that it meant that art stopped trying to do something it really couldn't do adequately in the first place. Adorno thought that Hegel reached this conclusion because of his inappropriate focus on the plastic arts (and thus on sensory appearance as an essential feature of art), rather than on the more abstract art of music. The "end of art" (in its highest vocation) didn't in any case for Hegel mean that there would be no more autonomous art, or that art would stop satisfying the highest formal canons. Nor did he think that it meant that art would become just a form of entertainment. Nor for that matter would he have thought that good entertainment was inherently heinous.

I have claimed that Adorno wanted to embed some Kantian themes about the importance and centrality of aesthetic form in a basically Left Hegelian philosophical view: a strictly formalist aesthetics isn't required by the inherent nature and invariant structures of the human cognitive apparatus, but it can be the most appropriate way for art to attain its highest vocation under certain historical circumstances. This doesn't, of course, mean that he wants to get a dialectical synthesis of Kant and Hegel. To think about it that way is to revert to Hegelian "positive" dialectics, where the synthesis overcomes in thought previous contradictions. Adorno assumes Marx was right to hold that contradictions often result from the real state of the world and can't be overcome through conceptual means alone. The best thing to do about some contradictions is to realize that they are rooted in the way the world is, and observe them, rather than trying to resolve them. The tension between Kant's view about formal freedom in the aesthetic experience and Hegel's concern with the histor-

---

[29] W. Benjamin (1955), p. 254.
[30] Hegel (1970), vol. 13, pp. 140 ff.

ical vocation of art is, I assume, one Adorno thinks reflects a real contradiction in our fallen world. The appropriate way to deal with it is not to try to get a "resolution" at some higher dialectreal stage, but to recognize Kant and Hegel as the two poles between which reflective activity must tack. Perhaps the use of the principle of internal criticism and the appeal to the "other" are similarly irreducible poles between which reflective criticism must move.

Adorno accepts a version of the end-of-ideology thesis—this is one of the implications of the distinction between stages 3 and 4 (see above)—that is, he recognizes that it is in fact correct that ideologies have lost their bite in the twentieth century and become both implausible and ineffective. This would be a good thing if it resulted from the fact that we had succeeded in constructing an ideally free utopian society, but as things stand it is a regrettable development. No matter how distorted some past ideologies were, and no matter how much real oppression they legitimized, they did at least provide some resources for forms of radical criticism of society. Perhaps Christianity was a racket that taught people to accept social oppression, but it did so through reference to certain standards of justice, love, brotherhood, etc., and these provided at least the possibility of a critical view of society. What he fears most is the aesthetic equivalent of the end-of-ideology. The total elimination of the autonomy of art of the kind that threatened it when Adorno was writing (i.e., in 1950) was that of the systematic reduction of all art to entertainment. Since any art that does not attempt to satisfy its highest vocation (by criticizing our society in an appropriately radical way) is morally reprehensible, destruction of the autonomy of art would be unmitigatedly bad. One might argue that it makes sense to think that entertainment is inherently reprehensible only if the position from which art could exercise its highest vocation is in some sense accessible. If it isn't, then the automatic devaluation of entertainment lapses. The question is what "accessible" means. For Adorno, as I have said, in the study of cultural phenomena impossible aspirations are in some sense just as important as realities. Art may reach for a kind of uniqueness *it* will never attain, to a fully noncommunicative autonomy, etc., even if those ideals are inherently unrealizable. I assume Adorno would apply a version of this doctrine here. Art is a necessary failure—it can't fully occupy a high ground from which it could realize its highest vocation, but the vocation is nonetheless important, and as such gives us good grounds for the denigration of mere entertainment.

That Adorno recognized the impossibility of this project perhaps explains the hopelessness of his position in the last years of his life. It has sometimes been said that the late Adorno "retreated" from the world of politics and action into the contemplation of art, but the situation for him was even more desperate than that would suggest, because there was no *inherent* aesthetic sphere into which he could really withdraw. Schopenhauer had the view that art was "timeless" and so he could end his ethics with a call to engage in contemplation of this timeless world. For Adorno, as for Hegel, however, art is necessarily in time and related to an audience, and, in contrast to Hegel, for Adorno "all art is *new* art,"[31] so if there is no avant-garde with the appropriate qualities, this affects *all* "art." It isn't just that no new art is produced, but "old" art remains as it was, as a set of objects of loving but socially irrelevant contemplation; rather, there is *no* art at all (in the emphatic sense), because part of what it was to be art in the emphatic sense was *not* to be socially irrelevant. So there is no coherent aesthetic sphere into which Adorno could retreat, but only the doomed attempt to recapture that wonderful avant-garde moment around the First World War when art could be a metaphor for society and Schönberg could speak of his compositions as "emancipation of dissonance" and associate that with real political emancipation. Adorno's whole philosophical work is an attempt to think through that equivalence between aesthetic radicalism and political progressiveness.

From the naive empirical point of view the equivalence just doesn't seem to hold. To stay with composers of whose work Adorno was aware, and adopt, as far as possible, the standards of aesthetic quality and political correctness Adorno would have used, the correlation between "progressives" in music and genuine opponents of instrumental reason seems no more than random. The politically most robust and heroic opponent of fascism was Bartók, for whose music Adorno can muster at best a kind of grudging acceptance as the work of an artistic also-ran, but no enthusiasm.[32] If recent research is correct,[33] the most rigorously consistent student of Schönberg and the man whose music in some way epitomized the modernist avante-garde, Webern, was, shall we say, a less than wholehearted opponent of the National Socialist regime. One might reply that Webern's *music* was banned in the Third Reich, and that it is the music rather than Webern's personal opinions that are at issue, and his music is an *"objective answer to an objective social constellation"*[34] even if he knew nothing about society and had reprehensible political opinions. Of course Stravinsky's music, or for that matter jazz (of any kind), was banned, too. Ah, Adorno will reply, but jazz is lousy *music*. It seems to me that all this shows is that whether or not the Nazis banned a certain kind of music was no way to tell, positively or negatively, whether it was any good. Adorno, of course, at one level *does* take this point and in fact makes it

---

[31] i.e., "Kunst heißt neue Kunst," Schönberg (1976), p. 26.

[32] Adorno (1968), p. 178. (Note that I see nothing in the text printed in Adorno (1984), p. 296, that is incompatible with the account I give.)

[33] Bailey (1998).

[34] *"Während die Kunstwerke diese [die Gesellschaft, RG] kaum je nachahmen, und ihre Autoren vollends nichts von ihr zu wissen brauchen, sind die Gesten der Kunstwerke objektive Antworten auf objektive gesellschaftliche Konstellationen."* Adorno (1958), p. 125.

with all requisite definiteness[35]—after all, it is just another way of expressing the autonomy of art. What is the point of insisting that *"objectively"* Webern's music isn't just aesthetically revolutionary but also politically progressive, if that political progressiveness has no actual empirical counterpart or embodiment, if we have no reason to expect it ever to have such an embodiment, and if we can't even envisage a way of acting that would give it such an embodiment?

The answer that it would or could have such an embodiment in a messianic future seems unhelpful because it just admits the point—that there is no empirical correlation—while mystifying it, and no amount of repetition of the word "objective" will help here, either. It is hard to avoid the conclusion that to say that an aesthetically radical work of art is "objectively" politically progressive really just means (a) that it is aesthetically to be very highly valued (perhaps by specifiable "objective" criteria), and (b) that we would very much *wish* and hope that people would interpret this work in a Left Hegelian way and that this would coincide in some way with appropriately progressive political beliefs. Given the strictures against reducing art to propaganda or connecting it too closely to instrumental forms of reasoning, we can't even say anything sufficiently nonmetaphorical about what this connection is or how we hope it could be realized. This doesn't in the end seem to me an aesthetic view but a religious one.

References

Adorno, T. (1951). *Minima Moralia*. Frankfurt/M: Suhrkamp.

———. (1958). *Philosophie der neuen Musik*. Frankfurt/M. Europäische Verlagsanstalt.

———. (1964). *Moments Musicaux*. Frankfurt/M: Suhrkamp.

———. (1966). *Negative Dialektik*. Frankfurt/M: Suhrkamp.

———. (1968). *Einführung in die Musiksoziologie*. Frankfurt/M: Suhrkamp.

———. (1970a). *Ästhetische Theorie*. Frankfurt/M: Suhrkamp.

———. (1970b). *Gesammelte Schriften*. Frankfurt: Suhrkamp.

———. (1978). *Klangfiguren*. Frankfurt/M: Suhrkamp.

———. (1984). *Musikalische Schriften*. Vol. V. Frankfurt/M: Suhrkamp.

———. (1993). *Beethoven*. Frankfurt/M: Suhrkamp.

———. (1993). *Adorno-Benjamin: Briefwechsel 1928–1940*. Frankfurt/M: Suhrkamp.

Adorno, T., and M. Horkheimer (1944). *Die Dialektik der Aufklarung*. New York: Social Studies Association, Inc.

Bailey, K. (1998). *The Life of Webern*. Cambridge: Cambridge University Press.

Benjamin, W. (1955). *Illuminationen: Ausgewählte Schriften*. Frankfurt/M: Suhrkamp.

Geuss, R. (1999). *Morality, Culture, and History*. Cambridge: Cambridge University Press.

---

[35] For instance, Adorno (1964), pp. 153 ff, but also in any number of other places.

Hardimon, M. (1994). *Hegel's Social Philosophy: The Project of Reconciliation*. Cambridge: Cambridge University Press.

Hegel, G.W.F. (1970). *Werke in zwanzig Bänden*. Frankfurt/M: Suhrkamp.

Marx, K. (1983). *Karl Marx und Friedrich Engels, Werke*. Vol. 3. Berlin: Dietz.

Schönberg, A. (1976). *Stil und Gedanke*. Frankfurt/M: Fischer.

11

Poetry and Knowledge

OVER TWO THOUSAND YEARS AGO Plato spoke of an "old" disagreement (παλαιὰ διαφορά) between poetry and philosophy (*Republic* 607b).[1] This was construed by Plato as a struggle about authority. One can reconstruct his argument as proceeding in three steps:

1. Authority by its very nature must be moral authority;

2. Moral authority must be able to give a self-warranting or self-validating account of itself (λόγον διδόναι);

3. The only such appropriately self-validating procedure is a process of philosophical argumentation which is essentially informed by correct representation of the real world, and which thereby grounds itself as a form of true knowledge.

To this Plato adds a fourth step that expresses his own radical antidemocratic belief:

4. Only a small group of people with special intellectual talents will be able to attain correct representations of which they will be able to give an adequate account.

Therefore, he concludes, a small group of philosopher-kings should in an ideal world be invested with all moral and political authority. Poetry, like everything else, could count as being *inherently* important if and only if it gave a self-validating, correct representation of the real world, and only then would it have an automatic warrant to continue to exist. The poet (and the expert on poetry), however, Plato claims, cannot provide an adequate account of his activity.[2] Since, then, poetry isn't a vehicle of knowledge, it can be no more than a knack for giving pleasure—or, as we would say, a form of "entertainment."[3] Since pleasure is inherently dangerous, and giv-

This is a slightly revised and much expanded version of a paper for a symposium at Princeton University in spring 2003. I am very grateful to Zeev Emmerich, Hilary Gaskin, Istvan Hont, Nicholas Poburko, Quentin Skinner, and Cain Todd for discussions of the topics treated here, from which I have benefited greatly.

[1] The clear upshot of the discussion in Andrew Ford's marvelous *Origin of Criticism* (Princeton: Princeton University Press, 2002) is that this way of seeing the situation is anachronistic and misguided, but it has been the dominant mode of perception since the ancient world.

[2] See Plato's *Ion*.

[3] I am, of course, slightly running together here the analysis of art (in such works as *Republic*) with the criticism of rhetoric (in such works as *Gorgias* 462–66). For the purposes of this paper, that seems to me legitimate.

ing way to it clearly a moral evil, poetry requires the continual tutelage of philosophy.

Starting in the late eighteenth century, Romanticism tried to reverse this Platonic judgment. Friedrich Schlegel claimed that poetry was self-evidently a thing of self-sufficient and infinite value.[4] The young Schlegel was an admirer of ancient democracy and of the egalitarian ideas of the French Revolution.[5] The rehabilitation of poetry should, he thought, go hand in hand with the removal of authoritarian moral and political structures to which Plato gave his unconditional approval. Unfortunately, although the Romantics pursued the laudable goal of revising Plato's denigration of art, they tried to do this while still playing Plato's game by the rules he had set up. If art is a thing of infinite value, they held, that *must be* because it really is (a form of) "knowledge"; if it were *not* knowledge, it would be, as Plato thought, no more than a harmless but useless game or a promiscuous vehicle for purveying dangerous pleasure.

The idea that poetry is a form of knowledge is, however, by no means self-evident, or one to which there is no alternative; it is not even the obvious default assumption to which one must automatically revert if one finds no other plausible view. Poetry might easily be considered a form, not of knowing, but of making (as indeed the word "poetry" itself indicates), or it could be seen as a kind of performance, a mode of expression, a type of action, etc.[6] In what sense, then, could poetry be supposed to be a form of knowledge? Philosophers have distinguished three kinds of knowledge: propositional knowledge, knowledge-as-skill, and knowledge-as-acquaintance.[7] Propositional knowledge or "knowing that" takes its name from the usual grammatical form in which such a claim to knowledge is expressed: the use of the verb "know" plus "that" plus a propositional clause, as in "I know *that* Edinburgh is north of Paris." I can also say I know *how* to ride a bicycle, or to speak French; this is knowing-how or skill, usually expressed by the use of "know" plus "how" plus an infinitive.[8] Finally, I can say I know Tony or Edinburgh or the poems of

---

[4] Friedrich Schlegel, *Kritische Friedrich-Schlegel-Ausgabe*, ed. E. Behler (Munich: Schöningh, 1981), Part 1, vol. 2, 148.

[5] See ibid., 198 [= fragment 216]; also, Schlegel's *Versuch über den Begriff des Republikanismus*, in *Kritische Friedrich-Schlegel-Ausgabe*, Part 1, vol. 7, 11–25. Throughout his early writings on ancient literature he emphasizes the rootedness of the best of Attic literature in the democratic political constitution of Athens.

[6] See, for instance, Andrew Ford, *Origin of Criticism*. Also, to take only two examples, Rilke sees poetry as a way of "praising" or "celebrating" ("*rühmen*")—see his *Sonette an Orpheus*, part 1, sonnets 7 and 8. Heidegger obviously thinks that poetry is essentially a matter not of knowledge, but of a human activity which, following Hölderlin ("*Andenken*"), he calls "*stiften*"—establishing, founding, opening up, grounding—and which is *prior* to knowing (see his *Erläuterungen zu Hölderlins Dichtung* [Frankfurt: Klostermann, 1951], 38–39).

[7] For a contemporary philosophic discussion of the issues here, see Michael Williams, *Problems of Knowledge* (Oxford: Oxford University Press, 2001), 1–47.

[8] Thus when one of the earliest lyric poets known to us, Archilochus, tells us that he knows

Sulpicia; this is knowledge in the sense of acquaintance-with. Here "know" usually takes a noun or pronoun as direct object, although in some cases this noun or pronoun can be replaced by an appropriate clause.[9] Thus instead of "I know the smell of a rose" or "I know the sound of an oboe," I could also say "I know how a rose smells" or "I know how an oboe sounds."[10]

Is, then, poetry close enough to one of these three phenomena—the entertaining of a well-supported, propositionally structured belief, a skill, or an acquaintance—for us reasonably to call it a "form of knowledge?" The differences between most forms of poetry and forms of propositional knowledge seem prima facie much more striking than any similarities. Canonical instances of propositional knowledge have a detachable content. If I know that Edinburgh is north of Paris, the clause "that Edinburgh is north of Paris" can be extracted and reidentified when it occurs as a constituent part of propositions involving a different attitude toward it. Thus: "I do not believe that Edinburgh is north of Paris"; "I hope that Edinburgh is north of Paris"; "I regret that Edinburgh is north of Paris," etc. It is hard to see anything parallel to "propositional content" in most forms of lyric poetry.

One might think that a case could be made that some kinds of narrative poetry, perhaps including epic, do have a content because each poem has a "plot" and this plot could be summarized, detached, and identifiably reused. Furthermore, there is a genre of poetry, didactic poetry, which has as its acknowledged intention to expound various philosophical, medical, astronomical, or agricultural truths, and these truths could presumably have been extracted and reformulated in another poem or in prose. Lucretius at the beginning of book 4 of *De rerum natura* is exceptionally clear about this feature of didactic poetry. Epicureanism is like the bitter medicine administered by doctors to children—hard to take at the moment, but beneficial in the long

---

how to do two things: wreak vengeance on his enemies (ἐπίσταμαι [+ acc.]: W126/D66) and strike up the dithyramb (οἶδα [+ inf.]: W120/D77; see also W1/D1 [ἐπίσταμαι + acc.]), both of these are instances of knowing-how. The use of the direct object after these verbs of "knowing" (see also W201/D103) is suggestive of a certain priority given to direct acquaintance, and an attempt to model all knowing on this. See discussion of "the idea of the good" below.

[9] It is an accident, that is, a complete quirk of the English language that we even use the same word "know" in all three of these contexts. Thus, French has two distinct words where we have one (*"connaître/savoir"*) and German uses three distinct words (*"wissen/können/kennen"*).

[10] There is a slight complication here in that the second form is used particularly in contexts in which what is at issue is the exercise of discriminating skills based on direct acquaintance. Thus, I will be likely to say "I know how an oboe sounds" if you question my claim that the instrument now playing is an oboe (rather than, for instance, a clarinet). This means only that in many, probably most, cases one kind of knowledge will be accompanied by others. If I am acquainted with the sound of the oboe, then I will also have a certain skill, that of being able in a wide range of cases of distinguishing the sound of the oboe from that of the clarinet. The fact that types or kinds of knowledge generally occur together is compatible with it being important to distinguish them analytically.

run. Lucretius is like a doctor who smears the rim of the cup with honey to make the bitter medicine more palatable. The poetic mode of expression of the doctrine is the honey (*"volui tibi suaviloquenti / carmine Pierio rationem exponere nostram / et quasi musaeo dulci contingere melle,"* 20–23).

Few, however, would wish to claim that the plot of an epic is the most important element in it, much less that it has the utterly overwhelming significance for the poem that the "content" has for propositional knowledge. In addition, at least one very strong aesthetic current in the West has held it to be absolutely central to a proper understanding of art that in a successful work of art the "form" and "matter," or "treatment" and "content," are *uniquely* suited to each other. This would seem to imply that no such *detachable* and repeatable content exists.[11]

As far as didactic poetry is concerned, even if one grants that it is possible to construe the relation of the poetic treatment and the "content" in the external way that Lucretius suggests—the "content," a philosophical doctrine like Epicureanism that could be stated in discursive prose, and the poetic treatment, Latin dactylic hexameter—this does not seem to give much real comfort to those who wish to claim that poetry is a "form of knowledge." They presumably wish to say that there are some truths to which access can be had *only* through poetry. Given, however, that Epicureanism existed as a body of prose propositions before its poetic expression by Lucretius, there is no sense in which his poem is a unique or even cognitively privileged mode of access to it.

Propositional knowledge is inherently connected with a whole apparatus of objective assertion, representation of reality, and truth, etc., which Western philosophy and science have developed during the past two and a half millennia. To claim to have propositional knowledge is to assert the content of what one claims to know. What I assert can in principle be true or false, better or less well supported, more warranted or less warranted.

Poems, however, don't necessarily make assertions about the world of any kind. Thus, the whole point of Pound's poem "In a Station of the Metro"

> The apparition of these faces in the crowd;
> Petals on a wet, black bough.

[11] See Søren Kierkegaard, *Either/Or*, trans. D. F. Swenson and L. M. Swenson, rev. H. Johnson (Princeton: Princeton University Press, 1944), vol. 1, 43–135, "The Immediate Stages of the Erotic or the Musical Erotic," about why *Don Giovanni* is the perfect opera. This perfect unity of treatment and content is, of course, presented as a *desideratum* of art, not a minimal condition that anything must satisfy in order to be a work of art. This in itself might be a characteristic difference between art and some other things: art might *inherently* contain a teleological orientation toward certain goals, so that one could not understand art except as something aspiring to be good/perfect art. A value judgment was built into the specification of what could, even minimally, be counted as art. Note the difficulty we have even today in distinguishing between the claim "That is not art at all" and "That is bad/poor/revolting art."

is precisely *not* to make an assertion. In fact, the haiku is a whole poetic genre the point of which is to fail to assert, or to refrain from asserting. It is as if the haiku were trying linguistically to operate *below* the level at which assertion takes place.[12] What proposition is being asserted in one of Apollinaire's *calligrammes* or in various of the poems of Jandl?[13] Are questions of truth, falsity, or evidence even relevant to them?

"Propositional knowledge" is connected with "objective" assertion. Speaking and writing, however, are actions, but objective assertion is by no means the only possible function or goal of these actions.[14] Asserting something about how the world is constituted is one kind of action I can perform in the world, and if I perform this action, then what I assert can be evaluated in various ways, including whether it is true or false. However, in addition to making assertions about the world, I can use language for a variety of other purposes, such as to make requests, ask questions, or issue orders. Philosophers call these activities "speech-acts," different things one can do with words. If I say to you "Down with Pierrot" or "Please close the door" or "Do you take sugar?" or "If only I were home in Cambridge," or, if I say about a child (in the right circumstances) "I name you 'Tom,'" I am not asserting anything about the world, I am performing the acts of execrating, giving an order, asking a question, expressing a wish, or naming a child respectively. To be sure, in each case I may be *assuming* various things about the world, such as that in the case of "Please close the door" or "Do you take sugar?" there is a door or a cup of tea in front of us, but that is a different matter. There are at least two kinds of questions I can ask about a given speech-act. First, I can ask what assumptions the speech-act makes, and whether or not these are true. If the assumptions are not true, the act may not make sense, but to say that an act makes no sense in a particular context is not to say it asserts something that is false. If I make a false knowledge claim like "Edinburgh is south of Paris," you may reply: "No, it isn't." On the other hand, if I were to ask you to open the door while we were standing in the middle of a desert, an appropriate response would be for you to ask me what the hell I meant, not to say "No, it

---

[12] It is thus a Kantian art form *par excellence*.

[13] For instance, Ernst Jandl, *Idyllen* (Hamburg and Zurich: Luchterhand, 1992), 170, 172.

[14] See J. L. Austin, *How to Do Things with Words*, ed. Urmson and Sbià, 2nd ed. (Oxford: Oxford University Press, 1980). There has been a certain discussion of literature as a form of acting rather than asserting propositions. Sartre seems to think that this is a special property of prose, rather than of poetry (*Qu'est-ce que la littérature?* [Paris: Gallimard, 1948], pp. 13–40). Heidegger's discussion of poetry as an initiating act (see note 6 above) does not construe it as a speech-act in the proper sense, but as an act which is prior to and constitutes the space within which speech-acts can be performed. Poetry, that is, is not like the action of the priest in the Catholic Eucharist who turns the water and wine into the body and blood of Christ, but like the action of Christ at the Last Supper (as construed by traditional Catholic theology) in founding or initiating the Eucharist. Furthermore, Heidegger thinks that this initiating act is one of *naming* the gods, etc. (not, for instance, of asserting anything).

isn't." For you to say "No, it isn't" in this context would be just as peculiar as was my asking you to close the door in the first place.

The second kind of question I can ask about the performance of a speech-act is an evaluative one. I can ask whether it was polite,[15] or a good idea, or morally and legally permissible for me to tell you to shut the door. If I try to name the child, do I have the power and authority to do that? In saying the polite thing, such as "How do you do?" when I meet someone, I may be expressing or exhibiting a knowledge I have of what is appropriate or polite, but that is not the same as claiming that what I *say* is a form of knowledge. The polite thing to do, after all, might be to shake hands, but shaking hands is surely not itself a form of knowledge.

Poetry is most plausibly taken to have its origins in such things as children's games, riddles, spells and incantations, rhythmical work songs, lullabies, invective, religious chants entreating aid from the gods, panegyric, and hymns in praise of dead heroes. In none of these would the expression or transmission of *knowledge* be likely to have a high priority, or even much relevance. Does a rhythmical lullaby ("La la la la la . . .") have to be composed of statements that are *true*?

Many poems seem to be virtually pure speech-act with no asserted content at all, such as one of my favorites:

Twang!
Yeah for Herakles, the King, the Champ!
Twang! The Champ!
You and Iolaos, what a pair of rough-necks!
Twang!
Yeah for Herakles, the King, the Champ![16]

One should resist the temptation to say that this poem is a form of knowledge on the grounds that, if I read it with comprehension, there is something I come to know, namely that the poet, or those who perform this poem, ap-

---

[15] See Andrew Ford, *Origin of Criticism*, for discussion of noncognitivist early Greek approaches.

[16] Τήνελλα
ὦ καλλίνικε χαῖρ' ἄναξ Ἡράκλεες,
τήνελλα καλλίνικε
αὐτός τε καί Ἰόλαος, αἰχμητά δυο.
τήνελλα
ὦ καλλίνικε χαῖρ' ἄναξ Ἡράκλεες

I follow Diehl (120), who accepts the attribution of this to Archilochus, for the text. West (alas!) lists it under "Spuria" (324) and gives a slightly different, and less full, text. The first word of the poem, "τήνελλα," is said to be an onomatopoetic invention imitating the sound of the plucked string of a lyre or the sound of an αὐλός (see testimonia collected at *Iambi et Elegi Graeci*, ed. West, 2nd ed. [Oxford: Oxford University Press, 1971], 1.104–6.)

prove of Herakles. I don't know this at all; poets, after all, often write to commission in praise of people and things they in no way think are especially praiseworthy, and performers are sometimes professionals who, within reason, will perform whatever they are given. A further example is the so-called "Carmen Arvale":

> Help us, Lares!
> Marmar, do not allow pestilence or catastophe to fall on the people.
> Be sated, wild Mars, jump on the boundary mark and stay there.
> Call in turn all the Semones.
> Marmor help us!
> Hurray! Hurray! Hurray! (Hurray! Hurray!)[17]

This song also has the property that, as far as we can tell, it contains no assertion at all, only exhortations and entreaties. In addition, we have reason to think that the *collegium* of priests who had it inscribed on a piece of stone in the third century AD and who performed it regularly had only the vaguest idea of what it meant. To cite the luminous words of one commentator, this ritual text "had become mere gibberish to those who pronounced it."[18] So what did those priests who had this poem inscribed know about it and what did they know by "knowing" it? What might we be said to know by knowing it? Was "Mars" the "same" deity as "Marma(r)" / "Ma(r)mor?" Would the priests have known that? Up to what period in Roman history would they still have known what the song meant? Is any of this terribly important? Anyone who has learned a foreign language will have noticed that many of the most powerful poetic effects do not depend even on a full or correct comprehension of the

---

[17] *enos Lases iuuate,*
  [e]nos Lases iuuate,
  enos Lases iuuate.
  neue luae rue Marma sins incurrere in pleores
  neue lue rue Marmar [si]ns incurrere in pleoris
  neue lue rue Marmar sers incurrere in pleosis
  satur furere, fere Mars, limen [sal]i, sta berber,
  satur fu, fere Mars, limen sali, sta berber,
  satur fu, fere Mars, limen sa[l]i, s[t]a berber.
  [sem]unis alternei aduocapit conctos
  semunis alternei aduocapit conctos
  simunis altern[ei] aduocapit [conct]os
  enos Marmor iuuato
  enos Marmor iuuato
  enos Mamor iuuato

  triumpe, triumpe, triumpe trium[pe tri]umpe

Text from L. R. Palmer, *The Latin Language* (London: Faber and Faber, 1954), 346–47. Translation basically follows Palmer, 63.
[18] L. R. Palmer (note 17), 63.

meaning of the text, much less on a recognition of whether the text transmits a cognitively correct representation of the world or indeed a truth of any kind. We nowadays don't even think that the god Mars exists, so how could my reading this poem, even if I enjoy and appreciate it as performance or a work of literature, count as a "form of knowledge?" The frequency with which nonsense passages occur in ancient magical spells suggests that the dissociation of comprehension of the meaning of the poem or the cognition it "embodies" from its effectiveness or power is a relatively old phenomenon.[19]

Clear understanding is thus a much overrated virtue that has limited application to poetry. Some of the best lyric poetry is characterized by irremediable obscurity or systematic and deep ambiguity, and this gives it a density of texture that is an aesthetic virtue.[20] Unclarity or ambiguities in meaning, however, are grave defects in propositional forms of investigation and argumentation, and most disciplines of knowing emphasize the need to adopt the most stringent measures to eliminate them as completely as possible.

Is poetry, then, knowledge in the sense of a knowing-how or a skill? In one sense, of course, it obviously is. Just as a swimmer knows how to do something nonswimmers cannot do, namely swim, so a poet knows how to do something nonpoets do not, namely how to write a poem. At certain periods in the past this aspect of poetry may have seemed even more salient and may in fact have been more important than it is now. The highly trained ἀοιδός in an illiterate society was an oral performer whose ability to tell a coherent, engaging, longish story in correct dactylic hexameter would have marked him out very noticeably from those who did not have this skill.[21] In early literate societies even the ability to read poetry aloud fluently from a text that had no punctuation or even word breaks would also have been a highly visible, and highly distinctive, skill. Although this is perfectly true, for two reasons I think it points us in the wrong direction if we wish to understand some particularly important things about poetry. First, we generally speak of a person having a skill only if he or she is able to be reliably successful in bringing about a certain result. The person who has the skill must be able to bring about something *others* can recognize as a successful outcome according to relatively clear socially recognized criteria. Thus in the nineteenth century you could lock schoolboys up in a room and ask them to write Latin hexameters. Some would be more skillful at this than others, and the difference would depend partly on the length of experience the individual boy had had, partly on his level of application, and partly on various more intangible gifts. The ones who were regularly most successful could be said to know how to write grammat-

---

[19] John Gager, *Cursing Tablets and Binding Spells from the Ancient World* (Oxford 1992). See also, Alf Önnerfors, *Antike Zaubersprüche* (Stuttgart: Reclam, 1991). See, finally, J. Hörisch, *Die Wut des Verstehens* (Frankfurt, 1998).

[20] See W. Empson, *Seven Types of Ambiguity* (London: Penguin 1961).

[21] See Andrew Ford, *Origin of Criticism*, Princeton University Press, parts 1 and 2.

ically and metrically correct Latin. The existence of a clear set of rules and expectations gave firm meaning to the notion of having "skill at writing poems" (or perhaps we might prefer to say in the case of the schoolboys, "skill at versification"). All of this means that the exercise of a skill has a kind of repeatability: the person who has the skill can deploy it again and again to get the same reliable success. This repeatability does not exclude certain kinds of innovation, especially in methods. However, even at their most extreme, innovations will be variations within an existing overall pattern. Poetry in the post-Romantic world, however, is particularly committed to originality, and that means focusing on departure from expected patterns and nonrepeatability. Ideally a post-Romantic work is not aspiring to be a success by preexisting criteria, but to create new criteria by which works are to be judged.[22] That does not mean that patterns and repeatable features do not play a crucial role in it, as they must do in any use of language; but construing poetry as *essentially* a matter of knowing-how or skill would focus attention precisely on those aspects of it that most contemporary people who are interested in poetry would find least interesting.

Furthermore, under contemporary conditions at any rate, one must distinguish two distinct groups of people. There are people who produce poetry and people who consume it: poets and readers of poetry (or, listeners to poetry).[23] Members of each of these two groups need to have certain skills in common, but it is by no means exactly obvious that the members of each group need exactly the *same* skills in all respects. It is not obviously the case that the ability to write a good poem is at the same time the ability to read or understand, or appreciate it—or whatever word one wants to use for the consumption side of the poetry-process. Not every good critic is a good poet, and vice versa. So if poetry is a form of knowing, and that is taken to mean a form

---

[22] Obviously the very idea that there is or could be a strict and simple dichotomy between "classic" art—devoted to the repeated attempt to realize a fixed and pre-given "κάνων" of excellence—on the one hand, and "Romantic" art—committed to "absolute" originality—on the other, does not make sense. Perhaps some forms of sub-artistic activities, like stenciling decorations on a wall, might approximate sheer repetition, although even in cases like that there would be likely to be variations in the placement of the stencil on the wall. No art, however, certainly not Homer, or anything we would call "classic" art, could be *simply* a matter of repeating existing patterns. Equally, the idea of an absolutely original art owing *nothing* to preexisting forms is incoherent. Repetition/deviation represents at best a kind of spectrum on which different works of art, ideals, and movements can be located, but this spectrum is like what mathematicians call an "open interval" in that the two endpoints—complete repetition and absolute deviation—are not points in the interval because they do not themselves designate positions that could be occupied by possible forms of art. For an early philosophical discussion of the issues involved, see I. Kant, *Kritik der Urteilskraft* (1799; modern edition: *Kant-Werke: Akademie Textausgabe* [Berlin: de Gruyter, 1968], vol. 5, 43–50). See my *Morality, Culture, History* (Cambridge: Cambridge University Press, 1999), 140–66.

[23] See the enlightening remarks by Sartre, *Qu'est-ce que la littérature?* (note 14), 48–49, although, again, Sartre seems to be speaking of prose rather than poetry.

of knowing-how, which of these distinct skills is that knowing? This specific problem does not arise with propositional knowledge: the person who *discovers* a new truth may need a different set of skills from the person who simply *learns* that truth, but in some sense what it is they know—that Edinburgh is north of Paris—is the same thing.

Perhaps poetry is a form of making us acquainted with something. This is pretty unspecific. Under the right circumstances anything in the world can be said to make us acquainted with *something*, minimally with itself. If I stub my toe on a stone this may be said to make me acquainted with the rough surface of that stone; seeing a pink flamingo makes me acquainted with the color pink and with flamingos. The rumbling of my belly may be said to make you directly acquainted with an unpleasant sound. Reading or hearing the *Iliad* can, of course, be said to give one knowledge by acquaintance in that if one has read the *Iliad*, one is acquainted with the *Iliad*, but for obvious reasons this is a completely uninteresting connection between poetry and knowledge. Even if one says that poems do not merely happen to make us acquainted with various things, but are specifically designed to make us acquainted with things, this will not help. After all, the ability to give a good massage may be a matter of skill or know-how, and the massage itself may be designed to make me aware of certain muscles and acquainted with feelings of muscular tension and relaxation I have never felt before, but few would call the rumbling of my belly or a massage a poem, or a form of knowledge.

One tack a supporter of the view that poetry gives us knowledge (in the sense of acquaintance) might take would be to claim that the model of "acquaintance" that has been presupposed up to now is too narrow. It has been tacitly assumed that what someone can "know" (in this sense) is either a simple sensory quality, as in "I know the smell of a rose," or an object or person, as in "I know Edinburgh" or "I know Tony." However, the appropriate model, these theorists might claim, ought to be something like "I know what it is like to be poor" or "I know what it is like to be a victorious Roman general celebrating a triumph" or "I know what it is like to be in the grip of pantheistic exaltation."[24] Knowing what it is, or would be like, to be a victorious Roman general is not at all a matter of acquaintance with any simple sensory property or with any particular individual human being. Still, it is not whimsical to say that this is a sort of knowing. If one is committed to defending the claim that poetry is a form of knowledge, this does seem to be one of the more promising lines to pursue, but it is still unconvincing. On the one hand, lots of works of prose may be just as capable of making me feel I know what it

---

[24] The philosophical significance of questions like "What is it like to be . . . ?" was a central concern of the classic paper by Thomas Nagel entitled "What Is It Like to Be a Bat?", originally published in 1974, now most easily available in his *Mortal Questions* (Cambridge: Cambridge University Press, 1979).

would be like to be, say, poor, as a poem would. A novel by Dickens or, for that matter, prose reportage, may be more effective in transmitting this than any poem one might name. On the other hand, although *some* poems might be intended to show us what it would be like to be, say, poor, and others may be interpreted in this way even if they were not originally so intended, it seems obvious that this is not a universal property of all poetry. To recur to previously mentioned examples, Apollinaire's *calligrammes* don't have this property, nor do various bits of didactic poetry. So giving us knowledge of "what it would be like to be . . ." seems neither a necessary nor a sufficient condition for something to be poetry.

It seems, thus, that poetry is not a form of knowledge in any of our normal senses of "knowledge." There will, then, be a strong temptation for those who cannot give up the Platonic model to claim that poetry must therefore be a wholly new, as yet unclassified, (fourth) kind of knowledge of a metaphysical entity with its own distinctive mechanism of self-validation. Obviously, I cannot describe the "metaphysical entity" in question ("Reality," "the Absolute," "the Truth," etc.) in a clear discursive way through a set of propositions. If I could, that in itself would refute at least the more extreme versions of the Romantic view which claim that the *only* modes of access to and expression of this entity are nondiscursive or "poetic."[25] The conception of a new, fourth form of "knowledge" is usually also conceived following Plato as model. The knowledge of "the idea of the good" in the *Republic* seems to be a kind of direct intuitive acquaintance, which both requires and makes possible propositional knowledge, and which gives those who have it skill at being a good person.

The "knowledge" to which the Romantics aspired was also a type of intuition which in some way put together acquaintance and propositional knowledge or was perhaps the common ground of both; it was usually also thought to have a strong moral dimension. The mechanism for the "self-validation" of this Romantic knowledge which paralleled the Platonic "λόγον διδόναι" was "feeling,"[26] or to use the currently more fashionable term, "emotions."

Those who take the Romantic view generally make two points. First, they

---

[25] Thus Hegel had a complex theory of what he called "the speculative proposition" which was not at all like what we normally call a "proposition," but had a kind of conceptual "motion" built into it. It could be understood only relative to its position within a much larger structure of continuous argumentation, a perpetual argument during the course of which the meaning of all the terms involved was constantly changing in a structured but not independently specifiable way. For more on this, see my "Dialectics and the Revolutionary Impulse," in *Cambridge Companion to Critical Theory*, ed. Fred Rush (Cambridge: Cambridge University Press, 2004). For Adorno, this metaphysical entity can be "named" but not described; see his *Negative Dialektik* (Frankfurt: Suhrkamp, 1966), 59–61.

[26] This is put especially succinctly in the posthumously published poem by Novalis that begins: "*Wenn nicht mehr Zahlen und Figuren / Sind Schlüssel aller Kreaturen, / Wenn die, so singen oder küssen / Mehr als die Tiefgelehrten wissen.*" For the manuscript version of this, see Novalis, *Schriften*, ed. P. Kluckhohn and R. Samuel (Stuttgart: Kohlhammer, 1960), 344–45.

emphasize the role that feelings or emotions play in usual processes of perception and cognition. Emotional responses focus our attention, and our feelings influence what we decide to pursue cognitively, what questions we ask, and, to some extent perhaps, also the direction in which we choose to pursue answers to questions. This, I take it, is intended to soften up the Platonic distinction between strict perception/cognition and emotional response. Second, they introduce notions like "appropriateness" or "fittingness" or "suitability" and claim that they can play something like the role for feelings that "true/false" or "warranted/unwarranted" play for propositional judgments. If I am stroking a cat and look at it very carefully, this very strikingly fails to warrant the knowledge-claim "This is a toothbrush," but it does warrant "This is a cat." Similarly, the Romantics claim, under most circumstances, hilarity is not an appropriate reaction to encountering a large predator in a forest unexpectedly; fear is.

Feelings should be considered to be *self*-validating, on this view, because one cannot tell whether or not an emotional response to a state of affairs is "appropriate" by reference to any form of propositional cognition. There are "sciences" that will tell you whether the substance in front of you is or is not gold, but there is no corresponding science[27] which will tell you whether you ought to be disappointed by this result or pleased, or experience feelings of greed, elation, hatred, disgust, depression, or contempt. Whether a response is or is not "appropriate" or "fitting" is a matter for second-order feeling; it depends essentially on having a particular positive or negative emotional reaction to the original reaction. Being afraid is an "appropriate" reaction to some situation because I *feel* it to be appropriate. In most sophisticated versions of this view it is accepted that these feelings can be trained or educated, and much of that training may well consist in imparting bits of knowledge—it is not appropriate to fear *this* type of snake because it is not venomous—but the "knowledge" employed here is distinctly subordinate to the structure of feelings and the way it reflectively and autonomously organizes itself. Eventually all of these elaborations come down to a final emotional reaction.

Emotional responses are responses *to* the world *as perceived*, not as it is. I am not afraid provided I do not see the tiger, even if it is about to pounce. To be more exact, in one sense fear is or would be appropriate—the tiger is there—while in another it is not, because in an obvious sense, given that I don't see it, I have no subjective reason to be afraid. That emotional response

[27] Perhaps in a very few extreme cases biology will tell us that humans are physiologically constituted so as to experience fear or anger under certain specifiable conditions; these, however, so runs the argument, are at best only the basic constituents of truly human emotions, not the emotions themselves. This assertion is subject to the qualification that another part of the agenda of many early Romantics was to expand the concept of "*Wissenschaft*," which even in normal everyday usage is wider than that of the English "science," to include their new fourth kind of knowledge.

is appropriate to *that* perceptual state (whether the perception is correct or not). Thus, at the beginning of the *Pisan Cantos*, Pound writes a threnody for the death of his hero, Mussolini.[28] Many might think that, although death is always a dreadful thing, Mussolini was not a hero, and his life was not one that should motivate anyone to think that his passing deserves special mourning. Nevertheless, the Romantic might claim, even if one disagrees with Pound's view of Mussolini and his career, one may still agree that the threnody was an appropriate reaction to that death *as Pound saw and evaluated it*.[29] If we disapprove of Mussolini, we presumably engage in a bit of make-believe ourselves here: "*If* Mussolini had been the heroic and tragic figure Pound took him to be, *then* this would have been an appropriate response to his death."

One can see how, extending this analysis even further, one might arrive at something very much like the Platonic view *in some respects*: there might be a state in which a person had the correctly appropriate feeling-based response to a Platonically correct set of perceptions or representations of the world. An ideal work of art would both express and generate these feelings in response to these true representations. This could still be a "Romantic" view, because it could give priority not to the correctness of representation while tacitly assuming, as the Platonist would, that if one had the representation right, one would also automatically have the emotional reaction right. Rather, the Romantic would claim that one had to have the feelings and emotions "right" in order to attain the correct representation of the world,[30] and that feelings can therefore in some sense be said (finally) to legislate themselves, independently of the antecedent correctness of perceptions.

Another way to put what I am getting at in the last paragraph is something like this: In his study of Descartes, Bernard Williams describes Descartes's commitment to an "absolute conception" of the world.[31] There is a world "out there" which has the properties it has "anyway," i.e., independently of our contingent and context-dependent modes of access to it or our modes of knowing it. In principle we can get a correct representation of that world, and when we do we represent it nonrelatively. This "absolute" conception has

[28] *Canto LXXIV*, 1–12.

[29] I merely note that this argument is highly condensed. Actually one would have to begin a full philosophical discussion by distinguishing at least three things: (a) Pound's perceptions or prepositional beliefs about Mussolini—he did this and that at this and that time; (b) Pound's "evaluation" of Mussolini—it was a good (or bad) thing that Mussolini did this or that; (c) Pound's "emotional response" to Mussolini. It is an open question whether these three are all distinct, or whether they are inherently connected, and, if so, how. I can't pursue this philosophical issue here, and only hope that my further claims about emotion and poetry will survive whatever the truth of this matter is.

[30] This is a Christian motif. In Augustine, one must love God in order to *know anything*. See my *Public Goods, Private Goods* (Princeton: Princeton University Press, 2001), 58–63.

[31] Bernard Williams, *Descartes: The Project of Pure Enquiry* (London: Penguin, 1978), 64–67.

been the object of some discussion, and so it is not universally admitted, but let us for the moment *assume* for the sake of further discussion that this is the right way to think about the world and our knowledge of it. Making this assumption, there seem to be three possibilities. First, there is the view attributed to "Plato" which is roughly that if one attained correct knowledge of the world, that in itself would restructure one's feelings and emotional reactions so that *they* would be correct, appropriate, and "absolute" too. The second, which I have associated with early Romanticism, agrees with the Platonist that there is (finally) an absolute set of correct, suitable feelings and emotions that are appropriate responses to the world, but denies that these responses can be, as it were, simply read off the dispassionate results of our cognitive inquiry into the state of the world. When I know that iron is heavier than water, this does not in itself tell me at all what my response to this ought to be, and no further accumulation of knowledge about the world will finally help. Rather, to know the world we need to be appropriately emotionally oriented toward it, and that means that emotion has at least independence if not priority. Acquiring this emotional attitude might take the form of something like a relatively brief, intense transformation—a conversion like that of Saul/Paul on the road to Damascus—or it might be the result of a long training of the will, such as that described by Foucault in various of his works.[32] Furthermore, once I know the facts, there is an inherent logic of (informed) feeling that dictates what response is suitable or proper or appropriate. Perhaps, then, in the end, the process would look like a historically extended or dialectical series of steps in each of which emotion played an independent part and which ended in convergence on the set of fully and absolutely "correct" and appropriate feelings.

A third possibility is that, even if one grants the assumption of an absolute conception of the world, there is no absolute system of feelings and emotions; there are only whatever various feelings people have. Perhaps in some cases one can say that some are fundamentally incoherent, or not humanly possible, not really livable, or not appropriate, but even when these are excluded there is still just a great, virtually unsurveyable variety of different, unobjectionable configurations of human emotion that cannot be reduced to some organized set of acceptably suitable or "correct" ones. Even if (*per impossibile*) we knew absolutely how the world was constituted, this would not tell us in all cases what state or set of states of feeling or emotional and voluntative reaction was uniquely appropriate as a response. It is this third position I support, and which I am suggesting is incompatible with traditional Romanticism.

This whole discussion of feelings still leaves open the question of the relation between emotional appropriateness and such things as the specific form

---

[32] Particularly his *L'herméneutique du sujet* (Paris, 2001).

of expression, the use of language, rhythm, style, sound, and all the "literary properties," which many people think are central to all forms of literature. Curzio Malaparte was at least as devoted to Mussolini as Pound was, and could also have written a threnody on his death. It might have been just as "suitable" to Malaparte's perception, and we have no reason to think it would not have been just as genuinely felt, but, given that Malaparte was a writer of *prose*, it is highly unlikely that any poem he might have written would have been as good, *qua* poem, as one of Pound's *Cantos*. One can try to deal with this by discounting or even denying the difference between emotional appropriateness and form of expression, roughly speaking, by claiming that the emotion does not exist unless in some sense adequately expressed, but surely that is so implausible as to be a counsel of despair.[33] Is it at all plausible to think I cannot cheer Herakles unless I know the (pseudo-) Archilochean tune, or that a better structured cheer necessarily means a "truer" emotion?

Feelings have neither the determinacy nor, in most cases, the clear binary structure that assertions do, and their relations to "the world" seem infinitely looser than those a proposition has to its object. If I am stroking a cat, "This is a cat" will recommend itself to me as true, and "This is a toothbrush" as false, but there does not seem any analogy at all between this and any *particular* feeling I might have as a reaction to the *Pisan Cantos* or to Paul Celan's poem about the assassination of Rosa Luxemburg and Karl Liebknecht in 1919 and the execution of the conspirators involved in the plot against Hitler of 20 July 1944.[34] Celan's poem reads:

[33] Croce and Collingwood seem to have held a view like this.

[34] "Du liegst im großen Gelausche" in *Schneepart* (Frankfurt: Sahrkamp, 1971), 8:

> Du liegst im großen Gelausche,
> umbuscht, umflockt.
>
> Geh du zur Spree, geh zur Havel,
> geh zu den Fleischerhaken,
> zu den roten Äppelstaken
> aus Schweden—
>
> Es kommt der Tisch mit den Gaben,
> er biegt um ein Eden—
>
> Der Mann ward zum Sieb. die Frau
> mußte schwimmen, die Sau,
> für sich, für keinen, für jeden—
>
> Der Landwehrkanal wird nicht rauschen.
> Nichts
>   stockt.

See also the remarkable analysis of this poem by Peter Szondi in his *Celan-Studien* (Frankfurt: Suhrkamp, 1972), 113–25. Sartre correctly recognizes the deep connection in the contemporary world between poetry and failure: *"le poète authentique ... c'est l'homme qui s'engage à perdre ... c'est son choix le plus profond, non pas la conséquence, mais la source de sa poésie. Il*

You lie in the ample listening place
surrounded by bushes, by flakes.
Go to the Spree, go to the Havel
go to the butchers' hooks
to the red apple-stakes
from Sweden—
The table with gifts is coming,
it curves around an Eden—
The man turned into a sieve, the woman
had to swim, the cunt,
for herself, for no one, for everyone—
The Landwehrkanal won't rustle,
Nothing
            stands still.

In fact, in this poem, Celan seems to be using some of his usual strategies of minimalism, condensation, superimposition of one motif on another, and extreme compression to put together as many diverse elements—historical, geographic, seasonal, mythic—that can be expected to call up contradictory emotions as possible, and almost surely not the *same* emotions in all readers. The "Eden" in line 8 is the Garden of Eden, but also the former Hotel-Eden in Central Berlin which in 1919 served as the headquarters of the cavalry unit whose members took Liebknecht and Luxemburg prisoner. The two of them were executed in the hotel and their bodies dumped into the Landwehrkanal. Finally, "Eden" is the name of the modern luxury apartment building which now stands on the same site as the old Hotel-Eden.

Luxemburg herself was well known for her view that revolutions were "*necessarily* premature," but that unavoidable and even completely predictable short-term failure was essential to eventual success, and she saw the Spartacus uprising, which she led and in which she was killed, in this light.[35] Even those with no sympathy whatever for her political views might admit that hers was a more complex form of failure than Mussolini's, and one that was more correctly designated a "tragedy" than his was.

Celan's friend and interpreter Peter Szondi provides some further biographical information about the trip to Berlin during which Celan wrote the poem. The red "apple-stakes" are small wooden sticks for affixing apples to an Advent wreath that Celan saw during a visit to Berlin just after visiting the memorial to the executed conspirators against Hitler in Plötzensee Prison.

est certain de l'échec total de l'entreprise humaine et s'arrange pour échouer dans sa proper vie, afin de témoigner, par sa défaite singulière, de la défaite humaine en général." *Qu'est-ce que la literature*, 43.

[35] See Rosa Luxemburg, *Sozialreform oder Revolution* (originally 1899) in her *Politische Schriften I* (Frankfurt: Europäische Verlagsanstalt, 1966), esp. 112–22.

That is, these sticks are part of the decorations for Christmas. However, they are also the stakes on which the decapitated heads of some of the conspirators against Hitler were stuck, and so they are made to rhyme with the meat hooks ("butchers' hooks") from which other conspirators were hung (*"Fleischerhaken"/"Äppelstaken"*).[36]

To say that some determinate, coherent (or, for that matter, incoherent) "feeling" or even range of feelings is fitting as a response to this poem is like saying that there is one proper emotional response to human life in the twentieth century. The poet might, to be sure, have had a reaction he *felt* or *thought* was unique. It might be important in *some* contexts to understand that (although not necessarily to agree with it or endorse it). Pound, who, as we know from his biography, was a supporter of the extreme political Right, may have felt that his feelings about Mussolini's fall were in some sense the only fitting and correct ones. Celan, an anarchist[37]—or perhaps a communist,[38] at any rate a man of the Left—perhaps also "felt" that his own complex reactions to Luxemburg's death were fitting, although, as we will see later, probably not "uniquely" fitting. Abstracting from what are called the "personal" or "private" feelings of Celan and Pound, a certain uniqueness of affect *might* be built into the poems themselves. Some poems might be structured in such a way that they seemed to assume or presuppose that some reaction was the only fitting one, or even that they presented some reaction *as if* it were the only one suitable. First of all, however, this need not be true of all poems. Second, as I have already said, the uniqueness of reaction would not, in general, be something the poems in question *asserted*, in the way in which I might assert, for instance, that this is the only copy of the *Iliad* I possess, or that 7 is the only whole number between 6 and 8. Finally, even if a claim to uniqueness or special appropriateness were made more or less directly or explicitly, that would be a particular claim that a particular poet made in a certain context, perhaps for a particular aesthetic effect, and may be no more. It would not follow that the claim was "true" or had any kind of binding power over me even if I am fond of the poem in question, feel "moved" by it, and judge that it is a good poem. Even if one were to accept for the sake of argument that Homer in the *Iliad* tacitly claimed that violence was admirable and celebrated it, I can love the poem and reject the sentiment.

[36] The biographical details are provided in Szondi's essay "Eden" in his *Celan-Studien*, 113–25. This set off an extremely vigorous discussion about the role of such "extraneous" biographical information in the interpretation of poetry. Some of the discussion is summarized by Jean Bollack in his "'Eden' nach Szondi," *Celan-Jahrbuch* 2 (1988), ed. M. Speier, *Beiträge zur neuen Literaturgeschichte*. series 3. vol. 1 (Winter 1988), 85–105.

[37] Paul Celan, *Der Meridian* (Frankfurt: Suhrkamp, 1999), 3.

[38] Thus in a letter written in 1962, Celan attributes to himself a *"vieux coeur de communiste."* See Marina Dmitrievna-Einhorn, "'Einhorn: du weißt um die Steine,' Zum Briefwechsel Paul Celans mit Erich Einhorn," in *Celan-Jahrbuch* 7, ed. H. M. Speier (Winter 1999), 8 n. 5.

In the real world of politics, the Fascist Mussolini and the Spartacist Rosa Luxemburg exclude each other. If one is right, the other is wrong; if one is in power, the other is not. Various of the knowledge-claims Luxemburg made, for instance her theory of capital accumulation, are either true or false.[39] *If* feelings have anything like the kind of structure they would have to have in order for the Romantic project of a self-validating realm of the emotions to be plausible, something similar must be true of them. Pound and Celan can't in some sense *both* be right. *If* the Romantics are right, one poem is (or at any rate some kinds of poems are) "true" (or even "good") and others "false" (or "bad"), one a vehicle of knowledge of the world and the others errors, deceptions, or lies. I suggest that the "if" clauses above are false, but that, in turn, does not mean that Pound and Celan are *both* "right." Rather, the notions of being "right" and its dichotomous opposite, being "wrong," either do not make sense at all in this context, or are at best crude, unhelpful, and misleading, because if we want to explain what sense they do make, we must construe them so differently and so idiosyncratically that they lose all significant touch with binary distinctions like "true/false."

My choice of Celan as an example might be thought to be disingenuous, as indeed it is. I find Celan's poetry especially congenial to my views, but do not see that as in any way discreditable, or problematic. Celan's friend and interpreter, Peter Szondi, suggested that Celan intended specifically to combine in his poems as many disparate and conflicting associationally charged semantic elements as possible—Eden as both paradise and the gates of hell—because for Celan "the moral world was not divided into good and evil, nor into a set of transitions between the two, but the good is at the same time evil and the evil, one way or another, always had its good aspect."[40] If Celan had an attitude toward the world, it was, Szondi is suggesting, one of "indifference,"[41] a fundamental nondistinguishing. This presumably does not mean that Celan was not willing to make *any* distinction between Rosa Luxemburg and those who killed her. Nor, presumably, does it designate a kind of Stoic imperturbability (ἀταραξία), a stable state of mind based on a clear understanding of the rationality of the universe and an active embracing of it.

It may be no accident that another of Celan's most powerful poems deals with the nineteenth-century poet Hölderlin, who went insane. At the end of his life, Hölderlin's favorite word was one of his own invention: *"Pallaksch,"*

---

[39] This, of course, is slightly more complicated in reality because many economic theories are "models" that show themselves to be more or less useful as representations, rather than determinate assertions. I cannot pursue this any further here.

[40] Peter Szondi, *Celan-Studien*, 123.

[41] Szondi (*Celan-Studien*) says this twice on page 123, using both *"Gleichgültigkeit"* and *"Indifferenz."* The notion of *"Indifferenz"* has a dense set of historical and philosophical uses in the German philosophy of the early nineteenth century, especially Schelling, but I cannot pursue that here.

which, according to observers, could mean either "yes" or "no." Celan's poem on Hölderlin ends with the suggestion that the only possible comment on our time would be a series of broken, compulsively repeated, half-articulate noises and then: "('*Pallaksch. Pallaksch*')."[42]

Is metaphysical-moral "indifference" or "*NO/YES*" (and/or "*YES/NO*") to the world and to every element in it—the repetition of a nonsense word invented by an insane nineteenth-century poet—the only suitable response to human life?[43] I have myself very considerable sympathy for this view, but I don't think it is the *only* one anyone could properly take. I hope Celan did not think so, either.

One can analyze a poem like Celan's and say various things about the elements of which it is composed, about the use of rhyme, language, history, verbal and syntactic structure. One can also discuss the various emotional responses people have to these elements, to their synthetic or paratactic conjunction, and to other aspects of the poem. One can analyze the cognitive or propositional beliefs with which various emotional reactions are contingently or inextricably intertwined in the given case, presuppositions the poems seems to make. From the denial that poetry is a form of knowledge, it need not follow that a poem is a completely closed semantic entity, a self-enclosed little world which can be understood without reference to anything else.[44] One can look at the embeddedness of poems in history and politics, the biographies of poets (to the extent to which they are accessible), their roles in the development of genres, etc. Sometimes poems or parts of poems have referential properties; sometimes they make assertions or have truth-values, and when this is the case, one can study these. The truth-values of such assertions may be more or less relevant to other aspects of the poem or to the various ways in which we might wish to use or relate to the poem.[45] Fi-

---

[42] Käme,

> käme ein Mensch,
> käme ein Mensch zur Welt, heute, mit
> dem Lichtbart der
> Patriarchen: er dürfte,
> spräch er von dieser
> Zeit, er
> dürfte
> nur lallen und lallen,
> immer—, immer—
> zuzu.
> ("*Pallaksch. Pallaksch.*")

Paul Celan, "Tübingen, Jänner," *Die Niemandsrose* (Frankfurt: Fischer, 1964), 24.

[43] Perhaps this is what Celan means when he writes: "*es sind / noch Lieder zu singen jenseits / der Menschen,*" *Atemwende* (Frankfurt: Suhrkamp, 1967), 22.

[44] Hans Georg Gadamer makes a series of characteristically fatuous remarks along these lines in his book on Celan, *Wer bin ich? Wer bist Du?* (Frankfurt: Suhrkamp, 1973), 110–30, which Bollack refutes elegantly in his paper "'Eden' nach Szondi," in *Celan-Jahrbuch* 2.

[45] Thus in a famous poem by Sappho (fragment 31, *Poetarum Lesbiorum Fragmenta*, ed. E.

nally, one can moralize about how a person with these reactions would be likely to act in the world, whether having these emotions and beliefs is a good thing or a bad thing for the person concerned or for others with whom that person is likely to come into contact. This is a highly complicated and very useful task, but it does not seem best understood according to some purported reductive logic of the "appropriate/inappropriate" which is claimed to parallel that of "true/false." The more one enters into any serious poem, the less useful such a simple binary framework becomes.

Much of the rhetoric of Romanticism is one of expanding human capacities and releasing the restrictive grip purportedly exercised by systematic forms of empirical and rational cognition on the human psyche. Romantic poetry, as one of its earliest programmatic statements put it, was to be an open-ended and "progressive universal poetry" that positively encompassed "everything poetical" from the most various systems of art to "the sigh, the kiss that the poetically active child breathes out into artless song."[46] The inclusion of the "poetically active child" is part of the potentially democratic, anti-Platonist political strand of this early Romantic view. This kind of synoptic intent stands in stark contrast to another that is more characteristic of one strand of modernism, and which finds its expression in Sartre's statement that every work of art wishes to destroy every other.[47] I take this to designate a certain extreme aesthetic claim to uniqueness that modernist works make—each one wants itself to be the final or canonical or indeed only work of art; it encom-

---

Lobel and D. Page [Oxford: Oxford University Press, 1955], 32), she describes watching a girl she was in love with flirt with a man and the effect this has on her. Among other things, she says it causes her to turn "greener than grass" (χλωροτέρα δὲ ποίας ἔμμι, 14–15). Or perhaps this means "paler than grass"—thus Page, *Sappho and Alcaeus: An Introduction to the Study of Ancient Lesbian Poetry* (Oxford 1955), 20—the use of color words in ancient Greek being notoriously peculiar, at least to modern European sensibilities. "Longinus," who transmits this text to us (*Libellus de sublimitate*, ed. Russell [Oxford 1968], chapter 10) praises it for its accuracy of observation (ἀλήθεια). Perhaps it might be of some interest to know from chemists and physiologists what hue the skin really takes on when a person is in the grip of a combination of lust (ἐρωτική μανία, "Longinus" calls it) and jealousy, and this might not be strictly irrelevant to an appreciation or evaluation of the poem. If people really did turn the color of grass when in the grip of certain acute passions, this might show that the poem really was in part the result of especially close observation, especially if this fact were not a matter of common knowledge. This might be thought, in turn, to accord well with the emotional intensity of the situation being presented: jealousy does perhaps focus the attention and sharpen certain kinds of perception. Still, the fact that the poem might give us "knowledge" of certain phenomena of human coloration is of fairly subordinate significance, if one is trying to evaluate this text as a poem. "Longinus" himself, for instance, does not praise it *merely* on the grounds that it is an accurate and truthful report of a set of symptoms, but also because of the way in which Sappho skillfully selects the most striking effects of passion and combines them ("τὰ ἄκρα αὐτῶν καὶ ὑπερτετάμενα δεινὴ καὶ ἐκλέξαι καὶ εἰς ἄλληλα συνδῆσαι"). This may be an extremely rudimentary form of criticism— Page is caustic about it (*Sappho and Alcaeus* [Oxford 1955], 20)—but it already goes beyond treating the poem simply as a transmitter of true propositions.

[46] Schlegel, *Kritische Friedrich-Schlegel-Ausgabe*, 182–83 [= fragment 116].

[47] *Qu'est-ce que la littérature?*

passes everything by destroying all competitors, reducing them to mere pale reflections or approximations of itself. This is a striking phenomenal property of much modernist art, but one should see that it is a specific aesthetic *gesture* which is constitutive of art of a particular kind, not a universal property of all poetry. There are, that is, *other* gestures poetry can make. The same is true of the Romantic aspiration to encompass everything in an uncoerced, continual process of organic appropriation.

One would obviously have to have a rather excessively puritanical view to think that one and only one emotional reaction is "fitting" or "suitable" to every given state of the world, and accepting such a view would have very repressive and constrictive consequences; but even a more liberal view—that "appropriateness" marked out antecedently a wide but determinately delimited set of responses—would seem to get the structure wrong. Rather than relaxing restraints and *expanding* the realm of knowledge, this would seem rather to be a way of trying to introduce restraints on emotions or regimenting them by enforcing on the realm of the emotions a dichotomous channeling (appropriate/inappropriate) which is parallel to the one that holds for knowledge-claims (true/false), and is perfectly warranted there, but distinctly and unnecessarily repressive in the realm of feelings.

All things considered, then, it seems hard to countenance "feeling" or "emotion" as the requisite kind of self-validating mechanism, and, if this is the case, it is equally difficult to see the point of a new, fourth notion of "knowledge."

I can't refute those who feel the metaphysical need and seek to satisfy it through reading or writing poetry, but I suggest that there is an alternative to Romanticism which would consist in rejecting the Platonic game and changing the rules entirely. No one can be prevented from using the word "knowledge" in a new way to refer to some purported amalgam of acquaintance with something and the sense for what is appropriate, but the compulsion to speak in this way seems so peculiar that a disinterested observer is more likely to want to ask why people continue to feel impelled to cling so ferociously to the word "knowledge." Nietzsche thought that the motive was partly weakness and evasion, but partly a residual asceticism.[48] To say "I know" rather than "I wish" or "I want" is to pretend that matters are out of my hands—it is the world, not me, that is responsible for what is going on; I'm not pleasing myself here, because knowledge is something completely impersonal.[49] If, how-

[48] Nietzsche, *Jenseits von Gut und Böse*, 1–23; *Zur Genealogie der Moral*, Dritte Abhandlung; both in *Kritische Studien-Ausgabe*, ed. G. Colli and M. Montinari (Berlin: de Gruyter, 1980), vol. 5.

[49] Nietzsche does not hold, as he is sometimes taken to hold, that whenever I say "I know," this is *always* a *mere* mask for something that ought really to be expressed as "I want." To want to know is to want to get away from mere personal desire, and people are sometimes successful in that. The "will-to-truth" is *not* a mere generator of illusions, but it is something that arises

ever, there is nothing inherently wrong with pleasure, and certainly nothing wrong with *feeling* "what I want to feel," there would be nothing inherently wrong with an art that was (merely) entertaining, and no one would need to claim that poetry is knowledge in order to defend it. Besides, why accept the dichotomy: either knowledge and therefore useful, or pleasure and therefore dangerous? Might there not be an indefinite number of further possibilities?

What we call "poetry" is a complex, historically changing body of performances, institutions, and practices. To be sure, like everything else in the human world, this historical corpus is connected in different historical periods in a variety of ways with forms of propositional knowledge, with the exercise of various skills, and with modes of making humans acquainted with various aspects of their lives and their world. The modern world is deeply immersed in and devoted to the acquisition, testing, transmission, and application of bodies of propositional beliefs in a highly self-conscious way, and it would be extremely strange if modern poetry, too, were not implicated in various forms of propositional knowledge. Some poetry may contain straightforward assertions or knowledge claims, but not all poetry does, and even in poems that do contain such claims, the cognitive aspects of the claims may not be the most important thing about them.

The corpus, or field, or family of practices which is poetry is also complexly related to forms of pedagogy, the exercise of social power, religious practices, regimes of pleasure, the cultivation of regional, national, and international solidarity, the expression of human aggression, etc. Obviously, poetry is an important part of human life for many people, and we can learn a lot from studying it, as we can learn a lot from studying virtually any form of human behavior, any institution, or any human artifact. Saying poetry is a form of knowledge, however, is no more informative than saying that it is a form of social control or, for that matter, saying that massage is a form of knowledge because it requires skill to administer and can make the receiver more aware of the world. We should follow Nietzsche's lead and give up the view that there is any such a thing as "the essence" of poetry,[50] thus a fortiori rejecting the whole question of whether poetry is or is not essentially a form of knowledge.

---

historically and psychologically from particular empirical sources that can be studied and understood.

[50] Nietzsche, *Jenseits von Gut und Böse*, 45–62, 186–203; *Zur Genealogie der Moral*, Zweite Abhandlung, 12–13; both in *Kritische Studien-Ausgabe*, vol. 5. See also my *Morality, Culture, History*, 1–28, 167–70. Heidegger, that is, is not giving a correct or incorrect answer to the right philosophical question when he asks what the "essence" of poetry is (Heidegger, "Hölderlin und das Wesen der Dichtung," *Erläuterungen zu Hölderlins Dichting* 31–45), but is asking the wrong question, a question that presupposes that there is some single "essence" of poetry, rather than a historical variety of practices some of which are sufficiently similar to others for us to group them together.

12

Plato, Romanticism, and Thereafter

In the 1880s a discovery was made that would have profound implications for the course of human thought in the second half of the twentieth century. A virtually blind, syphilitic, petit bourgeois Swiss rentier who led a peripatetic existence in a series of *pensioni*, cheap hotels, and furnished bed-sits in southeastern France, northern Italy, and Canton Graubünden began to see through a set of interconnected and highly constricting illusions that had dominated Western thinking for over two millennia. Friedrich Nietzsche— for he it was—gradually came to realize that Plato had made two mistaken assumptions about the world and our knowledge of it. These assumptions were taken over and developed by later philosophers, and through a gradual process of sedimentation eventually came to form the basis of Occidental "common sense," and thus to be deeply embedded in most of our institutions and practices. Systematically rejecting these two errors thus would be extremely difficult and profoundly unsettling, requiring us to revise fundamental ways of thinking, feeling, and acting. These patterns of feeling and thinking were rooted in psychological habits that had become second nature to us and were reinforced by vivid social sanctions.

Plato's first mistake, Nietzsche thought, was to hold that everything in the world had a fixed essence that could (and, as we will see later, in some sense "should") be specified in a formal definition. Thus, the aspiration of the character "Socrates" in the Platonic dialogues is to find a definition of "courage," "temperance," "justice," or whatever that would grasp the essence of each, and allow any person in possession of this definition reliably to distinguish instances of "courage" in the world from instances of "temperance," of "justice," of "cowardice," etc. Human thought took place in language and was a mirroring activity; in speaking, we were trying to get a grip on the essential structure of our world. When we succeeded, what we asserted was "true." The existence of fixed essences in the world was a precondition of any even minimally coherent linguistic activity. Without them language would have, as it were, nothing to latch on to.

Plato's second erroneous assumption was to put "knowledge" in general, and a highly specific kind of propositional knowledge in particular, into the absolute center of human life, assigning it virtually unlimited value, and call-

I'm greatly indebted to Zeev Emmerich, Hilary Gaskin, Istvan Hont, Robert Pippin, Nicholas Poburko, and Quentin Skinner for discussion of the topics treated in this essay.

ing upon us to see the worth of everything else in relation to it. Living a good life, being a good person, was a question of having the right kind of knowledge: knowledge of these essences. This knowledge was a propositional knowledge of the definitions of the most important features of the human world and human life which would allow one to recognize each for what it was and distinguish it from everything else. To say that the knowledge in question is of a propositional kind is to say that the definition can be expressed in a fixed form of words.[1] For a person with such knowledge no confusion was possible. The morally serious person thus should make great efforts to acquire the knowledge embodied in these definitions.

The application of this Platonic approach to poetry is clear. One must seek a formal definition of it that gives its fixed essence, and one must investigate the relation in which poetry stands "essentially" to knowledge. Plato in fact thought that poetry was not a reliable vehicle for correct knowledge, and hence that it had a highly fragile and dubious value-status. This specific claim about the real essential nature of poetry is in fact less important that the two assumptions he made. Romantics tried to reverse Plato's specific account of poetry and its valuation, claiming that it was an important kind of knowledge, but they did this while taking over unquestioned Plato's two crucial assumptions. That is, they shifted the idea of what "knowledge" was supposed to be from something propositional to something more intuitive, and tried to construe poetry as knowledge in this new sense. However, they continued to think that poetry had an essence and that the proper approach to it was through an exploration of its relation to knowledge (in some sense of "knowledge").

What Nietzsche realized in the mid-1880s was that this Platonic (and then Romantic) view of the relation between language and the world was a restrictive delusion. First of all, Nietzsche suggests that one look at language as a kind of human practice; speaking is usually intervening, not mere mirroring. Speaking is *doing* something; expressing true propositions, transmitting knowledge, mirroring the world was one of the things language could be used to try to do, but only one among many. In addition, even when what was at issue was mirroring, there were no fixed essences associated with language use; the distinction between literal and metaphorical usage was not fixed. Any fixation of terminology is an expression of an act of decision, or will (which Nietzsche had an unfortunate tendency to assimilate to an act of violence; a clear mistake this). Second, Nietzsche rejected the centrality of knowledge. If there *is* no essence or essential definition, then there is no knowledge of it that could be as uniquely important as Plato claimed. Nietzsche himself, for instance, thought instinct was much more important than propositional

---

[1] Some qualifications of this might be needed to take account of the exact nature of knowledge of the idea of the good.

knowledge. Just as there is no "essence of religion"—just a historically changing set of institutions, practices, forms of linguistic usage, etc.[2]—so there is no essence of poetry. There is no reason to be *especially* interested in the relation of poetry to knowledge. Poetry stands in shifting relations to varying kinds of knowledge and has value in itself independent of that relation.

Nietzsche's potential "revolution" in philosophical thought had little immediate effect.[3] He had an inkling of this, predicting that in the medium term he would be greatly influential for the wrong things, and that his major insights would be accepted only gradually, with difficulty, and after much time. European thought continued to be dominated by the view that poetry had an essence and that this was the attempt to give some kind of knowledge of the world; usually it was the Romantic rather than the more strictly Platonic form of this view that dominated. One might even speak here of the formation of a "Romantic common sense." Then during the period of World War II Ludwig Wittgenstein remade the revolutionary discovery, seemingly independently of Nietzsche.[4] Language, he claimed (as Nietzsche had), was best understood as a kind of action, a set of what he called "language-games."[5] It could only be understood relative to its mode of embeddedness in a set of historically constituted and changing social practices. Only some kinds of language-acts—by no means all—were part of one of the language games that involved using concepts to subsume individual cases or make statements or assertions. Much of the use of language consisted in issuing orders, posing questions, expressing

[2] Friedrich Nietzsche, *Jenseits von Gut und Böse*, in *Kritische Studien-Ausgabe*, ed. G. Colli and M. Montinari (Berlin: de Gruyter, 1967–77), vol. 5.

[3] There are several reasons for this failure. First of all, this insight was one over which Nietzsche did not himself have full control. It breaks through fragmentarily in *some* of his writing, such as the early "Über Wahrheit und Lüge in einem außermoralischen Sinne" (in *Kritische Studien-Ausgabe*, vol. 1, pp. 873–91) where, however, it is still mixed up in a confused way with Kantian motifs with which it is actually not compatible—but is covered over in others. This is not unusual, especially in the case of genuinely novel and deeply unsettling insights. Second, the "revolution" went virtually unnoticed. Nietzsche became fantastically influential, but for *other* aspects of his doctrine, such as his misleading theory of the "will-to-power." The potential significance of his mature approach went especially unnoticed in its application to poetry because his most influential work on this subject was taken to be *The Birth of Tragedy*, a juvenile work which he wrote in his 20s *before* making the revolutionary discovery just described. As he himself puts it later, in his retrospective preface to a second edition of *BT*, this book is a work of Romanticism. The mature thought of Nietzsche is *post*-Romantic precisely in breaking with Plato's two assumptions.

[4] It seems incredible that someone who grew up as a member of the Viennese upper classes at the turn of the nineteenth to the twentieth century, and who was also an avid reader of Schopenhauer, will not have been very familiar with Nietzsche's work and ideas. On the other hand, I am unaware of any direct evidence that Nietzsche's views about language and history had any direct influence on Wittgenstein, who does seem to have developed a remarkably similar view quite independently.

[5] Ludwig Wittgenstein, *Philosophische Untersuchungen* (Frankfurt: Suhrkamp, 1971), §§ 1–24.

sympathy, asking for help, joking, and so forth. Even when assertions were being made, there was a looseness about the relation of language to reality, because of the nonexistence of essences—a nonexistence that is intolerable to the Platonic sensibility. In place of Plato's theory of essence and definition Wittgenstein presents his famous view about "family resemblance" as the model for the relation between the many instances of a single concept.

Plato assumes that for a concept to refer at all, it must refer to a single essential property common to and shared by all the things to which it refers. Thus, for there to be a cognitive use of "cat," there must be some essential features common to all cats in virtue of which "cat" correctly applies. If I use "cat" correctly, I am picking these common features out. Wittgenstein, in contrast, holds that the various phenomena to which a single concept applies are more usually united not by a common feature, but by a "family resemblance."[6] A group of people who show a family resemblance to one another need not necessarily share a *single* common feature, but merely partially overlapping sets of different properties. Some may have the same kind of nose; others a characteristic configuration of eyes, eyebrows, and mouth; others may have strikingly large, bat-like ears with tiny lobes and Hapsburg lips; others again may have the ears and the nose, but not the lips. This theory depends, then, on notions of "similarity," of "likeness," of what is "striking." Consistently Wittgenstein gives these notions, too, a non-Platonic analysis. When I say that John, Jean, and Mary have a nose "of the same kind" or a "similar nose," the "similarity" or "sameness" involved is not an instantiation of a pure Platonic essence. There is no saying *in general* or in an abstract way how much similarity or likeness two noses must exhibit in order to count as "of the same kind." I start by noticing very superficial similarities between three sisters: same blonde hair, same blue eyes, same general shape of face. I can then begin to notice more subtle facial similarities between one or the other of the sisters and the mother who does not have blonde hair and blue eyes, or with the brother. Finally I may begin to see rather unobvious similarities among the cousins; they can all begin to have traces of "*that* look." How far can I move out from this? There is nothing like a determinate answer to that question; it is a bit like the question "How long is a piece of string?" It depends on accidental features of my perceptual apparatus, how attentive I am able (and motivated) to be, what opportunities of observation I have, and a variety of further particular facts about the situation.[7]

---

[6] Ibid., §§ 65–67.

[7] Two further points. First, this example is only an example and cannot be pressed too hard. In many cases I will know beforehand that X is the cousin of Y, independently of the observation of similarity, and will then be looking for a similarity I assume will be likely to exist. This is not a feature of some of the other examples Wittgenstein uses, e.g., the concept of "game," and will not be a general feature of thinking about concepts and that to which they apply. Second, this is not a form of "idealism" because the similarities exist prior to being recognized.

Again, if this line of argument is correct, both of the Platonic assumptions are rejected. The right way to approach poetry is not to look for essential definitions, but to immerse oneself in the practices of listening to, reciting, reading, and writing poems. One will no doubt be very likely to start with writings commonly accepted as poems, and gradually learn "how to go on." Which new poems one will add to the corpus of those one already knows will depend on a variety of factors, including in particular whether or not one is able to recognize some new phenomenon (text, performance, etc.) as sufficiently similar to what one already calls "poetry" for it to count as poetry too. How much similarity of what kind something has to have with the existing things that form part of the canon that we call "poetry" is a matter of history, social practice, and decision, not of ontological compulsion.

My paper "Poetry and Knowledge" (in the spring/summer 2003 issue of *Arion*) was an attempt to draw some consequences from this philosophical revolution for the way in which we should think about poetry. I assumed that this Platonic-Romantic conception still dominated thinking about poetry among a wide swathe of opinion, so I decided to *start from it*, adopting it for the sake of argument, and give it the best run I could for its money. I try out various ways of giving this claim substance and find them all wanting. At the very end I sketch briefly a non-Platonic/post-Romantic approach (found in Nietzsche) and the sketch of an analysis of why this incorrect view could have persisted (human weakness, the metaphysical need, etc.)

Professor Glenn Most has recently[8] expressed a number of reservations about my account.[9] I found his article puzzling because his main reservation depends on attributing to me a position I don't hold, namely the view that "reading a poem" provides no knowledge whatsoever, but is "purely a source of pleasure and entertainment" (p. 112). In my original essay, however, I was concerned to make three points. First, contrary to what a number of philosophers from Plato to Heidegger believed, there is no fixed essence of poetry, but rather a shifting variety of practices in which *different* elements are present in different combinations at different times (p. 205 above). The best approach to poetry, then, will be one that is similarly encompassing of diverse aspects; "sometimes poems . . . make assertions or have truth-values, and when that is the case one can study these. The truth-values of such assertions may

---

[8] In an article in *Arion*, vol. 11, no. 2, autumn 2003.

[9] Professor Most also objects to a number of "inconsistencies" in my account. I suspect that the impression of inconsistency may arise from my procedure: for most of the essay I am arguing from a position which I don't myself hold, but which I have adopted "for the sake of argument," the Romantic view. I am trying out a variety of very different possible strands of argument, all of which I think fail. Many of these strands, and the various interpretations I try to put on them, *are* inconsistent with each other. As it were, that is not my problem, but an artifact of constructing a discussion which is dialectical, that is, taking over and presenting positions and arguments others might present, and following them out as far as I can.

be more or less relevant to other aspects of the poem or to the various ways in which we might wish to use or relate to the poem." Second, "Why accept the dichotomy: either knowledge . . . or pleasure . . . Might there not be an indefinite number of further possibilities?" Third, there is something repellently puritanical about the obsession some theorists have with the claim that poetry *is* (essentially) a form of knowledge and *not* "mere entertainment." As against this, I claim that "there is nothing inherently wrong with pleasure, and . . . there would be nothing inherently wrong with an art that was (merely) entertaining."

I am unable to see how any of these points or the conjunction of all three of them could be taken to imply that poetry is, or should be, a source of pleasure and entertainment only, which provides no knowledge whatever. Professor Most in his reply ignores my second and third points completely, so in what follows I will concentrate on the first.

Because I have the strong suspicion that resistance to my thesis arises from confusing it with a number of other claims, let me try to clear the air. In saying that poetry is not (essentially) knowledge, I am not committing myself to any of the following highly unpromising theses:

1. poetry can *never* be used to transmit knowledge
2. poetry *never* contains any true statements
3. poetry *never* expresses any general human truths
4. poetry *never* makes us acquainted with anything
5. it makes no sense ever to say that one has understood a poem correctly (or has understood it incorrectly)
6. understanding (or writing) poetry is possible without the activation of any human cognitive capacities
7. there can be no knowledge *of* poetry
8. no one can ever learn anything from (reading, studying, listening to) poetry.

Since my view is precisely that poetry at different times and different places has had a variety of different functions—not the single one of being a vehicle for truth—it is easy for me to accept the negations of (1) through (4): *some* poetry can *in some particular contexts* be used to transmit *some* (forms of) knowledge truths (e.g., if one assumes that Epicureanism gives one "knowledge," I can transmit this to you by reading *De rerum natura* aloud to you); *some* poetry contains true statements, etc.

To see that (5) is not implied by my claim, just consider one of Wittgenstein's model of an elementary language game.[10] One builder asks another to hand him a brick by saying "Brick" (or: "Please hand me a brick"). If the second builder hands the first a nail instead of a brick, the second builder has made a mistake in understanding, or is perhaps expressing rebelliousness, etc.

---

[10] Ludwig Wittgenstein, *Philosophische Untersuchungen*, §§ 19–21.

We know how we would go about determining whether this was a case of mis-understanding or rebelliousness. It does not follow from any of this that "Brick" (or, as we would say: "Please hand me a brick") is in any sense a knowl-edge-claim or a speech-act that has a truth-value. "Please hand me a brick" is neither true nor false, and it is not a knowledge-claim. To be sure, it may be an inappropriate thing to say—perhaps the first builder made a mistake, and *ought* to have asked for a nail, which is what is really required for the job at hand. "Brick" is embedded in a human network which is drenched through with various forms of human knowing: the knowledge of the language on the part of both builders, their knowledge of their trade, tacit knowledge they have built up about what to expect of each other. None of this amounts to say-ing that "Please hand me a brick" is an assertion of a bit of knowledge, rather than a request,[11] which may, of course, be correctly understood or misinter-preted by the person to whom it is directed. Similarly, from the fact that I can understand or interpret a poem incorrectly, it does not follow that it is a ve-hicle of knowledge.[12]

As far as theses (6), (7), and (8) are concerned, it is important, I think, to see that the issues they raise are also completely distinct from the traditional issue of what poetry is and how it is best to be understood and evaluated.

Let me start with (8). In the course of his account Professor Most formu-lates a fundamental tenet of Romantic common sense. He writes that "for sev-eral thousand years very many readers of poetry have been convinced that they learned something interesting and important from it" and seems to take this as some kind of argument for thinking poetry is a form of knowledge. There are at least two difficulties with this. First of all, and trivially, the fact that many people for thousands of years have believed something does not make it true. For over a thousand years large numbers of people have be-lieved they learned something interesting and important from the doctrines

---

[11] Of course, it can be an *expression* of the knowledge the builder has of what is needed at this moment. Expressing something and asserting something are two different things, as are as-serting something and presupposing something, see Raymond Geuss, "Poetry and Knowledge," pp. 188–89 above.

[12] If the example of the request for a brick fails to convince, think of a question. In ordinary parlance the sentence "2 + 2 = 4" is distinct from "How much is 2 + 2?" in that the first is an instance or a vehicle of knowledge in a way in which the second is not. This issue is completely distinct from (a) the issue whether both of these do not presuppose certain forms of knowledge—of course, they do (knowledge of English)—and (b) the issue whether it is possible to say one has understood each of the two sentences correctly or incorrectly. I can understand "How much is 2 + 2?" correctly or incorrectly. That in itself tells me nothing about whether it is itself an in-stance of knowledge or an assertion of a truth. If one says it *is* an assertion of a truth because it presupposes various bit of "knowledge" on the part both of the questioner and the person to whom the question is directed, for instance, knowledge of the English language, then that is cor-rect, but one has changed the original terms of discussion in such a way as to make the whole issue trivial.

of Christianity, such as the Incarnation, without, despite the views of certain Protestant theologians, that being grounds to hold that these doctrines were true or that apprehension of these doctrines was knowledge.[13] Second, and much more importantly, from the fact that I can learn something from studying X, it in no way follows that X is a kind, instance, or vehicle of knowledge. This is a form of inference that I wish most vehemently to reject, because otherwise it will cause infinite confusion: "Reading/studying *Hamlet* gives me knowledge, therefore *Hamlet* is (a form, a kind, or an instance of) knowledge." This seems parallel to "Studying mathematics gives me knowledge (say, of numbers), therefore mathematics is a form of knowledge." Why, though, assume that this is the relevant parallel rather than "Studying beetles gives me knowledge (of bugs), therefore beetles are (instances of?) knowledge," or "Studying the palms of people's hands gives me knowledge (say, of the variation of human pigmentation), therefore the palms of people's hands are knowledge?"

To move on to (7), not everything that can be an *object* of knowledge is thereby shown to be an instance of knowledge. I can have knowledge of rock formations, the meteorological conditions of a certain country, etc. which is as objective as anything is, without a rock formation itself being in any way "knowledge." Similarly, nothing in what I have claimed suggests that the study of literature is not in principle just as objective a form of knowledge as geology is. I may have other independent grounds for doubting that literature is an object of knowledge, but that is another issue. Still, this in no way supports the claim that poetry itself is knowledge.

That leaves (6). Not everything which requires the activation of cognitive human capacities to understand, is *itself* a form of cognition. In order to understand *Hamlet*, I must, of course, probably exercise various visual capacities—I must be able to watch the performance—and some minimal linguistic skills. Even if I don't need to understand the language at a very high level, I must be able to do some minimal cognitive processing of the language. Therefore, one might be tempted to conclude, *Hamlet* gives us knowledge, but that would be a mistake. Again, to study geological stratification, I must perhaps exercise various visual and linguistic skills. This does not make a rock formation an *instance* of knowledge, but at best an *object* of knowledge.

So in one sense I can agree completely with Professor Most: we can learn various things, perhaps some of them interesting and important, from reading *Hamlet*, just as we can learn various things, some of them interesting and important, by studying cloud formations (allowing us perhaps to predict the weather) or by having a massage (which will make us acquainted with mus-

---

[13] One might, of course, want an explanation of the persistence of a false belief. This is what I try to provide at the end of my essay with my references to the "metaphysical need" and various Nietzschean doctrines.

cles of which we were unaware). For me the discussion only becomes interesting and important if it is claimed that for most poetry there is some form
of knowledge or acquaintance that goes *beyond* these kinds of banal cases.
This approach would become interesting only if it were possible to say *in what
specific way* poetry gave us acquaintance with something—in what way *that
was distinctive* of poetry, and not shared by empirical observation, human
empathy, and basic skills of language comprehension that are activated when
we hear any speech. One does not need to be a "formalist" in any very substantial sense to feel that *how* something is said is at least as significant as what
is said. Failing any account of this, I find the claim that poetry "gives us acquaintance" empty.[14]

Even if one accepts this clarification of my basic claim, one would surely,
and correctly, point out that this cannot be the whole story, if what I am saying is to have any real interest for students and critics of literature. My claim
that the *essence* of poetry is not knowledge is perfectly compatible with the
view that *some* poems are instances or vehicles of knowledge; I neither asserted not denied that. Surely, for my thesis to be of interest to people concerned with literature, rather than being of merely technical interest to some
philosophers, it must have some more distinctive first-order content.

One might object with some justification that what looked like and was presented as a potentially interesting but unfortunately (for me) false thesis:

"poetry is not knowledge" = "no form of poetry has any relation to cognition, truth,
knowledge at all"

actually turns out to be a thesis which may or may not be correct, but which
in any case is not terribly interesting:

"poetry is not knowledge" = "there is no essence of poetry by virtue of which it
must be a vehicle of truth"

We are all familiar with philosophical claims that have this built-in disap-
pointment. When Kant says that the world we know is "appearance" and not
a reality in itself, the immediate impulse is overwhelmingly to read this as if
it meant what Schopenhauer did mean when he said various similar things:
The world we know is *nothing but* a tissue of insubstantial illusion. Disap-
pointingly, it then turns out that "appearance" is a Kantian technical term,
which means, roughly, "located in space and time and subject to categories
such as 'causality,' 'substance,' and so forth." So "Our world is appearance"
means: "Our world is extended in space and time, subject to laws of causality, etc."

---

[14] There is in principle a further possibility, which is that poetry has a distinctive object. Most
people who hold this will also hold that there is a distinctive form of access to this object or way
of presenting the results of acquaintance with it.

Wittgenstein at one point says that philosophical problems arise when "language throws a party,"[15] i.e., when it steps out of the practical, everyday contexts in which it has a clear use and meaning, kicks over the traces, and begins to do silly things. This leads to errors and confusion. The only positive task for contemporary philosophy is to point this fact out and reduce language use to its practical context, a context in which it functions perfectly well.[16] Philosophy, then, "leaves everything as it is."[17]

I very explicitly do *not* wish to endorse this aspect of Wittgenstein. Why, though, should these apparently scholastic concerns about the definition (or the impossibility of giving a definition) of poetry matter for actual literary criticism? There are two related reasons. First, I think that there is room (in some cases) for distinguishing between correct and incorrect philosophical views, and whether one has a correct or an incorrect general view should have an effect on one's actual practice in writing, interpreting, and performing poetry. Second, the issue of definition is the traditional locus of engagement for various evaluative issues. Part of the Platonic model is that the value of something consists in the extent to which it realizes its essence. If the essence of poetry is knowledge, the best poetry will be that which is truest. A *good* poem was one that did well what its definition prescribed, that is, it was a good vehicle for knowledge.

If the first of these reasons is right, I must also be calling on people to change their practice of writing, listening, reading, thinking, and speaking insofar as it concerns poetry. It would be too simple, and completely uninformative, to say "poetry is not *essentially* knowledge (but in any given case you care to mention it is perhaps accidentally, but extremely importantly, knowledge)." I am suggesting a turn away from the traditional practice of looking for a "truth about the world or the self" purportedly embodied in poetic works. I think that the search for "truth" in poetry distracts from much more significant things: the study of the expressive, formal, rhetorical, and pragmatic features of poetic language, including meter, rhythm, syntax, and figuration, the study of the social context, the study of genres, etc. I also hold that the results that arise from the search for "truth" tend to be exceedingly thin: etiolated, uninteresting, empty, and boring.

For those who feel pained by the denial that poetry is knowledge (in any special or interesting sense) it will perhaps take a bit of the sting out of the claim to note the parallel with music. Traditional Western music is a possible object of a highly articulated science. One can explain what a diminished seventh chord is in such a way as to distinguish it from a minor third. One can recognize a certain progression as a "Dresden Amen." One can analyze the

---

[15] Ludwig Wittgenstein, *Philosophische Untersuchungen*, § 38.
[16] Ibid., § 109–116; 301.
[17] Ibid., § 124.

number of voices present in a piece, locate *stretti*, etc. From the fact that there is a highly structured quasi-scientific knowledge *of* music, it does not follow that a given piece of music is *itself* an instance of knowledge of the world (or of anything else). Schopenhauer was wrong to think music gave us quasi-cognitive, immediate access to Reality. Similarly, I can give a highly technical account of the metrical structure of certain kinds of poetry, even discovering things about it of which those who practiced the form were most probably not themselves consciously aware (such as Porson's bridge in iambic trimeter). Music, however, is not knowledge, although there is knowledge of music, and the understanding and production of music requires activation of highly complex human cognitive faculties. It does not follow from the fact that music is not knowledge that it is not of great importance.[18] Precisely the structured release from linguistic discursivity, the practical imperatives of action, and acquaintance with real or imaginary people and things can be experienced as pleasurable and significant.

In conclusion let me explain my basic intention in a slightly different way, which may make it easier to understand for those who had difficulty with the first formulation in "Poetry and Knowledge." Imagine a *very* pious Protestant scholar who wished to write a history of visual art in the twentieth century from the point of view of a theology based on the literal interpretation of the New Testament.[19] Every artist, movement, and work would be discussed in relation to the Christian Good News. Of course, one could do this; it is not impossible. Such a work might well contain a lot of highly interesting insightful analysis, perhaps, for instance, of paintings by Rouault, and it needn't contain any errors. However, much would be liable to be left out—what exactly would the author have to say about Kandinsky, apart from some commonplace remarks about "the discovery of the infinite wonders of pure color and pure shape in God's most marvelous creation: space itself, uncluttered by humanly recognizable objects?" We would be likely to feel that the author was not treating the paintings "as paintings" (which is again an appeal to a *different* kind of common sense, the common sense of a secularist society). In addition, those of us who do not share this specific Protestant perspective would be likely to find the whole treatment highly peculiar and arbitrary. Why emphasize *this* point rather than *that*? Should we really be looking for the religious truth in every painting? Is this the most enlightening and useful way to proceed? The basic question, however, would be, why start from the assumption that the doctrine of the New Testament is the final framework for interpreting everything? What I was trying to say in my original paper was

---

[18] Note, I am *not* saying here that poetry is *just like* music. See Adorno, "Fragment über Musik und Sprache," in his *Quasi una Fantasia* (Frankfurt: Suhrkamp, 1963).

[19] The account I give here is deeply influenced by Max Weber's discussion of meaning and interpretation in the study of history. See the essays in his *Gesammelte Schriften zur Wissenschaftslehre* (Tübingen: Mohr, 1973).

that there is a similar cognitivist framework that was installed by Plato: Interpret everything in terms of its relation to possible cognition.[20] Some poetry in some dimensions responds to such an analysis, but this is not true of all poetry in all its aspects. And why accept the cognitivist framework in any case? Of course, since human beings are creatures who, among other things, are trying to come to terms with their world by coming to know it, *any* human phenomenon one might name will be, as it were, swimming in a sea of various modes of knowing. If you are really looking, you will probably be able to force even lullabies and nonsense verse into *some* relation to knowing, just as the Protestant art historian will be able to force anything into his schema, although for those of us who do not share his religious commitments the result will be likely to be grotesque—not "false" in any very obvious sense, but radically deformed. Once you begin trying to see poetry through the lens of its conformity or deviation from cognitive paradigms, the effect will be both constricting and distorting. Both the constriction and the distortion are unnecessary.

Of course, one can try to extend the meaning of "true/false," "cognition," and "knowledge" so as to include all the phenomena that I described as "grotesque," "deformed," and "distorted." Given the Nietzschean/Wittgensteinean theory of language I sketched earlier, no one can prevent[21] anyone from trying out such an extension. There is no clear ontological boundary between night and day. There is not, that is, a particular moment at which day ceases and night begins, but it does not follow from that that there is no difference between night and day. At a certain point in the past people might have argued that the correct extension of "bridge" reaches exactly *thus* far and no further, so you can't call the piece of wood on a cello its "bridge." The OED gives 1607 as the first occurrence of the word "bridge" in its specifically musical usage. This argument might, then, have been plausible in the fifteenth century AD, and no longer plausible in the seventeenth. The reasons for the

---

[20] John Dewey (*Art as Experience*, New York: Capricorn, 1958, p. 291) speaks of an "overintellectualized conception of art."

[21] In fact my own views are the result of having spent about 30 years of my life reading and rereading, off and on, the aesthetic writings of Hegel and Adorno, trying to make sense of their claim that art is essentially the presentation of Truth. I was especially interested in the plausibility of this claim, particularly in the case of music. In two papers, "Art and Theodicy" and "Form and 'the new' in Adorno's *Vers une musique informelle*" (both published as chapters of my *Morality, Culture, and History* [Cambridge: Cambridge University Press, 1999]) I tried to explain this claim as plausibly and sympathetically as I could. My present view is that one can torture the terms "true," "cognition," "knowledge" into shape so that the required statements "Art presents the truth," "Art is a form of knowledge" come out true, but (1) they have then departed so far from ordinary usage that these statements are uninformative, and (2) using them requires accepting an enormous metaphysical apparatus that one can have strong reservations about on other grounds. For a good introduction to the strand of aesthetics I have in mind here, see Max Paddison's superb *Adorno's Aesthetics of Music* (Cambridge: Cambridge University Press, 1993).

change will have been very complex. The Nietzschean/Wittgensteinean theory of language does not imply that in language usage anything goes, or that any extension of the use of any term at any time is realistically possible and illuminating. Rather it implies that argumentation about the usefulness of such extension is contextual, and boundaries are unclear. We understand very imperfectly the conditions that must be satisfied for a new extension to establish itself. Social habit most likely plays an important role. What I find striking is that we *have* had a social habit among a large group of people professionally interested in the study of art, who in the wake of Romanticism have had an interest in this extension, and yet we can see that it hasn't worked. It adds nothing and sows confusion.

Nietzsche and Wittgenstein invite us to expand our horizons and throw off certain puritanical and constricting illusions. I know that this freedom can seem terrifying—there can be gripping, imaginative constructions that cannot be disciplined into structures of knowledge—but if we can face down this terror, that can lead to a genuine liberation of the human spirit. I invite all those who hold onto the more repressive forms of the "poetry is knowledge" ideology to free their minds instead.

13

Thucydides, Nietzsche, and Williams

WHO IS A BETTER GUIDE to human life, Plato or Thucydides? Given this choice, virtually all European philosophers for the past two thousand years would have chosen Plato. Indeed one might almost say that to exhibit this preference defines what it is to be a philosophically minded person in the traditional mold. Plato has fascinating things to say about the human soul as an entity composed of parts that can conflict, about the nature of knowledge and the authority it should have in human life, and about how human excellence is related to the demands imposed on us by the necessity of living together. Even more significantly, Plato has presented all philosophers since his time with the model of what it is to "have a philosophy" at all: it means having a systematically interconnected, abstract overview of and position on *all* the important features of human life which is argued for and justified in (purportedly) absolutely general terms. How could anyone think that the narration of a highly specific sequence of events that took place very long ago involving small groups of technologically rather primitive people squabbling in an obscure corner of the Balkans could conceivably compete with Plato's glorious project?

In the late nineteenth century Nietzsche broke radically with this founding assumption of Western philosophy. He did this not by developing one line or another of argument against Plato, but merely by raising the question about Plato's presumed self-evident superiority over Thucydides in a way that revealed that there was an issue of real philosophical substance and significance in the relation between the two on which it was possible to disagree. One way in which a philosopher can be original—many would say, the most profound way in which a philosopher can be original—is not by giving an ingenious or particularly well-grounded or especially convincing answer to a pre-existing question, but rather by asking a novel question or finding an issue where no one before has seen one. Thus Nietzsche thought it was one of his

Sir Bernard Williams, FBA (1929–2003) was Professor of Philosophy successively at University College/London, Cambridge, Oxford, and the University of California, Berkeley. From 1967 to 2003 he was a Fellow—and from 1979 to 1987 Provost—of King's College, Cambridge. In spring 1989 he gave the Sather Lectures at the University of California, Berkeley which were subsequently published as *Shame and Necessity* (Berkeley and Los Angeles: University of California Press, 1993). This essay is a slightly expanded version of a contribution to a memorial booklet printed privately by the Fellows of King's College. I am very grateful to Hilary Gaskin, Peter Garnsey, Jeremy Mynott, and Quentin Skinner for helpful comments on the original draft.

strongest claims to originality that he for the first time explicitly and persistently asked questions like "What is the value of our morality?" or "Why do we assume that truth will always be of greater value than error?" and did not simply presuppose that the value of truth and morality was self-evident.

Nietzsche found Thucydides more illuminating about human life than Plato for two reasons. First, he held that Thucydides had an unprejudiced theoretical sympathy for, and hence understanding of, a much wider spectrum of possible human motivations than Plato had.[1] *All* the characters in his history are allowed to exhibit the highest possible intelligence, clarity, and rationality in pursuing their respective enterprises, regardless of the judgments representatives of conventional morality would make on them.[2] Socrates, however, "dragged moralizing into science," and Plato followed in his wake.[3] Such moralizing, Nietzsche thought, was a result of weakness, of a deep-seated inability to bear looking the facts of the world in the face;[4] it crippled Plato intellectually and prevented him from ever developing that most highly prized of Nietzschean traits: *"Tatsachen-Sinn,"*[5] a "sense for the facts," that steely realism that is so abundantly evident on every page of Thucydides. Characters of whom Plato ethically disapproves, such as Thrasymachus or Callicles, are always shown in his dialogues to be confuted by Socrates. Vicious people, however, as we all know, do *not* always lose the argument. What Plato takes to be morally reprehensible behavior *must*, he thinks, finally be a form of irrationality that is self-defeating, and this puts such narrow limits to his ability to understand humans that it renders him unfit to be a serious guide to the world in which we live.

Another way of putting this might seem to be to claim that Plato could not have written such a characteristically clear-sighted, analytically rigorous, and uncompromising Thucydidean text as the Melian dialogue. Bernard Williams quite rightly corrects the implication this might be naturally taken to have when he points out that what is really at issue is not the empathetic, literary,

---

[1] Friedrich Nietzsche, *Morgenröthe* § 168 (= *SW, Sämtliche Werke: Kritische Studienausgabe*, ed. G. Colli and M. Montinari [Berlin: de Gruyter 1980], vol. 3, pp. 151–52).

[2] Nietzsche, *SW*, vol. 11, p. 58: 25 [187].

[3] *SW*, vol. 11, p. 554: 36 [11].

[4] See Nietzsche *Götzendämmerung*: "Was ich den Alten verdanke" § 2 (= *SW*, vol. 6, pp. 155–56). I note that in this passage Nietzsche does a little rhetorical counter-moralizing himself, calling Plato not merely "weak" and "unable to face the facts," but "a coward in the face of reality." Needless to say, for reasons some of which emerge later in this essay, I do not think there is anything incoherent about this. At least one very important strand in Nietzsche is by no means opposed to any form of morality, but rather seems devoted to constructing a more realistic morality than that of Plato and the philosophical tradition (see Nietzsche, *Der Antichrist* § 59, *SW*, vol. 6, p. 248; etc.)

[5] See Nietzsche, *Der Antichrist* § 59, *SW* vol. 6, p. 248; see also *SW*, vol. 10, pp. 335–40: 8 [15], and Nietzsche, *Zur Genealogie der Moral* : "Vorrede" § 7 (*SW*, vol. 5, p. 254). See, finally, Williams, *Truth and Truthfulness* (Princeton, NJ: Princeton University Press, 2002), pp. 12–19.

hermeneutic, expository, or other human capacities of the individual Plato but what the explanatory motivational apparatus he recognizes and develops in his work would structurally require or admit: "Thucydides' conception of an intelligible and typically human motivation is broader and less committed to a distinctive ethical outlook than Plato's; or rather—the distinction is important—it is broader than the conception acknowledged in Plato's psychological theories" (*Shame and Necessity*, pp. 161–62). Nietzsche is, of course, keen to connect these two—the man Plato and the Platonic philosophy—as closely as possible. Williams proposes a more subtle account of a kind with which we are familiar in other contexts. Many have thought that Freud the clinical practitioner exhibited a higher, deeper, or fuller "understanding" of the human psyche than he was able to articulate in his theoretical constructs, so that the "real" Freud is the Freud of the case histories, not the Freud of the meta-psychological writings. Hegel very clearly taught that any form of spirit (except his own) appealed to, used, and exhibited more complex structures than it could explicitly give an account of. So similarly, one might try to claim, Plato was, after all, an extraordinary literary and philosophical genius, who was capable even of the apparently deeply un-Platonic performance of depicting Alcibiades (in *Symposium*) as attractive; it might then well be the case that he exhibited in his dialogues—although he could not articulate—a much more subtle, flexible, and insightful practice of philosophy and understanding of human nature than his theories would have allowed. It was, of course, Plato's *theories* that were historically more influential than the practice, so in one sense it makes perfect sense to focus on them.

The situation here is further complicated by Nietzsche's claim that he had a low opinion of Plato's literary and stylistic gifts.[6] This, however, is such an extraordinarily obtuse or willfully perverse judgment that one suspects that it must be a pose adopted for some strategic purpose or simply for effect, as when Nietzsche claims to prefer the music of Bizet to that of Wagner.[7] If Nietzsche really did find Plato "boring," then perhaps there is simply nothing more to say about this particular lapse on his part, but there are clear ways, or at any rate the germs of ways, in which one could come to a very different judgment of Plato within a basically Nietzschean way of looking at the world. After all, in *Birth of Tragedy* Nietzsche emphasizes that tragedy in some sense killed itself ("*sie starb durch Selbstmord*");[8] Euripides was the main executioner, with some help from Socrates. Tragedy, however, one could argue, was only really "dead" when it was *replaced* by something else. In one sense what replaced it was Socratic rationalism and its extension, what came to be "Western philosophy," but the process by which the replacement was effected re-

[6] See Nietzsche, *Götzendämmerung*," Was ich den Alten verdanke" § 2 (*SW*, vol. 6, p. 155).
[7] See Nietzsche, *Der Fall Wagner*, "Vorwort" and §§ 1–2 (*SW*, vol. 6, pp. 11–16).
[8] *Geburt der Tragödie* § 11 (*SW*, vol. 1, p. 75).

quires a deeper account of how it took place than is often given. Excitable Hellenic youth did perhaps turn its back on the theater because it had become boring,[9] but this does not yet explain why it chose to embrace the chaste and austere delights of linguistic analysis, logical argumentation, and (potentially) the Life of Reason instead. As Plato clearly realized (see the *Symposium*), the erotic fascination Socrates exercised during his life had something to do with this, but Nietzsche adds to this an observation about the important role the "image" or "picture" (*Bild*) of the dying Socrates played.[10] Plato was "enchanted"[11] by Socrates and "threw himself down before this image,"[12] and this quasi-erotic, quasi-religious bondage had significant historical consequences. As Nietzsche puts it in *Human, All-Too-Human*: "It is by no means an idle question whether Plato, if he had remained free of enchantment by Socrates, might not have found an even higher type of philosophical man, which is lost to us forever. When one looks at the period before Plato one seems to be gazing into a workshop for forming such types (*Bildner-Werkstätte solcher Typen*).[13] While the emphasis here is on Plato *finding* a type of philosopher, as if that were like a block of stone already roughed out for a statue in a mason's yard and needing simply to be discovered, this almost certainly underestimates the active shaping that would be required if the rough-hewn original were to be finished off, taken out of the shop, and set up so as to attract the appropriate continuing attention. There is a sense in which the image of Socrates is a fetish which Plato himself at least partly *created*. Socrates' impact, Nietzsche tells us, was in fact so overwhelming, that in order to tolerate him, Plato had to *transform* him ("*umbilden*"),[14] to produce a very free portrait, a picture of Socrates that suited *Plato* ("*Plato's freie Art, . . . sich Sokrates zurecht zu machen*").[15] To present Socrates, whose life was essentially devoted to conducting private conversations with individuals,[16] as a figure who dies in some sense "heroically" because of his commitment to the Life of Reason requires at least minimal artistic structuration and stylization of the material a real human life provides. Only when this image of the death of Socrates supplants those of the deaths of Patroclus, Ajax, and Hector can Reason really take over from myth, and Western philosophy succeed tragedy. Philosophy as we know it established itself as a continuing presence in Western culture partly because in his dialogues Plato was able to embody the erotic charge of Socrates in a striking image that transmitted it down the ages and

---

[9] As indicated by Dionysus's reaction at the start of Aristophanes' *The Frogs*.

[10] *Geburt der Tragödie* § 13 (*SW*, vol. 1, p. 91).

[11] See Nietzsche, *Menschliches, Allzumenschliches I* § 261 (*SW*, vol. 2, p. 216).

[12] *Geburt der Tragödie* § 13 (*SW*, vol. 1, p. 91).

[13] See Nietzsche, *Menschliches, Allzumenschliches I* § 261 (*SW*, vol. 2, p. 216).

[14] See *SW*, vol. 10, p. 337.

[15] See *SW*, vol. 10, p. 338.

[16] See *Apology* 23b, 31c. *Gorgias* 484c–86d (admittedly by a hostile witness).

hooked successive generations on the dialectic. This can be seen as a kind of artistic creation, a skilled production of highly and long-lastingly effective *Schein*, and it would, then, seem to be perfectly possible to find this achievement neither boring nor lacking in artistic merit.

The antecedent moralization of the basic categories in Plato's theory of human psychology vitiates his own positive ethical proposals. If he really has merely smuggled a set of tacit moral assumptions into his basic psychology, then it is not surprising that he can victoriously draw them out again as conclusions. To the extent to which Plato, and most philosophers after him, have done this while pretending to be engaged in some kind of disinterested inquiry, they are violating their own ostensible standards of good faith, truthfulness, and noncircularity of argumentation.

Nietzsche's second reason for preferring Thucydides concerns the issue of optimism or pessimism as the appropriate human attitude toward the world. Nietzsche correctly diagnosed the philosophical tradition as deeply optimistic.[17] This optimism had several related aspects. First of all, traditional philosophers assumed that the world could be made cognitively accessible to us without remainder: it was in principle possible to come to know any part of the world as it really was. Second, they assumed that when the world was correctly understood, it would make moral sense to us. Third, the kind of "moral sense" which the world made to us would be one that would show it to have *some* orientation toward the satisfaction of some basic, rational human desires or interests, that is, the world was not sheerly indifferent to or perversely frustrating of human happiness.[18] Fourth, the world is set up so that for us to accumulate knowledge and use our reason as vigorously as possible will be good for us, and will contribute to making us happy. Finally, it was assumed that there was a natural fit between the exercise of reason, the conditions of healthy individual human development, the demands of individuals for satisfaction of their needs, interests and basic desires, and human sociability. Nature, reason, and all human goods, including human virtues, formed a potentially harmonious whole.[19] There was one human state and one course of human development which was "correct" (or, as Aristotle would put it, "natural") for us. "Natural" human development would lead to a full development of human rational capacities. This is turn would make humans disposed toward socially desirable forms of conduct, and also individually and collectively

---

[17] Nietzsche thinks this is part of the legacy of Socrates; see *Die Geburt der Tragödie aus dem Geiste der Musik* § 15 (*SW* 1:97–102).

[18] Note that there are three distinct ideas here: (a) the world makes *some* kind of sense, (b) the world makes "moral" sense, (c) the world makes a kind of moral sense in which human needs and at least some human aspirations have *some* standing.

[19] One of Williams's principal teachers, Isaiah Berlin, was a subtle analyst and highly outspoken critic of precisely this strand of traditional moral thinking in all its forms. See his *Four Essays on Liberty* (Oxford: Oxford University Press, 1969), esp. pp. li, 8, 167–72.

happy. Over the last two thousand years, there have been different accounts given of what "correct" or "natural" means, and there have been any number of minor reinterpretations of and deviations from the above scheme, but the basic structure of a philosophy centered around the claim of a harmonious fit between what is rational, what is good for us, and what is good for our society has been very widely retained. If one excludes a few Gnostics, the odd skeptic, and marginal figures like Schopenhauer, few philosophers or religious thinkers in the West have not been guided by it, at least as a tacit ideal.

In one respect the "rationalism" of Socrates is, however, peculiar. Plato's Socrates may be wiser than others in that he does not think he knows what he does not know (*Ap.* 21d), and he may strive constantly for greater knowledge and greater self-clarity, but his life is also fundamentally structured not around a form of well-grounded prepositional knowledge, but rather around what he himself calls a "great hope" (πολλὴ ἐλπίς *Ap.* 40c4; also *Phaedo* 67b7–c3), the almost ludicrously optimistic belief that nothing bad can befall a good man. If Plato's account in *Apology, Crito*, and *Phaedo* is to be believed, in his last days Socrates refused to save himself by availing himself of existing possibilities of avoiding conviction and the death penalty, and then of escaping from prison, and succumbed to bouts of preachiness during which he exhorted his companions to be of "good hope" (". . . ὑμᾶς χρή . . . εὐέλπιδας εἶναι" *Ap.* 41c8; compare also *Phaedo* 63b4–c7) with regard to death: it cannot be an inherently bad thing because it befalls both good and bad people alike. It is striking how heavy a weight this "ἐλπίς" is made to bear.

The contrast with Thucydides could hardly be starker. The power of "ἐλπίς" is a recurrent theme in his history, but ἐλπίς for him is almost invariably deluding and its power is overwhelmingly destructive.[20] "Hope (ἐλπίς) and desire (ἔρως), the latter leading the way, cleverly hatching the enterprise, the former following, suggesting that chance will make the circumstances propitious for success (τὴν εὐπορίαν τῆς τύχης ὑποτιθεῖσα), between them cause the greatest destruction" (III.45.5; see also V.103). This view of "ἐλπίς" is also not simply an "opinion" expressed by various speakers in the history, but Thucydides himself seems to delight in demonstrating its validity through the juxtaposition of speech and narrative. Thus, when Nicias in Sicily appeals to "hope" (VII.77) in addressing his troops, the reader can hardly avoid feeling sure that he and they are about to suffer complete destruction, as in fact they do, and it is hard to believe Thucydides did not intend this sinister effect.

Thucydides seems largely immune to any of the forms of wishful thinking associated with Platonic optimism. He knows that good men suffer unde-

---

[20] For the best treatment of this aspect of Thucydides known to me, see Hans-Peter Stahl, *Thukydides: Die Stellung des Menschen im geschichtlichen Prozeß* (Zetemata, Heft 40; Munich: Beck, 1966). See also discussion of Ἐλπίς in Hesiod, *Works and Days*, ed. M. L. West (Oxford: Oxford University Press, 1978) pp. 169–70 and further passages and modern works cited there.

served, irremediable, definitive catastrophic failure (Nicias); unworthy men reap the benefit of others' achievements (Cleon in Pylos); men exhibit pre-eminent virtue in some contexts and fall into decadence in others (Pausanias); there is no preexisting "meaning" in the world, only what we humans can construct by our weak powers and flawed efforts. Human rationality is real, but its motivational power is extremely weak, particularly in the face of human hopes, loves, desires, and fears, and the success of even the most well-founded and rational plan is at the mercy of external chance. Donald Rumsfeld, regardless of what one might think of the rest of his politics, is making a good Thucydidean point when he emphasizes the importance not just of "known unknowns" in war and politics—factors for which some rational provision can be made, even if only on the basis of educated estimates—but also of "unknown unknowns" which cannot be subjected even to crude rational approximation because they cannot be envisaged at all, and which thus lie strictly beyond the possibility of human ratiocination.

In what is in many ways his most impressive book, *Shame and Necessity*, Bernard Williams cites and endorses the above Nietzschean account: Thucydides should be seen to stand with Sophocles as the major representative of an attitude toward the world which is realistic, values truthfulness, and is lacking in the shallow "optimism" of later philosophy (*SN* pp. 163–64). This coupling of Thucydides and Sophocles might seem rather odd, and thus warrants some further attention.

We are used to believing that there was an "old quarrel" between poetry and philosophy in pre-Socratic Greece,[21] although, as Andrew Ford in a recent work[22] has persuasively shown, there is no evidence that this was the case and the claim is perhaps best understood as a bit of Platonic invention or disinformation. In the original published version of *The Birth of Tragedy* Nietzsche accepts this bipartite structure of the argument, although, of course, he wishes to reverse Plato's valuation and argue for the superiority of poetry over Socratic philosophy. Thucydides, who might have been thought to represent a third option, is not even mentioned in Nietzsche's text. After the publication of *The Birth of Tragedy*, however, Nietzsche does seem to have gradually become aware that reading the history of Greece simply through the lens of the struggle between Homer/Sophocles, on the one hand, and Socrates/Plato, on the other, leaves out something important. Thus in a note from 1885, he calls the attitude exhibited by the philosopher Democritus, the physician Hippocrates, and Thucydides the high point of scientific-mindedness (*Wissenschaftlichkeit*) that was attained in Greece, and speaks of the opposition between the ethical philosophy of someone like Socrates and "science."[23]

---

[21] Plato, *Republic* 607b.
[22] Andrew Ford, *The Origins of Criticism* (Princeton, NJ: Princeton University Press, 2002).
[23] *SW*, vol. 11, p. 554: 36[11].

"*Wissenschaftlichkeit*" means careful, methodical attention to the real facts of the situation being investigated. As Williams points out (*Truth and Truthfulness*[24] pp. 12, 152–53), however, it does not necessarily imply commitment to the ideals of positivism to the extent to which these represent a code of restrictive practice. This negative canon would have it that a "scientific" account must restrict itself to a purportedly value-free registering of observable facts, to the formulation of generalizations that have their full meaning by virtue of being connected to sets of observable facts, and to the use of conjunctions of fact and generalization for the purposes of causal explanation and prediction.

Thucydides' way of approaching his subject is like that advocated by the positivists in that his treatment is radically nonmythic,[25] nontheological, and nonliterary. Although he uses the Homeric poems as material to be studied in the interest of forming plausible hypotheses about certain aspects of earlier societies,[26] he shows disdain for the exaggerations, inventions, and factual insouciance of poets,[27] and specifically disclaims any intention of trying to increase the appeal of his work by giving it a literary polish.[28] His project is to exhibit what really moves people to act, and what then happens to them and to others as a consequence of how they act, not to write an edifying treatise or a partisan tract. Thucydides' account differs, however, from anything that positivists of the stricter observance would countenance in taking human beliefs, attitudes, emotions, valuations, even superstitions[29] very seriously indeed as things that need to be considered if one wishes to have a genuine understanding of what happens in the human world. His impartiality between the two warring sides in the conflict between the Athenians and Peloponnesians should also not be confused with a positivist commitment to an ideal of "value-freedom." He is in no way reluctant to express value judgments of his own when it suits him. These include not only low-level technical judgments such as praise of Pericles for his "foresight"—in that the Athenians would have won the war if they had consistently followed his initial strategy (II.65)— but also overall moral evaluations such as that Nicias was a man who did not deserve the end he suffered (VII.86).

The work Thucydides wrote is not "history" at all in the most usual sense in which we use the term, that is, a work that is centrally or specifically concerned with a study of the *past*.[30] Thucydides is specifically interested not in the *past*,

[24] Princeton University Press, 2002.

[25] I. 20–22.

[26] I.3.

[27] I.10.

[28] I.22.

[29] II. 54 (plague and oracles); VII.50 about Nicias.

[30] Although we still use the term "history" in a wider sense in expressions like "natural history," the Greek word (ἱστορία) from which ours is derived has a very broad extension, meaning any kind of "investigation," "inquiry," or "research." Furthermore, we have no idea what, if any-

but in understanding those forms of collective human behavior that are re-current and thus comprehensible.[31] He pursues this aim by giving a narrative account of what was for him the present: current affairs, in some of which he was himself an actor. Part of this narrative account is an analysis of the motives and reasons of various individual and social agents. One could then say that he is trying to do something like what we might call "social and political theory" or even "behavioral science" (if the later term could be cleansed of all the as-sociations it has acquired during the past century or so), but *only provided* one keeps clearly in mind that he does not think there are "laws" of history or so-ciety which we can formulate abstractly and the mastery of which will allow us to control our fate.[32] One of the most important things one can learn from the study of "human nature" is that this kind of control is an illusion.

Understanding human nature as exhibited in large-scale human action re-quires the correct sequencing of complex, spatially distant events, placing them in their proper order through time, and as Williams emphasizes in chap-ter 7 of *Truth and Truthfulness*, this requires having a general notion of a single, measurable historical time within which events in different places can be located. This is not a triviality because "human beings can live with-out the idea of historical time" (*Truth and Truthfulness*, p. 169), and in fact they did so in Europe until the fifth century BC. Thucydides is extremely self-conscious and careful in introducing a single chronological scheme which will allow clear and unambiguous coordination of the diverse local calendars used in the different Greek cities.[33] Williams seems to go so far as to attribute to Thucydides the "invention" of the "objective" conception of time (*Truth and Truthfulness*, pp. 154, 169–71). Again, this invention might be an essential precondition for doing history (rather than narrating stories of indeterminate historical location), but to invent a very conception of objective time is not, by itself, to do history, as we understand it.

It is a commonplace in the secondary literature on Thucydides that, in con-trast, for instance, to Plato, he stands alone. There were plenty of followers of Plato, Platonists of one kind of another, in antiquity, but no Thucy-dideans.[34] In the strict sense Thucydides had no successors in doing his spe-

---

thing, Thucydides himself would have called his work, had he finished it. In the text we have he never refers to it by using the word "ἱστορία," and in any case the whole issue of the titles of works from antiquity is highly complex and obscure. In the late fifth century BC the giving of ti-tles to works seems to have been a significantly more casual matter than it later became, and cer-tainly not the object of sustained authorial concern.

[31] I. 22.

[32] On the non-instrumentalist nature of Thucydides' conception of understanding and expla-nation, see Hans-Peter Stahl, *Thukydides: Die Stellung des Menschen im geschichtlichen Prozeß.*

[33] See A. W. Gomme, *A Historical Commentary on Thucydides* (Oxford: Oxford University Press, 1945), vol. 1, pp. 1–8.

[34] Philistius is mentioned as *"Thucydidi imitator"* (Quintilian X,74; see also Cicero, *Brutus*

cific kind of "investigation." There were those who "continued" his narrative, telling the story of the war between the Athenians and Peloponnesians from the point at which his (unfinished) account breaks off to the final destruction of Athens, but each of these "continuators" had his own very different agenda, different aims, different literary styles and modes of proceeding from Thucydides. It is often claimed that the reason for this lack of direct influence was the extreme success of the discipline that came in some sense to be a competitor to Thucydidean "inquiry": rhetoric. Rhetoric was in some ways the most immediately advantageous, practical skill a young man in a πόλις could learn, and thus came to be an increasingly powerful influence on the education of the young. For various reasons Thucydides' work was not especially useful for those wishing to learn to speak well in public. For one thing, his style did not lend itself at all to emulation: it was too difficult and too obscure. Even Cicero, who was a fluent speaker of Greek and encountered it as a fully living language, calls the speeches in his work almost unintelligible. This was no model for clear, persuasive, public discourse. (*"Ipsae illae contiones ita multas habent obscuras abditasque sententias vix ut intellegantur; quod est in oratione civili vitium vel maxime." Orator* 30).

There is perhaps also a second reason that is connected with a more deep-seated incompatibility between the spirit of Thucydides' work and the demands of rhetorical training. In Book 3 (82–84) Thucydides describes the long-lasting internal unrest in Corcyra. One result of this state of civil war is that the accustomed meaning of words shifts. What used to be called "senseless rashness" (τόλμα ἀλόγιστος) now came to be called "a manly spirit that looks out for its friends" (ἀνδρεία φιλέταιρος), and "circumspection in every regard" (τὸ πρὸς ἅπαν ξυνετόν) came to be considered to be, and was called, "complete laziness" (ἐπὶ πᾶν ἀργόν). This shift in the application of customary evaluative terms was considered by Thucydides to be a clear sign of a seriously pathological state of society.[35] For the rhetorician, on the other hand, the fact that the same situation or character traits admits of a variety of different designations, each with a completely different moral and affective coloration—I am prudent; you are cautious; he is a coward—is a *precondition* of the exercise of his art, not a sign of degeneracy. Thucydides' final value judgments may be unconventional and hidden so deeply in his harsh and obscure prose as to require sustained attention and effort to comprehend them, but they are not, finally, slippery and ambiguous. He clearly did not think that

---

66), but so little of his work has survived we cannot know on what basis this judgment was made or whether it was well founded.

[35] One might claim that modern political thought begins when Hobbes, who translated Thucydides, decides that the "pathological" state Thucydides describes in Corcyra is the natural state from which the study of politics must begin. On these issues, see the seminal paper by Quentin Skinner, "Hobbes on Rhetoric and the Construction of Morality," in Skinner, *Visions of Politics*, vol. III (*Hobbes and Civil Science*) (Cambridge University Press, 2002), pp. 87–141.

THUCYDIDES, NIETZSCHE, AND WILLIAMS

by judicious redescription one could make the same course of action either good or bad, and surely one of the lessons one can hardly fail to learn from his work, if one studies it carefully and understands it correctly, is that it is, therefore, highly inadvisable in the long run to try to make actions *seem* good or bad ad libitum, even if one can succeed in producing an effective appearance. As long as rhetoric dominated political life and education there was no room for Thucydides' unique combination of superficial, analytic detachment from the demands of immediate political partisanship, compressed and convoluted literary style, and deep-seated, if idiosyncratic, moral realism.[36] In the final analysis Nietzsche is closer to the mark when he connects Thucydides with incipient forms of "*Wissenschaftlichkeit*" such as one finds in Hippocrates[37] than when he calls him a representative of the "culture of the sophists."[38]

Nietzsche's *Birth of Tragedy* is equally about the death of tragedy. One might think that a more complete account of that crucial period between the middle of the fifth and the middle of the fourth century BC when so many of the most characteristic European modes of thinking become visible would require, as a supplement and pendant to *The Birth of Tragedy*, a treatise on the murder by starvation of early Greek "*Wissenschaftlichkeit*." One might call it "*Ugolino graecus, oder der Hungertod der frühgriechischen Wissenschaft*." Instead of Nietzsche's stark Aeschylean drama of two actors: tragedy and Socratic philosophy, there would have to be a more Wagnerian drama with a fuller cast including two sets of infant-victims: the potential unborn children of Sophocles and those of Thucydides, and two murderers: Socratic philosophy and rhetoric. That Socratics and rhetoricians were also enemies is true, but irrelevant to the larger story; Plato's unrelenting guerrilla war against rhetoric (and the sophists) must not divert attention completely from the role he played in doing in and supplanting both tragedy and Thucydidean "enquiry." Thucydides' work instantiated and was clearly aimed at the cultivation of a kind of practical reasoning and political—and "moral," if one wishes— judgment, which was supposed to have general scope; it was not positivist science. However, the nourishment his form of "inquiry" absolutely needed was a keen interest in understanding clearly and exactly (τὸ σαφές and τὸ ἀκριβές) the *real*, causal details of human motivation, the contingencies of particular political situations, the historically and geographically specific structure of existing human institutions, topography (Sphakteria, Syracuse), dialectology (VII.44), etc. In a society in which a very large number of the most active political agents devote themselves to trying to learn how to put together words pleasingly and convincingly so as to persuade their hearers, with little regard

---

[36] See Williams, *Truth and Truthfulness*, chapters 7 and 10.
[37] *SW*, vol. 11, p. 554: 36[11].
[38] Nietzsche, *Götzendämmerung*: "Was ich den Alten verdanke" § 2 (*SW* 6:156).

for truth, and the most reflective members are committed to the search for abstract definitions, general principles, dialectically sustainable hypotheses, and perhaps, in some cases, a "vision of the idea of the good," Thucydidean political thinking informed by a study of the reality of what actually happens will be likely to wither away.

During the 1870s and early 1880s Nietzsche kept a series of notebooks in which one can find a large number of sketches, drafts, and plans for a more comprehensive treatment of "the Greeks" than that given in *The Birth of Tragedy*. None of these ever materialized, but if one reads the notebooks, it seems clear that he became increasingly aware of the importance of the strand of realist and empiricist[39] thinking that Thucydides represents, and of seeing the demise of tragedy and of Thucydidean "inquiry" synoptically.[40] What I am suggesting is that Bernard Williams's later work can be seen as in some sense trying to do this.

Williams agrees with Nietzsche that there can be no simple return to ancient "pre-Socratic" conceptions (*SN* pp. 6–7, 9–11); he knows as well as Nietzsche did that his own form of consciousness is possible only because of developments about which he has serious reservations (*SN* p. 9), and that this by itself would make simple return impossible, even if it were desirable on other grounds (which for many other reasons it is not). We have no alternative but to use the techniques of reflective analysis, formal argumentation, and modern, mathematically structured, empirical science that have been developed by representatives of post-Platonic philosophy, but we can try to use them to break through the bad faith on which traditional ethics rests.

To return to the two ways in which Nietzsche thinks Thucydides surpasses Plato—his more open-minded psychology, and his resistance to unfounded optimism (see above)—each of them might contain a hint about how we could advance our own understanding. Although there can be no value-free psychology, not *all* values are "moral" values, and not all moral values are of the kind originally recognized by Plato (and then bequeathed to the rest of the main-line of Western philosophy). We can also try to become aware of the extent to which we presuppose certain values, and try to make our assumptions as realistic as possible. We can, that is, try to be as truthful and truth-loving as possible in developing an alternative to the deceitful, hypermoralized views of Plato, Aristotle, Kant, and the other major figures in the history of Western ethics. There is a story inspired by Christianity and sharpened by

[39] These terms, like many of the others I am compelled to use, are philosophically loaded because of their later history. I must ask the reader to try to suspend as many of those later associations as possible.

[40] The parallel between the fate of tragedy and that of Thucydidean investigation is not exact. For instance, tragedy was a long established institution with religious roots and an important civic aspect which was supported by public funds; "inquiry" on the other hand, was a socially and politically much more fragile construct of uncertain standing.

Kant which makes us look down on the ancients and especially ancient ethics for its deficient concept of will, or failure to put volition in the center of human life. A complementary story, presented in a classic way by one of Williams's predecessors as Sather Lecturer, E. R. Dodds, in his book *The Greeks and the Irrational*,[41] denigrates ancient Greek culture as one based on "shame"—the highly primitive reaction to loss of face vis-à-vis one's compeers—rather than on "guilt," which is considered to be a more sophisticated and morally sensitive reaction. Contrary to this line of thought, Williams proposes that a psychology which is not based on notions of "volition" (*SN* p. 36), the will (*SN* pp. 41–46), the distinction between the voluntary and the involuntary (*SN* pp. 66–68) or the idea of "guilt" (*SN* pp. 75–102), but is centered on an expanded and reflectively clarified concept of "shame," will actually contribute to a more realistic, substantial, and socially enlightened form of ethical thinking.

Williams, then, invites us to reflect on a possible historical path not taken, one from ancient shame, tragedy, and Thucydidean "inquiry," rather than from Plato, Christianity, and guilt; not, of course, with the intention of inviting us to try to turn the clock back or embark now on the path not taken two thousand years ago—it was *not* taken and history cannot be turned back—but in order to inform our imagination for positive transformations of our own moral thinking.

On the question of optimism or pessimism, there are two different ways in which one could depart from the consensual optimism that characterizes most traditional philosophy. First, one could think that the world had a purposive structure, perhaps imposed on it by a malicious creator-god who delights in tormenting humans and who set it up in order to thwart essential human aspirations. The second view is that there is no inherent, discernible purposive structure, sense, or meaning to the world at all, and no guarantee that the items in the optimists' package—rationality, individual happiness, natural human development, socially desirable action—are all compatible. To think either that these items are set up so as to cohere, or that they are "by nature" ineluctably fated to conflict in an unresolvable way—to be either an old-style philosophical optimist or a dogmatic pessimist—is still to be prey to notions that are theological in their origins and implications. When Nietzsche wrote that "the Hellene was neither an optimist nor a pessimist,"[42] this is what I assume he meant, and no Hellene could illustrate this more exactly than Thucydides. As Williams puts it, the world is not "intrinsically shaped to human interests" (*SN* p. 163), either for good or ill. This is a bleak view only relative to a set of exaggerated expectations about how the world *ought* to make sense that are themselves highly questionable (*SN* p. 68).

---

[41] Berkeley and Los Angeles: University of California Press, 1951.
[42] *SW*, vol. 7, p. 77: 3[62].

None of this at all suggests any serious form of "Cartesian" skepticism about our knowledge of the world, the existence of truth, the importance of truthfulness, or our ability to make sense of our world and our lives (as opposed to discovering a preexisting "meaning" in the universe). This is the burden of Williams's final book, *Truth and Truthfulness*. Of course, we can know all sorts of things, and the very project of criticizing the Platonic-Aristotelean-Kantian tradition in ethics would be impossible without the apparatus of systematic inquiry and the evaluation of cognitive claims which philosophy, and latterly also science, have done so much to develop. There are some "universal materials" out of which particular human ethical conceptions are constructed (*SN* p. 56), and Williams believes that there is no special problem in claiming that we can know this or what these materials are. However, he also holds that, contrary to what Plato and Kant thought, investigation of these universal materials *alone* will not throw adequate light on any particular concrete form of human ethical thought because there is no unique path from these materials to any particular historical conception. A more traditional philosopher would be inclined, I think, to suggest that this is merely a limitation, not an invalidation of the claim to preeminence of strictly philosophical analysis; abstract philosophical accounts give only an outline, which of course needs to be filled empirically, but this outline is a delineation of what is essential. Williams, I think, would have rejected this suggestion. Thus, to take one case he treats in some detail in *Shame and Necessity*, the concept of "responsibility" has been an extremely prominent part of much ethical thinking during the past few hundred years, especially in the Kantian tradition. This concept puts together a number of different elements, which refer to universal features of human action: facts about causation, human intention, social needs for predictability, etc. There is, however, no unique way to put these elements together into an ethical or legal concept of responsibility. "There is not, and there could never be, just one appropriate way of adjusting these elements to each other—as we might put it, just one correct concept of responsibility . . . in different circumstances [we] need different conceptions" (*SN* p. 55). The particular way in which the elements are connected will depend in a substantive or—if one wishes to use this term—an "essential" way on the particular social structure, political institutions, and vagaries of the human history of the society in which the concept has arisen and is used. The history, sociology, and politics of the case do not simply fill in the details of the picture: they are the picture. This is the most important thing we can learn from Thucydides, and we can perhaps learn it more easily from him than from Plato.

Given that our main source of knowledge about Socrates is through the Platonic dialogues, it is not surprising that there is a tendency to treat "Socrates-Plato" as a single unitary philosophical personality, but, of course, in their better moments everyone knows that this is incorrect. We have seen that

Nietzsche accommodates a recognition of their duality through his account of the way in which Plato "transformed" Socrates. In *Ethics and the Limits of Philosophy*[43] (chapter 1) Williams claims that the genuinely philosophical impulse is the Socratic impulse of questioning, in particular asking the question how one should live; this is presumably intended to imply the possibility of distancing oneself philosophically not merely from Socratic optimism but also from the Socratic form of rationalism, especially as these are developed by Plato and the Western tradition. How then can this impulse be prevented from running away with itself and dissipating its energies in the sands of excessive abstraction, as it did in traditional forms of post-Platonic philosophy? At various points in *The Birth of Tragedy* Nietzsche appeals to the ideal of a "Socrates who makes music." In this essay I have been trying to claim that Williams's later work is similarly inspired by the ideal of what one might call a "Thucydides who philosophizes."

[43] London: Fontana, 1985.

14

Adorno's Gaps

WHILE EXILED IN THE UNITED STATES during the 1940s, the German philosopher Adorno wrote the three books on which his lasting reputation rests. The first, *The Philosophy of New Music*, presented a remarkably Whiggish theory which set the terms for all of his later and very extensive writings on art. Adorno believed that musical techniques developed historically, more or less in the way in which industrial techniques and forms of scientific knowledge did. Over time musical forms became more complex, more sophisticated and flexible, and more suited to their task of representing the "truth" about the world. He also believed in a convergence or parallelism between the historically progressive and the aesthetically satisfactory. The *only* way to comprehend and evaluate a particular piece of music properly was to understand it formally *and also* to locate it in the history of music, and this history had to be read backwards, starting from the "most advanced" contemporary practice. Adorno had also been trained as a composer in Vienna by Alban Berg, and so it comes as little surprise that he thought the "most advanced practice" was instantiated in the Schönberg School. In particular any form of neoclassicism, such as that represented by Stravinsky and his followers, was historically retrogressive, aesthetically deficient, and politically suspect.

Given this general view, it would not be strange if Adorno had little interest in the ancient world. If, as he claimed, serious music starts in the eighteenth century, with perhaps an exceptional "honorable mention" for Bach, because that is as far back into the past as the reflected insight of Schönberg's music reaches, one should not be surprised to find Adorno writing essays on Proust, Beckett, Stefan George, Valéry, and Kafka,[1] but exhibiting no equally

This is a slightly expanded version of a talk I gave in November 2003 at the Tate Modern in London as part of their day-long event, "T. W. Adorno: Music and Philosophy." I am extremely grateful to John Dunn, Zeev Emmerich, Hilary Gaskin, and Istvan Hont for discussion of the topics treated in this paper. I use the following abbreviation for referring to Adorno's works:

ÄT   *Ästhetische Theorie* (Frankfurt: Suhrkamp, 1970)
Beethoven   *Beethoven: Philosophie der Musik* (Frankfurt: Suhrkamp, 1993)
DA   *Dialektik der Aufklärung* (Frankfurt: Fischer, 1969)
GS   *Gesammelte Schriften* (Frankfurt: Suhrkamp, 1970–) [cited by volume and page]
MM   *Minima Moralia* (Frankfurt: Suhrkamp, 1973)
ND   *Negative Dialektik* (Frankfurt: Suhrkamp, 1966)

[1] Essays on all these writers are contained in the four volumes of Adorno's *Noten zur Literatur* (Frankfurt: Suhrkamp, 1958–74).

detailed engagement with Archilochus, Sophocles, Virgil, or Catullus (or, for that matter, with Walther von der Vogelweide, Dante, Rabelais, Shakespeare, or Racine).

The second of Adorno's major works, *Dialektik der Aufklärung*, written jointly with Max Horkheimer, to some extent, then, seems to violate this expectation in that it contains an extended interpretation of Homer's *Odyssey*. To be sure, this is systematically interpreted in a way that must be intentionally anachronistic as one of the earliest documents of "bourgeois-occidental civilization" (*DA* p. 6) in which Odysseus is interpreted as the "archetype of the bourgeois individual" (*DA* p. 50), but this kind of anachronism is an integral part of the basically Hegelian framework Adorno uses. All of Western history is a single story of increasing technical control over nature and concomitant Enlightenment. Such control, however, is purchased at a very high price which we have come systematically to underestimate: at the cost of self-repression, alienation, and the exploitation of inferiors in a social system divided into classes. In particular the story of Odysseus and the Sirens is an image of the process of Enlightenment: Odysseus gains knowledge, control over nature (and aesthetic satisfaction)—concretely, the ability to sail by the island of the Sirens, while hearing their song—by virtue of self-repression, being bound to the mast, and by virtue of reducing his sailors to the status of (temporarily) mutilated slaves, who must row with stopped ears.

The title of the third book, *Minima Moralia*, recalls the (probably pseudo-) Aristotelian *Magna Moralia* (i.e., Ἠθικὰ μεγάλα).[2] Although in the case of the pseudo-Aristotelean writing "μεγάλα"/"*magna*" almost certainly does *not* express a judgment about the contents ("*Moral Writings on Topics of Great Importance*"), but is a bookseller's or a librarian's term referring to the sheer physical size of the rolls of papyrus (or whatever): ("*Writings on Ethical Matters* [Format: Large"]),[3] Adorno exploits the possible ambiguity of the Latin form of expression, because he specifically intended this to be read both as "*Tiny Moral Writings*" and "*Writings on Moral Minutiae*." *Minima Moralia* is "tiny" because it is a collection of just over 150 extremely short disquisitions, most of them only two or three pages long. In addition, the ostensible topics are not the grand topics of academic theorizing—the concept of a moral obligation, the goal of human life, or the role of universal rules in ac-

---

[2] Adorno seems to have had a distinct penchant for this form of title. One of his last completed works uses it again: *Ohne Leitbild: Parva Aesthetica* (Frankfurt: Suhrkamp, 1969).

[3] Prima facie it seems odd that of three treatises on ethics in the traditional Aristotlean corpus (*Eudemian Ethics, Nichomachean Ethics*, and *Magna Moralia*), by far the *shortest* in total length should have acquired the name "The Large Ethics," but this has been plausibly explained by the fact that although the *Magna Moralia* is shorter overall, it is composed of only two books, each of which is thus over twice the length of an average book, e.g., of one of the books of *Nichomachean Ethics*. See the treatment of the issue of the title in Aristoteles, *Magna Moralia*, ed. Franz Dirlmeier (Berlin: Akademie-Verlag, 1966), pp. 97–99.

tion—but such apparently trivial matters as whether doors have handles or knobs (*MM* § 19), publishers' advertising (*MM* § 133), the discovery of a "well-preserved dinosaur" in Utah (*MM* § 74), why one does not need a dictionary to read de Sade (if one is a German speaker reading it in French) (*MM* § 27), occultism (*MM* § 151), film (*MM* § 131), running (*MM* § 102),[4] gift-giving (*MM* § 21), house-guests (*MM* § 114), etc. The cultivation of the fragment or aphorism as a literary or philosophical form has a reasonably long history in German,[5] and the idea that what Adorno calls "micrology,"[6] the study of the seemingly trivial details of life, could be of great philosophical significance is one he took over from his two older colleagues, Ernst Bloch[7] and Walter Benjamin.[8] The best way to avoid the ideology-laden world of abstractions, they thought, was to cultivate sharp observation and spontaneous reaction to concrete objects and situations, to the "apparently most banal and indifferent things,"[9] and Adorno for most of his life tried to follow this policy. This is connected with Adorno's attempt to break with many of the traditional ways of doing philosophy. Traditional academic philosophers seek to convince others of the rightness of their views by presenting logically irrefutable arguments. The coerciveness of this project, even if it is a highly sublimated form of coerciveness,[10] is part of the general obsession with control that is charac-

---

[4] Not, of course, "jogging" which did not exist in the 1940s (even in California).

[5] Friedrich Schlegel, *Athenäumsfragmente*, fragments 25, 77, 206, 225, 259, in *Friedrich Schlegel: Kritische Schriften und Fragmente*, ed. E. Behler and H. Eichner (Paderborn: Schöningh, 1988).

[6] See Susan Buck-Morss, *The Origin of Negative Dialectics* (New York: Free Press, 1977).

[7] See Adorno's two essay on Bloch: "Henkel, Krug und frühe Erfahrung" (*Noten zur Literatur IV* [Frankfurt: Suhrkamp, 1974]) and "Blochs Spuren" (*Noten zur Literatur II* [Frankfurt: Suhrkamp, 1961]).

[8] Many of Adorno's works on Benjamin are collected in Adorno, *Schriften über Walter Benjamin* (Frankfurt: Suhrkamp, 1970).

[9] Ibid., p. 69.

[10] Habermas, who is widely seen as a representative of the "second generation" of the Frankfurt School, and thus as a kind of successor of Adorno, in fact holds views on two central issues diametrically opposed to those Adorno held. First, Habermas believes that "argumentation" exerts a characteristically *noncoercive* form of coercion on people ("*der zwangslose Zwang des besseren Argumentes*"), and that therefore it is an unequivocally good thing that society become more discursive. Adorno, on the other hand, thinks this kind of logically compelling argumentation is itself a part of the apparatus of self-preservation which the Enlightenment developed, and that it is both in some sense unavoidable and also distorting, alienating, and oppressive. It must be handled with great care. Second, "consensus," especially one reached on the basis of full communication and mutual understanding (and rational argumentation), is for Habermas a kind of positive ideal. For Adorno, on the other hand, the complete communicability of thought is a "liberal fiction" (*MM* § 50), and "consensus" is more closely connected with "conformism" than with human freedom (*MM* §§ 44, 93). In particular, Adorno thinks it a mistake to understand poetry as a form of communication. There is an "irreconcilable" contradiction between "language that has poetic integrity" and "communicative" language (*Noten zur Literatur II*, [Frankfurt: Suhrkamp, 1961], 8; see also the essay "Voraussetzungen" in *Noten zur Literatur III* [Frankfurt: Suhrkamp, 1965]).

teristic of the Enlightenment. Adorno wished to practice a "post-Socratic" form of philosophizing which would not be motivated by the compulsive need to be in the right and convince all possible opponents like a lawyer arguing a case (*MM* § 44). The micro-treatises that constitute *Minima Moralia* then are supposed to be series of images, suppositions, insights, even "arguments" (of a kind), etc. that do not demand agreement, but which have other kinds of plausibility.

The section of *Minima Moralia* entitled "Gaps" is one of a series of meditations on the dichotomies between the successful and the failed, the adequate and the inadequate, the perfect and the imperfect, the sound and the damaged, as they apply to art and thought, and also to a human life considered as a whole. These "Reflections *from* a Damaged Life," as the subtitle of *Minima Moralia* calls them, are also reflections *on* what it is for a life to be damaged, and thus also, *ex negativo*, on what it would be for it to be sound. To put it this way is not incorrect, but suggests a more detached and even-handed attitude toward the success or failure of a human life than will survive a careful reading of any of Adorno's works. Adorno was, after all, a philosopher whose ethical thinking revolved around the claims that nothing in the contemporary world is harmless (*MM* § 5), that it isn't really possible to live the right life in our society because it is so thoroughly evil, and that it is a part of morality not to feel at home with oneself (*MM* § 18). When Adorno describes the relation of mutual envy that existed between Schönberg and Berg, Schönberg envying Berg his public success with *Wozzeck*, and Berg envying Schönberg his numerous public failures (*GS* 13.360; *GS* 18.492), there is no doubt that officially Adorno stood with Berg, on the side of the *prima facie* superiority of failure. One's first reaction to public success,[11] at any rate in a society like ours, should be that it is something too disgraceful to bear, and indeed apparent success of any kind is to be treated with great suspicion. In various everyday, comparative, or context-dependent senses we may distinguish relative success from relative failure, but "in an emphatic sense no work of art can be a success" (*ÄT* p. 87), and the same is true of a life (*MM* § 18).

To speak of the failure or the inadequacy of a human life is to measure it against something[12] which it lives up to or fails to live up to. That "something" is a construct of our imagination. Thus, a life can be imagined as potentially having a structure like that of a train of consecutive thoughts and therefore

---

[11] Adorno, who was involved in the preparation for the premier of *Wozzeck* in Berlin, reports that after the performance Berg was very upset because it was so well received, thinking that "if a piece of music nowadays won over the public so immediately, there must be something wrong with it" (*GS* 18.492). That it pleased the public was "an argument against the opera" (*GS* 13.336).

[12] Friedrich Nietzsche, *Zur Genealogie der Moral* (in *Sämtliche Werke: Kritische Studienausgabe*, ed. Colli and Montinari [Berlin: de Gruyter, 1980], vol. 5) : "*der Mensch bezeichnet sich als das Wesen, welches Werthe misst, werthet und misst, als das 'abschätzende Thier an sich'*" (Essay 2, section 8, p. 306).

potentially as exhibiting the same kind of coherence, closure, and validity that such a train of thought has. That is, since a human life evolves through time, it is tempting to look for some kind of analogy in the imagination to this temporal extension, and the consecutiveness of thought seems to provide that. This temporally extended aspect is intensified if what I am thinking about is a sequence of ordered, practical steps to be taken to attain a goal; and if this ordered sequence is constructed in my mind before being realized, what I have is a plan of action. The ordered stages of my thinking through the plan are to be mirrored in the steps taken in the real world to execute the plan. My life is construed as the attempted execution of an imaginatively entertained plan. This attempt retains enough residual connection with the world of consecutive thought for it to be appropriate to evaluate it as if it were a deductive system. Adorno speaks of the "line of life"—like a line of argument—that may follow along or stray from the path indicated by its "premises."[13] If I begin to think of my life in this way, then in addition to all the other ways in which I can speak of it as a success or a failure, there are several highly specific kinds of failure I can envisage. I can fail to attain the goal, or I can deviate from the path marked out by the plan, whether or not I eventually attain the end. Or I can attain the goal, whether I followed the path or not, and discover it was not at all what I thought it was going to be. This, in turn, can be because it has properties I had not expected or because the properties I correctly thought it had turn out not to please me, perhaps because I have changed.[14] I can change my mind about whether attaining the goal actually constituted "success." Given the facts of temporal succession and the context-dependency of much human judgment, it is not a forgone conclusion that my judgment when I have attained the goal will be the same as the prospective judgment I made about it when I began to plan.

Adorno was, of course, far from the only one ever to be fascinated by deficiency, imperfection, and failure. Arguably the same was true of the ancients. The ancients' obsession with failure, however, was based on extreme fear, certainly not on anything like admiration. Partly this was the perfectly realistic general fear on the part of relatively weak animals in an unpredictable world. Sometimes it was a specific fear of a success or prosperity that could be thought to be excessive. This kind of fear, too, can be empirically well-grounded because in small face-to-face societies the envy visible prosperity can provoke among the less fortunate is a serious danger; but in the case of

[13] Leibniz takes this thought to its extreme: everything that happens to me can be formulated in a sentence which could in principle be deduced from my concept, but only God grasps my concept and has the infinite intellect necessary to do the requisite deduction; everyone else must be satisfied with empirical approximations of my "concept" given through normal experience.

[14] This last, that my life fails because I get what I always wanted, but have so changed during the process of getting it that it no longer satisfies me, is a staple of much modern literature, see, e.g., Samuel Beckett, *Proust* (New York: Grove Press, 1931), pp. 3–4.

the ancients it also partly took the form of a paranoid fantasy that "the gods" would begrudge humans any signal success they might have.[15]

The ancients then in no sense *glorified* failure per se, nor indeed attributed any special positive value to it. Some ancient heroes were admired although they (finally) failed, and heroes precisely because of their documented success in many encounters, and the possible envy attached to that, were especially at risk of catastrophic failure, but no hero was glorious *because* he failed.

Just as all political careers in a sense end in failure, so too all human life is radically deficient and a failure, if only because all humans in the end die, and thus fail to live up to the imaginary standard of continuing to last at least a bit longer. No matter how long it has lasted already, one can always imagine it lasting a *little* longer.[16] This fantasy takes its most concrete shape in the contrast between human life and that of the gods who "live for ever" ("θεοὶ αἰὲν ἐόντες" *Iliad* I. 290, etc.). In a famous passage of the *Odyssey* (Book XI, ll. 471–91) Odysseus congratulates the shade of Achilles because of the superlatively blessed life he has had. He was supremely honored while he was alive, and now in the underworld he is powerful among the dead. Achilles does not deny that his life on earth was all that Odysseus says it was, but now he is in Hades and virtually *any* life on earth is better than the best life possible after death.

Not only, however, is the end—a certain kind of failure (death)—common to all humans, but life and prosperity are highly precarious and unpredictable while they last. Croesus and Priam are the *non plus ultra* of success and happiness: wealthy, established, politically overwhelmingly powerful men. The only question about Priam's good fortune is: how long will it last? Croesus has various proactive plans for increasing his prosperity; will they work? Priam's good fortune does not last to the end of his life, and Croesus's plans backfire: crossing the River Halys to attack the Medes lands him on a heap of faggots waiting to be burned to death. Both suffer startling and sudden reversals of fortune; what can happen to them can happen to anyone, so even while you live in prosperity, never trust your luck. Achilles' problem was not that he trusted his luck or his ability to plan cleverly when he ought not to have. That is not the point in his life. Achilles, Priam, and Croesus represent three slightly different variants on the general theme of the imperfection and inadequacy of human life.

Sophocles' Oedipus represents a significant increase in complexity over other archaic conceptions and is perhaps an even more appropriate point of reference for this Adorno text, because "Gaps" begins with a discussion of "intellectual honesty" and what it requires. Oedipus is overwhelmingly a man of rational plans and intellectual honesty—he knows the line he wishes his life

---

[15] See LSJ *sv* "φθόνος."

[16] But compare Cicero, *De senectute*, and Seneca, *De brevitate vitae*.

to track and thinks he is very much on that track—and his plans all go awry for him in a way that is both spectacular and partially self-induced.

As Aristophanes' Aeschylus points out (*Ranae* 1181ff.), it would not be exactly right to call Oedipus "happy" (εὐδαίμων) even at the beginning of a play about his discovery of his own identity: he is married to a woman old enough to be his mother—she *is* his mother, he had to flee from his home in Corinth because of fear of a horrible fate that was predicted for him, he had bad feet, etc. Nevertheless, he is famous ("ὁ πᾶσι κλεινὸς Οἰδίπους καλούμενος," *OT* l.8) and trusted to be competent by the citizens of Thebes (*OT* ll.31–51). There is a plague, to be sure, but Oedipus has dealt with seemingly insoluble external situations before, most notably by removing the Sphinx, and this time, too, he has a plan and everyone seems moderately confident that he will manage again. Will the plan work? In one sense it works only too well; this is part of the problem: according to the poet Hölderlin, "King Oedipus has one eye too many perhaps."[17] He does find out exactly who killed Laius, and is put in a position to end the plague. On the other hand, discovering who killed Laius turns out to be a less satisfying outcome than he imagined, and, precisely the success of that project—"success" if one construes it in the limited terms in which it was originally envisaged—retrospectively demonstrates that the apparent success of his life never was substantial and real.[18] The events of the play show that his initial state was a complete illusion and that he *never really was* leading a "successful," "adequate," "sound" human life.

The ancient world was haunted by a double pessimism. A relatively shallow pessimism concerned the brevity of life, the general mutability of human affairs, and the particular fallibility of human plans. This form of pessimism is often associated with the paranoid fantasy that great success actually attracts failure. The second and more deep-seated pessimism is the one that finds expression in what Nietzsche called the "wisdom of Silenus,"[19] the view

[17] "*Der König Oedipus hat ein Auge zuviel vieleicht* [sic]." At the end of the prose-poem "In lieblicher Bläue" (in Friedrich Hölderlin, *Sämtliche Werke*, "Frankfurter Ausgabe," ed. Franz and Sattler [Frankfurt: Roter Stern Verlag, 1983], vol. 9, p. 35), Hölderlin's highly idiosyncratic view takes Oedipus's tragedy to consist in his trying to totalize or go beyond the boundaries, as it were trying to be a Hegelian philosopher. There is, Hölderlin thinks, no reason for Oedipus to jump to the conclusion that the oracle is referring to the murder of Laius. The oracle merely says to purify the land. Oedipus "interprets" this in "too infinite" a way so that it becomes *nefas* ("Anmerkungen zu Oedipus" in *Sämtlichte Werke*, "Frankfurter Ausgabe," vol. 9, pp. 249–58).

[18] Although it would probably not be compatible with a widespread shift in human sensibility of the type suggested by Brecht ("Kleines Organon für das Theater," in *Schriften zum Theater* [Frankfurt: Suhrkamp, 1957], esp. pp. 16–23, 40–41) in which failure of plans had *no* effect on us except to motivate us to make better, technologically superior plans. An audience of thoroughgoing human engineers could not understand, much less love, tragedy. The continued availability of ancient tragedy depends on it being easy for us to accept the unavoidable failure of human plans, that is to our not being engineers.

[19] Friedrich Nietzsche, *Die Geburt der Tragödie* § 3 (in *Sämtliche Werke: Kritische Studienausgabe*, ed. Colli and Montinari [Berlin: de Gruyter, 1980], vol. 1, p. 35).

that human life, correctly understood, is even at its best never worth living. We know perfectly well what an adequate life would be—one like that of the gods—but no form of that life is accessible to humans at all. Among other advantages, only the gods possess sufficient strength and longevity to be able to have coherent plans they can have any expectation of carrying out successfully on their own terms. Our inherent and painful inadequacy, as the creatures we are, means that the only sensible human attitude toward the world and our own lives in it is one of complete rejection. As Silenus tells us, the best thing for us would have been never to have been born, and that is always already beyond our grasp; the second best thing for us is to die as soon as possible.

It is the observation of this contrast between Silenus and Achilles, who thinks that *any* life is better than being dead, that motivates Nietzsche's claim in *The Birth of Tragedy* that there was not one pre-Socratic Greek worldview, but two diametrically opposed ones: the "Dionysian" wisdom of Silenus, and the "Apollonian" view of Homer. Both of these views are deeply pessimistic, the Dionysian for obvious reasons, and the Apollonian because life, though good in itself, is, even at its best, short and then gone forever.

Christianity, of course, brought a change to all of this. Its main historical significance lay in two paradoxical claims. First of all, the Christian claims that life in this world is generally less vivid and substantial than something else which is to come. Our life in the everyday world is a mere, pale shadow of a Life-to-Come; it is like a watercolor whose colors have faded, but which will be restored to its original state after death, or like the faded photo of a person whom one will eventually meet face to face (1 Corinthians 13:12).[20]

The second claim is that one of the most striking kinds of definitive failure, a particularly humiliating form of public execution generally reserved for slaves, could be seen as in some sense the greatest success, thus opening the way to a form of cosmic optimism that must otherwise seem demented, or, as Saint Paul called it, a "folly" (1 Corinthians 1:18–31). What seems complete failure in every respect here in this life can be seen to be, or made to be, a success *there* in a life beyond. It becomes possible to think a radical reversal of valuation. This, of course, is a potentially extremely subversive element in the Christian synthesis. Repeatedly in history, groups have taken the view that the first shall be last and the last shall be first, and have drawn from this view political implications that were upsetting for those in positions of power and authority. Without it, the Christian prospect of a future life can become comfortable, if not to say complacent.

The Christian theme of this life as a vague approximation of one to come was one that found repeated expression in the poetry of German Romanticism, for instance in the late poem which Hölderlin wrote, after he had gone mad, to the carpenter Zimmern in whose house he lived:

[20] *Odyssey* Book XI (especially ll. 488–91).

Die Linien des Lebens sind verschieden
wie Wege oder wie der Berge Grenzen
was hier wir sind, kann dort ein Gott ergänzen
mit Harmonien, und ew'gem Lohn und Frieden.[21]

What is deficient about life is not its brevity or uncertainty, as in the case of
Croesus or Priam, but its internal constitution, as in that of Oedipus or
Silenus. The orthodox Christian view, to be sure, even in its more austere
forms that emphasize that this life is a vale of tears, is distinct from that of
Silenus. The Christian could never accept that it would have been better not
to have been born; if God has caused us to be born, that *must be* for the best.[22]
However, Hölderlin is here presenting the more comfortable version of
Christianity:[23] life is not inherently horrible, rather it is simply "not perfect
enough"; it is pale and disappointing, and needs supplementation. For the
Christian no human state on earth is "perfect." Our life is like a sketch that is
incomplete and needs filling in; God will finish the job. Or rather, it is like a
single line of music to which God adds the appropriate "harmonies." Life is
still structured as a plan, and, as Oedipus discovered to his cost, it is (finally)
someone else's plan. Furthermore, our inability to execute the plan fully here
is in one sense absolute, as Silenus taught, but that is no grounds for pessimism, because the Christian god is all-powerful and cares intensely for his
children, so in the end all will be well.

In "Gaps" Adorno takes up this theme of the inadequacy of the "lines of
life" but moves it in a post-Christian direction. Our conception of a fully successful life is that of a life that is happy, *although* spontaneous, and unregi-
mented (*MM* §§ 12,38; *Klangfiguren*, p. 125 f). To say that it is "unregi-
mented," however, is to say it does not make itself conform to any pre-given

---

[21] The lines of life are various; they diverge and cease
    Like footpaths and the mountains' utmost ends.
    What here we are, elsewhere a God amends
    With harmonies, eternal recompense, and peace.

Translation by Michael Hamburger, *Friedrich Hölderlin: Poems and Fragments* (London: Anvil
1994), p. 671. It will not, I hope, be taken as a sign of lack of appreciation for the extremely impressive translations of Michael Hamburger if I point out that he has slightly changed the meaning, making it slightly more Christian. What Hölderlin says the god does is "supplement" or
"make whole" our gappy, fragmentary life; the possible moral overtones of "amend" (= correct)
in English are absent.

[22] This is not, of course, true of Gnostic versions of Christianity. See Jochen Hörisch, *Es gibt
(k)ein richtiges Leben im falschen* (Frankfurt: Suhrkamp, 2003).

[23] Some of the *"poète maudit"* mythology associated with the likes of Baudelaire and Rimbaud can be seen as a development of the reversal topos. Lyric poetry as a genre becomes
tremendously bourgeois in Germany in the nineteenth century. It comes as something of a shock
to realize that Mörike is a contemporary of Baudelaire. The closest parallel to the French development in German art, as various French writers pointed out, was not a form of literature but
Wagner's music.

standards of coherency, consistency, progression, or achievement. We want, that is, coherence without regimentation.[24] Logical inference, discursive argumentation, or fully transparent, consistent, self-grounding thought are thus bad models to understand an "adequate" human life from the very start, because they are *supposed* to be "regimented" in this way. Since art is a *"promesse de bonheur"* (*ÄT* p. 128), a promise of happiness *in life*, discursive systems are also a poor model for art. The line of an "adequate" life does not run straight, like a series of inferences from a set of premises. The very idea that a good life in this world would be one that went perfectly according to plan—to *anyone's* plan, even my own—is a mistake. That things do not go according to plan, and that my life is deficient in various ways, may be the condition of my attaining the highest state of freedom from regimentation that is possible for me. A "perfect" life would not be a perfect life.

In a final dialectical twist, Adorno adds that if human life is not structured like a formal argument, then neither is serious creative thought. Euclid and Descartes are just as bad models for actual thinking as they are for art or life. Real thinking, too, is never fully self-transparent, fully self-grounding, and never fully direct and coherent in its progress. It is at its best when not being perfect.

Adorno ought then to have emphasized that optimism and pessimism, hope and despair are equally inappropriate philosophical attitudes to life as a whole, because each depends on antecedently attributing to human life a kind of potential "completeness"[25] which is drawn from logical inference, that is, from thought, and which is not true even of unformalized thought, much less of a human life. This is related to the Nietzschean insight that without God neither pessimism nor optimism as they were traditionally construed, namely as attitudes that are *appropriate* because grounded in a correct appreciation of the very nature of reality, makes much sense. Either optimism or pessimism, if they are to be more than *merely* psychological categories, requires a theological framework which no longer exists. If there is no God, there is no reason, apart from the vagaries of one's own psychology and particular accidental[26] details of one's situation, to be basically optimistic or pessimistic.[27]

---

[24] Kant tried to square the circle by claiming that for a life to be free it *had to* be one in which the agent gave himself a law which would be identical with the law every other rational creature gave itself—the moral law—but this is ludicrous. Unless one presupposes Kant's baroque metaphysics, this thought simply does not make any sense at all.

[25] There are some similar reflections in Heidegger's discussion of the incompleteness of human life (*Sein und Zeit* §§ 46–53), although Heidegger thinks that the "inappropriate" conception of wholeness comes from the idea of a whole *object* rather than from the idea of the completion of a deductive system. See also Jonathan Lear, *Happiness, Death, and the Remainder of Life* (Cambridge, MA: Harvard, 2000).

[26] "Accidental" in one sense, not all; see Jonathan Lear, *Love and its Place in Nature* (New York: Farrar, Straus, and Giroux, 1990).

[27] In one of the pieces in his collection *Die Lücke die der Teufel läßt* (Frankfurt: Suhrkamp,

Adorno himself comes very close to making this point in his interpretation of the last scene of Goethe's *Faust*, when he observes that it is equally impossible to attribute any "meaning" to that which exists (*"was irgend dem Daseienden Sinn zuschriebe"*) and to deny such meaning (*"Verleugnung"*).[28] Having seen this Nietzschean truth, however, he seems at the final moment to pull back and suggests that the response to the loss of "transcendence" is to read profane texts as if they were sacred texts, and in general, as we will see, he continues to use patently religious vocabulary.

There was a strong movement in Central Europe in the nineteenth and early twentieth centuries to split up the historical conjunction between religion and theology. Christianity, it was felt, had become a religion of abstract dogma: of scholastic arguments, speculative systems, and metaphysical beliefs. At the very latest with Kant, these beliefs had all become rationally completely untenable. What was one to do? The Christian religion played a very significant part in social and to some extent even political life, and provided all kinds of services the society could ill afford to do without. Not merely hospitals, bureaus of vital statistics, schools, and mediation services for minor dis-

---

2003, pp. 190–93), Alexander Kluge tells the story of a Russian émigré to Berlin during the 1920s named Leschtschenko who opened a studio for producing Russian versions of American (silent) films for distribution in the Soviet Union and American versions of Russian (silent) films for distribution in the United States. One major difficulty was that all the American films had happy endings that would have been considered silly and superficial in Russia, while the Russian films had melancholy endings that were not appealing in the United States. My suggestion is that this difference is no more than a difference of national temperament, i.e., the sediment of particular differential historical experiences, not matters which one group or the other "got right." Optimism and pessimism are matters for the psychoanalyst and historian, not the philosopher (or theologian). The Russian émigré thus had the task of filming new "happy endings" for the Russian exports to the United States and new "unhappy endings" for the U.S. exports to Russia. This was a slightly tricky task, since the original actors were never available. How then could one film a convincing new final scene? He had to become very adept at using various dodges, illusions, and suggestive techniques. Fortunately, Leschtschenko discovered, by the last scene a film has built up a certain momentum, which will carry audiences along and cause them to "supplement" what they actually see in the direction of the expected coherence (*"Der Zuschauer verzeiht. Er geht mit. Er ergänzt,"* p. 192). In fact, the audience would do almost anything rather than find their expectations (for a happy ending or a sad ending, as the case may be) disappointed. To be forced to confront an inappropriate ending, however, is something an audience would *never* forgive.

[28] *Noten zur Literatur II*, p. 7. There is a common confusion between "meaning/sense" and *"positive* meaning/sense." Thus, "I can give my life no meaning / I can find no sense in my life" means either: (a) I am confused, like Durkheim's anomic individuals who do not know what moral and social prescriptions hold for them, or I do not know what is happening to me, etc., or (b) I know perfectly well what is happening to me and I *do not like it one bit*. Thus, the absolute antithesis of the modern disoriented individual is the believing Calvinist. The Calvinist knows exactly what is what: most of humanity is condemned to roast for all eternity in the fires of the divine wrath. Life has a perfectly clear meaning, but it might be one that is unwelcome to most of humanity. "Optimism" would require "meaning" in *both* senses.

putes, but psychologically and social-psychologically important services like provision of meaningful markers for human life, consolation in cases of bereavement, social forms in which to celebrate changes of status, ways for groups to express human solidarity, etc. Some theorists suggested discarding the theology altogether and retaining a purified and radically a-theological religion: either a religion of pure rational morality (Kant), or a naturalized way of celebrating important anthropological features of human life on earth (Feuerbach), or a return to the vivid immediacy of primitive Christian forms of faith, unspoilt and undistorted by the inappropriate theoretical categories of Greek philosophy and its descendents (young Heidegger). Adorno takes the opposite tack. He vociferously rejects religion:[29] Beethoven's *Missa Solemnis* is a failure because religious belief became impossible in the nineteenth century, and it became impossible quite simply because it is a "lie" and had come to be seen as one (*Beethoven*, Fr. 363, p. 251). On the other hand, he does seems to have an appropriately dialectical, but in the final instance positive, attitude toward theology (*Beethoven* Fr. 363, p. 251; see also *Briefwechsel mit Benjamin*).

Now, of course, there is nothing in any way inherently bizarre about a theology without religion. For millennia people have speculated about a variety of subjects: rain, tides, the characteristic difference in tessitura of the male and female voices, the reproductive systems of eels—a subject of special interest to Aristotle and Freud—why not also about gods? If one thinks of gods as simply large, powerful creatures in the world, that is a reason to come to know as much as one can about them—they might be dangerous. That is no reason to worship them, or even to have any particular respect for them. Philosophers over the centuries have discussed the idea of an unmoved mover or a cause of itself or a supreme being without it being the least obvious that any particular human attitude should necessarily be appropriate to this entity, if it were to exist. What, after all, would be so wonderful about being bigger or stronger than anything else or the cause of oneself?[30]

So it is perfectly possible to do theology, as the purported study of a postulated entity, without being in any way committed to anything like a religious attitude toward it. Theology is then a form of pure speculation, a particularly disembodied kind of metaphysics. This was, to be sure, a highly peculiar kind of metaphysics which ostensibly took on board Nietzsche's criticism of every form of appeal to a *"Hinterwelt"*—a world "beyond" the sensible world in which we live—but retained a place for some "metaphysical experiences" that

---

[29] See Hörisch, *Es gibt (k)ein richtiges Leben im falschen*, esp. pp. 60 ff.

[30] Frank Ramsey, the brilliant but overweight Cambridge philosopher who died in 1930 at the age of 27, notoriously wrote: "Where I seem to differ from some of my friends is in attaching little importance to physical size. I don't feel the least humble before the vastness of the heavens. . . . I take no credit for weighing nearly seventeen stone." *The Foundations of Mathematics* (London: Routledge, 1954), p. 291.

were not specifically religious. These experiences are supposed to be analogous to the childhood experiences described by Proust, experiences of the intense meaningfulness of certain concrete places, persons, or things, a meaningfulness that manifests itself with particular intensity, when they are *not* actually present (*ND* 364–66). These are to be interpreted neither as reflections of some objective meaningfulness, nor as a mere subjective "addition" to the world that can be simply dismissed, nor finally as mere illusions.[31]

Adorno's particular version of nonreligious theology derives from his general anti-Kantian epistemology. Kant rejected theology because he believed that one had to have reasons for believing things to be true. In the case of cognitively contentful beliefs, these reasons had to be connected in an appropriate way with the possibility of human experience. Theological beliefs, Kant thinks, fail to have the appropriate structure, and thus are untenable as claims about the world.

In contrast to this, Adorno holds that *all* thinking is exaggeration, and that fantasy, wishful thinking, irresponsible running on ahead of the evidence, and desperate non sequiturs are all integral constituents of substantive cognitive processes. Theology, then, can be seen as one further imaginative extension of our normal forms of thinking, and is as such unobjectionable. It is no mistake to speculate—that is not only unavoidable in any case, but it is a good thing. The mistake would be to *adore* the object of such wishful thinking; that would be to give to fantasy a significance which it does not deserve. If the model of "metaphysical experience" is the child's imaginative projection of a quasi-paradisical state onto that which is designated by certain names of places—Amorbach, for instance—then what the child discovers when he arrives is not a town that is literally "out of this world" but a real place which he has qualitatively transfigured in the imagination.

"Gaps" has a highly ambiguous ending. No serious thought can avoid bearing on itself the marks of its own partial groundlessness, its lack of a full legitimation. Equally, however, every thought is "waiting to be awakened" by a "recollection" of what is missing from it which will turn the thought into a "*Lehre*," a doctrine that has apodictic certainty because it follows from absolutely certain premises, as in mathematics. The use of "recollection" ("*Erinnerung*") alone ought to rouse suspicions because of its associations with the metaphysical elaboration of Plato's epistemology which was of such importance in giving form to later Christian views of an afterlife.

Adorno probably took over this use of the term "*Lehre*" in an emphatic sense from his friend Walter Benjamin, who held the highly implausible view that our intellectual life should be directed at attempting to formulate a "*Lehre*." For Benjamin the archetype of a "*Lehre*" was the traditional Jewish

---

[31] Beckett, too, describes this element in Proust, but he calls a spade a spade, or in this case, a fetish a "fetish" (*Proust*, pp. 23 ff).

Law,[32] a closed apodictic body of prescriptions that can be detached from any justificatory argument and presented as something simply to be followed,[33] if necessary to be followed blindly. In the case of Benjamin the religious motivation for this view is clear. The question is how we are to understand the notion of "*Lehre*" in this passage by Adorno. One would have thought that this Benjaminian doctrine was completely contrary to Adorno's own most deeply seated views, as expressed in *MM* § 43 (or *ND* 27–64), that there is no "thesis" that can be extracted from a philosophical argument, no "summary" of philosophical thought that is possible because the process of thinking and the "conclusion" are too intimately intertwined.

Perhaps it is the case that human nature in some sense requires us, or at least strongly induces us, fantastically to project for ourselves an exaggerated idealized conception of a perfect life, but it is also true that this can be seen through as a complete illusion. To begin to live seriously is to see both the psychic temptation—perhaps even the psychic unavoidability—of these fantasies and *also* their thoroughly delusional nature. Romantics tend to use this as an argument to retain as much of the fantasy as possible, even the completely incredible parts, like religion. One can accept the general point about our inability *fully* to live without fantasies without thereby endorsing every particular one. Freud's life, one would have thought, was a sufficient proof that a long, highly productive, basically benevolent existence is perfectly possible without giving way to religious illusions. Life is not a matter of logic and mathematical certainty, of the executing or failing to execute a single life-plan, of living up to or failing to live up to a fixed moral code, or indeed of success and failure in any globally significant sense. To think it could be is an archaic remnant. Adorno was fond of citing Rimbaud's famous injunction from the end of *Une Saison en enfer*: "Il faut être absolument moderne" (One must be absolutely modern). He set out to be an absolutely modern philosopher. The next line of that Rimbaud text, however, runs: "Point de cantiques: tenir le pas gagné" ("Absolutely no more religious songs: maintain the advance that has been achieved).[34] It would be a shame if it turned out to be the case that Adorno remained dependent on the tired, diffuse Romantic religiosity from which it was one of the glories of the twentieth century to have freed us.

[32] Walter Benjamin, "Über das Programm der kommenden Philosophie; Nachtrag," in *Angelus Novus* (Frankfurt: Suhrkamp, 1966) pp. 39–41.
[33] This is, of course, the exact reverse of Adorno's usual view. See *ND*, pp. 41–43.
[34] Arthur Rimbaud, *Oeuvres completes*, ed. A. Adam (Paris: Gallimard, 1972), pp. 116–17.

Index